# CHALLENGING HISTORY

# THE GREAT POWERS 1814 – 1914

## ERIC WILMOT

Head of History, John Port School, Etwall

Nelson

**Thomas Nelson and Sons Ltd**
Nelson House  Mayfield Road
Walton-on-Thames  Surrey
KT12 5PL  UK

**Thomas Nelson Australia**
102 Dodds Street
South Melbourne
Victoria 3205  Australia

**Nelson Canada**
1120 Birchmount Road
Scarborough  Ontario
M1K 5G4  Canada

© Eric Wilmot 1992

First published by Thomas Nelson and Sons Ltd 1992

I(T)P  Thomas Nelson is an International
      Thomson Publishing Company.

I(T)P  is used under licence.

ISBN 0-17-435056-2
NPN 9 8 7 6 5

Designed by Roger Walker

Printed in China

# Contents

# Author's Acknowledgements

I am grateful to many people for the expert advice and guidance given during the writing of this book. In particular, the suggestions made by John Jones, Michael Jones, Beverley Tarquini and John Traynor have been invaluable. I wish to acknowledge the contribution of my students, past and present, whose enthusiasm and criticism have helped to shape the final text. I also wish to thank my family and friends for their enduring interest and support.

I am particularly indebted to Christine for her help and encouragement in the preparation of this book.

FOR CATHERINE MARY                                   EW

# Editor's Preface

This book offers you the challenge of history. It encourages you to engage with the past in a creative and personal way; it also presents you with the many challenges which the past provides for present-day students. It demands a rigorous and scholarly approach. In return, we expect that you will increase your understanding, improve your skills, and develop a personal involvement in historical study.

The challenge is presented to you through the different components of each chapter:

**Preview**    Each chapter begins with a presentation which is designed to arouse your interest, and alert you to one or more of the major themes of the chapter.

**Text**    The text demands an active response from you. The book has been carefully written, designed and fully illustrated to develop your learning and understanding. Photographs, artwork, cartoons, statistical tables, maps, graphs are among the many visual images that reinforce the quality of the text.

**Examining evidence**    These sections present a wide variety of Historical sources, both primary and secondary. They encourage you to analyse the opinions of others, to assess the reliability of evidence, and to formulate and test your own personal views.

**Focus**    Focus sections zoom in on, and highlight, particular events, people and issues of the period. They are designed to enable you to see these more clearly and to find your way through the complexity of historical problems.

**Talking Points**    They are scattered widely throughout the book. By talking and listening, we can all learn about the major issues which translate the past into the present. In doing so, we question our own perceptions, test out our ideas and widen our range of interests.

**Questions**    Throughout the chapters, questions encourage you to consider what you see and read. They invite your personal response and encourage you to share it verbally with your fellow students, and in writing with your teachers.

**Review**    Each chapter contains an exercise, often a formal essay or question, which enables you to revise the learning and understanding of the whole chapter. You will find supporting ideas and structures to help you to formulate your answer.

This book offers you many experiences of History. It opens up to you the thoughts and feelings of contemporaries; it classifies the distinctive nature of your period; it places people, events and issues in the context of the flow of History. Just as important, it invites and encourages you to formulate your own personal insights and opinions in a living and developing debate. The Challenge of History is essential to the vitality and well-being of the modern world.

J.A.P. Jones

General Editor

*Titles in the series*

EUROPE 1890–1990
John Traynor

THE GREAT POWERS 1814–1914
Eric Wilmot

INDUSTRIALISATION AND SOCIETY 1750–1914
Neil Tonge

BRITAIN 1815–1914
Howard Martin

THE TUDOR CENTURY 1485–1603
Ian Dawson

EUROPE 1500–1600
J.A.P. Jones

# Dedication

*Challenging History* is dedicated, with affection, to the memory of Vince Crinnion. It was inspired by his humanity, and his vision, and by his belief that the study of history is an enjoyable, creative experience, through which we can challenge both our concept of the past and present, and our understanding of ourselves.

# 1 The European Peace Settlement 1814–15

## PREVIEW

THE RETREAT FROM MOSCOW

### The collapse of Napoleon's empire

Early in 1814 a momentous era in European history began drawing to a close. For more than two decades the French, first in the name of the Republic and then on behalf of Napoleon Bonaparte, had attacked and subjugated huge areas of the European continent. Now the tide was turning. During the winter of 1812 Napoleon's armies had been driven back from Moscow, the Russian troops and the fierce eastern cold taking thousands of French lives. Six months later Napoleon's Iberian possessions were lost to a combination of British, Spanish and Portuguese troops. In October 1813 he had been resoundingly defeated at Leipzig by the Allies of the Fourth Coalition (Russia, Britain, Austria and Prussia) and the French army was thrown into perpetual retreat. Finally, on 1 April 1814, in a graphic illustration of the French collapse, the citizens of Paris watched aghast as the Tsar of Russia, the King of Prussia and Prince Schwarzenberg of Austria paraded through the streets of their city.

# The Abdication of Napoleon

Shortly after the Allies began their occupation of Paris, Napoleon publicly acknowledged defeat and offered to abdicate:

'Since the allied powers have proclaimed the Emperor Napoleon the sole obstacle to the re-establishment of peace in Europe the Emperor Napoleon, faithful to his oath, states that he is ready to relinquish the throne...'

Quoted in Vincent Cronin, *Napoleon* (1971)

A replacement for Napoleon was quickly found:

'The French people freely call to the throne of France Louis Stanislas-Xavier of France, brother of the last king – and after him the other members of the House of Bourbon in the old order.'

Part of the Second Article of the new French Charter (constitution) introduced on 6 April 1814. Quoted in Harold Nicolson, *The Congress of Vienna* (1946)

With Napoleon defeated and exiled to the island of Elba, the Allies began the complex task of restructuring Europe in an effort to secure a just and lasting peace. The main problems they faced in dismantling Napoleonic Europe can be considered in the following Focus section.

THE EMPEROR NAPOLEON

## 1.1 Problems facing the peacemakers

**The Principal Decision-makers**

- Britain
- Russia
- Austria
- Prussia

**The Principal Objectives**

- Secure peace
- Contain France
- Restore the balance of power

Napoleonic Empire

**Dependent states**

1. Rhine Confederation
2. Switzerland
3. Grand Duchy of Warsaw
4. Kingdom of Italy
5. Kingdom of Naples
6. Spain

## France

Substantially enlarged through Revolutionary and Napoleonic campaigns with extensions into the Italian peninsula and the Low Countries.

To what degree should the peacemakers reduce France? What should be done with the territory removed from French possession? What might be the dangers of punishing France too severely? How could France be confined within her new borders?

> If you were one of the principal peacemakers what role would you allow France in the discussions?

## Grand Duchy of Warsaw

Formerly Poland but renamed by Napoleon and made into a puppet state of the French Empire. In the Eighteenth Century Poland had been partitioned between Russia, Austria and Prussia. In 1814 it was occupied by Russian troops.

Should the Tsar be allowed to keep Poland or should it be repartitioned? Should the wishes of the Poles be considered?

> Why might there be objections from Prussia and Austria to the suggestion that Russia should keep Poland?

These questions are intended for discussion. At this stage the results of your debates should not be considered as definitive solutions to the problems facing the peacemakers.

## Kingdom of Italy

Napoleon had conquered the whole of the Italian mainland by 1799. Thereafter, either directly or indirectly, the Italian peninsula came under French control. Italian nationalists had been encouraged by this example of the potential of national unity.

Should the peacemakers allow Nationalism to develop in Italy by creating an independent and unified state? Would it be preferable to restore Italy to its pre-Napoleonic position with numerous small states each with their own absolutist monarch?

> How could these restored monarchs be guaranteed against further French aggression?

## Rhine Confederation

Created by Napoleon in 1806. United 17 German states into an association under direct French control.

Should the Confederation be preserved as an independent state by the peacemakers? Should it be broken up and the component states restored to their legitimate rulers? Should it be a source of territory for Prussian expansion?

> Given the geographical position of the Rhine Confederation, what advantages might there be in extending Prussian influence here?

# The settlement of France

Between April 1814 and November 1815, representatives of the major Powers met to determine the new territorial arrangements for Europe. Three stages in the settlement are discernible: the first Peace of Paris (May 1814), the Treaty of Vienna (June 1815) and the second Peace of Paris (November 1815). The most pressing decisions to be made following the defeat of Napoleon concerned the fate of France. Negotiations between the Allies produced the first Peace of Paris, signed on 30 May 1814. The treaty was exceptionally lenient. France was restored to her frontiers of 1792 and accepted the termination of all claims over Italy, Switzerland, Belgium, Holland and Germany. Britain received the former French colonies of Santa Lucia, Tobago and Isle de France. There was to be no occupying army and no indemnity was levied; the French were even allowed to retain art treasures looted from the cities of Europe during the Napoleonic conquests. Appended to the treaty were a number of secret articles. These detailed the Allies' proposals for disposing of confiscated French territory. At Britain's insistence it was decided that Holland would be enlarged by the addition of the former Austrian Netherlands (Belgium). Prussia was to be allowed territory in the Rhineland and it was proposed to restore Austrian influence in Northern Italy. In addition the French were required to agree to the independence of Switzerland. The astonishing leniency of the French settlement was not the product of international benevolence. It was a deliberate manoeuvre by the Allies to ensure an enduring period of peace and repose in Europe.

'The... [first Peace of Paris] bore the stamp of the moderation of the monarchs and their cabinets – a moderation which did not arise from weakness, but from the resolve to secure a lasting peace to Europe... The Peace to be concluded with France could only be looked at either as a revenge on the country, or as establishing the greatest possible equilibrium between the powers.'

Metternich, *Memoirs,* quoted in Edward Vose Gulick, *Europe's Classical Balance of Power* (1955)

THE BATTLE OF WATERLOO

The Allies understood that a harsh settlement would only serve to direct resentment against the newly-restored Bourbon monarchy and could well result in a revival of Bonapartism.

However, the treaty was soon amended. On the evening of Sunday 19 March 1815, Louis XVIII left his rain-swept capital and struck north for Ghent in Belgium. On the following night Napoleon Bonaparte, having escaped from Elba, entered Paris and renewed the war against the Allies. Napoleon's 'Hundred Days' ended decisively at Waterloo on 18 June 1815. He was incarcerated on the island of St Helena in the South Atlantic where he remained until his death from stomach cancer in 1821. The revival of Napoleon's ambitions and French support for them invalidated the first Peace of Paris. It was replaced in November by the second Peace of Paris, a more punitive settlement than the first. Once again the Bourbons were restored to the French throne but this time an Allied army of occupation was imposed. The frontiers of France were reduced to those of 1790, an indemnity of 700 million francs was demanded and stolen works of art began to be returned to the cities from which they had been plundered.

ST HELENA, NAPOLEON'S EXILE HOME

## The Congress of Vienna

Five months before Napoleon's escape from Elba the sovereigns, states-men and nobility of Europe began to congregate in Vienna. This splendid assembly was in accordance with Article 32 of the first Peace of Paris which made provision for a congress to settle the European state system. In six months (November 1814–May 1815) the Congress of Vienna held 41 sessions at which an enormous amount of work was transacted. The culmination of these meetings was the signing of the Treaty of Vienna on 9 June 1815 which settled the main issues affecting Central and Eastern Europe.

Five nations dominated the proceedings: Russia, Britain, France, Austria and Prussia. They were bound together by certain broad princi-ples but differed in the specific aims and ambitions which formed their national interests. What were these general principles and national ambi-tions, and who voiced them at Vienna?

## 1.2 The aims of the peacemakers

### Castlereagh

British Foreign Secretary (1812-22) and chief British representative at the Congress of Vienna.

Devoted to the principle of a European balance of power. He arrived at Vienna with the intention of making 'the establishment of a just equilibrium in Europe...the first objective of my attention'. With this aim he hoped to create the basis of an enduring peace to serve the general interests of war-weary Europe and the particular needs of British commerce. As an island power Britain had no territorial ambitions in continental Europe. However, Castlereagh was determined to resist claims for land being voiced most noticeably by Tsar Alexander of Russia. He was also committed to the containment of France in order to prevent her from ever again menacing the peace of Europe. Castlereagh was convinced that any future challenge to the peace and stability of Europe would come from either France or Russia. Accordingly, he had as one of his aims the creation of a strong, independent Central Europe designed to resist aggression from both east and west. Initially, he believed that both Austria and Prussia would together be able to provide the central counterbalance to future French and Russian ambitions.

### Talleyrand

Formerly Napoleon's Foreign Minister (1799-1807). Instrumental in securing the restoration of Louis XVIII, and the King's representative at the Congress. Talleyrand was concerned to convince the Allies that his country no longer posed a threat to them. In his memoirs he wrote: 'France wanted nothing more than she possessed...she had sincerely repudiated the heritage of conquest...she considered herself strong enough within her ancient frontiers...she had no thought of extending them...she now took pride in her moderation.' However, Talleyrand was determined that French interests would be recognised by the Congress and that France would be restored to an equal footing with the other European Powers. He opposed the Russian claims on Poland and did not wish to see Prussia strengthened on the eastern frontier of France. Talleyrand was the chief exponent of the principle of legitimacy believing that, wherever possible, rightful rulers should be restored to their thrones.

## Tsar Alexander

Tsar of Russia from 1801 to 1825. The only sovereign among the great Powers to represent personally the interests of his country at Vienna. Alexander was quite prepared to use the Congress to pursue the traditional aims of Russian foreign policy, in particular the aim of westward expansion. This was translated into one very specific purpose: the complete absorption of Poland and its subjection to Russian authority. Alexander was well placed to achieve this with some 600,000 men in occupation of the former Napoleonic state. However, in acquiring Poland for himself, Alexander was proposing to deprive Austria and Prussia of the Polish lands they had obtained in the eighteenth-century partitions.

## Metternich

Austrian Foreign Minister (1809-21) and principal representative of the Austrian Empire at the Congress. Like Castlereagh, Metternich was interested in a settlement which would establish a just equilibrium between states and would preserve the peace of Europe. He hoped to see France and Russia confined to their ancient frontiers and was especially concerned to obtain security for Austria against the westward ambitions of Tsar Alexander. He believed in the creation of a strong Central Europe and saw Austria as the logical director of this power group. He was not at all inclined to accept the consolidation of power in the German states by Prussia. Metternich wished to re-assert Austrian authority over the Italian states and was totally opposed to the granting of concessions to Nationalism and Liberalism.

## Hardenberg

Prussian Chancellor (since 1810), he acted on behalf of King Frederick William III at Vienna. Prussia was a rising power in 1815 but was not well placed to make particular demands at the Congress. Defeat at the hands of Napoleon left the Prussians dedicated to recovery and this Hardenberg hoped to achieve by augmenting Prussian territory in Germany. However, he found his diplomatic options restricted. King Frederick William regarded the Tsar as his 'divine friend' and was excessively grateful to Alexander for liberating his country from Napoleon's grip. Hardenberg was accordingly compelled to follow the Russian line. Nevertheless, he was not prevented from demanding Saxony as compensation for the possible transfer of Prussian Poland to the Tsar.

## QUESTIONS

**1** Summarize the principal aims of the statesmen who attended the Congress of Vienna.

**2** In order to achieve their aims, it became apparent that individual states would have to combine with others of like ambition. In these 'power combinations' states would be able to outflank opponents and achieve mutual benefits. The diagram below represents power combinations which seemed possible at Vienna.

Using the information from this section:
(a) explain in each case why such a combination seemed likely;
(b) detail any areas of possible dispute between the member states.

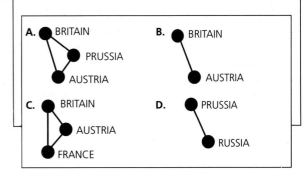

# General principles

Aside from the specific aims and ambitions of the Great Powers at Vienna, it is clear that there was some general agreement about the nature of the final settlement all wished to see. The negotiations of the Congress were based around certain fundamental principles which determined the overall complexion of the final treaty.

## 1 The balance of power

The Vienna peacemakers subscribed to the Eighteenth Century concept of international relations commonly known as 'the balance of power'. At its most elementary level this held that the ideal state system was one where no single Power was able to exercise influence or control over the others. The period of Revolutionary and Napoleonic France had upset this balance and it was now the task of the peacemakers to restore an 'equilibrium' in Europe.

Unfortunately, this was no easy assignment as the historian Douglas Dakin points out:

'This idea [the balance of power] was as old as the hills, but so various were its expositions that there was no consensus of opinion on what constituted a balance of power. For Britain a balance of power implied a state system, a series of frontiers and stable alignments containing France within her historic frontiers. To the Austrians it meant a state system and frontiers which gave her predominance in Central Europe, and security against a Russia seeking to encroach on Poland and the Ottoman Empire and to extend her dynastic influence in the German Courts... As for Russia, her conception of a balance of power was of a quite different order: as a spasmodically expansionist power she regarded a balance of power as something to be manipulated to facilitate the fulfilment of her designs. The balance was not for her, as for Austria and Britain, a system of repose – not as Castlereagh, Metternich and Talleyrand would have termed it 'a just equilibrium'.'

Douglas Dakin in *Europe's Balance of Power* (ed. A Sked, 1979)

## 2 A lasting peace

Establishing a balance of power was part of a wider design to create a settlement which would offer security from a future war. After 20 years of armed conflict the Congress statesmen looked to return to the period of harmony which they believed had existed before the upheaval of the French Revolution.

## 3 Compensation

Although not specifically mentioned at the Vienna Congress, this principle was implicit in the negotiating positions taken by the statesmen as they discussed the territorial reshaping of Europe. The first Peace of Paris had already agreed to the compensation of Holland with Belgium (formerly the Austrian Netherlands). Austria, who surrendered this province, looked to be compensated in Italy. Prussia wished for compensation in return for Russian absorption of her Polish lands. Even Britain, who came to Vienna with no territorial claims on Europe, had achieved compensation through the acquisition of colonial bases.

The following items might be regarded as elements which make up the international balance of power: population; commercial trade; industrial capacity; troops available for mobilization; territorial extent.

In groups discuss the implications for the balance of power of a substantial increase in each of these elements in one country. Which do you think would have the most significant impact on the other countries?

## 4 Legitimacy

The restoration of rightful rulers to their thrones has become a principle commonly linked with the work of the Vienna statesmen. This has largely arisen due to Talleyrand's insistence on the idea during the time of the Congress. However, the principle was far less frequently applied in practice as the historian LCB Seaman notes:

'The notion that Vienna was solely concerned to restore legitimate rulers breaks down after only the briefest examination. It was ignored in Western Germany, in Poland, in Saxony, Norway, the Austrian Netherlands and Northern Italy. It was most conspicuously applied to the French Bourbons; but it was almost exclusively in their interest that the slogan was invented.'

LCB Seaman, *From Vienna to Versailles* (1956)

## 5 Containment

In order to establish a lasting peace, the statesmen at Vienna sought to obtain security against the French. It was not enough that France was the defeated nation in 1814; a very real fear existed that, given the right opportunity, the French would once again invade and disrupt Europe. The statesmen were determined that this should not happen and planned to erect a chain of buffer states along the entire French frontier to contain her aggressive ambitions.

# The work of the Congress

The Congress of Vienna began in dispute. Under the terms of a secret article of the first Peace of Paris, the Four Great Powers of the Quadruple Alliance (Britain, Russia, Austria, Prussia) had allocated to themselves the right to decide the future of the European state system. This agreement excluded significant nations such as Spain, Portugal and Sweden; it offered only spectator status to the numerous Minor Powers who had arrived in Vienna; above all France, still one of the most important states in Europe, was to be denied the role of Great Power. It was a danger Talleyrand fully recognized:

'It was very tempting and very easy for the Governments which had so long been hostile to keep her [France] excluded from the major questions affecting Europe. By the Treaty of Paris France had escaped destruction, but she had not retained the position that she ought to occupy in the general political system. Trained eyes could easily detect in several of the principal plenipotentiaries the secret desire to reduce France to a secondary role.'

From Talleyrand's *Memoirs*, quoted in Duff Cooper, *Talleyrand* (1932)

Talleyrand was determined to prevent the dilution of French power and skillfully set about exploiting the disappointment of the Minor Powers:

'France alone the great powers might afford to ignore, but France at the head of the rest of Europe became at once a formidable antagonist.'

Duff Cooper, *Talleyrand* (1932)

At a private meeting with the 'Big Four' and the representative of Spain on 30 September, Talleyrand methodically dismantled the plans laid by

**1** Suggest reasons why the Four Great Powers might have wished to exclude France from negotiations to decide 'the major questions affecting Europe'.

**2** What arguments might Talleyrand have used to obtain the inclusion of France in these negotiations?

**3** What 'position' do you think Talleyrand intended France to occupy in the 'general political system'?

the Great Powers, at one point berating them for their use of the term 'Allies': 'Let us speak frankly, gentlemen, if there are to be Allies in this business then this is no place for me.' He subsequently secured a Committee of Eight consisting of the Powers who had signed the first Peace of Paris (the Big Four plus France, Spain, Portugal and Sweden) to direct the proceedings at Vienna. More importantly, be obtained the admission of France into the discussions of the Big Four, now transformed into the Big Five. Thereafter he abandoned the Minor Powers and laboured ceaselessly in pursuit of French interests.

Talleyrand's diplomatic accomplishments had important consequences. As the former allies began to split over the Polish-Saxon issue, Talleyrand found himself able to promote French interests by offering his support to the highest bidder.

## Poland and Saxony

The Polish-Saxon issue dominated the work of the Congress from October 1814 to January 1815. The focal point of this protracted dispute was Poland. Tsar Alexander was determined to convert his occupation of the former Napoleonic state into full ownership, incorporating Poland into the Russian Empire. The Tsar and his occupying armies were in a strong position and his message to the Vienna statesmen was clear: 'Poland is mine. There can be little negotiation with 600,000 men.'

Alexander completed his proposals by offering Saxony to Prussia in compensation for her loss of Polish territory. Immediate resistance to these plans came from Castlereagh and Metternich. The latter feared an enlarged Russia so close to the north and north-east boundary of the Austrian Empire and was equally opposed to any extension of Prussian power in the German states. Castlereagh too objected to Russian encroachment into Eastern Europe. In his quest for a European balance of power, Castlereagh was especially concerned to sabotage Alexander's Polish-Saxon proposals. The British Foreign Secretary feared that if these proposals succeeded, Russia and Prussia would be bound so closely together as to render his aim of a strong, independent Central Europe impossible.

Amidst this atmosphere of conflicting ambition the diplomatic bargaining began. It soon became apparent that for Castlereagh and Metternich, the prevention of Russian westward expansion was a priority. Accordingly, the two statesmen looked to Prussia for assistance against the Tsar. Hardenberg was offered Saxony in return for full co-operation with Austria and Britain against Russia. On 24 October 1814, the three statesmen met and mutually approved the plan. However, this three-power bloc was short-lived. Upon hearing of the opposition to his Polish designs, Alexander flew into a rage causing the Prussian King Frederick William to buckle and order Hardenberg to abandon his arrangements with Metternich and Castlereagh.

With the former allies now split into two rival camps over the Polish-Saxon issue, Talleyrand was able to play an important role in helping to settle the dispute. Talleyrand feared the knock-on effect of the Polish issue in Western Europe, being especially worried about the consolidation of Prussian power in Germany. He was therefore inclined to work with Britain and Austria, and on 3 January 1815 the Triple Alliance was created. This provided for mutual assistance if any of the three were attacked. Alexander now faced the formidable combination of Britain, Austria and France aligned against his Polish designs. Accordingly, he began to soften and the threat of war receded.

The final settlement was a compromise. Prussia received about three-fifths (by area) of Saxony. Poland became an independent kingdom with its own constitution but was ruled over by the Russian Tsar. Some Polish territory was relinquished to Austria and Prussia and the Eighteenth-Century principle of partitioning Poland was restored.

### The 'Cordon Sanitaire'

Following the conclusion of the Polish-Saxon affair, rapid progress was made towards resolving the other outstanding territorial questions. The decisions made regarding the Netherlands, the German states, Switzerland and Italy had important consequences for France who found herself contained, along the entire length of her European frontier, behind an arc of hostile buffer states. The first Peace of Paris may have been lenient, but the Powers were taking no chances by leaving unprotected the borders across which France had launched her invasions of Europe in the Eighteenth Century. The map below shows the features of this 'Cordon Sanitaire'.

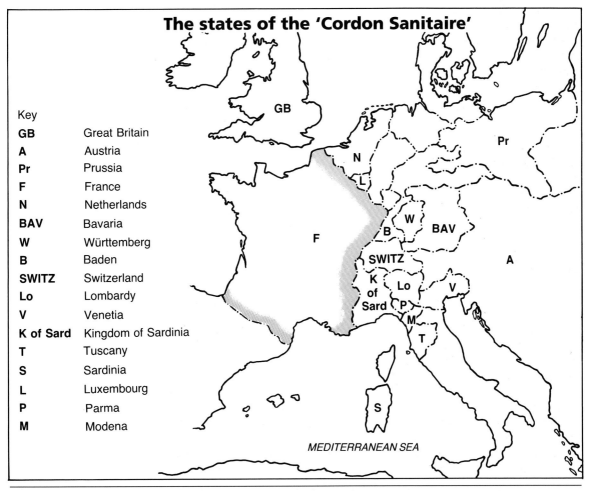

The states of the 'Cordon Sanitaire'

**Key**

| | |
|---|---|
| **GB** | Great Britain |
| **A** | Austria |
| **Pr** | Prussia |
| **F** | France |
| **N** | Netherlands |
| **BAV** | Bavaria |
| **W** | Württemberg |
| **B** | Baden |
| **SWITZ** | Switzerland |
| **Lo** | Lombardy |
| **V** | Venetia |
| **K of Sard** | Kingdom of Sardinia |
| **T** | Tuscany |
| **S** | Sardinia |
| **L** | Luxembourg |
| **P** | Parma |
| **M** | Modena |

MEDITERRANEAN SEA

**The Netherlands** Holland was united with the former Austrian Netherlands (Belgium) to form a new Kingdom of the Netherlands ruled over by the King of Holland. Britain had already agreed to provide £2 million towards the cost of constructing defensive fortresses along the vulnerable Franco-Dutch border. The King of Holland also received the Duchy of Luxembourg.

**Hanover** Established as an enlarged and independent kingdom but retaining close dynastic links with Britain. (Hanover had, since 1714, been the source of the British monarchy.)

**Prussia** Given extensive territory in the Rhineland and expected to garrison the area with a large number of troops.

**Bavaria, Württemberg, Baden** Incorporated as part of the new German Confederation. This consisted of 39 independent units (including Prussia) under the Presidency of Austria.

**Switzerland** Constituted as an independent state. Her neutrality was guaranteed by the Big Five Powers.

**Lombardy, Venetia** These two north Italian states were linked together as the Lombardo-Venetian kingdom and placed under the direct rule of the Austrian Emperor.

**Kingdom of Sardinia** An enlarged Piedmont incorporating Sardinia, Savoy, Nice and Genoa.

**Tuscany** Given to the brother of the Austrian Emperor. The two minor Italian states, Parma and Modena, were also placed in the hands of the Austrian Habsburgs.

---

1 What was the purpose of:

(a) uniting Belgium with Holland?

(b) enlarging the Kingdom of Sardinia?

**2** Why were Lombardy, Venetia, Parma, Modena and Tuscany all linked to the Austrian throne?

**3** What strategic considerations lay behind the decision to allocate territory in the Rhineland to Prussia?

**4** 'Security not revenge,' claimed Castlereagh, was one of the principal aims of the Vienna Congress. How 'secure' was continental Europe from future French aggression following these new territorial arrangements? Consider these scenarios and suggest the likely outcomes:

(a) French attack launched on Europe through Luxembourg;

(b) French violation of Swiss neutrality;

(c) French attack on Europe via the Kingdom of Sardinia.

**5** How did these new territorial arrangements help to secure a 'balance of power' in Europe?

**6** What do you suppose was the French reaction to these arrangements?

---

# Examining the evidence
## Verdicts on Vienna: contemporary views

### Source A

The object [of the Congress], as all gentlemen must be aware, was to gain and permanently secure greater safety on both flanks of the two States which were to form the immediate bulwarks of Europe [Austria and Prussia], to give adequate power by means of the additional strength which they should supply to that State of North Germany which would be charged with the preservation of that portion of the Continent. It was also desirable that a strong barrier should be interposed between the States of Italy and France, to prevent them also from arraying themselves against each other. It was further wished that Switzerland should be re-established in her influence and independence, to keep up the chain of communication, and that Germany might be again confederated in the same system, to render it an impregnable bulwark between the great States in the East and West of Europe.

*Speech by Castlereagh in the House of Commons, 20 March 1815. Quoted in CK Webster, British Diplomacy 1813–1815 (1921)*

### Source B

The object of the new system is to crush the weak by the combination of the strong; to subject Europe in the first place to an oligarchy of sovereigns, and ultimately to swallow it up in the gulf of universal monarchy; where civilization has always perished, with freedom of thought, with controlled power, with national character and spirit, with patriotism and emulation, in a word, with all its characteristic attributes, and with all its guardian principles.

I am content, Sir, that these observations should be thought wholly unreasonable by those new masters of civil wisdom, who tell us that the whole policy of Europe consists in strengthening the right flank of Prussia, and the left flank of Austria; who see in that wise and venerable system long the boast and the safeguard of Europe, only the millions of souls to be given to one power, or the thousands of square miles to be given to another; who consider the frontier of a river as a better protection for a country than the love of its inhabitants; and who provide for the safety of their states by wounding the pride and mortifying the patriotic affection of a people, in order to fortify a line of military posts.

*Speech by Sir James Mackintosh in the House of Commons, 27 April 1815. Hansard, Parliamentary Debates (vol. XXX. 918)*

---

**1** Identify the 'great States in the East and West of Europe' mentioned in Source A.

**2** What was the main object of the Vienna negotiations according to:

(a) Castlereagh (Source A)?

(b) Mackintosh (Source B)?

**3** What specific criticisms does Mackintosh make about the actions of the Vienna peacemakers?

**4** What kind of settlement do you suppose Mackintosh would have preferred?

**5** Castlereagh in Source A speaks in support of the settlement on behalf of the Tory Government which despatched him to Vienna to help arrange it.

What inferences can you make from Source B about the political affiliations of Sir James Mackintosh?

In what ways are these sources biased?

How useful are these sources to the historian who wishes to discover the nature of contemporary reactions to the Vienna settlement?

## Verdicts on Vienna: historians' views

### Source C

The conclusion of this tremendous treaty [Treaty of Vienna] attracted but slight attention. Castlereagh himself predicted that it would maintain the peace of Europe for at least seven years. As a matter of fact all the main provisions of the Vienna Final Act remained unaltered for a space of forty years; and the settlement arrived at preserved Europe from any general conflagration for all but a century.

Harold Nicolson, *The Congress of Vienna* (1946)

### Source D

...the Vienna settlement must not be regarded as having of itself prevented a European war for a century. It is possible to say instead that it contained in none of its provisions the seeds of a future war between the great powers...

...ultimately, wars are neither caused nor prevented by treaties, but by policies. What prevented major war until 1853 [Crimean War] was the determination of the great powers that there should not be such a war.... If there was peace in Europe for forty years after 1815, the credit must go mainly to Metternich, but also to Palmerston [British Foreign Secretary, 1830–41] and to Nicholas I [Tsar of Russia, 1825–55]. That there were wars between 1853 and 1871 was due mainly to Napoleon III [Emperor of France, 1852–70]. That there was no general war between 1871 and 1914 does not mean that peace prevailed in any sense in that period. There might have been war in 1875, 1878, 1885, 1887, 1898, 1906, 1908, 1911 or 1912. That it was avoided on each of these occasions has nothing to do with the Congress of Vienna.

LCB Seaman, *From Vienna to Versailles* (1956)

### Source E

It is further to be observed that none of these three treaties [first and second Paris Treaties and the Treaty of Vienna] contain any express guarantee, general or special, by which their observance is to be enforced...There is no doubt that a breach of the covenant by any one State is an injury which all the other States may, if they shall think fit, either separately or collectively resent, but the treaties do not impose, by express stipulation, the doing so as a matter of positive obligation.

Memorandum on the Treaties of 1814 and 1815 submitted by Britain, 1818. Quoted in
Sir Charles Webster, *The Congress of Vienna* (1919)

### Source F

They [the Vienna statesmen] were limited in outlook, too prone to compromise, lacking in faith and courage. None, except Alexander – and he only fitfully and irresolutely – made any attempt to do more than the obvious. They were content with expedients. They were men of their own generation; and, though they secured for Europe a breathing-space of peace, and in one or two minor points, such as the regulation of International Rivers, did much for the future government of Europe, they did little else to win the gratitude of posterity.

Sir Charles Webster, as above

### Source G

The central European arrangements made after the Napoleonic Wars proved to be the weakest feature of the new order. The weakness arose out of the fact that Austrian power was over-stretched. She was made into a buffer state defending the status quo against future French aggression from the west and Russian aggression from the east...she did not have the means to sustain this burden...The central problem of the Vienna states system was how to strengthen Austria to enable her to fulfil the tasks which had been imposed upon her. Castlereagh and Metternich tried to solve this question by leading the four-power alliance and using it to control both France and Russia. When this failed Metternich was forced to rely exclusively on Russia to keep the empire intact and defend the monarchy against the revolutionary threat from below and the French threat from the west. When this also failed Austria was vulnerable to her enemies.

FR Bridge and Roger Bullen, *The Great Powers and the European States System 1815–1914* (1980)

### Source H

Like a collection of rooks' nests, which a gust of wind dislocates, these little principalities [the numerous states of Italy and Germany] are liable to be over-run and plundered in every political squall. Were there no such clusters of small independencies in Germany and Italy, there would be no commodious theatre for war; powerful princes would be obliged to attack the territories of powerful princes, and the simple construction of the European system would not only be better understood, but fewer clashing interests would exist...

Gould Francis Leckie, 'Historical Research into the Nature of the Balance of Power.' Quoted in Edward Vose Gulick, *Europe's Classical Balance of Power* (1955)

### Source I

During the latter part of the nineteenth century, after the great nationalistic triumphs that the unifications of Italy and Germany represented, the shortcomings of Vienna were largely emphasized. In our time of greater trouble and uncertainty, when the nineteenth century as a whole appears by contrast with the present as a period of relative stability and minor disturbances, the point is often made that, altered as they had become by 1914, the settlements of 1815 served Europe for a century; the contrast certainly is arresting between the mere twenty-year truce that followed the

1919 settlements [concluding the First World War] and the story enclosed by the years 1815 to 1914. Metternich's stock has risen as a consequence and some have rediscovered the merits of the conservative outlook that was his. History is forever rewritten.

René Albrecht-Carrie, *A Diplomatic History of Europe Since the Congress of Vienna* (1958)

---

**1** Using Sources F, G and H, identify and detail the criticisms of the Vienna settlement.

**2** Source G identifies a fundamental weakness of the Vienna arrangements. What combination of Powers resulted from this weakness? Explain why this was detrimental to the interests of British foreign policy.

**3** Source H suggests that a better solution to the problems of multiple states in Italy and Germany could have been devised at Vienna. What is the nature of the solution offered in this source?

**4** What general compliment is paid to the settlement in Sources C and I? How does Seaman (Source D) challenge this view of the settlement?

**5** How does Source E help to support Seaman's contention that war was avoided until 1853 because of the attitude of the Powers and not because of the Treaty?

**6** Consider this information:

Castlereagh: born 1769; son of an aristocrat, the Marquis of Londonderry.

Metternich: born 1773; son of a Count. Imbued with conservative principles during his youth.

Talleyrand: born 1754 into the aristocratic family of Talleyrand-Perigord.

Alexander I: born 1777. Frederick William III: born 1770. Both ruled as absolute monarchs.

How can this information help us to understand the criticisms of the peacemakers made in Source F?

Why is it important for the historian to recognize the backgrounds and attitudes of individuals who are subject to historical assessment? What is the danger of seeing the past from a modern perspective?

**7** Copy out the chart opposite. Using Sources C and I show how the general perception of the Vienna settlement changed according to the features of the period from which it was viewed.

**8** What does Albrecht-Carrie mean by the phrase 'History is forever rewritten' (Source I)?

---

| Time period | Features | General attitude to Vienna |
|---|---|---|
| 1815–53 | Peace | |
| 1859–71 | Wars of Nationalism | |
| Twentieth Century | First and Second World Wars; persistent conflict. | |

## Defending the settlement

During the Nineteenth Century the Vienna settlement was subjected to a barrage of hostile criticism. The chief complaint was that the statesmen who had devised the new territorial arrangements had failed to acknowledge the principles of liberalism and nationalism. Hundreds of thousands of people, representing entire national groups, had been transferred into the possession of remote kings without the slightest regard for their wishes, political rights or feelings. However, such criticism originated at a time, in the latter half of the Nineteenth Century, when the forces of nationalism and liberalism were beginning to overcome the conservative ideals so beloved of the Vienna statesmen. How fair and appropriate then, is such criticism? The historian Frederick Artz offers this defence of the settlement:

'In 1815 neither the statesmen nor the peoples of Europe had any thorough understanding of the vague principles of nationalism and democracy. Moreover, there was, at the time of the Vienna Congress, a widespread distrust of these revolutionary ideas. It is as incredible that the statesmen of 1815 should have made them the basis of a reconstructed Europe as that the delegates at the Conference of 1919 [the Versailles negotiations to settle Europe after the First World War] should have revamped Europe in accordance with the precepts of communism. After the overthrow of Napoleon the diplomatists quite naturally resorted to the familiar ideas of the balance of power and to the notions of legitimacy, and tried to fuse them into some sort of compromise that would guarantee Europe a period of peace. Whatever may be said against them, they were, most of them, reasonable, fair minded and well-intentioned.'

Frederick B Artz, *Reaction and Revolution* (1934)

---

**1** According to Artz, why did the peacemakers ignore the principles of nationalism and liberalism?

**2** How does Artz defend the work of the statesmen?

---

'In 1815 the ideas of nationalism and liberalism were in their infancy. They were associated in the minds of the peacemakers with the chaos of the French Revolution and the subsequent Continental wars. In their desire to obtain peace and security it would have been unthinkable for them to encourage such ideas. Thus the national interests of the Belgians were not considered because the primary objective was to secure the north-eastern border of France. Belgium by herself would have been considered dangerously vulnerable to future French aggression. The transfer of the north Italian states to Austrian control was partly motivated by the desire to prevent these places from falling into the hands of the French as they had done under Napoleon. Similarly, the national aspirations held by some Germans were ignored. The unification of those states was completely out of the question in 1815. As the historian LCB Seaman explains: 'Diplomats cannot be criticized for not wanting to negotiate their countries out of existence; and the creation of a unitary Germany would have involved the representatives of Austria and Prussia in doing precisely that." (*From Vienna to Versailles,* 1956).

When assessing the settlement then, it is important to understand what was practical for the time. After the domestic upheaval of the French Revolution and the international violence of the wars which followed, the priority was to establish a workable peace; in this at least, the peacemakers were generally successful.

# REVIEW

The list below describes the principal actions of the Vienna peacemakers.

**1** The fusion of Belgium with Holland to form the Kingdom of the Netherlands.

**2** The allocation of territory in the Rhineland to Prussia.

**3** The creation of the German Confederation under the Presidency of Austria.

**4** The creation of the Lombardo-Venetian Kingdom under the direct rule of the Austrian Emperor.

**5** The enlargement of the Kingdom of Sardinia.

**6** Tuscany, Parma and Modena placed under the control of relatives of the Austrian Habsburgs.

**7** The transference of three-fifths of Saxony to Prussia.

**8** The creation of the Kingdom of Poland ruled over by the Tsar of Russia.

Consider the following question which is taken from an Advanced Level examination paper:

**'National rather than international interests determined the actions of the peacemakers at Vienna.' Discuss this statement. (JMB)**

Which of the actions listed above could be said to have been motivated by national self-interest? Which were inspired by broader international considerations? In each case your task is to try to determine what the peacemakers hoped would be achieved by their actions. An example is provided for you on the page opposite.

**Example**

**1** The fusion of Belgium with Holland to create the Kingdom of the Netherlands.

The principal purpose of this action was to protect the vulnerable northeastern frontier between France and the Low Countries. It was believed that a larger, united state would stand a better chance of resisting possible French aggression than two smaller, independent states. The peacemakers looked to the new Kingdom of the Netherlands to help secure the general European peace. In this sense it could be argued that the fusion of Belgium with Holland was part of an international strategy to ensure the long-term survival of peace in Europe. Of course national interests were served by such a policy. The European Powers were financially exhausted by years of war and commercial prosperity depended upon the open exchange of goods and services. It was therefore in the national interest of each of the Powers to establish and help protect the general European peace.

In your review of this chapter you should aim to provide a similar analysis for each of the actions listed opposite.

Is it always possible to distinguish between national and international interests?

On balance, would you agree or disagree with the claim made in the essay question?

# 2 The Congress System: Great Power Diplomacy 1815–30

## PREVIEW

### The Congress System: myth or reality?

Most historical studies of the Nineteenth Century employ the term 'Congress System' when discussing the style of Great Power diplomacy following the collapse of Napoleonic France. So frequently does the expression arise that it is easy to assume the existence of some form of nineteenth-century United Nations charged with the task of regulating international affairs. Such an impression would be quite incorrect. The historian LCB Seaman offers sound advice on this issue:

'Perhaps the most useful service a student can do himself in attempting to study Great Power co-operation in the years immediately after the Napoleonic Wars is to dismiss from his mind altogether the notion that there ever was such a thing as a Congress System. He may then have some chance of realizing that although there were Congresses after 1815 there was little that was systematic about them. There was no agreement between the powers as to what the Congresses were for, and there was no permanent organization for international co-operation such as was set up after each of the two German wars of the twentieth century. Like so many of the 'systems' in history, the Congress System is an invention of historians.'

LCB Seaman, *From Vienna to Versailles* (1956)

## TALKING POINT

**Terms of convenience**

Why do historians 'invent' devices such as the Congress System? How can such devices (a) be helpful, and (b) cause difficulties in the study of history? Try to think of some comparable terms used by historians. If you find this exercise difficult, look out for such terms during the course of your wider reading.

THE CONGRESS OF VERONA IN SESSION

# Great Power co-operation

If the Congress System never really existed, what do historians mean when they use the phrase? Stephen J Lee, in his book *Aspects of European History,* offers an alternative term and an appropriate definition:

'The Concert of Europe is the term used to describe various attempts made by the major powers to co-operate, after 1815, in settling possible causes of conflict between themselves in order to prevent the possibility of another large-scale war.'

The Congress System and the Concert of Europe; both terms apply to the period of attempted co-operation among the Major Powers following the conclusion of the Napoleonic Wars. The basic idea behind this co-operative venture was that, having defeated France through concerted effort, the Powers might best maintain the peace they had created at Vienna through sustained co-operation. Initially, this collaborative exercise was conducted through the medium of periodic meetings known as Congresses. Four such Congresses were held: at Aix-la-Chapelle in 1818; Troppau, 1820; Laibach, 1821 and Verona in 1822. Such meetings gave rise to the term 'Congress System', and were an ambitious attempt to conduct international diplomacy across the conference table.

During the 1820s the Congress System collapsed. Britain refused to attend the meetings, believing that the original purpose of the co-operative process had been betrayed by Powers who sought to use their combined strength for selfish ends. Those Powers which remained, Austria, Russia and Prussia, were subject to their own rivalries and found it difficult to co-operate effectively on the issues which faced them.

## Holy Alliance and Quadruple Alliance

The success of Great Power co-operation, first in the war against France and then during the peacemaking process at Vienna, led the statesmen to conclude that great benefits could be derived from similar co-operation in peacetime. During the latter part of 1815 two documents appeared which gave expression to the desire for continued co-operation. The first of these emerged from the increasingly mystical mind of Tsar Alexander. Encouraged by the religious zealot Baroness von Krüdener, Alexander looked to involve his fellow sovereigns in a moral and spiritual association based on Christian principles; the result was the Holy Alliance.

'Art. 1. Conformably to the words of the Holy Scriptures, which command all men to consider each other as brethren, the Three Contracting Monarchs [of Russia, Austria and Prussia] will remain united by the bonds of a true and indissoluble fraternity, and considering each other as fellow countrymen, they will, on all occasions and in all places, lend each other aid and assistance; and, regarding themselves towards their subjects and armies as fathers of families, they will lead them, in the same spirit of fraternity with which they are animated, to protect Religion, Peace and Justice.'

Part of the Declaration of the Holy Alliance, 26 September 1815. Quoted in René Albrecht-Carrie, *The Concert of Europe* (1968)

The Holy Alliance was signed by most European sovereigns with the exception of the Sultan of Turkey, the Pope and the Prince Regent (who,

BARONESS VON KRÜDENER

according to the British constitution, did not possess the authority to endorse such a treaty). The Holy Alliance came to be associated in the minds of European liberals with the repressive actions of the three eastern autocracies in the 1820s and beyond. However, Alexander had not devised the Alliance with this in mind, a point conceded by Metternich who was to use it for that very purpose:

'The Holy Alliance was not founded to restrain the rights of the people nor to encourage absolutism and tyranny in any form. It was simply the expression of the mystical sentiments of the Emperor Alexander and the application of Christian principles to politics.'

Metternich, quoted in G de Bertier de Sauvigny, *Metternich and his Times* (1962)

At first only Alexander took the Holy Alliance seriously. Castlereagh called it 'a piece of sublime mysticism and nonsense'. The Austrian Emperor signed it only to avoid offending the Tsar while Metternich described it as 'a loud-sounding nothing'. However, as revolutionary outbreaks began to disturb the European peace after 1820, the Alliance was redefined and directed against those who would dare to challenge the existing political order.

Two months after the creation of the Holy Alliance, Castlereagh presented the Powers with his own version of co-operative diplomacy. The Quadruple Alliance, signed between the four wartime allies, looked to maintain the settlement with France and to guard against a revival of Bonapartism. However, the most significant aspect of the Alliance was contained in Article VI. (For the text of Article VI see Source A under *Examining the Evidence* on page 28.) This made provision for the calling of periodic meetings to discuss issues in which the Powers shared a common interest. Here was the origin of Congress diplomacy.

After 1815 then, there were two rival alliances each with the declared purpose of promoting international co-operation. However, both were vague when it came to defining their precise functions and the scope of their operations. This lack of clarity proved to be one of the major causes of the Congress System's demise.

## The Powers divide (1815–18)

In spite of the high-sounding principles of the Holy Alliance and the general undertaking of the Quadruple Alliance to consult upon 'common interests', divisions between the Great Powers were becoming apparent even as the ink dried on the peace treaties of 1815. With Napoleon across the ocean on St Helena, the Powers had lost their one unifying cause. France, until recently the dominant force in Europe, was now defeated, contained and isolated. The years after 1815 were to witness an Anglo-Russian contest to fill the vacuum left by the collapse of French hegemony. In this atmosphere the mood of international co-operation began to recede as the Powers looked to align themselves with one or other of the contenders for European supremacy.

# POWER ALIGNMENTS (1815–20)

The dominant powers in Europe after 1815. Both aspired to direct and control the affairs of the new Europe. They had little in common; their only real shared aim was the desire to keep France in her place.

## Britain

Britain's main concern was with her economy. She maintained an unrivalled navy to protect her global commerce. Wished to see peace maintained in Europe and so resisted the ambitions of Russia. However, she was not especially concerned about the manner in which peace was preserved. To Britain the important thing was that peace should prevail in order to allow her economy to flourish.

## Russia

Resented Britain's clear attempt to keep a check on Russian ambitions while at the same time advancing British power through naval supremacy. Believed Britain was intent on relegating Russia to a secondary role in postwar affairs. Aware of Anglo-Austrian co-operation and looked to align with other Powers (notably France) to break their control of the Alliance.

## Austria

As the central anchor of the newly-constructed Europe, Austria had cause to fear both France and Russia. Metternich favoured close relations with Britain as her security against the threat from east and west. Sought to work with Britain through the Quadruple Alliance to restrain Russia. However, did not wish to see Russia and France pushed together as a reaction to Anglo-Austrian co-operation. Therefore, looked to maintain good relations with Russia – a difficult and sometimes impossible task.

## Prussia

Fearful of a French attack, particularly across her new Rhine territories. For security she looked primarily to Russia, with whom close links had been forged during the war and at Vienna. Also favoured the idea of closer ties between Austria and Russia which would result in a powerful combination against France.

## France

Acutely aware of her isolation in Europe. Looked desperately for an ally to assist her in revising the Vienna settlement. Wished to fracture permanently the coalition of Powers ranged against her. Saw in Russia's discontent an opportunity to link the two greatest military forces in Europe in a partnership which could be directed against Britain.

**1** What appeared to be the only shared aim of the four wartime allies after 1815? In what way was this common objective threatened?

**2** In postwar Europe a number of factors began to place barriers in the way of Great Power co-operation. The diagram below identifies some of these factors; in each case explain how international co-operation was made less likely by their existence.

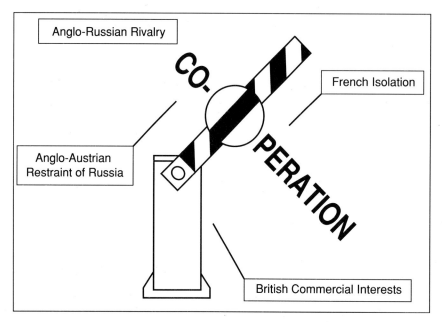

## The Congress of Aix-la-Chapelle (1818)

Prior to the first Congress being convened in 1818, the main instrument of the Quadruple Alliance was a Council of Ambassadors which met for weekly conferences in Paris. They were charged with the task of regulating French domestic affairs and were especially concerned with supervising the Allied army of occupation and ensuring that the war indemnity was paid. With a common and limited function, the Council was able to operate successfully so that by 1818 the time had come to review the relationship between France and the Allies. This was the declared purpose of the Congress of Aix-la-Chapelle.

Before the Congress assembled it had already been decided to withdraw the army of occupation from France and this decision was formalized at Aix-la-Chapelle. Beneath the co-operative surface, however, there lurked steadily-deepening divisions. Alexander hoped to use the Congress to obtain the unconditional admission of France into the Alliance. Metternich and Castlereagh recognized the danger of a Franco-Russian entente and opposed the proposal. In the end a compromise was arranged. Accordingly the Quadruple Alliance was renewed to ensure continued vigilance against possible French aggression. In addition, France was admitted into a new Quintuple Alliance and henceforth Congress diplomacy was to be conducted by five Powers.

**1** Suggest why the Tsar wished to admit France into the Quadruple Alliance in 1818.

**2** Was the Congress of Aix-la-Chapelle a success or a failure?

In their deliberations at Aix-la-Chapelle, the Powers went on to reveal the poor prospects for future international co-operation as the search for common ground proved fruitless. Alexander, for example, raised the question of disarmament but was unable to find any consensus on the issue. Castlereagh tried and failed to secure joint action against the slave-trade and the Barbary pirates. The Tsar called for the creation of an international army to protect Europe's existing frontiers; both Castlereagh and Metternich dismissed the proposal. The same fate befell another of Alexander's plans, this time for a general union of sovereigns sworn to act against revolution. Congress diplomacy had got off to an uninspiring start and the Alliance looked disturbingly fragile.

## Revolution: redefining the Congress System

In 1820 and 1821 revolutionary outbreaks occurred in several parts of Europe. (See map below.) The differing responses of the Allies to these revolutions had profound effects on Congress diplomacy and led to a reshaping of the Great Power alignments.

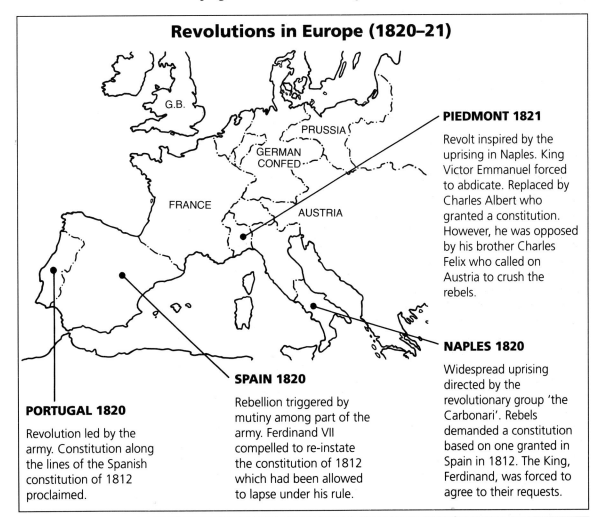

### Revolutions in Europe (1820–21)

**PIEDMONT 1821**

Revolt inspired by the uprising in Naples. King Victor Emmanuel forced to abdicate. Replaced by Charles Albert who granted a constitution. However, he was opposed by his brother Charles Felix who called on Austria to crush the rebels.

**NAPLES 1820**

Widespread uprising directed by the revolutionary group 'the Carbonari'. Rebels demanded a constitution based on one granted in Spain in 1812. The King, Ferdinand, was forced to agree to their requests.

**SPAIN 1820**

Rebellion triggered by mutiny among part of the army. Ferdinand VII compelled to re-instate the constitution of 1812 which had been allowed to lapse under his rule.

**PORTUGAL 1820**

Revolution led by the army. Constitution along the lines of the Spanish constitution of 1812 proclaimed.

News of the revolutions greatly alarmed Metternich. He knew that if the revolutionary infection was not halted promptly, it could spread uncontrolled into the Austrian Empire with its wide assortment of national groups. It was a prospect he feared as much as the threat of French or Russian invasion. Metternich came rapidly to the conclusion that the power of the Alliance should be harnessed and directed in a united effort against the forces of revolution.

Tsar Alexander was also disturbed by these challenges to monarchical authority. Increasingly he was coming to regard France, and the revolutionary ideals in which she had recently indulged, as being the inspiration for the latest wave of revolts. Accordingly, he began to sever his connections with France and to join with Austria in promoting the use of the Alliance against the rebels. Castlereagh objected strongly to the suggestion that the Alliance should be used in this way and, in his State Paper of May 1820 (see Source F under *Examining the Evidence* opposite), he outlined British opposition to the intervention of the Alliance in the affairs of other states. At the Congress of Troppau, convened to discuss the revolt in Naples, the three eastern Powers declared, through the Troppau Protocol (see Source G opposite), their intention to resist revolution wherever it occurred in Europe. Britain now dissociated herself from the new style of Congress diplomacy and the Congress System began to expire.

# TALKING POINT

## Revolutions of 1820–21

What did these revolutions have in common? In what ways had the Powers created the conditions which made revolutions likely? Why did revolution alarm Metternich and Alexander so much? Why do you think Britain's attitude to the revolts was different?

# EXAMINING THE EVIDENCE
## The issue of function

The Congress System began to fail after 1820 because the Powers were unable to agree on the central purpose of Congress diplomacy. What was the original aim of the Congress System and how did its function change over time?

### Source A

Article VI. To facilitate and to secure the execution of the present Treaty [second Peace of Paris], and to consolidate the connections which at the present moment so closely unite the Four Sovereigns for the happiness of the World, the High Contracting Parties have agreed to renew their meetings at fixed periods, either under the immediate auspices of the Sovereigns themselves, or by their respective Ministers, for the purpose of consulting upon their common interests, and for the consideration of the measures which at each of these periods shall be considered the most salutary for the repose and prosperity of Nations, and for the maintenance of the peace of Europe.

> Part of the Treaty of Alliance and Friendship (Quadruple Alliance) between Britain, Austria, Prussia and Russia which established the idea of regular Congresses (signed at Paris, 20 November 1815). Quoted in René Albrecht-Carrie, *The Concert of Europe* (1968)

### Source B

The coalition only survives because the governments of the Great Powers see in it an instrument of high policy, a common expedient against the restlessness of the masses and the disorders of our time. If it did not have a much wider object than the re-establishment of order in France, dissolution would not be far off.

Friedrich von Gentz, Metternich's secretary and publicity agent, in a memoir of August 1816. Quoted in G de Bertier de Sauvigny, *Metternich and his Times* (1962)

## Source C

The Quadruple Alliance as it exists today acts as a brake on the actual or potential plans of the Emperor Alexander.

Metternich in a letter to Paul Esterhazy (Austrian ambassador at London), 26 March 1817. Quoted in G de Bertier de Sauvigny as above

## Source D

Each day brings me fresh conviction that the remedy for this evil [the threat of revolution] which threatens the tranquillity of every State can only be found in perfect understanding between all the Powers. They should openly pool their resources and their energies to stifle everywhere that revolutionary spirit which was developed more powerfully and more dangerously during the three months of Napoleon's reign than it ever was during the first years of the French Revolution...The conference of Ministers in Paris could become the centre of a system of surveillance over these revolutionary intrigues both at home and in other countries, a surveillance which would be instructed to consider and put forward repressive measures to be adopted against them.

Metternich, 22 June 1817, quoted in G de Bertier de Sauvigny as above

## Source E

That if...the Powers...should judge it necessary to establish particular meetings...and that in the case of these meetings having for their object affairs specially connected with the interests of the other States of Europe, they shall only take place in pursuance of a formal invitation on the part of such of those States as the said affairs may concern, and under the express reservation of their right of direct participation therein, either directly or by their Plenipotentiaries.

Part of the Protocol of the Congress of Aix-la-Chapelle, 15 November 1818. Quoted in René Albrecht-Carrie as above

## Source F

In this Alliance [Quintuple Alliance], as in all other human arrangements, nothing is more likely to impair, or even destroy its real utility, than any attempt to push its duties and its obligations beyond the sphere which its original conception and understood principles will warrant. It was a Union for the re-conquest and liberation of a great proportion of the continent of Europe from the military domination of France; and having subdued the conqueror, it took the state of possession, as established by the peace, under the protection of the Alliance. It never was, however, intended as a Union for the government of the world, or for the superintendence of the internal affairs of other states...We shall be found in our place when actual danger menaces the system of Europe; but this country cannot, and will not, act upon abstract and speculative principles of precaution. The Alliance which exists had no such purpose in view of its original formation.

Part of Castlereagh's State Paper of 5 May 1820. Quoted in Sir AW Ward and GP Gooch (eds.), *The Cambridge History of British Foreign Policy 1783–1919* (1923)

## Source G

States which have undergone a change of Government due to revolution, the results of which threaten other states, *ipso facto* cease to be members of the European Alliance, and remain excluded from it until their situation gives guarantees for legal order and stability. If, owing to such situations, immediate danger threatens other states, the Powers bind themselves, by peaceful means, or if need be by arms, to bring back the guilty state into the bosom of the Great Alliance.

Part of the Troppau Protocol, 19 November 1820.
Quoted in René Albrecht-Carrie, as above

---

**1** Article VI of the Quadruple Alliance (Source A) is commonly regarded by historians as representing Castlereagh's initial hopes for the Congress System. From this source identify:

(a) the two aims which lay behind the decision of the Great Powers to 'renew their meetings at fixed periods';

(b) the principal purposes of those periodic meetings.

**2** In subsequent years the initial functions of the Congress System, as declared in Article VI, became subject to interpretation and redefinition. This movement away from Castlereagh's original plan is central to your understanding of the collapse of the Congress System. Sources B, C, E, F and G trace some of the major developments in this process of change. Using these sources complete your own copy of the chart opposite.

**3** Using your chart explain how Castlereagh's initial hopes for the Congress System had been changed by 1820.

**4** What clue is offered in Source D for the reason behind this change of function?

---

## Troppau and Laibach

The divisions within the Alliance were signalled at the Congress of Troppau as the governments of Britain and France refused to send official delegations. Instead, observers were present; spectators to the proceedings with no powers to act. The Troppau Protocol, proclaimed by Austria, Russia and Prussia, was rejected by Britain and France; the new power alignments were beginning to take shape. After an adjournment the Congress reconvened at Laibach where it was agreed by the three eastern Powers that Austria should dispatch an army to Naples to crush the revolution. During March 1821 Austrian soldiers stamped out the last smouldering remains of the Carbonari's rebellion and restored King Ferdinand to his throne. In the following month the rising in Piedmont suffered a similar fate. Elsewhere in the Italian states liberals were arrested, imprisoned and even executed. Although Castlereagh agreed that

| Developments | Declared function of Congress System |
|---|---|
| *Interpretation 1* (Source B): suggested by Friedrich von Gentz (August 1816) | |
| *Interpretation 2* (Source C): suggested by Metternich (26 March 1817) | |
| *Redefinition 1* (Source E): understanding reached by the Powers on the issue of intervention at the Congress of Aix-la-Chapelle (15 November 1818) | |
| *Redefinition 2* (Source F): Castlereagh's State Paper (5 May 1820) expressing Britain's attitude to growing demands to use the Congress System as a means of regulating the affairs of other states. | |
| *Redefinition 3* (Source G): Troppau Protocol (19 November 1820), expressing the attitude of the eastern autocracies to revolutionary activity in the European states. | |

Austria had the right to intervene in Naples as a domestic concern, he objected to her doing so in Italy, or anywhere else, in the name of the Alliance. This was the fundamental issue which split the Quintuple Alliance and which led to the collapse of the Congress System.

## Greece, Spain and the Congress of Verona

As the Congress of Laibach drew to a close, news reached the conference that the Greeks had revolted against their Turkish masters. Metternich feared that Alexander would damage the anti-revolutionary stance of the eastern Powers by supporting his fellow Orthodox Christians in their fight against the Moslem Turks. In addition, and in common with Castlereagh, Metternich was worried that a successful challenge to the Ottomans might result in Russia expanding into the Turkish Empire. The brutal nature of the Turkish response to the uprising, including the massacre of some 25,000 people on the island of Chios, meant that Russian sympathy for

THE RETURN OF KING FERDINAND I TO NAPLES (MARCH 1821)

the Greek cause was strong. However, to Metternich the struggles of the Greek people were unimportant: 'Over there, beyond our frontiers, three or four hundred thousand individuals hanged, impaled or with their throats cut, hardly count!' For the time being Alexander was prevailed upon by Metternich to adhere to the anti-revolutionary principles of the Troppau Protocol and not to lend assistance to the Greeks.

In Spain, the revolution had developed into a civil war. The French looked set to intervene and Alexander was proposing to send Russian troops into the Iberian peninsula. Neither prospect appealed to Metternich and Castlereagh, and it was agreed that a Congress be held in Italy in 1822 to discuss the issue. However, before the Verona Congress assembled, Castlereagh had committed suicide. Metternich was dismayed when he learned of the tragedy:

'It is one of the worst catastrophes that could have befallen me. He was devoted to me heart and soul, not only from a personal attachment but also from conviction. Many matters which would have been easy with him are going to need fresh study and renewed effort with his successor, who-ever he may be.'

Metternich, quoted in G de Bertier de Sauvigny, *Metternich and his Times* (1962)

The new Foreign Secretary was George Canning (see *Focus* section 2.1). He possessed no commitment to the collective diplomacy of the Congress System and believed in the simple rule: 'every nation for itself.' For the time being, however, there was little difference in the approach taken by

Canning over the main issues of the day. Wellington was dispatched to Verona with instructions drawn up by Castlereagh before his death. At Verona the French sought and obtained the permission of the eastern Powers to send an army into Spain to restore the King to his throne. In response Canning declared:

'If...there is entertained by the Allies a determined project of interference by force, or by menace, in the present struggle in Spain...I am to instruct your Grace [the Duke of Wellington] at once frankly and peremptorily to declare, that to any such interference, come what may, His Majesty will not be a party.'

Canning to Wellington, 27 September 1822, quoted in Harold Temperley,<br>The Foreign Policy of Canning (1925)

Canning's 'come what may' instruction shattered any remaining hope of the Alliance being able to co-operate on Spain and marked Britain's decisive withdrawal from the Congress System. Canning, however, was not pursuing a novel policy; he was quite clearly following the pattern of gradual separation from the Alliance which Castlereagh had, unhappily for him, inaugurated in 1820. The only real difference was that Canning felt not regret at the collapse of the Congress System, but relief.

In April 1823, 100,000 Frenchmen crossed the mountains into Spain. By the end of September King Ferdinand had been restored. Prompted by the governments of Prussia, Russia and Austria to destroy completely the forces of revolution, Ferdinand embarked upon an orgy of violence directed against the former rebels. Riego, the ex-President of the revolutionary Chamber was publicly butchered in a Madrid square. The five pieces of his dismembered body were set on display in the five towns which had provided him with his most enthusiastic support. It was a savage reminder to the constitutionalists that in the present international climate the forces of reaction possessed both the will and the resources collectively to stamp out the hopes of the liberals. The French invasion of Spain was a blow to British pride, and Canning was determined that it should go no further. He obtained assurances from the French, in the shape of the Polignac Memorandum, that they had no intention of assisting Spain in recapturing her former South American colonies. The 'New World' had become increasingly important to British trade in the post-Napoleonic period as the figures below show.

*Value of exports of British manufactures to Central and South America*
1818–21      £12 million
1821–25      £19 million

Canning was determined to protect this trade and in 1825 the British government officially recognized the independence of Mexico, Colombia and Argentina. In the following year Canning made his celebrated boast on the apparent success of his Latin American policy: 'I resolved that if France had Spain, it should not be Spain with the Indies. I called the New World into existence to redress the balance of the old.'

What did Canning mean when he made this statement?

# **F**OCUS

## 2.1 Canning

GEORGE CANNING

George Canning became British Foreign Secretary for the second time in 1822. He had first occupied the position in 1807. However, following profound disagreements with Castlereagh, he remained out of the Cabinet from 1809 to 1816. Unlike Castlereagh, Canning was a gifted speaker. Through the Press and by public speaking he courted popularity. In 1824 the *Morning Herald* commented: 'It strikes us that no Minister, since the Revolution, excepting only the great Lord Chatham, has acquired the same national popularity which is at this moment possessed by Mr Canning.' Part of Canning's popularity was that he believed passionately in the pursuit and protection of national interest. He distrusted intervention, preferring 'neutrality in word and deed'. He had no interest in maintaining the Alliance and was suspicious of Congress diplomacy, a point outlined in a letter from Lord Bathurst to Castlereagh in 1818:

> He thinks that system of periodical meetings of the four great Powers, with a view to the general concerns of Europe, new, and of very questionable policy; that it will necessarily involve us deeply in all the politics of the Continent, whereas our true policy has always been not to interfere except in great emergencies, and then with a commanding force.
>
> Quoted in H Temperley,
> *The Foreign Policy of Canning* (1925)

When Canning saw the content of Castlereagh's famous *State Paper* in 1820 he remarked with considerable satisfaction: 'Yes, we shall have no more congresses, thank God!'

The compact made by the three eastern Powers at Troppau to guarantee the territories and political systems of existing rulers was categorically refuted by Canning:

> The British Government will not, in any case, undertake any guarantee whatever, either of territory or of internal Institutions.

Such statements led to a popular misconception that Canning was a champion of liberal and constitutional causes. However, this was not the case. He described the Portuguese revolutionaries, for example, as 'the scum of the earth...fierce, rascally, thieving, ignorant ragamuffins...' In fact Canning objected equally to the excesses of revolution and to the unrestrained power of despotism. Britain's association with liberal and constitutional causes was not due to ideological commitment but to the calculation that such contacts best suited British interests.

Canning was not well disposed to Metternich, calling him 'the greatest rogue and liar in Europe, perhaps in the civilised world'. The feeling was mutual and Metternich found it impossible to work with Canning as he had done with Castlereagh. In the period after 1822, therefore, Britain, under Canning's direction, moved further away from her original Alliance partners.

## QUESTIONS

**1** How did Canning's approach to European diplomacy differ to that of Castlereagh?

**2** How could Canning be said to have contributed to the failure of the Congress System?

# Old problems, new solutions: European diplomacy (1824–30)

Although the formal period of Congress diplomacy ended at Verona, attempts were continued to organize international responses to events deemed to be threatening to European stability. However, the pattern of such responses was changing. In 1825 Tsar Alexander died and was succeeded by Nicholas I. The new emperor was remote from the Quadruple Alliance, having played no part in its creation and subsequent activities. He was far less inclined to be directed by Metternich and favoured an immediate response in support of the Greek revolutionaries now being cruelly subdued by the Sultan's vassal, Mehemet Ali of Egypt. At the same time Canning was busy pursuing policies designed to dismantle further the European Concert and to diminish the influence of Metternich. In 1826 he had directly intervened in the affairs of Portugal where Britain enjoyed considerable influence. A detachment of troops was sent to Lisbon in support of the constitutionalists. In the same year Canning rejected Metternich's call for a five-power conference to discuss Portugal, thus emphasizing Britain's commitment to independent action in the protection of her interests.

TSAR NICHOLAS I

The Greek revolt inspired Canning to pursue a novel course: co-operation with Russia. He was certainly aware of popular opinion in Britain which strongly favoured the Greek rebels. However, what really drove him to his new policy was the desire to drive a wedge between the Austro-Russian partnership and to restrain Russian ambitions in the Turkish Empire. Accordingly, the St Petersburg Protocol of 1826 was arranged between Tsar Nicholas and the Duke of Wellington. This document called for the establishment of self-government in Greece and made vague threats about joint intervention if this were not achieved. The Turks remained unmoved and in 1827 Canning went further by calling on the Great Powers to join Britain and Russia in forcing the Sultan to accept mediation. France responded and the Treaty of London was signed. Austria and Prussia chose not to become involved and once again the pattern of Great Power co-operation changed. In October 1827 the Turkish-Egyptian fleet was destroyed by Allied warships at Navarino. This incident, and the death of Canning the previous August, heralded another change in Great Power relations. Russia followed up Navarino by going to war with Turkey. Wellington, now Prime Minister, was suspicious of the Tsar's actions and withdrew from co-operation with Russia. Only after peace had been made between Russia and Turkey at Adrianople in 1829 was the Greek question settled. By the London Protocol of 3 February 1830, Greece was declared an independent kingdom with its status guaranteed by the signatures of Britain, Russia and France.

MEHEMET ALI OF EGYPT

DESTRUCTION OF THE TURKISH FLEET AT NAVARINO (OCTOBER 1827)

# REVIEW
## Why did the Congress System collapse?

**Source A**

History teaches us...that Coalitions begin to disintegrate from the moment that the common danger is removed. With Napoleon at St Helena and Louis XVIII back in the Tuileries France had ceased to be a menace to the peace of Europe; it was before long agreed to withdraw the armies of occupation and to readmit France into the comity of nations. The original purpose of the Coalition having thus disappeared, it soon became evident that the three main partners to the Alliance interpreted its future in different ways.

Harold Nicolson, *The Congress of Vienna* (1946)

**Source B**

The Quadruple Alliance would thereafter [following the discontinuance of the Council of Ambassadors in Paris] be without a fixed meeting-point, and it would be hard to avoid the realization that a moral institution deprived of a central and visible representation must sooner or later fall into disuse.

Metternich, quoted in G de Bertier de Sauvigny, *Metternich and his Times* (1962)

**Source C**

By 1823... the idea of relating diplomacy to regular councils had to be abandoned. A major reason for this was that a gap opened between Britain and the continental autocracies of Austria, Russia and Prussia, caused largely by different policies over the question of intervention against revolutionary movements.

Stephen J Lee, *Aspects of European History 1789–1980* (1982)

## Source D

...both documents [Article VI of the Quadruple Alliance and the Holy Alliance] left nearly everything uncertain. It was not clear which of them was to serve as the basis on which international co-operation was to proceed. The League of Nations had one Covenant, the United Nations one Charter. The so-called Congress System had two covenants or charters and nobody knew for certain which of them was to be the basis of action. It is not surprising therefore that what could not be done after 1919 or 1945 on the basis of a single document could not be done after 1815 on the basis of two.

LCB Seaman, *From Vienna to Versailles* (1956)

## Source E

After the control of British foreign policy had fallen into Canning's hands in August 1822, it was only too obvious that England would refuse to have a part in the action that was being taken by the Continental allies against the liberal revolutions in Italy and Spain. Castlereagh would have sought to play down this difference; but Canning paraded it and used it to win golden opinions from his countrymen.

G de Bertier de Sauvigny, as above

From the evidence contained in the sources, provide information to show how the following factors contributed to the collapse of the Congress System.

**1 Institutional/organizational difficulties** What were the basic weaknesses of the administration of the Congress System? How was it prevented from functioning efficiently?

**2 Internal disagreements** What issue drove a wedge between the Powers and ensured the failure of continued co-operation?

**3 Extinction of common purpose** How was the solidarity of the Powers undermined? What were the dangers of continuing with an alliance which had no common purpose?

**4 Influence of individuals** How did the attitude of individual statesmen help to weaken Allied co-operation?

From your reading of this chapter, can you identify any other factors which helped to bring about the collapse of the Congress System? If so, add them to the list you have just compiled.

# TALKING POINT:

## Debate

'The Congress System was an admirable and enlightened attempt to regulate international affairs through peaceful discussion.'

'The Congress System was a cynical attempt to impose outdated values on groups who tried to challenge the existing political and social order.'

Work initially in a group of four. Allocate one of the above interpretations to each of the pairs in your group. Each pair should prepare a case supporting the interpretation they are given. As a four, debate the arguments used by each pair.

# 3 Metternich and the Austrian Empire 1815–48

## Metternich: the arrogance of power

Metternich was the principal statesman of the Austrian Empire in the period 1815–48. It has sometimes been said that Metternich's favourite topic was Metternich, and his arrogance has become legendary.

'People look on me as a kind of lantern to which they draw near in order to see their way through the almost complete darkness.'

'My mind is not narrow in its conceptions. I am always either short of or beyond the preoccupations of most statesmen. I cover a much wider ground than they either want to or are capable of seeing. I cannot help telling myself twenty times a day: "O Lord! how right I am and how wrong they are!"'

'The visit which General Orloff has just paid us must have left him with a flattering impression. He said as he took his leave of me, and I believe in the sincerity of his words: "I have learned more in the ten weeks that I have spent with you than in the thirty years I spent as an observer of or a participant in the affairs of the world."'

'Men like Canning fall twenty times and recover themselves as often; men like myself have no need of recovery because they are not subject to falls.'

But in 1848 Metternich did fall. The revolutions which swept across Europe in that year brought angry crowds onto the streets of Vienna and sent Metternich into exile. How did it happen that a man so confident in his own abilities and ideals, and so respected by his contemporaries, was removed from high office by a wave of popular protest?

PRINCE CLEMENS METTERNICH

# The Empire in 1815

In 1804 the Austrian Habsburgs, who had dominated the lands of Central Europe since the Sixteenth Century, brought their scattered territories together under a common name: the Empire of the House of Austria. However, it was not until 1815 and the conclusion of the Treaty of Vienna, that the regions comprising the Empire were formally established. There were five principal components (see map on page 41): the central portion was dominated by the Hereditary Lands (Upper and Lower Austria) and the Lands of the Hungarian Crown (which included Croatia-Slavonia and Transylvania); to the north lay the Lands of the Bohemian Crown (Bohemia, Moravia and Upper Silesia) and in the north-east was the region called Galicia; Lombardy and Venetia, the recent Italian acquisitions in the south, completed this vast and improbable collection of possessions presided over in 1815 by the Emperor Francis I.

In the years which followed the Treaty of Vienna, one issue dominated Austrian internal affairs: how to ensure the survival of such a large and unco-ordinated empire? It is true that between 1815 and 1848 the Empire remained territorially unchanged and was even viewed as a 'European necessity', vital to the preservation of the new European order created at Vienna. However, this was not enough. The historian Andrew Milne sets out what was needed after 1815:

> How did the Treaty of Vienna (1815) recognize Austria as a 'European necessity'?

'If the Empire were to survive there must be a major effort made to revitalise the ties which held it together. The faith of the Great Powers in the idea of an Austrian Empire, with a vital role to play in central and eastern Europe, must be matched by a new and dynamic loyalty to that same Empire on the part of the provinces which comprised it.'

A Milne, *Metternich* (1975)

Metternich, as Foreign Minister from 1809 and State Chancellor from 1821, was certainly alert to such needs and recognized that decisive measures would have to be taken if the forces of nationalism and liberalism were to be prevented from tearing the Empire apart.

# Obstacles to change

The task of transforming the Empire into a more coherent unit was fraught with difficulties. The map opposite graphically illustrates some of the fundamental problems which lay at the heart of any attempt to generate greater loyalty to the authority of the Emperor.

### 1 Lack of unity

The Empire was the product of historical accretion. Centuries of gradual expansion through treaties, marriages, partitions, wars and conquest shaped the rambling geography of the Habsburg lands. Carinthia was acquired in 1335, Bohemia in 1526, Hungary and Transylvania were added in 1699, Bukovina in 1775; a sequence of additions which offers just a few examples of the prolonged and random construction of the Empire. The region was devoid of any economic or geographical unity. In fact the only real binding agent was the dynastic link which all shared with the Habsburg Crown and it was precisely this connection which was most in need of reinforcement.

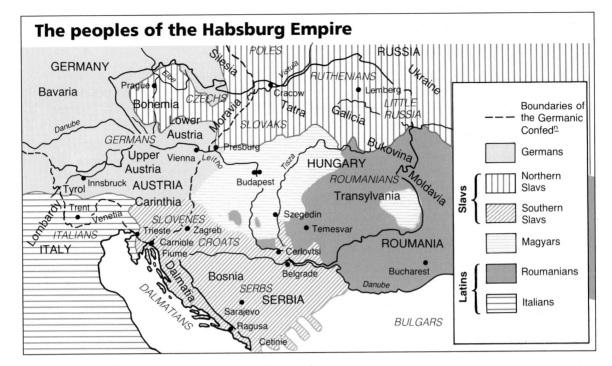

### The peoples of the Habsburg Empire

Why was nationalism seen as such a danger to the Austrian Empire?

## 2 Administrative nightmare

The Empire was large and unwieldy. It was composed of eleven distinct national groups. There was no common language, culture or religion and little by way of shared experience save that of being acquired by the crowned head of Austria. The Empire presented Vienna with an enormous administrative problem. How was it possible to find common ground between such diverse national groups as Italians, Poles, Germans, Czechs and Magyars? How could the particular needs of Lombardy-Venetia be met and reconciled with those, for example, of Hungary? Developing an administrative system which catered for all fairly and efficiently was a monumental task.

## 3 The problem of minorities

It was clear also that an administrative solution which dealt with the Empire on a regional basis was no solution at all. Minorities were to be found throughout the Habsburg lands and their existence served to complicate the situation still further.

The survival of the Empire depended on the discovery of a radical and imaginative political formula which could be applied as an antidote to the potentially fatal effects of internal division. The challenge was to persuade the people that their national identities were less important than their loyalty to Vienna. Changes in the internal structure of the Empire were desperately needed if this were to be achieved. However, it soon became apparent that language, geography and regional diversity were not the only obstacles to the much needed Imperial overhaul. The principal objector to any reforming scheme was the Emperor himself.

# 3.1 Emperor Francis I

FRANCIS I, EMPEROR OF AUSTRIA (1792-1835)

Francis assumed the Habsburg Crown in 1792 following the premature death of his father Leopold II. Within three months the 24-year-old monarch found himself at war with revolutionary France; he was 47 before Austria could truly count herself at peace once more. The experience of this fiery baptism left a lasting impression on the Emperor. The wars were disastrous for Austria; she was expelled from Italy, lost her possessions in the Rhineland and suffered the ignominy of seeing the capital, Vienna, twice occupied by the French. Francis, buffeted through his early reign by a series of military defeats, territorial losses and personal humiliations, emerged into middle age with an unshakable hatred of anything which challenged stability. He despised change and was hostile to new ideas; presented on

one occasion with a plan for railway construction in Austria he responded 'No no. I will have nothing to do with it, lest the revolution might come into the country.' Francis may be appropriately described as the arch-conservative of his time. From 1810 he followed a strictly personal form of government, demanding total obedience from his subjects and advisers. He alone made the decisions, accepting or ignoring advice from whoever he chose. Yet he was incapable of grasping complex ideas and was perpetually suspicious of advisers with original thoughts. He was not completely without intelligence and possessed a strong sense of duty, but he was unimaginative and lacked vision. His refusal to delegate even the most trivial matters of business was enormously time consuming and wasteful of the undoubted talents of such men as Stadion, Gentz and Metternich. Ultimately Francis was not interested in what such men might offer the Empire by way of reconstruction. He wished only for their approval and assistance in his principal aim of preserving the *status quo*. Ironically, his only concession to change was the desire to see his own monarchical absolutism extended more comprehensively to his dominions. He abhorred nationalism and liberalism, seeing them as the dual sponsors of revolution. According to the historian Von Treitschke, he

> ...saw in all of the revolutionary and national ideas which moved the new century nothing but wickedness and stupidity, nothing but criminal rebellion against the pious archducal House.
>
> C.A. Macartney: *The House of Austria* (1978)

Such was the man who piloted the Austrian Empire through the first 35 years of the Nineteenth Century; a period so static, according to the historian CA Macartney, that:

> ...March 1848 found Austria in all respects which government ingenuity could contrive in the condition in which Francis had found it in March 1792.

If securing the future of the Empire meant making changes to its internal structure, it was to the Habsburgs' everlasting misfortune that Francis I was the man with the ultimate responsibility for those alterations. Metternich's plans for improvements were rejected or ignored. The Emperor's personal obstruction of reform can be clearly witnessed in the following anecdote from Metternich's memoirs:

> ...I handed it [a reform proposal] over to the Emperor at the beginning of 1817 and he put it into his drawer.
>
> When the Emperor had begun his convalescence, following his serious illness in 1827, he sent for me one day at eight o'clock in the morning.
>
> When I had seated myself by him he began by apologising for having sent for me at such an early hour, then he said: 'I have a confession to make to you: I am returning to life after an illness from which I thought I should never recover. I tell you that while I was ill I felt guilty because I had not looked at your work. As soon as I am up and about again, I shall nominate a commission to study the question and you shall preside. Give me a list of the men you would like as colleagues.'
>
> On December 31, 1834, I visited the Emperor to wish him a happy New Year. 'Once again you see in me a repentant sinner', he said. 'Your work has not been taken out of the drawer yet. I give you my word of honour that the year 1835 shall not pass until the body is set up.' Two months later the Emperor was dead.

Metternich, quoted in G de Bertier de Sauvigny, *Metternich and his Times* (1962)

Confronted with such calculated obstruction, it is not surprising that the changes required within the Empire were never realized and that in March 1848 the region was convulsed by revolution.

---

## QUESTIONS

**1** How would you account for the Emperor's fear of change and his insistence on stability?

**2** Explain why Francis regarded nationalism and liberalism as the 'dual sponsors of revolution'.

**3** What do you see as being the disadvantage of the Emperor's insistence on making all executive decisions himself? Discussion of the following support questions should help you to frame an answer:

(a) What were the Emperor's priorities for internal policy? Did these priorities match the needs of the Habsburg Empire?

(b) Was the Emperor sufficiently talented to deal effectively with all matters relating to the government of such a diverse empire?

(c) On a practical level, would the Emperor ever have had enough time to consider thoroughly all items of Imperial business? If not, what effect would this have on the transaction of such business.

## The 'Metternich System'

The difficulties which Metternich faced as State Chancellor were certainly considerable. In response to these problems he has been credited by some historians with having devised a method of working, known as the 'Metternich System'. This 'System' represented Metternich's efforts to maintain the 1815 settlement through an alliance of European monarchies and by the comprehensive repression of nationalism and liberalism within states. The principal motive behind the scheme was the protection of the old social and political order against the threat of revolutionary disruption. Whether or not Metternich consciously pursued such a calculated strategy remains an area of some debate amongst historians. Metternich himself denied the existence of any 'system' and spoke instead of the simple application of his 'principles' to the political circumstances of the time. An appreciation of these principles is central to any understanding of Metternich's Austrian policies.

## Metternich's political ideas

Metternich's political outlook was firmly rooted in the Eighteenth Century. He perceived the physical world as being governed by certain fundamental laws which held opposing forces together in a natural state of balance. His principal objective was to achieve such a balance in the conduct of international relations and between the different classes and interests within particular states. Yet such a balance was always difficult to maintain. In the political world as in nature, disruptive forces were constantly at work, seeking to upset the ideal balance. Metternich's philosophy viewed history as being composed of a series of contests between chaos and stability. Periodically there arose times of calm and repose when society was held in a state of equilibrium. At such times Man followed the guidance provided by morality and the natural law. However, such times were merely intervals between the high drama of repression and anarchy, features which characterized the disturbed balance.

In his own time Metternich found the balance tipped in the direction of anarchy. The Vienna settlement had provided a material solution to the aftermath of war but had failed to solve the underlying problem of moral decay which, in Metternich's view, had promoted the French Revolution and the chaos which followed. Thus in the postwar period the foundations of ordered society – religion, morality and authority – continued to be assailed by revolutionary forces demanding rapid and comprehensive change. Faced with the ideological challenges of the day, how did Metternich respond?

**T**ALKING POINT

**Causes of political instability**

Through discussion identify those factors which can cause political instability in a country. Examples might be 'war' or 'harvest failure'.

# EXAMINING THE EVIDENCE
## Social and political change: Metternich's views

**Challenge** *Society should move towards popular representation; extending to its citizens the responsibility of political participation in state government.*

**Metternich's response** 'The people let themselves be duped easily enough; you cannot exaggerate the goodness of the people; but their ignorance is great; therefore they must be led.'

*Memoirs of Prince Metternich* translated by Mrs A Napier (1880)

'It is true that I do not like democracies. Democracy is in every case a principle of dissolution, of decomposition. It tends to separate men, it loosens society. I am opposed to this because I am by nature and by habit constructive. That is why monarchy is the only government that suits my way of thinking...Monarchy alone tends to bring men together, to unite them in compact, efficient masses, and to make them capable by their combined efforts of the highest degree of culture and civilization.'

Metternich to the American G Licknor

**Challenge** *All men are created equal and are entitled to certain basic rights including life, liberty and the pursuit of happiness.*

**Metternich's response** 'Two words suffice to create evil; two words which because they are devoid of any practical meaning delight the visionaries. The words are liberty and equality. The word liberty conjures up nothing in the mind; it indicates something excellent if it is in the right place, something detestable if it is in the wrong. Liberty of what? Liberty to do good (but the whole world enjoys that faculty) or to do evil? The word liberty is like the word religion. To what religion do we refer?'

'...Never will I be persuaded that there is equality between a fool and an intellectual, between a pauper and a rich man, or between a hunchback and a man of noble and pleasing physique. Equal before God and the law, but not from the point of view of their social existence.'

**Challenge** *The traditional system of government with an absolutist monarch exercising sole power should be dismantled. In its place should be erected a new constitutional system with shared powers.*

**Metternich's response** 'A king must never sacrifice any part of his authority...There may be delegation of certain branches of public authority (that of making laws, for example) to bodies existing by virtue of ancient institutions or established for this purpose by the sovereign himself. But delegation is not alienation, neither is it sharing...delegated power necessarily carries with it the condition that the foundation, the substance, and capital of power invariably remains in the hands of the sovereign. The only possible meaning of the word constitution in connection with the monarchical system is that of an organization of public powers under the supreme, indivisible and inalienable authority of the monarch...In any other context constitution is the equivalent of anarchy, and the so-called division of powers spells the death of monarchical government.'

Metternich to Wellington, 1822

**1** What type of government did Metternich regard as ideal?

**2** Outline Metternich's objections to popular political representation.

**3** Why did Metternich object to the concept of 'liberty'?

**4** Describe Metternich's perception of the natural social order.

**5** What were Metternich's views on the concept of 'constitutional monarchy'?

# Metternich and revolution

In 1832 Metternich wrote, 'There is only one serious matter in Europe...and that is revolution.' The idea of popular challenges to legitimate authority both frightened and appalled him. He described 'proper revolutions' as being characterized by 'the spectacle of devastation and the spilling of blood'. He regarded revolution as the natural consequence of three centuries of human progress. Developments in science and technology, the discovery of the New World and the Reformation in religion had led to rapid advances in learning and the acquisition of knowledge. But to Metternich these were hollow achievements, releasing ambitions which Man lacked the wisdom to restrain. The result was a Man fattened on knowledge, arrogantly confident in his own abilities and contemptuous of the foundations upon which society had been built. In short, Man had become guilty of presumption and this had led directly to the French Revolution. In 1820 Metternich set out his political views in a lengthy statement intended for Tsar Alexander I. Here he described in detail what he saw as the principal characteristics of the so-called 'presumptuous man'. (See chart below.)

To Metternich the attitudes and aspirations of the 'presumptuous man' lay directly behind the chaos of the recent French Revolution, and threatened, if left unchecked, to plunge Europe once more into turmoil. In his political statement to Alexander in 1820, Metternich was quite prepared to identify what he regarded as the principal source of this revolutionary danger. In his examination of the three great classes in society he came to the conclusions outlined in the chart opposite.

**Authority**

Dismissed as being unnecessary: he is his own regulator. He sees no need to give in to the rule of others. Such a system he sees as useful only to restrain those who lack knowledge – he possesses sufficient wisdom to govern his own actions.

**Laws**

Regarded as meaningless since he did not participate in their making. He feels no compulsion to abide by the restrictions devised by people remote in time and governed by different values.

**THE PRESUMPTUOUS MAN**

**Morality**

Sees standards of morality as being flexible. He constructs his own moral standards and encourages others to determine their own, providing they do not infringe his basic rights of life and property.

**Faith**

Has no meaning to him. In its place he substitutes a so-called private conviction which he assembles from the facts at his disposal.

| The Masses | The Middle Class | The Aristocracy |
|---|---|---|
| Largely unaffected by revolutionary ideas. Their chief task was the humble duty of provision: the supply of food and shelter for the family. This was time consuming and left no opportunity for them to become moved by vague ambitions and ideals. | The main source of trouble: the civil servants, lawyers, professors and financiers etc. They were politically ambitious in order to complement their rising social status. Their calls for constitutional changes stood at the core of their thirst for power, prestige and fortune. | Most were naturally opposed to disorder. The minority who occasionally flirted with revolutionaries, either out of some romantic notion or in the hope of gain, rarely survived beyond the first wave of reforms. |

Metternich's response to the challenge of the middle class was simple and direct: repression. He believed the first duty of any government was to maintain control and to preserve the existing order. Sudden and far-reaching reforms were not to be considered in a climate of political uncertainty. Stability was the watchword of Metternich and his conservative peers, and change was *their* responsibility; concessions were not to be granted to those who sought the rapid overhaul of society through illegal methods.

**1** In the first half of the Nineteenth Century liberalism and nationalism shared common goals, and Metternich associated both with the promotion of revolution. Given this, why was he so keen to clamp down on the demands of the middle class? You may find it useful to refer back to the map on page 41.

**2** In what circumstances might the masses become attracted to revolutionary political ideas?

## Metternich's internal policies

Metternich's consuming fear of revolution and his commitment to preserving the authority of the Emperor led him to adopt that time-honoured strategy practised by monarchs throughout Europe: political repression. His determination to re-align forcefully the disturbed equilibrium in the direction of order and stability caused one historian to describe the Austrian Empire under Francis as 'the classic example of the police State'.

In a period of intense political repression throughout Europe, it was the Austrian secret police who were the most notorious. Under Metternich and the Chief of Police, Count Sedlnitzky, a network of informers was established. Particularly useful were those in positions of public service; waiters, doormen, servants and even prostitutes were all hired to report on the activities and conversations of the Austrian public.

Official instructions to regional police forces, especially those in remote and politically-sensitive areas such as Venetia, were comprehensive indeed. Their duties included the unmasking of conspiracies, close surveillance of targeted individuals, the scrutiny of newspapers, books and pictures, the observation of foreign consuls and diplomatic personnel, the surveillance of all public employees and the monitoring of private correspondence. This latter activity was the preserve of special mail-opening departments called *Logen* which were located at every major post office in Austria. Mail sent to persons on police lists was intercepted, copied and resealed. The information gathered was then directed to the highest levels. Each morning the Emperor Francis spent hours eagerly reading through the police reports in search of compromising items. The penetration of the police into all aspects of public life exerted a stifling pressure on the minds and activities of the Austrian people. This was complemented by rigid censorship, restrictions on freedom of movement and the forbidding presence of fortress prisons such as Spielberg and Kufstein; institutions dedicated to the incarceration of political prisoners.

STUDENT DEMONSTRATION AT WARTBURG CASTLE (OCTOBER 1817)

Perhaps the best example of Metternich's anti-revolutionary crusade can be found in Germany where he believed the stability of the Confederation to be under threat from a developing liberal and nationalist movement. Between 1814 and 1820, 13 of the 39 German states introduced constitutions, and in the universities the old order was under attack. On 18 October 1817 about 500 students of the University of Jena attended a festival at Wartburg Castle in Saxe-Weimar. Their joint anniversary celebrations in honour of the Battle of Leipzig and the beginning of the Reformation were concluded with the burning of reactionary books, together with some symbols of repression and censorship such as a policeman's pigtail. The Wartburg Festival was harmless enough but Metternich was sufficiently alarmed to be on the look-out for an excuse to bring the German states back to the conservative fold. His opportunity came on 23 March 1819 when Karl Ludwig Sand, a student of Jena University, stabbed to death the reactionary journalist and playwright August von Kotzebue. Metternich received the news of this politically-motivated murder with considerable satisfaction:

'All my efforts are directed towards giving the affairs the best possible sequel and to taking as much advantage of it as possible. I shall act vigorously to this end.'

Metternich, 9 April 1819

ASSASSINATION OF AUGUST VON KOTZEBUE (1819). METTERNICH USED THIS AS AN EXCUSE TO INTRODUCE THE REPRESSIVE CARLSBAD DECREES

The 'sequel' was a comprehensive counter-offensive designed to silence the German liberal movement. A package of measures known collectively as the Carlsbad Decrees was adopted by the frightened rulers of all the states of the Confederation. Several months before Sand fell victim to the hangman's noose, the Carlsbad Decrees had introduced nationwide censorship on all printed material under 320 pages, placed the universities under the strictest supervision and established a commission of investigation at Mainz to expose 'revolutionary plots and demagogic connections'. There followed a 'demagogue hunt' as the police turned their attention to liberal students and professors; even as late as the period 1832–38 there were 1200 prosecutions for membership of the outlawed Student Associations. Helplessly bound and gagged, the liberal movement ceased to be capable of voicing its demands and fell into decline.

# Attempts at reform

Although Metternich freely used repressive methods to keep revolutionary aspirations in check, he was never ignorant of the need to restructure the existing administrative system and to improve the relationship between Vienna and the outlying provinces of the Austrian Empire. However, Metternich very carefully defined the terms on which any reform programme would be developed. He believed that changes must be determined by the properly-instituted authority and must be gradual:

'I have been accused by those who run of remaining still: I do not know how to be stationary except on matters of principle. I cannot be stationary in the application of principles. I can move and stop as circumstances demand, but I have never believed that a hot pace was the one best suited to governments.'

Metternich to Sir Travers Twiss (11 February 1849)

Accordingly, Metternich made a number of serious attempts to improve the administrative system. Borrowing from the Napoleonic example which he openly admired, he set about the task of promoting administrative efficiency with a series of proposals for new streamlined institutions with clearly-defined functions. (See chart opposite.)

# Treatment of the nationalities

Metternich's abortive attempts to streamline the Imperial administration help in part to explain why, in the years before 1848, it became increasingly difficult to retain provincial loyalty to Vienna. Having no constructive alternative to the policy of repression, Metternich was compelled to witness the steady erosion of Habsburg authority upon which he had pinned all his hopes for the survival of the Empire and its values. Reflecting on this in later life, he often blamed his failure on forces which were beyond his direct control such as the attitude of the Emperor and the recalcitrance of the bureaucracy.

However, his attempt to revitalize the ties which held together the Empire did not stop at an administrative overhaul. Parallel to this was a calculated attempt to encourage regional contentment in the hope that the nationalities would be happy to maintain their Imperial connection. Instead, Metternich unwittingly promoted the very forces which were to plunge the Empire into revolutionary chaos in 1848.

Metternich had no plans to amalgamate the separate racial groups into a more unified Austrian State. Indeed, both he and the Emperor accepted the differences which existed and sought to exploit them through the traditional policy of 'divide and rule':

My people are strange to each other and that is all right. They do not get the same sickness at the same time...The one does not understand the other and one hates the other...From their antipathy will be born order and from the mutual hatreds general peace.

Emperor Francis to French ambassador

The attempt to generate local contentment arose initially out of Metternich's respect for regional traditions, in particular provincial

| Reform proposal | Result |
|---|---|
| **Imperial Council** In 1811, Metternich suggested the creation of an Imperial Council to be composed of all the chief officers of the State. Its purpose was to advise the Emperor on matters of State raised at the request of the Emperor. The Council was to have no executive authority but was a genuine attempt to improve the clumsy system of random consultation which the Emperor conducted with the many and varied elements of the Imperial administration. Allowed to function properly, the Council could have spared the Emperor and his advisers the time-consuming responsibility of considering every item of State business. | Given a trial run in 1814, the scheme failed. Members of the Council lacked the ability to co-operate effectively. Principally, however, it was the attitude of Francis which caused the assembly to expire. He could ignore the Council's proposals and was not obliged to adhere to the reforms he sanctioned. |
| **State Chancelleries** Metternich also suggested the creation of State Chancelleries to supervise the interests of the primary ethnic groups within the Empire. Two Chancelleries already functioned on behalf of Hungary and Transylvania; four more were to be added; Austria-Illyria; Galicia; Lombardy-Venetia; Bohemia-Moravia. In charge would be a Chancellor-in-Chief with deputies to administer the new institutions. Their task was to protect the interests of the nationalities they represented and to promote amongst their charges respect for and belief in the unity of the Empire. | Met with bureaucratic opposition and royal indifference, their principal effect was to add to the already complicated administrative system and render the goal of efficiency less attainable than ever. Francis rapidly abandoned the scheme. |
| **Council General of the Empire** In 1817, Metternich further proposed the creation of a Council General of the Empire. It was to be composed of Crown nominees and selected individuals from the provincial assemblies. It would function as a forum for discussion on the budget and general legislation. | Metternich's reform memo was filed by the Emperor upon receipt. A decision was promised on the idea in 1827 when Francis next considered the original draft. Eight years later, when the Emperor died, no progress had been made. |

institutions such as the local Diets. These bodies, composed of the local aristocracy, had been in existence for many years but were generally impotent. Many had lapsed altogether and those that *did* meet tended to do no more than endorse the tax demands and legislation proposed by Vienna. This constitutional sham appealed to Metternich who, while refusing to bestow any effective power on them, was inclined to have the Diets meet more frequently and to revive those which had fallen into disuse. His motive for this was clear enough: to stimulate regional contentment by offering the appearance of local participation in Imperial affairs. But Metternich underestimated the development of nationalism in the component parts of the Empire, and the Diets subsequently became centres of opposition to Imperial control.

However, before this became apparent Metternich had already embarked on another attempt to promote provincial identities; this time through the sponsorship of local cultural traditions. This too he hoped would lead to regional contentment within the context of the Empire while at the same time depriving German nationalism of its wider appeal by encouraging the separate characters of different national groups. Accordingly he backed a Czech revival in Bohemia which was characterized by renewed interest in language, literature and history. He also patronized the Croat national upsurge, even offering financial support to its primary exponent, the poet Ljudevit Gaj. Undoubtedly this encouragement of regional pride was part of Metternich's wider scheme to 'divide and rule'. He expected as a result to be able to neutralize the impact of excessive regional demands by allowing the nationalities to keep each other in check. Thus, in the wake of the European revolutions of 1830, he was able to claim:

Revolutions would not in our case mean a forest fire. If the Hungarian revolts...we should immediately set the Bohemian against him, for they hate each other; and after him the Pole, or the German, or the Italian.

Quoted in G de Bertier de Sauvigny, *Metternich and his Times* (1962)

But the practical effect of Metternich's short-sightedness was to encourage those very elements which provide the building blocks in the construction of any national state. By fostering regional language, history and culture, Metternich unwittingly awakened in many people the realization that they were not German. The next logical step was for them to question their status as subject peoples of the Habsburgs. The answers which emerged contributed significantly to the revolutions of 1848.

## The end of the Metternich System (1835–48)

The obsessive attachment of Emperor Francis to the *status quo* meant that Metternich's plans for reform were repeatedly frustrated. However, for some years the Emperor had been in poor health. A serious illness in 1826 had deprived him of much of his old enthusiasm and energy and finally, in March 1835, he died. According to some historians, Metternich was now presented with a clear opportunity to drive through the measures necessary to revitalize the Empire. To begin with, the Imperial throne was now to be occupied by Francis' eldest son, Ferdinand. Mentally feeble, physically weak and unfit to father children, Ferdinand was totally incapable of discharging the duties and shouldering the responsibilities of such elevated office. Describing him shortly after his installation as Emperor, the shocked Russian Empress wrote:

Good heavens, I have heard much of him, of his puny wizened figure, his great head devoid of any expression save stupidity, but the reality transcends all descriptions.

Quoted in RJ Goldstein, *Political Repression in 19th Century Europe* (1983)

Well before the death of Francis it was widely recognized that Ferdinand was not suited for his inheritance and there had been talk of finding an alternative. However, Metternich strengthened the resolve of Francis not to change the succession by emphasizing the need to uphold the principle of hereditary monarchy. There is no reason to doubt Metternich's sincerity on this matter of principle, but there was almost certainly a further

# TALKING POINT
**Building a nation**

What makes a nation? How do we distinguish France from Russia or Australia from China? We accept such places as distinct national entities, but what are their unique characteristics? Working as a pair or in a group of 3–4, try to identify those features which serve to give a people 'national status'. See how many 'bricks' you can lay towards building a nation…

FERDINAND I, EMPEROR OF AUSTRIA

motive for his insistence upon the legitimate succession.

Metternich calculated that in the absence of a monarch capable of governing, he would be compelled to take charge and at last be able to give the Empire the reforms it needed. He was given further encouragement in this direction by the contents of Francis's political testament (drawn up before the Emperor's death) which urged his successor to:

'...bestow on Prince Metternich, my most faithful servant and friend, the trust which I have reposed in him during so many years. Take no decision on public affairs, or respecting persons, without hearing him.'

Quoted in A Milne, *Metternich* (1975)

Metternich seemed to be on the threshold of a new era of conservative construction. His optimism, however, was to be shortlived. Metternich faced powerful rivals who challenged his new position in Austrian affairs. The chief of these were the brothers of Francis, Archdukes John and Charles, and the capable bureaucrat-administrator Count Anton Kolowrat. A third brother of the ex-Emperor, Archduke Ludwig, was Metternich's only ally. Metternich had sponsored the latter's selection as adviser to Ferdinand in the certain knowledge that he would be easy to dominate and would not obstruct Metternich's reform plans. But Metternich's scheming was short-sighted. What he needed was the support of a strong and capable ally, not the weak indifference offered by Ludwig. When, therefore, Metternich attempted in 1836 to reintroduce his ideas for a Conference of Ministers and a Reichsrat, the combined opposition of John, Charles and Kolowrat was sufficient to intimidate Ludwig into submission. Metternich's plans were aborted and Imperial power was transferred to a Council of Regency consisting of Ludwig, Metternich and Kolowrat. The result was the complete breakdown of the Austrian executive. Ludwig, as President of the Council, had no desire and no ability to lead, while Metternich and Kolowrat so despised each other that on the rare occasions one wanted to change anything, the other went out of his way to sabotage the move. Without the changes necessary to repair and revitalize the Empire, Austrian affairs moved inexorably towards March 1848 and the outbreak of the revolutions; small wonder that historians have chosen the term *Vor März* (Pre-March) to describe the 14 depressingly predictable years which followed the death of Francis. (For details on development during the *Vor März* see *Focus* section 3.2.)

ARCHDUKE JOHN

ARCHDUKE CHARLES

ARCHDUKE LUDWIG

The accession of Ferdinand was not the only opportunity missed by Metternich. Of all the provinces which made up the Austrian Empire, Hungary was the only one which had preserved for itself a degree of independence. The Magyar noblemen who constituted the ruling élite of the region proudly defended the rights of the Hungarian Diet against the encroachment of Habsburg authority. Between 1812 and 1825 Francis had ceased to summon the Hungarian Diet following the refusal of the Magyars to submit to a plan to devalue the Hungarian currency. However, the subsequent difficulties involved in extracting Hungary's valuable contribution of money and men forced Francis to recall the Diet in 1825. This success encouraged the Magyars to call upon Vienna to make reforming concessions to Hungary including the adoption of Magyar as the official language and the creation of a more meaningful role for the Diet in shaping Hungarian affairs. The principal exponent of these demands was Count Istvan Szechenyi; an enlightened aristocrat whose passion for his country had led him to donate one year's income from his estates to establish a Hungarian Academy. Szechenyi attacked the privileges of the nobles, arguing that concessions such as tax exemptions prevented the accumulation of capital which could be used to further Hungarian development. He founded the National Casino, a debating forum for the discussion of liberal ideas, proposed a series of imaginative economic schemes and called for the Diet to be given a more effective role in the government of Hungary. In spite of this Szechenyi remained loyal to the Imperial Crown. He was not a separatist and wished for his plans to be carried out gradually and within the context of the Empire.

However, Metternich's fossilized political principles meant that he opposed anything which resembled liberalism or social and political reform. As a result he refused to contemplate Szechenyi's moderate programme and this intransigence caused Hungarians to turn to the nationalist ambitions of Hungary's other outstanding nineteenth-century figure, Lajos Kossuth. Kossuth agreed with Szechenyi on the need to reform Hungary but ascribed its backwardness to the connection with the Austrian Crown. As a gifted writer and speaker, Kossuth persuaded many Hungarians that their only salvation lay in complete national freedom. Metternich's failure to offer timely concessions to Hungary along the lines of those proposed by Szechenyi allowed Kossuth to exploit the problems of the Empire and to mount a serious challenge to Vienna in the revolution of 1848.

### Count Istvan Szechenyi (1791–1860)

Szechenyi's contribution to the development of a distinct Magyar identity has led commentators to describe him as the founder of modern Hungary. He belonged by birth to the great landed aristocracy and was the champion of both liberalism and nationalism. He founded the Hungarian Academy to promote the Magyar language and culture and set up the 'casinos' to serve as a forum for liberal intellectual discussion. Szechenyi was contemptuous of the lesser nobility and insisted that it would require the leadership and example of the educated aristocracy to initiate and sustain the modernisation of Hungary. He argued that the aristocracy should abandon feudal privileges such as their traditional exemption from taxation and saw the future of Hungary as being dependent upon a marriage between his own class and the developing bourgeoisie. He wished as a priority to encourage economic progress in Hungary and embarked upon a number of imaginative and ambitious schemes. Perhaps the most enduring monument to his vision was the bridging of the Danube which achieved the economic unification of the twin cities of Buda and Pest. In spite of his passionate commitment to the Magyar cause, Szechenyi was never a separatist and wished to promote Hungarian development within the context of the Habsburg Empire.

### Lajos Kossuth (1802–1894)

Kossuth is perhaps the best known Magyar nationalist and is Hungary's most popular national hero. He came from a minor noble family and was a journalist by profession. His support came from the country gentry whom he lauded as the embodiment of the Magyar spirit and tradition. He was a gifted orator and writer and used his talents to encourage Hungarian nationalism. In the 1840's he edited his own newspaper, the *Pesti Hirlap*. Through the pages of this journal Kossuth popularised his view that the principal cause of Hungary's problems was inefficient government from Vienna. He dreamed of an independent Magyar state and proclaimed the cultural superiority of the Magyars over the Serb, Roumanian, Ruthenian and Slovak national groups. He wished to expand Magyar territory to incorporate the historic lands of St. Stephen, a proposal which threatened the autonomy of Transylvania and Croatia. Prior to the outbreak of the 1848 revolutions, one of his proudest achievements was to help secure a language law in 1844. This made Magyar the official language for use in the Hungarian administration, the judiciary and in public education.

COUNT ISTVAN SZECHENYI

LAJOS KOSSUTH

## 3.2 Economic and social developments during the Vor März

**1** The population remained chiefly rural and agricultural. In 1845 80% of the population lived in rural districts. 73.4% were engaged in farming, forestry or fishing.

**2** But, changes were beginning to happen. A movement to the towns was evident by 1845:

| Vienna | 400,000 | Pest | 80,000 |
| Milan | 150,000 | Trieste | 50,000 |
| Prague | 100,000 | Graz | 44,000 |
| Venice | 100,000 | Buda | 40,000 |

**3** Communications were improving: in 1839 an important line was opened between Vienna and Brunn. The network continued to expand:

| 1841 | 473 kms |
| 1848 | 1401 kms |

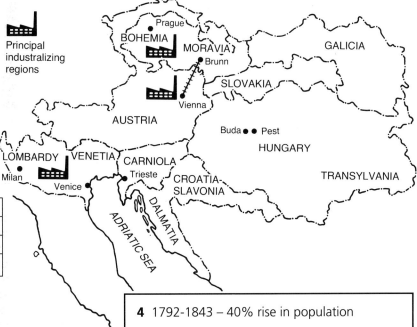

Principal industralizing regions

**4** 1792-1843 – 40% rise in population

### Urban housing problems

■ Pace of building unable to keep up with expanding populations. Eg Vienna – 45% population increase 1827-47; increase in housing – 11.4%.

■ Property owners charged high rents – frequently one-third of a family's total income.

■ Development of the 'Bettgeher' - the system by which a worker could hire a bed for a few hours a day.

■ Some workers remained in the factories and slept by their machines.

Increasing rural population led to extensive sub-division of land holdings; eg *Moravia-Silesia* in mid 1840s:

■ 6766 full holdings

◨ 3242 three-quarter holdings

◧ 26,935 half holdings

◩ 38,425 quarter holdings

☐ 132,493 holdings smaller than one quarter

In addition there were many peasants who were entirely landless. Eg 65,000 landless families in Lower Austria; 40,000 landless families in Styria.

**5** Improved communications assisted the development of industry by bringing in raw materials and transporting away finished products. *The Cotton industry* was especially important:

| Year | No. of cotton-spinning mills |
|---|---|
| 1829 | 110 |
| 1841 | 135 |
| 1843 | 149 |
| 1847 | 204 |
| **1835-42**<br>Imports of cotton yarn | increased × 8 |
| Imports of raw cotton | increased × 3 |

## Coal production   1 Zentner = 123.48 lbs

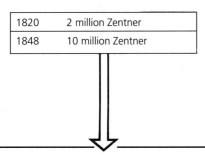

| 1820 | 2 million Zentner |
|---|---|
| 1848 | 10 million Zentner |

### Conditions in industry

Widespread employment of women and children. Eg in the cotton and paper industries of the western half of the monarchy in 1845 there were 433 men, 420 women and 147 children employed out of every 1000 workers.

Long hours were worked:
Children - 12.5 hours per day
Adults   - 13-16 hours per day
An adult was officially anyone over 12 years of age.

Technological unemployment resulted from introduction of machinery. Serious outbreaks of machine-breaking arose in 1842, 1843 and 1844.

## QUESTIONS

**1** The administrative stagnation caused by the advent of the Council of Regency should not cloud your perception of the Vor März. Use the information in points 1-5 to demonstrate that this was a dynamic period in Austrian history.

**2** The political effects of these social and economic developments were far reaching. In particular, two social classes began to multiply:

(i) an urban and rural proletariat;

(ii) a prosperous middle class of capitalist traders and manufacturers.

Consider the political implications for the Empire of the rise of these classes. Use the information below as a framework for discussion.

### Middle class

Educated, financially secure, even wealthy. Prominent in society, ambitious. What did this class aspire to in order to complement its rising social status? How did it threaten Metternich's established order?

### Urban proletariat

Try to assume the outlook of a revolutionary activist in Austria before 1848. In what ways could you expect to win the support of this class for your political ideas? In what circumstances might this class become revolutionary?

### Rural proletariat

In many areas this class lived near to starvation level - how had this situation arisen? What would you envisage being the political result of severe flooding or, worse, a failed harvest?

# EXAMINING THE EVIDENCE
## Two views of Metternich

Metternich has been the subject of assessment by many eminent histor-ians throughout the years. Two of the Twentieth Century's most prominent Metternich scholars were Heinrich von Srbik and Viktor Bibl, both pro-fessors of history at the University of Vienna. These men offered rather different views on the performance and motivation of Metternich. The two extracts which follow reproduce part of their debate.

### Source A: Heinrich von Srbik

History is not a court of justice for the world. The historian of a notable man has the duty of investigating his actions in their context and to explain their results, not, with the haughty bearing of a judge, deliver a judgement. Contemporaries already blamed Metternich and his system, and the princes who followed his principles for having prepared the way for the revolution [of 1848]...

The liberal and national opposition spoke through their mouths. It was they who accused Metternich of confounding cause and effect and of being a 'symptom doctor'. He denied this reproach, and could truthfully say that he looked upon the new ideas of the time as the real malady of the body social, and upon the political and social disturbances merely as their fruit and symptoms...Ultraconservatives and liberals as physicians for the state and society went out from completely different views as to the nature of the malady, and hence also of the symptoms. Liberalism saw the essence of the evil in the maintenance of obsolete conditions, and looked upon the eruptive movements as being the result of the suppres-sion of natural growth and any attempt to combat it as charlatanry. Thus in 1847 Richard Cobden called Metternich 'probably the last of those state physicians who, looking only to the symptoms of a nation, content themselves with superficial remedies from day to day, and never attempt to probe beneath the surface, to discover the source of the evils which afflict the social system. This order of statesmen will pass away with him, because too much light has been shed upon the laboratory of government, to allow them to impose upon mankind with the old formulas.' Ultraconservatives on the other hand, considered the tendencies towards change to be the disease, and combatted them preventively by the maint-enance of monarchical absolutism and the strength of the government, repressively and at the same time preventively by punishment...

It must never be forgotten that Metternich believed with the deepest conviction that the entire phenomenon of political and social desire for progress was only a temporary manifestation leading in the eternal cycle of things to the restoration of the old institutions governed by principles, and that he looked upon it as his fate to be the apostle of European social conservatism.

That is, in the deepest sense, his historical significance: the constant and consistent opposition throughout the world of European civilization to the levelling of democracy and the rule of the mobilized masses which threatened the historical order of states and society, and individual cul-ture. Thus from the point of view of the individualistic cultural aristocrat,

Jakob Burckhardt also hated and feared liberalism and the social levelling of democracy, and rejected the idea of progress, but also the unitary state and centralization. The great error of the statesman and the historian was that they did not recognize the irresistibility of elemental processes as a tragic necessity. Metternich who, in the field of foreign affairs, always knew how to comprehend the limits of the possible, as ultraconservative social statesman tried to do the impossible. He who set up timeless doctrines was overtaken by time. But his doctrines must be accorded objective significance: this system justifiably made the claim that it was a European and universal social system. It was a world-doctrine opposing, as an enemy, the new century and its dynamics, a primary heir of the international thinking of the pre-Revolutionary time, and the classical expression of the ultraconservative thought of the era of the Restoration; a *credo* which will always have its place in the history of political and social ideas, and in the great struggle of the spiritual forces of recent history…

Heinrich von Srbik, *Metternich, der Staatsmann und der Mensch* (1925), quoted in Henry F Schwarz, *Metternich the 'Coachman of Europe'* (1962)

## Source B: Viktor Bibl

The most serious reproach…which can be levelled against the Chancellor is the suspicion that in reality he was not at all 'blind to the movement of forces' or 'lacking in ideas' but rather that, contrary to his own better insight, he pursued a policy fatal to Austria. Can one suppose that he, a gifted man, really did not recognise what simpler minds at the Vienna court, such as the Archduke John, had long seen, namely, that it was wasted effort to oppose the world-moving force of new ideas? He himself admitted in 1820: 'The world moves forward amid storms: to try to oppose its violent progress would be a vain effort.' And in the same year he declared: 'My life has fallen in a horrible period. I have been born either too early or too late, now I feel myself good for nothing…today my life is passed in shoring up the mouldering buildings.'

But why did Metternich look upon it as his task to shore up the mouldering buildings rather than to follow the great example of his Rhenish compatriot Stein [in Prussia] and build anew?…In his reminiscences, Grillparzer explained the immobility of Metternich after Francis' death with the idea that the former critic of the narrow minded policy of the Emperor, now that he himself had grown old, went on in the same routine as a result of indolence, and dignified 'the measures which he had involuntarily adopted by giving them the honorary title of System.' In practice, however, the supple Chancellor had made this system his own while the Emperor was still alive, precisely because his criticism had had no effect…He avoided a struggle with his imperial master which would have cost him his position.

Does the sum total of Metternich's statesmanlike ideas really reduce to a single thought, the maintaining of himself in his office? His physician, Dr Jager, testified that in all his life he had never met a more thoroughgoing egoist than was the Chancellor. It would seem then comprehensible that Metternich placed his own welfare above that of the Empire, and for purely personal reasons conducted a policy which, according to his own conviction, must lead to the downfall of Austria…He must bear the entire blame for the outbreak of the March Revolution [1848] with all of its catastrophic results, and with the increasing difficulties with which Francis Joseph had to struggle, and which, in spite of never resting and most laborious work he never succeeded in overcoming. The peaceful, steady development of the Empire, which a renewal of the structure of the Estates at the right time would seem to have guaranteed, was prevented by Metternich, and thus also the free development of the peoples within the framework of the Danubean monarchy. The absolute, centralized state, the result of the preceding revolution, called forth the struggles of the peoples which crippled the inner strength of the Habsburg Monarchy. Metternich's unfortunate German and Italian policy led to the fateful days of Solferino and Koniggratz; the much delayed opening up of the Eastern Question, which he did not want touched, led to the World War.'

Viktor Bibl, *Metternich, Austria's Evil Genius* (1936.) Quoted in Henry F Schwarz, as above

---

Examine the two accounts above with care. Don't expect to understand the arguments instantly; be prepared to read them a number of times. Answer the following questions; they will help you to clarify the assessments of the two professors.

**1** Identify the broad group of 'contemporaries' (Source A) who would have 'blamed Metternich' for the revolutions of 1848.

**2** Suggest what Metternich meant by the 'mouldering buildings' referred to in Source B.

**3** Assessments of Metternich frequently employ the 'doctor' analogy used in Source A. The Chancellor is presented as a physician, diagnosing and treating the 'illness' which affects his patient: the Habsburg Empire.

The liberals and Metternich perceived the problems of society differently. Use Source A to complete your own copy of the chart opposite.

**4** Consider this view by Srbik: 'The great error of the statesman and the historian was that they did not recognize the irresistibility of elemental processes as a tragic necessity.'

(a) How might this be regarded as an 'apology' for Metternich's ultraconservative behaviour as Imperial Chancellor?

(b) How does Bibl challenge this view?

**5** Metternich claimed in 1820: 'today my life is passed in shoring up the mouldering buildings.' In response to this claim, Bibl poses an interesting question: 'Why did Metternich look upon it as his task to shore up the mouldering buildings…?'

Consider separately how each of these historians accounts for Metternich's self-appointed task.

**6** Consider the final paragraph of each assessment. How do they demonstrate the very different approaches taken by the two historians to their subject?

**7** Consider the first four lines of Source A. What does this preliminary statement suggest to you about Srbik's purpose in attempting his assessment of Metternich?

| | Metternich's diagnosis | Liberal diagnosis |
|---|---|---|
| Principal 'disease' of society | new ideas, liberalism, nationalism, the urge to change the existing social and political system | |
| Symptoms of 'disease' | revolutions, protest meetings, demagogic agitation, demonstrations | |
| Treatment/cure | repression, use of secret police, censorship, general maintenance of existing order | |

**8** What might be the dangers of writing history out of context?; for example, in passing judgement on Metternich's reactionary conservatism from the perspective of the Twentieth Century.

**9** Which of these historians would you consider to have been more objective in his approach? You might like to consider:

(a) the title each gave to his book;

(b) the degree of 'balance' in their analyses;

(c) the 'evidence' used in support of their conclusions;

(d) the language employed.

## Metternich: an assessment

In 1848 Metternich fell from office as the Habsburg lands were shaken by revolution. The popular verdict on his performance as chief Imperial minister was emphatic. After years of dedicated maintenance he had finally been unable to prevent the decaying edifice of Habsburg authority from crashing down. The fact that Metternich was one of the principal casualties of this collapse seems to suggest that he was substantially to blame for it and that the judgement of history should be simple and direct; Metternich was capable of achieving more, ought to have done so, but failed because he lacked the necessary commitment and enthusiasm for his appointed task. How far this is true depends upon an examination of the problems he faced and the practical alternatives open to him for dealing with them.

Metternich did not prevaricate in passing judgement on himself; in a line frequently quoted by historians he claimed: 'I have sometimes ruled Europe, but never have I governed Austria.' However, since Metternich was not given by nature to bouts of self-criticism, we can take this to represent not so much a comment on his own failings but on the political restrictions which he claimed had prevented him from functioning effectively. It is true that Metternich was confronted with real obstacles which left him little room to manoeuvre. Because of the intransigence of the Emperor, for example, he was never able to gain royal endorsement for his reforming efforts and could not therefore generate provincial loyalty to the Habsburg Crown. Metternich has been criticized, however, for failing to take a stronger line with Francis. He was an able diplomat and was highly regarded by the Emperor; in such circumstances he might have been expected to achieve rather more. However, as Metternich was keen to point out, his influence over Francis was limited:

'I know that the Emperor Nicholas has the idea that I can bend to my will the master whom I serve. But this is a wrong judgement upon the Emperor of Austria. His will is strong and no-one can make him do anything which he does not wish to. He overwhelms me with kindness, and gives me his confidence; but he does this because I follow the direction which he lays down for me.'

> Metternich to the Russian General Krasinski, quoted in EL Woodward,
> *Three Studies in European Conservatism* (1929)

Perhaps Metternich *did* lack sufficient personal influence over the Emperor to move him on reform issues; certainly Francis could be frustratingly single-minded at times. Yet it was quite apparent that Metternich shared the general outlook of the Emperor and was so committed to the principle of monarchical authority that he refused to challenge decisions made by Francis:

'Heaven has placed me next to a man who might have been created for me, as I for him. The Emperor Francis knows what he wants and that never differs in any way from what I most want.'

> Metternich describing the Emperor, quoted in Alan Sked,
> *Europe's Balance of Power 1815–1848* (1979)

If Metternich had been genuinely dedicated to the idea of reform why did he not resign in protest at the repeated dismissal of his schemes? The answer to this probably lies in Metternich's perception of his priorities. Commenting on his role in the years before 1848 he wrote: 'My task was not to govern nor to administer, but to represent the Empire to foreign countries.' Metternich regarded his concern with domestic affairs as being secondary to his role as Foreign Minister, and was not prepared to abandon his responsibilities to Europe by resigning over internal issues. Besides, he regarded himself, with typical arrogance, as being indispensable. Writing to his son Viktor in 1828 he observed:

'The world has need of me still if only because my place in it could not be filled by anyone else. To be what I am needs an accumulation of experience, and one could as easily replace an old tree as an old minister.'

> Metternich, *Memoirs*. Quoted in G de Bertier de Sauvigny,
> *Metternich and his Times* (1962)

The immobility of Francis and the refusal of Metternich to take a more forceful line are both factors which help to explain the absence of meaningful reform in the Habsburg Empire. Other factors also contributed. In the *Vor Marz* period the stagnation of the administration was further ensured by the rivalry between Metternich and Kolowrat. Even in better times Metternich was never able to secure the co-operation of the State bureaucracy, and his plans faced the open hostility of the aristocracy who saw any proposed change to the existing order as being directed against their interests.

Perhaps the greatest damage Metternich did to the Austrian Empire was to continue promoting her as a 'European necessity'. This self-imposed mission to uphold the Central European balance against encroachment from Russia and France, and to keep Italy and Germany within her conservative orbit, was beyond the resources of Austria to sustain. The Habsburgs had emerged from the Napoleonic Wars in a state of financial exhaustion. In the years which followed revenue *did* rise, thanks largely to the efforts of the minister Stadion. In spite of this, however, expenditure continued to outstrip income and a budget deficit was registered in most years. Metternich was thus unable to maintain Austria's pivotal role in European affairs but stubbornly continued to insist on scarce resources being diverted towards this responsibility. As a result other areas of domestic need went without and Metternich's true priorities were once again emphasized.

The enduring image of Metternich is of a man unable to adapt to the changing circumstances of his time. He believed himself to be living through one of history's transitional phases and recognized that society would inevitably jettison the values and beliefs which had shaped his perception of the world. Yet he was not prepared to go down fighting and accepted his own inevitable failure. When revolution broke out in France in 1830 he wrote to the Russian Foreign Minister Nesselrode: 'My most secret conviction is that the old Europe is nearing its end...I have determined to fall with it.' Again, in his *Memoirs*, Metternich suggested that his work was doomed to failure:

'My life has coincided with a most abominable time. I have come into the world too soon or too late; I know that in these years I can accomplish nothing...I am spending my life underpinning buildings which are mouldering into decay. I ought to have been born in 1900, with the twentieth century before me.'

Metternich, *Memoirs*, quoted in EL Woodward, *Three Studies in European Conservatism* (1929)

Whether Metternich could have made more of himself in the Twentieth Century would make an interesting academic debate. More immediately relevant was the fact that when Metternich fell from office in 1848 it was probably not much of a surprise to him. It is difficult to resist the conclusion that when the revolutions broke out he had been waiting for them to happen for some time. That Metternich was unwilling to devise any constructive alternative to the rigid conservatism which characterized his career of Imperial service is a damning indictment of a man described by the eminent historian AJP Taylor as '...the ablest man who ever applied himself to the "Austrian problem"' (*The Habsburg Monarchy 1809–1918* (1948)).

# REVIEW

## How successful was Metternich in dealing with the principal problems of the Austrian Empire in the period 1815–48?

This question requires a careful review of the whole chapter and is best tackled through discussion in small groups. It is suggested that you work according to the following procedure:

**1** Identify a significant problem which Metternich had to deal with.

**2** Give details of the action taken by Metternich in response to the problem.

**3** Describe the results of these actions.

**4** Evaluate Metternich's performance.

Clearly, steps 1 and 4 will be the most difficult to resolve with any certainty. These items should be the focus of the group's discussions. An example of how this procedure might work in practice is given below.

**1 Identify problem** The Empire was made up of different national groups each with different characteristics. Metternich had to keep these nationalities loyal to Vienna or risk the collapse of the Empire.

**2 Actions taken** Sponsored a 'divide and rule' approach; never attempted to impose complete unity on the peoples of the Empire.
Encouraged provincial institutions such as the local Diets.
Promoted local cultural traditions, language, history, literature.
Stood firm against any attempts to liberalize local government.

**3 Results** Allowed the nationalities to regard themselves as separate to the German Habsburgs.
Opened the eyes of many subject peoples to the rich diversity of their own cultural traditions.
Intransigence in the face of demands for liberal reforms drove the people away from moderates such as Szechenyi (Hungary) and into the arms of radicals such as Kossuth.

**4 Evaluation** Metternich sought to subvert nationalist tendencies by trying to encourage the subject peoples to feel content within the context of the Empire. But Metternich's plans were never more than cosmetic. He might sponsor national poets but he stopped short of giving any real power to the local parliaments (Diets). As a result his schemes served only to stimulate nationalist feelings. He showed the Czechs and Croats, for example, that they had an identity of their own which could be recognized and sustained through their language, history and culture. In the 1848 revolutions such characteristics were often emphasized. In addition, because Metternich remained anti-liberal in his approach to the component states of the Empire, a strong tradition of radicalism developed, particularly in places like Hungary. Here, concessions to the moderates might have been sufficient to hold the Empire together. When control passed to the radicals the question was not how much liberty Vienna might grant to the regions, but how soon the regions would be independent from Vienna.

# 4 The 1848 Revolutions

## PREVIEW

### The extent of revolution

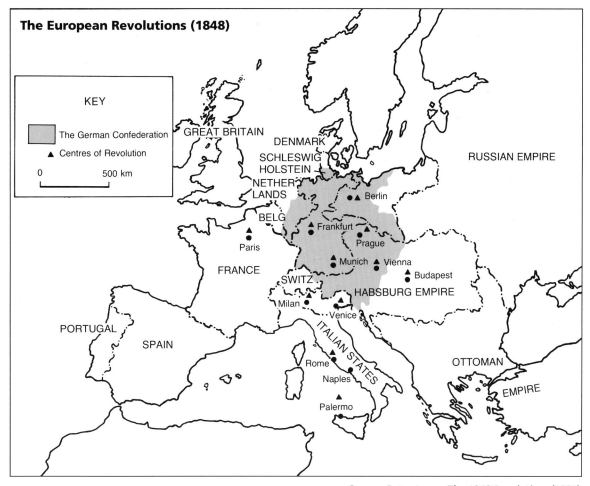

The European Revolutions (1848)

KEY

The German Confederation

▲ Centres of Revolution

0          500 km

GREAT BRITAIN

DENMARK

SCHLESWIG
HOLSTEIN

NETHER-
LANDS

BELG

Paris

FRANCE

SWITZ

Milan

Venice

PORTUGAL

SPAIN

Berlin

Frankfurt

Prague

Munich    Vienna

Budapest

HABSBURG EMPIRE

ITALIAN STATES

Rome

Naples

Palermo

RUSSIAN EMPIRE

OTTOMAN

EMPIRE

Source: Peter Jones, *The 1848 Revolutions* (1981)

'1848 was pre-eminently the revolutionary year when almost the entire
continent of Europe was swept by revolution. Russia escaped at one end
of the continent, England at the other except for the Chartist demonstration. Virtually every other state in Europe experienced a revolution,
political, social or both together.'

AJP Taylor, *Revolutions and Revolutionaries* (1981)

# The causes of the 1848 revolutions

Why were there so many revolutions in 1848? The causes of these widespread phenomena have become the subject of dozens of historical studies. Historians are in general agreement that the revolutions sprang from a context of long-term social, economic and political change which characterized the years after 1815. The effects of these changes were aggravated by a short-term crisis produced by acute food shortages after 1846. In these circumstances incidents occurred which then triggered the outbreak of the revolutions. The first part of this chapter will examine the problems facing European society in the period 1815–48.

## Long-term tensions

### Population growth and industrialization

**1 Population** One of the most important elements in the general development of Europe during the first half of the Nineteenth Century was sustained population growth (see graph). This long-term development placed enormous strains on the land. Although the productivity of agricultural land *did* increase, by 1840 many areas of Europe were quite unable to sustain their populations. Even at the best of times the common citizens of Europe lived at subsistence level only. Now, with cultivated land unable to yield adequate food supplies for a growing population, the potential for disorder during times of poor harvest became acute. In the 1840s there were major incidents of public disorder in Silesia, Posen, East Prussia and Galicia.

**2 Industrialization** During the first half of the Nineteenth Century, continental Europe experienced a modest degree of industrial development. In concentrated areas of France, Belgium and Germany the foundation industries – coal, iron and textiles – underwent steady expansion. Large-scale factories were not yet commonplace in Europe but industrial towns, with their numerous busy workshops, displayed rapid growth. This growth was stimulated by migration from the overpopulated rural districts. Industrial towns like Saint Étienne and Lille, and older centres such as Paris and Berlin, attracted a section of the European population displaced from their traditional agrarian base and compelled to seek an alternative livelihood in the new industrial enterprises. The urban conditions which resulted help to explain the long-term background to the revolutions of 1848. Housing was in desperately short supply, producing terrible overcrowding; the average life expectancy of an industrial worker in Lille was just 32. Inadequate sanitation encouraged disease; tuberculosis, typhoid and worst of all, cholera. Epidemics of this deadly disease ravaged France in 1831–32 and again in 1847–49; in Paris alone during the earlier of these outbreaks, 18,400 people were carried off in just six months.

Many of the migrants who flooded into the towns were uneducated, displayed criminal tendencies and were attracted to the cheap escape of alcoholic oblivion. The newcomers had little sense of loyalty to their adopted towns and were frequently unemployed. Tension between the migrants and the natives was in constant evidence. For the city authorities it became increasingly difficult to control this potentially explosive

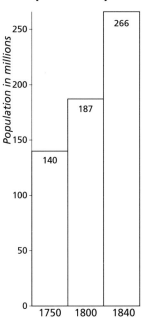

**Population of Europe (1750–1840)**

*Population in millions*

- 1750: 140
- 1800: 187
- 1840: 266

## Rising populations

*Paris*

| | |
|---|---|
| 1817 | 713,966 |
| 1846 | 1,053,897 |

*St Étienne*

| | |
|---|---|
| 1831 | 16,000 |
| 1841 | 54,000 |

situation. Strikes and riots amongst the urban working class multiplied in the years prior to 1848. Paris, Lille, Marseilles and Lyons all experienced civil disturbances which could be directly linked to the intolerable conditions existing in such centres.

A further source of discontent was the deteriorating position of the skilled artisan. Industrialization brought machines and constant supplies of cheap labour which placed great strains on the traditional hand-workers. Gradually the protection of the trade guilds was removed as unsympathetic governments passed legislation to render these organizations illegal. Increasingly the skilled artisan had to compete with immigrant workers prepared to work for low wages and with machinery which forced down the costs of production and made hand-produced goods relatively expensive. The social status of the artisan worker was threatened by industrialization, thus adding another source of discontent to an already restless Europe.

# TALKING POINT

## Urban Conditions in the Habsburg Empire (1845–48)

| | |
|---|---|
| Continuous inflation. | Typhoid. |
| No official relief provided for unemployed. | Factory workers' wages approx. 40 kr per day. |
| Vienna – 10,000 factory workers laid off in 1847. | 1846 – 1 lb of butter cost 66 kr. |
| Wood prices increase 250% in period 1836–46. | 1847 – 1 egg cost 6–7.5 kr. |
| No relaxation of taxes on consumables – including food. | Linz – ⅔ of population (26,000) were undernourished. |

**1** Discuss the effect such conditions were likely to have on the everyday lives of people in the Habsburg Empire.

**2** How far do you think revolution could be described as the inevitable result of such conditions?

**3** Ireland and Russia did not escape the experience of the economic crisis after 1846 – yet revolution did not break out in these countries. Does this information help you to clarify your response to question 2 above?

## The challenge to the 1815 settlement

The peace treaty which emerged at Vienna in 1815 settled the European state system following the collapse of Napoleon's empire. However, the settlement was more than a simple territorial reshuffle. Bound up in the settlement was a commitment to the power of monarchy and the Church, and the recognition of aristocratic privilege. Increasingly after 1815, these ideas, which predated the French Revolution, came to be challenged by groups representing new forces.

**Liberalism** The development of a European middle class during the first half of the Nineteenth Century produced an articulate challenge to the values of 1815. Educated professionals, such as lawyers, teachers, doctors, journalists and public officials, were openly critical of a system which denied them appropriate recognition and status in society. They were largely excluded from participation in politics, were discriminated against when in competition with the privileged nobility and were restrained from the free expression of their grievances by the censor and the secret police. Such people became attracted to the ideals of liberalism (see opposite).

Those who supported the liberal programme were not democrats. They looked to invest political power not in the people but in a parliament composed of an educated and responsible élite. Neither were they revolutionaries, wishing to achieve political change by force of argument not force of arms. Yet as the Nineteenth Century progressed, middle-class liberals made little progress against the entrenched opposition of men like Metternich. Governments consistently ignored the interests and grievances of this important and ambitious group; in 1848 they were made to pay for their neglect.

**Nationalism** East of the Rhine, nationalism was beginning to mount its challenge to the 1815 settlement. The belief that groups of people sharing a common language, culture and historical background should come together to form nation states had begun to develop in the Eighteenth Century. After 1815 the ideas of nationalism made steady if unspectacular progress. The Vienna settlement had charged Austria with the responsibility of overseeing the states of Italy and the German Confederation. In both areas, and also in Hungary, nationalists challenged the legitimacy of Habsburg rule. When revolution broke out in these regions in 1848 the principal aim was to obtain independence from Vienna.

## Short-term tensions

### The economic crisis (1845–48)

**1 The food crisis** Given time, European society might have peacefully assimilated the effects of industrialization and population growth had it not been for a severe economic crisis which developed after 1845. The social problems associated with the post-Napoleonic era were now greatly intensified. The predominant feature of this crisis was the widespread disruption of food supplies. In 1845–46 cereal harvests throughout much of Central Europe were very poor and the situation was made worse by the devastation of the potato crop. The yield of both these staples remained low during 1847 with catastrophic consequences for Europe's labouring classes. The principal effect was to inflate the price of basic foodstuffs to outrageous levels. Grain prices at Hamburg were 60 per cent higher in 1847 than they had been two years earlier, and in some parts of Germany the price of potatoes rose by 135 per cent in the space of 12 months. Parts of France, Eastern Europe and the Low Countries were also badly affected by the shortage of food.

Not surprisingly perhaps, incidents of civil disorder directly linked to the food crisis began to multiply. There were riots in The Hague, Delft, Leyden and Harlem in 1845 and in the rural district of Galicia the following year. In 1847 Stettin and Berlin both witnessed bread riots. The pressures which provoked these outbursts were clear enough. It has been estimated that around 70 per cent of working-class income was used to

> ### The principles of liberalism
>
> **1** Restrain the arbitrary power of the monarch and the Church.
>
> **2** Develop parliamentary government to allow sharing of political power.
>
> **3** Govern according to the rule of law.
>
> **4** Enact laws to guarantee civil liberties and freedom of speech.

buy food. Huge price increases and inadequate supplies pushed many peasants and town-dwellers towards starvation. The crisis compounded the effects of Europe's long-term social problems and produced an unpredictable and potentially revolutionary mass.

BREAD RIOT IN PARIS (OCTOBER 1846). SUCH SCENES WERE COMMON IN MANY EUROPEAN CITIES DUE TO SEVERE FOOD SHORTAGES

**2 The financial crisis** Food shortages were but one aspect of the general economic crisis evident after 1845. Businessmen and financiers found themselves in difficulties as a financial crisis descended on Europe. As food prices rose consumer purchases of manufactured goods declined. The result was substantial unemployment and the contraction of industrial output. Interest rates climbed steadily, gold reserves came under pressure to pay for expensive food imports and British capital, the mainstay of railway and general industrial investment on the Continent, began to be withdrawn. The result was a credit squeeze which forced many businessmen into bankruptcy.

The financial crisis was especially severe in France. Here, overproduction characterized industries such as coalmining and ironmaking. Encouraged by government-led investment in the railways, such industries had expanded their operations only to find that their increased output exceeded demand. In 1847 the iron industry was forced to cut production by 30 per cent; coal was reduced by 20 per cent. The result was unemployment and a loss of confidence in the government. Dramatic falls in the value of share prices shattered confidence still further. The middle class and the working class now constituted a huge body of discontent in Europe. A temporary alliance followed which in 1848 shook European society to its foundations.

# Case study 1: France

## Phase 1: 1847 to Provisional Government

The principal events in the French revolution of 1848 occurred in the capital city, Paris. Here, an increasingly active liberal opposition to the monarchy of Louis Philippe had emerged. Their appetite for change had been sharpened by the economic crisis which had developed after 1845 and they successfully exploited two government scandals to register their disgust over official corruption. At a criminal trial in 1847 it was revealed that the former Minister of Public Works had accepted bribes when allocating industrial concessions. More dramatic was the case of the Duc de Praslin who battered his wife to death for the love of his English mistress and then committed suicide before the conclusion of his trial. Both episodes were publicly exhibited by the opposition as evidence of the moral decay of the ruling class, and were used to question its fitness to govern.

But the overriding grievance of this predominantly middle-class group was its exclusion from government. The 200 franc tax qualification for voters produced a small electorate of about 240,000 drawn from the nobility and upper ranks of the middle class. The remainder of the middle class – the journalists, lawyers, doctors, shopkeepers and minor employers – was effectively disenfranchised. From this group developed demands for a change in the electoral law.

Early in 1847 a proposal to reduce the tax qualification to 100 francs was defeated in the Chamber of Deputies. Louis Philippe and his conservative Prime Minister Guizot were dismissive of the middle-class liberals and quite unprepared to offer concessions to them. Had they done so they might have been able to re-establish traditional middle-class support for the regime, now in serious jeopardy thanks to the effects of the financial crisis.

The liberal opposition now reverted to organizing activities away from the Chamber. Since political meetings had been declared illegal, the campaigners held 'reform banquets' where the after-dinner speeches focused on familiar demands for constitutional reform. Alert to the propaganda value of such meetings, the government banned a dinner planned for 22 February 1848. The moderate reformers who had made the arrangements accepted the ban without protest. But the intransigence of the government during 1847 had encouraged the radicals who now used the banning of the banquet to call for a protest demonstration. In circumstances of unemployment and food shortages the demonstration was well attended, and the police were forced to disperse an agitated crowd in the Place de la Madeleine.

On 23 February the situation in Paris deteriorated. Belatedly, Louis Philippe realized the need for concessions. He dismissed Guizot and replaced him with the more liberal Molé. The move came too late. That evening a crowd advancing on the Foreign Ministry was fired upon by nervous troops. Around 40 protestors were killed and within hours Paris was in open revolt. The Parisian public, incensed by the murder of fellow citizens, tore up trees and paving stones in a frenzy of barricade-building. Gunsmiths and barracks were looted for weapons as civil disorder gripped the city. National Guardsmen, called out to help restore order, defected to

**1** Which incident triggered the outbreak of revolution in Paris?

**2** Why did Louis Philippe face opposition from the middle class and from the Parisian workers?

the side of the reformers and the King was compelled to deploy regular troops under the command of Marshal Bugeaud to end the disturbances. Bugeaud's men, however, were unaccustomed to the complexities of tackling urban violence. The barricades held and the troops retreated in disarray.

Unable to suppress the revolutionaries, Louis Philippe was urged to abdicate. On 24 February he accepted this advice and abandoned his capital; that same afternoon, in front of the Hotel de Ville, the creation of a Provisional Government was announced.

### Phase 2: the seeds of defeat (24 February to the April elections)

**The dubious alliance** Success in the February revolution was not the result of long-term planning. The middle class certainly wanted change but on the whole its members were not revolutionaries; when the Parisian workers had set up their street barricades it was essentially a spontaneous reaction to the incident outside the Foreign Ministry. The revolution began by accident. From the ruins of the Orleanist monarchy arose the Second French Republic. Four years later the republican experiment ended with the French adopting a Bonaparte as their emperor. The seeds of the republican collapse were evident from the outset.

CROWDS WITNESS THE PROCLAMATION IN PARIS OF THE SECOND FRENCH REPUBLIC (27 FEBRUARY 1848)

The factor which had brought victory in February was the alliance between aspiring sections of the middle class and the discontent of the labouring masses. But this was essentially a marriage of convenience. The workers were determined to establish a social republic and their mood was menacing; the middle class was nervous about these ambitions. It wanted moderate political reform and the return of business confidence. Public order was essential; socialism was an unwarranted interference. The mutual suspicion felt by the partners in this flimsy alliance soon provoked hostility as the impulse to dominate the Republic developed.

**The Provisional Government** These divisions were evident in the composition of the Provisional Government. In the immediate wake of Louis Philippe's departure hopes were briefly entertained within the Chamber that the monarchy would survive in the shape of a Regency. Such hopes evaporated when the Paris mob descended on the Chamber and demanded the creation of a republic.

Seven leading, and essentially moderate, republican figures were nominated to set up a Provisional Government. But the moderates had rivals; radical left-wingers who demanded their right to be represented in the new government. Accordingly, four radicals – including the socialist Louis Blanc and a solitary worker, Albert – were accommodated by the moderates. According to the historian Anthony Wood:

'...from the beginning the provisional government consisted of an indigestible amalgam of two utterly different political groups.'

*Europe 1815–1945* (1964)

The principal source of contention was the vision each faction had of the transformation of France. The moderates wished only to establish constitutional parliamentary government; the left-wing radicals articulated the aspirations of the urban masses for a republic based on democracy and committed to extensive social reform. The search for common ground between these two groups became increasingly futile.

**The limits of social change** The principal task of the Provisional Government was to administer France until elections could be held to choose a Constituent Assembly. These elections were scheduled for April; in the meantime there were urgent problems which had to be confronted immediately. Under pressure from the Parisian masses the Provisional Government was required to initiate a political and social programme. Accordingly, a number of measures were taken. (See opposite.)

These measures raised the expectations of the labouring classes who saw in them the first steps towards social justice. In fact they represented stop-gap concessions to silence the immediate demands of the agitated masses and to divert them from their dangerous brand of political activity. The majority in the Provisional Government had no intention of moving further in the direction of social reform.

**Financial difficulties** The collapse of the monarchy did not herald a return of confidence among financiers and businessmen. In fact, the situation inherited from Louis Philippe continued to deteriorate. In three weeks the reserves of the Bank of France fell by 70 per cent and share values were cut by 55 per cent. Industrial output slumped and during

---

**The work of the Provisional Government**

**1** The National Guard was opened to all classes.

**2** Press freedom and individual liberties were granted.

**3** A commission was established at the Luxembourg Palace, headed by Louis Blanc, to investigate living and working conditions and to propose reforms.

**4** A reduction of one hour in the working day was secured.

**5** The right of all citizens to work was recognized.

**6** National Workshops were set up in order to assist the large number of unemployed workers in Paris.

---

March the government deficit rose sharply. The government tried to fill the budgetary gap by imposing a 45 per cent increase in direct taxation. Crucially, the bulk of this new burden fell on the peasants, already being squeezed by the continuing agrarian crisis. Peasant support for the Republic was badly affected and 50,000 troops were needed to police the countryside for the remainder of 1848.

**The April elections** One of the more enduring measures of the Provisional Government was to introduce the principle of universal male suffrage. In the rapidly-approaching elections every male over the age of 21 was to be allowed a vote. The electorate rocketed from around 250,000 to almost nine million! Universal suffrage provided an opportunity for provincial France to pass its verdict on recent events in Paris. But for the ruling groups in the capital, the nature of the new electorate raised worrying questions. By far the majority of voters now comprised peasants, many of whom were illiterate and without experience of political involvement. Faced with political choices they were likely to settle for the familiar; the guidance of the priest and the authority of the local notable. In addition they were already resentful of the tax increases, and suspicious of socialism which seemed to imply the nationalization of their lands. The disturbances in Paris alarmed them still further and provoked a consuming desire to see the restoration of order within French society.

The power and influence of the Church in the provinces was critical. Dismayed by the plans of the radicals to terminate Church control of education, the clergy came out in opposition to republicanism. Its campaign to persuade the peasantry to follow them was effective. On Easter Sunday 84 per cent of the new French electorate went to the polls. The day chosen for the elections was a mistake. Bishops had already prepared lists of acceptable candidates which the priests then made known to the peasants. Their final reminders came at morning mass on Easter Sunday; from the pulpit to the polling centre was but a short distance.

The results of the elections were very damaging to the republicans. The overwhelming complexion of the new Constituent Assembly was moderate and conservative. Out of the 900 deputies, 700 paid tax in excess of 500 francs per year; the traditional position of propertied classes in government had been categorically endorsed. Socialists and radical republicans won between 70 and 80 seats; only amongst this minority group was there any real sympathy for the kind of extensive social reforms envisaged by the spokesmen of the urban working classes. The majority of deputies were either monarchists or moderate republicans; social reform was absent from the political agendas of both groups. A clash between the left wing and the forces of conservatism now looked highly likely.

## Phase 3: counter-revolution

The results of the April elections frustrated the left and encouraged conservatives to seize the initiative away from the reformers. On 15 May an attempted coup by Parisian radicals led to the arrest of prominent left-wingers such as Blanqui and Albert. Shortly after, the work of the Luxembourg Commission was discontinued and its proposals were shelved.

The real body-blow to the radical movement was delivered on 21 June with the announcement that the National Workshops were to be closed down. Although they had only offered unskilled work to a minority of workers, and had been established simply as a mechanism through which the unemployed could be registered and paid a small dole, they were symbolic of the commitment to the principle of the right to work. While they existed they continued to offer hope that the economy would develop along socialist lines. To the conservatives they were associated with revolution and were an unnecessary financial burden on the government. The 120,000 men registered with the Workshops were now given the option of military service or removal to the provinces to labour on public works schemes.

Large numbers of workers regarded the decision to close the Workshops as a betrayal. The expectations raised during the first weeks and months of the Republic had been cruelly disappointed. On 22 June barricades once more were erected in working-class districts of Paris and an attempt was made to restart the revolution. This time, however, the forces of conservatism kept their composure. The National Guard supported the government as 30,000 regular troops were moved into the capital by train. In command of these forces was General Cavaignac and for the next six days, the so-called 'June Days', his men systematically and often brutally cleared the Paris streets of barricades and protestors. Around 3000 rioters were killed and some 12,000 arrested. Of those brought to trial 4000 were deported.

CAVAIGNAC'S TROOPS ROUND UP RIOTERS DURING THE JUNE DAYS (1848)

The June Days signalled the triumph of reaction over reform. The constitution of the Second Republic, which appeared in November, made no reference to the 'right to work' and placed executive power in the hands of a President to be elected by universal suffrage. Two months earlier the working day had been extended to 12 hours; the one specifically social reform of the Provisional Government had been cast aside. In December the French overwhelmingly elected Louis Napoleon Bonaparte, nephew of the great emperor, to the position of President. Under his direction the Republic finally collapsed.

| PRESIDENTIAL ELECTION RESULTS (DEC. 1848) | |
|---|---|
| **Candidate** | **Votes received** |
| Louis Napoleon Bonaparte | 5,400,000 |
| General Cavaignac | 1,500,000 |
| Lamartine | 17,000 |

## Case study 2: the Habsburg Empire

As news of events in Paris on 23–24 February began to spread across the Continent, European liberals were unable to contain their excitement. At meetings and demonstrations, middle-class reformers, disaffected workers and student radicals gave notice of their intention to force a change in the outdated system of government, discredited in their eyes after years of inaction and suffocating repression. In the Habsburg Empire, the added dimension of racial tension entered the frame as the grievances of various national groups gathered momentum. The guardians of the old order had hardly time to tremble before being overwhelmed by a huge wave of popular disapproval.

### Hungary

On 3 March Lajos Kossuth, Hungary's most prominent nationalist leader, delivered an impassioned speech before the Hungarian Diet meeting at Pressburg (Bratislava). He demanded an end to absolute rule from Vienna and outlined constitutional changes which would establish Hungarian autonomy. Kossuth's inspirational and persuasive appeal led the Pressburg Diet to pass the so-called 'March Laws'.

The fall of Metternich and the crisis in Vienna meant that the March Laws received Imperial approval from Ferdinand without dispute. The Emperor's authority over Hungary was terminated and power passed to an independent Magyar government headed by Count Louis Batthyany. The triumphant Kossuth became Minister of Finance.

### Vienna

In Vienna during the second week of March, it rained petitions. Middle-class liberals and radical students collected support for a broad package of progressive reforms: Press freedom, jury trials, emancipation of the peasants, civil rights and representative constitutional government. Then on 13 March the Lower Austrian Diet met in the capital to discuss the crisis

**The 'March Laws'**

● A national government, independent of Vienna was to be established.

● The Pressburg Diet was to be replaced by a parliament at Budapest, elected on a limited property franchise.

● The nobility were to lose their tax exemptions.

● The *robot* (a feudal survival obliging the peasants to provide labour services on the landowners' estates) was to be abolished.

● Freedom of the Press was to be granted.

● Transylvania and Croatia (non-Magyar kingdoms) were to be incorporated into the new Hungarian state.

● Knowledge of the Magyar language was to be required for candidates wishing to stand for election to the new parliament.

and to call for the dismissal of Metternich. Whilst the Diet was in session an expectant crowd began to assemble. Speeches were made, and leaflets bearing the text of Kossuth's radical address to the Hungarian Diet on 3 March were passed among the excited crowd. When Metternich was sighted at a window in the Chancellery the crowd turned their anger on the man who had come to symbolize the stifling conservatism of the Imperial government. Increasingly abusive and agitated, sections of the crown broke into the hall where the Diet was in session. Troops were now ordered to disperse the demonstrators using fixed bayonets and live rounds. The mood of anger spread as barricades were set up and thousands of people took to the streets adding their voices to the clamour for reform and the removal of Metternich. That same evening Metternich offered his resignation. Emperor Ferdinand accepted and instructed his ministers to 'Tell the people that I consent to everything.' The following morning Metternich left Vienna to seek refuge in England.

Although a major coup for the reformers, the departure of Metternich did not satisfy all their demands. There were further demonstrations on 15 March and Ferdinand was forced to agree to introduce a constitution. Meanwhile effective control of the city passed into the hands of students who formed the radical core of the Viennese revolutionaries. On 25 April a constitution was published and immediately rejected by the radicals. Further disturbances within the city caused the government to withdraw its constitution. It was proposed to hold elections (based on universal suffrage) to a Constituent Assembly which would draft a new constitution. On 17 May, two days after Ferdinand had agreed to these proposals, the Emperor and his royal entourage fled from Vienna to Innsbruck.

## Bohemia

The events in Hungary encouraged similar nationalist demands amongst the Czechs in Bohemia. On 11 March at a café in Prague, Czech intellectuals drew up a petition to present to the Emperor. A delegation headed by a university professor, Francis Palacky, was sent to Vienna to present the Czech demands. They requested a package of liberal reforms and, more significantly perhaps, the unity and independence of the 'lands of St Wenceslaus': Bohemia, Moravia and Silesia. In April, Vienna agreed to the liberal demands and promised to establish a parliament in Prague. The question of uniting Bohemia, Moravia and Silesia was placed on the agenda of the next Imperial parliament.

## Northern Italy

In Lombardy and Venetia, the expulsion of the Austrians was seen as an essential pre-condition to the development of liberal institutions and the improvement of economic conditions. The fall of Metternich provoked a violent response in Milan. On 18 March, 10,000 protestors presented a petition calling for freedom of the Press and elections to a parliament. Trouble quickly flared. Street battles between Austrian troops and the people of Milan raged for five days before the Austrian commander, Radetzky, was forced to withdraw from the city. In his diary for 22 March he wrote:

AUSTRIAN TROOPS BEING DRIVEN OUT OF MILAN BY ITALIAN REVOLUTIONARIES (MARCH 1848)

'It is the most frightful decision of my life, but I can no longer hold Milan. The whole country is in revolt...'

In Venice a similar fate befell the Austrian garrison under General Zichy. Here, a rising led by Daniel Manin led to the creation of an independent Venetian republic. Before the end of March, Piedmont had joined the anti-Austrian movement and, along with Lombardy and Venetia, declared war on the Habsburgs.

RADETZKY, AUSTRIAN MILITARY COMMANDER

CITIZENS OF VENICE TAKE UP ARMS AGAINST AUSTRIAN RULE (1848)

## 4.1 How did the Habsburgs survive 1848?

In the face of such a determined challenge the Habsburgs were rapidly forced to make concessions to the opposition. However, the Imperial authorities quickly regained the initiative and by 1849 the Habsburgs were back in control. How were they able to defeat the revolutionaries?

## Divisions among the revolutionaries

The activists who won the initial victories of the revolutions soon found themselves torn by internal disagreements. These appeared at two levels:

### 1 National rivalries

It soon became apparent that the gains made by some national groups threatened the position of others. This was especially true between Magyars and Croats and between Germans and Czechs. Soon after the Magyars had won independence the Croats and Romanians (in Transylvania) raised objections to the proposal to absorb them into the new Hungarian state. Jellacic, the Governor of Croatia, remained dedicated to the dynastic link with the Habsburgs and to the political unity of the Austrian Empire. He accordingly affirmed his loyalty to the Emperor and with the aim of returning the Magyars to the fold, invaded Hungary in September 1848.

Czech ambitions were also sabotaged by the issue of national claims. A revolution in the German states had produced the Frankfurt Parliament which met in May 1848. The Frankfurt delegates called for the union of all Germans in a Greater Germany. This was to include Bohemia, Moravia and Silesia. Since the Czechs also laid claim to these territories there was a clear tension between the Germans and the Czechs. Palacky refused an invitation to attend the deliberations in Frankfurt with the declaration `I am a Bohemian of Slav race.' In order to resist German national ambitions the Czechs sought the security of the Habsburg Empire. In his celebrated admission of the necessity of Habsburg authority Palacky announced: `If the Austrian Empire did not exist it would be necessary for us to create it.' In response to German nationalism Palacky developed the programme of Austro-Slavism. This aimed at transforming the Empire into a federation of independent subject peoples united under Habsburg protection. It was a vain hope and advertised to the Imperial authorities that the opposition they faced was superficial. In the final analysis the Czech leadership wanted to retain the dynastic link with the Habsburgs. A Slav congress aimed at promoting Austro-Slavism was convened in Prague in June. The congress served merely to reveal the divisions within Slav nationalism. Unable to agree on a common purpose, the congress broke up.

### 2 Liberals v radicals

The Imperial authorities had rapidly agreed to the removal of Metternich and the granting of liberal concessions. Those who had forced these changes now found themselves divided. The middle-class liberals were quick to affirm their attachment to monarchy, albeit in a constitutional form, and wanted only a limited extension of the franchise. Social change was seen as undesirable. On the other hand, radical democrats, urged on by workers' demands for social improvements, were keen to move towards a republic. These divisions became increasingly apparent within the Austrian Constituent Assembly where the majority of the 383 members were moderate and deeply suspicious of democracy. Worker protests in June and August in Vienna were violently suppressed by the middle-class National Guards. The differences between the liberals and the radicals came to a head on 6 October when the Minister for War, Latour, was lynched by a mob. The Constituent Assembly left the capital and moved to Kresmier, leaving the radicals behind to face Windischgratz and his troops.

A similar situation existed in Lombardy and Venetia, where the middle-class revolutionaries failed to address the common people. The revolutionary governments in cities such as Milan and Venice were dominated by property owners who refused to concede much needed agrarian reforms to the peasants. The potential of mass support withered away and the cities were left isolated: easy pickings for Radetsky and his troops.

THE EMPEROR OF AUSTRIA ABANDONS VIENNA AND MAKES FOR INNSBRUCK (MAY 1848)

In May the Emperor and the Imperial party had been allowed to leave Vienna and to establish themselves at Innsbruck. Here they were in no immediate danger as they had been in the capital. They were able from a safe distance to begin planning the counter-revolution.

## 4.1 How did the Habsburgs survive 1848? *continued*

### The Role of the Military

CZECH REVOLUTIONARIES
ERECT BARRICADES IN
PRAGUE (JUNE 1848)

On 12 June crowds began street protests in Prague. There were clashes with troops and barricades were erected as the city broke out into revolution. As few as 1200 persons played an active part in the violence; the population of Prague was around 100,000. In spite of the small scale of the rising, General Windischgratz authorized an indiscriminate artillery bombardment of the city. Within five days Windischgratz had subdued the rising and placed the city under martial law.

Charles Albert's military campaign against the Austrians was a disaster. On 23 July Radetzky won a decisive victory at Custozza and an armistice was arranged on 9 August. The Italian war against Austria was restarted by Charles Albert in March 1849. Within one week Austrian supremacy on the battlefield had been established with a conclusive victory at Novara. The Venetian republic surrendered on 24 August.

In September 1848 it was decided to send part of the Vienna garrison to assist Jellacic in the subjection of Hungary. This prompted demonstrations by the radicals in Vienna and violence erupted once more in the capital. On 6 October a mob seized Count Baillet-Latour, the Minister for War, and clubbed him to death. His mutilated body was hung from a lamp-post, a gruesome symbol of radical defiance to government authority. By the end of the month, 100,000 troops under the command of Windischgratz had surrounded the city. As with Prague four months earlier, Vienna was subjected to a prolonged bombardment. Troops advanced as the resistance of the radicals evaporated. Between three and five thousand people were killed in the 'October Days' rising and by 1 November the revolt had been crushed.

The restoration of Imperial authority owed much to the loyalty and discipline of the army. The officer class tended to be of noble origin and was generally committed to the values of the old order now being challenged by the revolutionaries. The High Command, under the direction of Radetsky, Windischgratz and Jellacic, was solid and experienced. Regular troops were kept separate from the civilian population and cut off from political debate. Faced with hostile crowds they rarely disobeyed orders.

HUNGARIANS PROCLAIM THEIR
INDEPENDENCE FROM VIENNA (1849)

Hungary proved to be the most difficult region to subdue. Budapest had been captured by the armies of Windischgratz and Jellacic in January 1849. By April, however, the invading troops had been driven out by the Magyar forces. Windischgratz was dismissed and replaced in May by the ruthless General Haynau. Of potential significance was an offer of help from Tsar Nicholas I of Russia. Nicholas acted in the broad interests of monarchical solidarity and also through a determination to sabotage the emergence of an independent and troublesome state so close to his own turbulent Polish lands. In the event, Russian intervention was not decisive and the principal engagements took place between Hungarian units and Austrian troops under Haynau. In these, the ill-equipped and poorly-trained Hungarians were systematically defeated. The Magyars surrendered at Vilagos on 13 August 1849.

In September 1848 the Constituent Assembly elected following the revolution in Vienna made a very significant decision. Delegates voted to abolish serfdom throughout the Habsburg Empire. This was one of the few lasting achievements of the revolution and ironically one of the reasons why it failed. By abolishing serfdom the revolutionaries removed one of the principal grievances of the peasantry and left them with little cause to oppose the Habsburgs. The revolutionaries effectively denied themselves the chance of developing mass support.

# REVIEW

**The revolutionaries of 1848 were responsible for their own failure.**

Does this assessment apply to the two case studies examined in this chapter? It is worth bearing in mind that such an emphatic historical judgement is unlikely to be completely satisfactory. We should not forget that historians thrive best where there is controversy. On this understanding it is advisable to approach such a question by systematically locating evidence which could be used to support the statement; and, using the same technique, by identifying arguments which could be directed against it. In this way you will be able to consider both sides of the argument. You can then decide clearly the merits of the case and in your written response identify where your own opinions lie.

Closely examine the details in *Focus* section 4.1 and the case study dealing with France. Now complete your copy of the chart opposite. Be prepared to include more than one item in each space.

# EXAMINING THE EVIDENCE
## Garibaldi: the making of a hero

Giuseppe Garibaldi was one of the great heroic figures of the Nineteenth Century. As a dedicated Italian patriot and follower of Mazzini he was forced to flee from Italy in 1834. He established himself in South America and won fame as a maverick military commander supporting Uruguay in its fight for independence from Argentina. In 1848 he returned to Italy to offer his services to the revolutionaries and in 1849 directed the defence of the Roman Republic against attack from the French. Garibaldi's defence of Rome, although ultimately a failure, helped to establish him as an Italian hero.

### Source A

I had no idea...of enlisting [in Garibaldi's brigade of volunteers preparing to defend the Roman Republic against French attack]. I was a young artist; I only went out of curiosity – but oh! I shall never forget that day when I saw him [Garibaldi] on his beautiful white horse in the market-place, with his noble aspect, his calm, kind face, his high, smooth forehead, his light hair and beard – everyone said the same. He reminded us of nothing so much as of our Saviour's head in the galleries. I could not resist him. I left my studio. I went after him; thousands did likewise. He only had to show himself. We all worshipped him; we could not help it.

Unknown artist describes the impact of his first view of Garibaldi in Rome (April 1849).
This story was related in the years after the collapse of the Roman Republic.
Quoted in GM Trevelyan, *Garibaldi's Defence of the Roman Republic* (1928)

Sources B and C comment on the behaviour of Garibaldi and his followers during their operations in South America.

Items 1–6 suggest that the revolutionaries of 1848 were indeed responsible for their own failure. Items 7–10 suggest that there were other factors which helped to bring about the failure of the revolutions.

Try to find examples from the two case studies in this chapter which can be used to support these 10 items.

| | France | Habsburg Empire |
|---|---|---|
| **1** Once in control, the revolutionaries were unable to agree amongst themselves. | | |
| **2** The revolutionaries raised expectations which they were unable or unwilling to satisfy. | | |
| **3** The revolutionaries introduced measures which directly undermined the security of their position. | | |
| **4** The political conduct of some revolutionaries isolated important social groups. | | |
| **5** The revolutionaries were guilty of miscalculations which acted directly against their interests. | | |
| **6** Some revolutionaries acted against their former partners. | | |
| **7** Continuing financial difficulties. | | |
| **8** Nature and role of the rural peasantry in the failure of the revolutions. | | |
| **9** Role of the armed forces in the failure of the revolutions. | | |
| **10** Essentially spontaneous nature of the revolutions. | | |

## Source B

As is well known and notorious, this bandit [Garibaldi], who has been proscribed in Italy on account of his crimes, sacked the shops and houses at the Cerro [a fortress], committing barbarous atrocities on the bloody days of 12, 13 and 14 June – deeds of prowess worthy of a well known pirate and murderer.

From an article in the *Gaceta Mercantil,* an Argentinian newspaper (5 July 1843).
Quoted in Jasper Ridley, *Garibaldi* (1974)

## Source C

The beautiful church of Colonia, so clean with its recently whitewashed walls, as simple in its style as a village chapel, did not escape the outrages. The victorious Condottieri [Garibaldi's men] established themselves there; they slept upon the marble floor of the choir, hanging up their caps and cartridge boxes on the blessed chandeliers; the vaults re-echoed the sound of muskets and swords which rolled on the floor in the midst of sacrilegious and profane shouts; the altar served as a table of orgies.

Extract from Portuguese newspaper, the *Restauracion* (18 September 1846).
Quoted in Jasper Ridley, *Garibaldi* (1974)

In 1848 Garibaldi returned to Italy with 169 volunteers. He offered his services to Charles Albert of Piedmont in the struggle for independence from Austria. In Source D below, Charles Albert confesses his reservations about accepting such an offer of help.

## Source D

I hasten to warn you that I have today received in audience the famous General Garibaldi, who has come from America and arrived at Genoa, where he left sixty of his disciples, whom he offered to me along with himself. The antecedents of these gentlemen, and particularly of the self-styled general, and his famous republican proclamation, make it absolutely impossible for us to accept them in the army, and particularly to make Garibaldi a general. If there were a naval war he might be employed as a leader of privateers, but to employ him otherwise would be to dishonour the army. As I think he will be going to Turin, where he will not lack supporters, be ready for his attack. The best would be if they went off to any other place; and to encourage him and his brave fellows they might perhaps be given a subsidy on condition that they go away.

Charles Albert, King of Piedmont, writing to the War Office (5 July 1848).
Quoted in Jasper Ridley, *Garibaldi* (1974)

## Source E

Garibaldi in the meanwhile, if the encampment was far from the scene of danger, lay stretched out under his tent. If, on the contrary, the enemy were at hand, he remained constantly on horseback, giving orders and visiting the outposts; often, disguised as a peasant, he risked his own safety in daring reconnaissances, but most frequently, seated on some commanding elevation, he passed whole hours examining the environs with the aid of a telescope...Garibaldi appeared more like the chief of a tribe of Indians than a General; but at the approach of danger, and in the heat of combat, his presence of mind and courage were admirable...

Emilio Dandolo, a volunteer from Lombardy, quoted in GM Trevelyan,
*Garibaldi's Defence of the Roman Republic* (1928)

## Source F

…no pillaging took place, and in that deserted village not a single door was forced. We sat down on the ground in the square; and, when the terrified inhabitants observed from the surrounding heights this admirable spirit of order and self-restraint, they hurried down to welcome us, threw open their houses and shops, and in a few minutes the whole village had regained its accustomed activity. They then related to us how many superstitious fables the Neapolitans had spread among them; according to which we were so many ogres let loose by the devil, to devour children and burn down houses; and the fantastic costumes of Garibaldi and his followers had contributed not a little to increase the ignorant fears of the natives.

Emilio Dandolo describing an incident in May 1849 when Garibaldi's men crossed into Neapolitan territory and arrived at the frontier town of Rocca d'Arce. Quoted in GM Trevelyan, *Garibaldi's Defence of the Roman Republic* (1928)

## T ALKING POINT

### The appeal of Garibaldi

Around 5000 volunteers went with Garibaldi into exile following his speech of 2 July 1849 (Source G). Suggest reasons why, in spite of the hardships promised by Garibaldi, so many were prepared to follow him.

## Source G

Soldiers! You who have shared with me the labour and the dangers of fighting for our fatherland, you who have won a rich share of glory and honour, all you can now expect if you now come with me into exile is heat and thirst by day, cold and hunger by night. No other wages await you save hard work and danger. You will have to live in the open, without rest, without food, and there will be long night watches, forced marches, and fighting at every step.

Let him who loves his country follow me.

Garibaldi's speech to his followers in St Peter's Square, Rome (2 July 1849) prior to his march into exile following the collapse of the Roman Republic. Quoted in Denis Mack Smith, *The Making of Italy 1796–1866* (1968)

---

**1** Compare the impressions given of Garibaldi and his followers in Sources A and F with those in Sources B and C.

**2** Which of the Sources (A, B, C and F) do you think gives the more reliable description of Garibaldi and his followers? Explain your answer carefully.

**3** How do Sources B and C help to account for the attitudes of Charles Albert in Source D?

**4** How do you think Sources A, E and G helped to foster the image of Garibaldi as a great Italian hero?

---

# 5 France 1814–48

## Preview
### Monarchy and revolution

**1814** THE BOURBON MONARCHY IS RESTORED TO FRANCE UNDER LOUIS XVIII

**1830** THE HOTEL DE VILLE IN PARIS IS ATTACKED AS THE BOURBONS ARE OVERTHROWN BY REVOLUTIONARIES

**1830** LOUIS PHILIPPE IS ACCLAIMED AS THE NEW KING OF FRANCE: THE JULY MONARCHY BEGINS

**1848** THE COLLAPSE OF THE JULY MONARCHY: REBELS IN THE THRONE ROOM OF THE TUILERIES IN PARIS

# The legacy of the French Revolution

The central feature of the French Revolution was the attack against privilege. From this struggle emerged groups which could be described as 'winners' and others whose experiences made them the 'losers'. The values and ambitions of these broad groups produced a lingering instability in French politics in the years after 1815, and help to account for the failure of the Restoration monarchy.

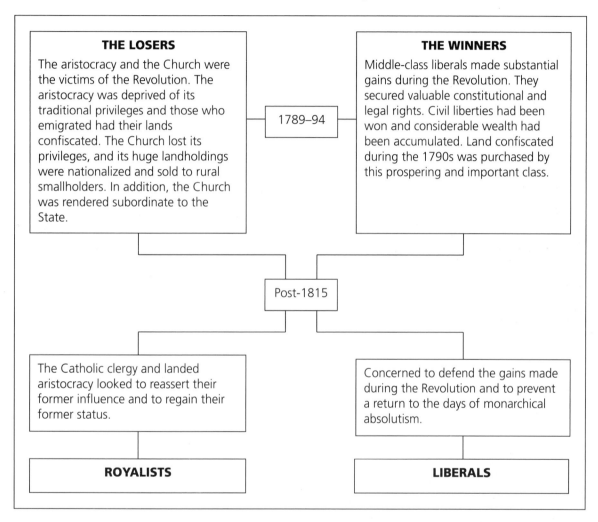

**THE LOSERS**

The aristocracy and the Church were the victims of the Revolution. The aristocracy was deprived of its traditional privileges and those who emigrated had their lands confiscated. The Church lost its privileges, and its huge landholdings were nationalized and sold to rural smallholders. In addition, the Church was rendered subordinate to the State.

**THE WINNERS**

Middle-class liberals made substantial gains during the Revolution. They secured valuable constitutional and legal rights. Civil liberties had been won and considerable wealth had been accumulated. Land confiscated during the 1790s was purchased by this prospering and important class.

1789–94

Post-1815

The Catholic clergy and landed aristocracy looked to reassert their former influence and to regain their former status.

Concerned to defend the gains made during the Revolution and to prevent a return to the days of monarchical absolutism.

**ROYALISTS**

**LIBERALS**

The Allied decision to restore royal government to France in 1814 provoked considerable concern amongst the middle class, the principal beneficiary of the French Revolution. No one in France had forgotten the execution of Louis XVI in 1793, and the death of his son in prison two years later served to emphasize the apparent rejection of hereditary kingship. Middle-class fears that the restoration of Bourbon rule to France would signal a return to eighteenth-century absolutism were very real. The gains made during the Revolutionary and Napoleonic periods appeared to be under threat.

The man chosen to resurrect the fortunes of the Bourbon dynasty was Louis XVIII, brother of Louis XVI. Viewed from the perspective of the middle class, the new king displayed some worrying characteristics:

- He adopted the traditional title, 'King of France and Navarre', and thus emphasized his attachment to the customs of his ancestors;
- He returned as Louis XVIII and insisted on dating his reign from 1795, the year in which Louis XVI's son and heir died in prison;
- He retained an unqualified belief in the divine right of kings;
- Louis' constitutional document, the Charter, was issued as a 'concession' to the French people. He did not regard it as something to which they had a natural right.

In spite of these pretensions, Louis XVIII recognized the need to be conciliatory. His task was to balance the interests of the royalists and the liberals in a compromise which would be generally acceptable. Accordingly he kept his opinions about divine right hidden from public view, and he accepted the need to rule as a moderate constitutional monarch. The Charter (see diagram opposite) represented a major departure from traditional Bourbon rule and appeared to suggest that a return to eighteenth-century absolutism would not occur.

LOUIS XVI, THE KING OF FRANCE, EXECUTED IN 1793 DURING THE FRENCH REVOLUTION

## The 'White Terror'

The difficult task of re-establishing the Bourbon monarchy seemed to have been made easier by three factors:

- The first Peace of Paris (May 1814) which settled French affairs following the defeat of Napoleon, was moderate and non-punitive (see page 6);
- Widespread acceptance of the new regime and the absence of any popular opposition to Louis XVIII;
- The prudent retention of the principal legal and administrative developments made during the Revolutionary and Napoleonic periods, and now embodied in the Charter.

However, the chronic insecurity of Louis XVIII's position soon became apparent. In late April 1815, Napoleon escaped from exile and returned to France. Announcing himself as a liberal constitutionalist, he attracted enthusiastic support not just from Bonapartists but also from liberals and republicans who had never really been comfortable with the Bourbon Restoration. Between 1 March and 15 July Napoleon directed the 'Hundred Days' revival before being overwhelmed by the Allies at Waterloo.

AN OFFICIAL PORTRAIT OF LOUIS XVIII. COMPARE THIS PAINTING WITH THAT OF LOUIS XVI. HOW MIGHT THIS HAVE ADDED TO FEARS ABOUT THE NATURE OF THE RESTORED MONARCHY?

An effective royalist response to the Hundred Days failed to materialize. Troops sent to halt Napoleon's advance defected to the command of their former emperor and Louis XVIII was forced to seek refuge in Belgium. The Hundred Days dealt a serious blow to the prestige and credibility of the Bourbon monarchy. The second restoration, which followed Waterloo, was greeted with derision. The King, it was claimed, had returned in the 'baggage waggon' of France's enemies. By September 1815 some 1,250,000 Allied troops were in occupation of France. In the countryside they raped and looted and compelled the local peasant populations to provide food, fuel and shelter. Resentment against these hardships was directed squarely at the Bourbon king who came to be associated with defeat and humiliation.

The Hundred Days did more than tarnish the reputation of Louis XVIII. They set in motion a royalist backlash directed against all those who had rallied to Napoleon. This was witnessed in electoral terms by the composition of the Chamber of Deputies following the election of August 1815. By lowering the qualification age for candidates from 40 to 25, Louis XVIII ensured the return of a Chamber in which young and extreme royalists – the Ultras – formed a huge majority. Away from the Chamber, royalist reprisals against the supporters of Napoleon had

## — THE CHARTER —

### The King

- Head of the Executive
- Solely responsible for proposing laws
- Chose ministers to form the government
- Could dissolve the Chamber of Deputies
- Commanded the armed forces
- Appointed judges
- Could declare war
- Could alter the electorate
- Could rule by ordinances in emergencies
- Could create peers

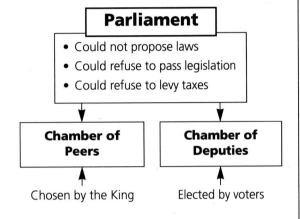

### Parliament

- Could not propose laws
- Could refuse to pass legislation
- Could refuse to levy taxes

**Chamber of Peers**

Chosen by the King

**Chamber of Deputies**

Elected by voters

### The electorate

**Candidates**

- Over 40 years of age
- Pay 1000 francs per year in direct taxes
- 12,000 citizens qualified

**Voters**

- Over 30 years of age
- Pay 300 francs per year in direct taxes
- 90,000 citizens qualified

### General principles

- Equality before the law
- Freedom of the Press
- Civil liberties
- Religious toleration
- Taxation according to wealth not status
- Equality of opportunity in State employment
- Guaranteed the land settlement made during the Revolution

1  Why do you suppose the middle class found the Charter generally acceptable?

2  To what extent was royal power restrained by the Charter? How might an unscrupulous king subvert the Charter?

3  The population of France at this time was around 25 million people. Comment on the size and nature of the electorate in view of this detail.

already commenced. The violence of this reaction, which persisted into 1816, has been termed the 'White Terror'. Unable to restrain their own supporters, the Bourbons appeared incompetent or else became identified with the excesses of royalist violence committed in their name.

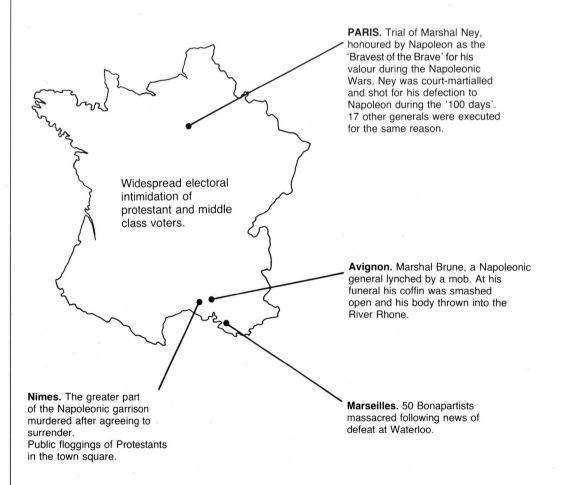

## The 'White Terror'

250     'Terror'-linked deaths
50,000  public officials purged
3,476   political convictions
3,382   arrests without trial
29      peers banished from the Chamber

**PARIS.** Trial of Marshal Ney, honoured by Napoleon as the 'Bravest of the Brave' for his valour during the Napoleonic Wars. Ney was court-martialled and shot for his defection to Napoleon during the '100 days'. 17 other generals were executed for the same reason.

Widespread electoral intimidation of protestant and middle class voters.

**Avignon.** Marshal Brune, a Napoleonic general lynched by a mob. At his funeral his coffin was smashed open and his body thrown into the River Rhone.

**Nimes.** The greater part of the Napoleonic garrison murdered after agreeing to surrender.
Public floggings of Protestants in the town square.

**Marseilles.** 50 Bonapartists massacred following news of defeat at Waterloo.

# The liberal revival (1816–20)

The activities of the Ultras alarmed both the King and his chief minister, the Duc de Richelieu. They feared that France might descend into civil war, and therefore in September 1816, Louis XVIII used the power conferred on him by the Charter to dissolve the Chamber by royal decree. In addition he restored the qualifying age for parliamentary candidates to 40. The election which followed reduced the Ultras to 90 deputies out of 238 and gave Richelieu a working majority. Between 1816 and 1820 the King was able – through Richelieu and, after 1818, Decazes – to steer a moderate course between the subversive intentions of the Ultras on the right and the extreme liberals on the left.

Indeed, during this period there were some impressive accomplishments, the most notable being the skilful handling of the nation's finances which enabled the government to pay off the war indemnity and secure the withdrawal of the army of occupation. Under Decazes, government restraints on the Press were relaxed and the army was reformed along more democratic lines. A change in the electoral law in 1817 which had increased the number of persons entitled to vote enabled the liberals to make steady electoral gains. With Decazes playing to the liberal gallery, the Ultras repeatedly warned that the values and authority of monarchical government were in danger of being overwhelmed. In the elections of 1819, the liberals made further gains. Then, in 1820, an event occurred which changed the whole tone of French politics and set in motion a conservative reaction which ended in the revolution of July 1830.

# The shift to the right

On 13 February 1820, the Duc de Berry, the nephew of Louis XVIII, was assassinated outside the Paris Opera House. Louvel, the Bonapartist fanatic who carried out the crime, acted alone. But the enraged Ultras quickly identified an accomplice: Decazes. His irresponsible liberal policies had, according to the extreme right, assisted this shocking act of terrorism just as surely as if he had provided the murder weapon. Indeed, the Ultra Press described the dagger which killed de Berry as a 'liberal idea'. The murder unleashed a storm of anti-liberal protest and forced the King to dismiss Decazes. The King's attempt to reconcile liberalism and royalism was henceforth doomed to failure. Richelieu was recalled and with him began a distinct shift to the right in French politics.

1820    • Richelieu's package of anti-liberal measures:
1. Detention of political suspects for up to three months without trial;
2. Reintroduction of Press censorship;
3. Electoral adjustments giving a double vote to the highest taxpayers (about 12,000 voters).

1821    • Secondary school education placed under the supervision of the bishops.

1822    • A Catholic bishop, Frayssinous, made Grand Master of the University of France – effectively the government minister for education.

| 1822 | • Richelieu forced to resign; replaced by the Compt de Villèle. |
|---|---|
| | • Villèle tightened the Press laws still further – it was now a criminal offence to write any article which carried the mere chance of provoking a public disturbance. |
| 1823 | • French troops sent across the Pyrenees to crush the Spanish liberals and to restore the Bourbon King Ferdinand VII to his throne. |
| • 1824 | • In the election to the Chamber of Deputies the number of liberal seats fell from 110 to just 19. (There were 430 seats in total.) |
| | • A decree scrapped interim elections and declared the current Chamber in session for the next seven years. |
| | • Death of Louis XVIII (16 September). |

## The accession of Charles X

The Comte d'Artois, brother of the late King, continued the Bourbon line under the title Charles X. Now aged 67, he was a devout Catholic and a known reactionary. He had been the leading figure in Ultra politics during the reign of Louis XVIII and was dedicated to the principle of monarchical authority. He regarded the Charter as a temporary concession whose interference in royal government could not be tolerated indefinitely.

THE RETURN OF CHARLES X TO PARIS FOLLOWING HIS CORONATION

One of the most curious and perhaps symbolic scenes played out in Restoration France was the five-hour epic of Charles X's coronation on 29 May 1825. The traditional medieval ceremony in Rheims Cathedral had not been used since 1775. Although Charles took an oath to defend the Charter, he also prostrated himself before an archbishop who had earlier used the occasion to condemn that same document. To Frenchmen who recalled the days before 1789 the relationship between Crown and Church was beginning to look uncomfortably familiar.

Under Charles X the monarchy quickly assumed a more definable shape than it had been possible to discern under Louis XVIII. This was not to be a regime of compromise and conciliation but one dedicated to repairing the damage done by the Revolution to the fortunes and power of the Church and landed aristocracy. In 1825 two measures gave notice of this intention:

- Sacrilege (the theft or vandalism of sacred objects used in Catholic services) was made punishable by life imprisonment, and in certain cases by death. Charles made it clear that the Church was untouchable and could expect the full protection of the State against those who opposed its role and influence in France.
- The confiscation and redistribution of property during the Revolution deprived the former landed aristocracy of its hereditary possessions. Charles saw this group – chiefly composed of returned *émigrés* – as victims, and wished to compensate them for their losses. One thousand million francs were allocated to this exercise though only about 630 million francs were actually paid out. In many ways the measure was a necessary one. Uncertainties surrounding the legal ownership of confiscated land had kept its value below true market levels. Compensation removed the doubts about ownership and increased land prices were expected to reflect this. However, the fact that the *émigrés* had been compensated with public money enraged many Frenchmen. The money was raised by lowering the interest rate on government bonds, infuriating the middle-class businessmen who tended to hold such securities.

## The rise of the opposition

The reactionary tone of the monarchy and its attempts to undo the work of the Revolution were highly provocative to the liberals. They were particularly stimulated by an anti-clerical impulse which was developing in response to increasing Church involvement in State affairs. Liberals feared the existence of a Jesuit-inspired conspiracy aimed at recapturing the wealth, power and privileges of the pre-Revolution Church. Liberal newspapers carried articles condemning the clerical revival and attacked as subversive religious societies such as the Congregation which printed and distributed religious propaganda throughout France. Church buildings were violated and there were anti-clerical demonstrations in Paris and other large cities. Anti-clerical protest was not the sole preserve of the liberals. Many royalists too were concerned by the ambitions of the clerics, and were determined to ensure that the Church remained subordinate to the Crown.

In the years 1825–30, liberal opposition to the regime of Charles X was both highly organized and far-reaching. In Paris the principal vehicles for this opposition were the liberal newspapers, *Le Constitutionnel* and *Le Courrier francais*. Funerals for public figures who had in life been critical of the regime were used by the opposition as occasions upon which to stage popular demonstrations. In the Chamber of Peers, which was less reactionary than the lower house, a number of important government proposals came to grief, much to the delight of the Paris crowds. In addition, the King faced continuous criticism from among the ranks of the Crown's most ardent supporters, the Ultras. They were disappointed that the land issue had been settled through compensation payments and not a full-scale reallocation of property to the 'victims' of the Revolution. They regarded Villèle as too moderate and were irritated at the lack of any real progress towards the restoration of aristocratic and clerical privileges. Assailed from both left and right, and distrusted by the defenders of the constitutional principle in the centre, Charles was increasingly losing his grip on his inheritance. A measure of his ability to alienate potential supporters came in March 1827 as he reviewed the Paris National Guard. Amongst the 20,000 assembled Guardsmen a minority shouted anti-clerical and anti-government slogans. The following day the King disbanded the Guard; now, in the event of civil disturbances in the capital, he had no armed and trained militia upon which he could call to restore order and defend his position.

By 1827 the government of Villèle was faced with a serious crisis as he struggled to find adequate support in parliament. Lacking in political imagination, the King and his minister turned first to repression and then to the electorate in the belief that fresh elections would restore a broad royalist base of support in the Chamber of Deputies. The move was a grave miscalculation. In preparation for the elections, the liberals – increasingly experienced as the political opposition – overwhelmed the incoherent and complacent right. Two liberal organizations, the Society of the Friends of the Freedom of the Press, and the *Aide-toi, le ciel t'aidera* (literally, 'Help yourself, and heaven will help you') swung into action, spreading propaganda and ensuring that all those entitled to vote were included on local electoral lists. The result of the elections caused the resignation of Villèle; liberal candidates won 180 seats and, in conjunction with conservative opponents of Villèle, secured a majority of 60. The liberal response to the policies of Charles X was unmistakable. Nor did the King's problems end here. In 1826 an economic recession struck France causing distress both in rural and urban districts (see margin).

## The July Revolution

Villèle was replaced with the moderate royalist, Martignac. He presided over a liberal interlude which lasted for less than 12 months. Charles X had no intention of developing a long-term relationship with the constitutionalists and used Martignac merely to buy himself time. When Martignac resigned in August 1829, the King launched his bid for absolute power. He called to office the notorious Ultra, Prince Jules de Polignac. A former *émigré* who had refused to swear the oath to the Charter, Polignac represented the perfect choice for a monarch who now sought to disengage himself from constitutional government and to halt

**Features of the economic recession (1826–32)**
- Crisis begun by a series of poor harvests.
- Food shortages led to high prices.
- Eastern France – 1826–30 wheat prices rose by 66 per cent.
- Riots against taxation and grain shortages.
- High unemployment, especially in manufacturing towns.
- Hunger aggravated problems such as poor housing, impure water and disease.
- July 1830 – more than 25 per cent of the population of Paris was receiving some form of charitable assistance.
- Credit crisis produced a large number of bankruptcies: this especially hit middle-class business interests, adding economic distress to political grievances.
- Government regarded itself as powerless to act in such circumstances, and failed to provide aid to assist those suffering from the recession.

the progress of liberalism: 'The French wanted a charter; they were given one...but in the end this charter cannot keep me from doing my will.'

For six months the new ministry did little on the domestic scene and was most active in foreign affairs. Then in March 1830, at the first session of parliament, the storm broke. By a majority of 221 to 181 the Chamber of Deputies voiced its insistence that the only legitimate government in France was that endorsed by a majority in parliament. This represented a defiant rejection of monarchical authority and a defence of the Charter with its principle of the sovereignty of parliament. Polignac dissolved the Chamber and called for fresh elections; the King's supporters hung on to 143 seats, the number of opposition deputies rose to 274. Ignoring the verdict of the electorate Charles X and Polignac set about organizing a royal *coup d'etat*. On 25 July, Four Ordinances – sometimes referred to as the Ordinances of St Cloud – were issued by the government. In the political atmosphere of 1830 they were quite astonishing:

- All publications of less than 25 pages to be officially authorized;
- The dissolution of the newly-elected Chamber of Deputies;
- A reduction in the electorate from 100,000 voters to 25,000;
- Fresh elections to be held in September.

Polignac, now regularly experiencing visions of the Virgin Mary who assured him of success, passed on these divine endorsements to the King who found time in the crisis to embark on a hunting expedition. This total disregard for the gravity of the situation was reflected in the lack of military preparation for the inevitable liberal backlash. The most

PARISIAN REBELS DEFEND BARRICADES AT THE RUE ST HONORÉ (1830)

experienced French troops – 40,000 of them – were in Algeria; only 12,000 troops were in the Paris area in July 1830. Urged on by liberal appeals to defend the Charter, rioters took to the streets of Paris on 27 July. They were joined by members of the disbanded National Guard, still in possession of their weapons. Troops sent to restore order lost control of the city during the 'Three Glorious Days' (27–29 July). Charles X, at last realizing the need for action, offered to withdraw the Four Ordinances and to dismiss Polignac. His concessions had no impact and he was forced to abdicate in favour of his grandson, the Duc de Bordeaux.

THE ARREST OF POLIGNAC

# EXAMINING THE EVIDENCE

Consider the judgements of the following historians on the reign of Charles X.

## Source A

Ultimately the combination of an unstable right-wing party, an articulate and well-developed urban liberal movement, and a chronically inept monarch brought the Bourbon dynasty down...success required a monarch with political acumen, which Charles X had not. He was as dangerous an ideologue as any of the extreme Ultras, but both he and the Prince de Polignac, his trusted adviser...lacked the capacity to see the political implications of their position. He charged the liberals head-on by trying, in effect, to dismantle the Charter by the ordinances of 24th July 1830. Yet he failed to back up his initiative by military force until it was too late and Paris was in arms.

*Christopher Harvie, Napoleon and Restoration Europe (1972)*

## Source B

Charles X....needlessly and provocatively alienated all social classes with his anachronistic coronation at Rheims, his extreme pro-Catholic policies, his...indemnity scheme for royalist emigres, and his crude attempts to stifle press and parliamentary criticism...The decision to form a reactionary ministry headed by Polignac was an act of political folly while the four ordinances virtually sealed his fate...Through sheer ineptitude and incompetence Charles X lost what a French historian has described as Europe's most glorious throne and most beautiful kingdom.

*William Fortescue, Revolution and Counter-Revolution in France (1988)*

## Source C

It is possible to imagine that had Charles X conducted his coup d'etat effectively he could have been successful, at least for the time being. Most of France was sufficiently lethargic in political matters to passively accept any action by the king which had a claim to legality and which did not directly affect their standard of living or way of life. It was only in Paris that there was a sufficient concentration of economic and political discontent to challenge the Four Ordinances with any hope of success. Had Charles arrested potential leaders of an uprising against him before the Ordinances were published, and brought large numbers of troops into Paris so that key positions, including newspaper offices, could be occupied on the morning of 25th July, the situation would probably have remained under control. As it was, few troops were in evidence in Paris (the pick of the army was in fact still in Algiers), opposition leaders were left at liberty, and the initiative was left to those who wished to make trouble.

*Keith Randell, France, Monarchy, Republic and Empire 1814–70 (1986)*

## Source D

Economic change was the essential factor which fuelled the political and social unrest which undermined the Restoration. The ultraroyalist attempt to create a stable regime on the basis of land, religion, hierarchy and deference proved futile because a period of peace allowed the acceleration of changes in market-relations, technology and organization of production which the laissez-faire legislation of the 1790s had encouraged. In the ultraroyalist stronghold of Gard the rapid growth of coal, silk, woollen textiles and wine-monoculture rendered abortive the efforts of the Catholic-royalist elites to turn back the clock. Economic development boosted the strength of the bourgeoisie, multiplied the numbers of cafés where politics were discussed, generated a demand for education among the petty bourgeoisie and popular classes.

Roger Magraw, *France 1815–1914: The Bourgeois Century* (1983)

### Source E

The Restoration had failed: this does not prove that it was from the beginning inexorably doomed to failure. On the contrary, the Revolution of 1830 seems at first impression rather the result of a series of accidents, and above all of the obstinacy of Charles X, who went from blunder to blunder as though driven by a blind fate, or as though the little sense there had ever been in that addled pate had entirely vanished with age. He was such a nonentity as to be hardly worth a revolution, and indeed looking behind the passing events of 1830, one can see that it was not really directed against him; it was against the anachronistic reappearance of a *noblesse* [noble class] which believed that the eighteenth century had never ended and a clergy which, since the eighteenth century was, so far as the church was concerned, a rather unfortunate episode, looked back to the [17th] century...On the other hand, an important section of the educated classes in France, even if they thought that religion might be good for the masses, did not intend that priests should rule, or that their own sons be educated by them. They turned against a regime in which the influence of the Church seemed to be increasingly dominant.

Alfred Cobban, *A History of Modern France Volume 2: 1799–1871* (1961)

# REVIEW
### Why did the reign of Charles X last for only six years?

**1** Carefully read the views of the historians given above.

**2** Working in groups, take turns to contribute one item from these assessments which could help to explain why the Bourbon Restoration failed in 1830.

**3** Keep a record of all the points contributed.

**4** When the group has exhausted the material in these assessments, break into smaller groups and attempt to arrange your points under broad headings. These headings should provide a structure to help you explain the failure of the Restoration. An example is provided for you opposite.

### The personal failings of Charles X

| Illustration | Location |
|---|---|
| Lack of political acumen | Harvie |
| Politically naïve | Harvie, Fortescue |
| Insensitive coronation | Fortescue |
| Advancement of Polignac | Harvie, Fortescue |
| Failure to prepare for opposition | Harvie, Randell |
| Blind obstinacy | Cobban |

**5** You should now be in a position to add to these lists and possibly to extend them by re-reading the material on pages 86 to 94.

## The July Monarchy (1830–48)

As Charles X made his way to England, ironically on board a ship belonging to the Bonapartes, the people who had engineered his downfall were faced with the problem of establishing an alternative system of government. Three possible options presented themselves:

- A regency until the Duc de Bordeaux, the nine-year-old grandson of the deposed king, came of age;
- A republic to replace the monarchy under the presidency of Lafayette, the hero of 1789;
- A continuation of the monarchy under Louis Philippe, the Duc d'Orleans.

The first option represented the wishes of Charles X and by this association was generally regarded as unacceptable. The creation of a republic was the popular choice amongst the common people of Paris but was regarded as too extreme by the moderate middle class which had orchestrated the resistance to the ex-king. It soon became clear that the most influential elements within the revolutionary movement would support the candidacy of Louis Philippe for the French throne. Through an efficient publicity campaign the Orleanist case was pressed. Determined to prevent the appearance of a republic, the wealthy and the influential hurriedly invited Louis Philippe to become their king.

### Why Louis Philippe?

The new king proved to be acceptable to a broad cross-section of French people. He had a true hereditary claim to the throne, being descended from the brother of Louis XIV. Monarchists accordingly found him to be a satisfactory alternative to the Bourbon line. Louis Philippe also had the advantage of being associated with the revolution. He had fought with the revolutionary armies and been a constant critic of Charles X. There were other, cosmetic attractions, which made Louis Philippe acceptable. (See left.)

### Practical changes

Of course, the architects of the July Revolution did not simply want a change of face at the royal palace. They expected measures which would reverse the Ultraroyalist policies of Charles X and secure their own social and political status. Accordingly, the new king introduced a series of changes designed to remove the worst excesses of Bourbon rule.

LOUIS PHILIPPE

HE ADOPTED THE REVOLUTIONARY TRICOLOUR AS THE FLAG OF FRANCE.

HE RETAINED HIS NAME, LOUIS PHILIPPE, RATHER THAN BECOMING LOUIS XIX OR PHILIPPE VII.

HE WAS CROWNED AS 'KING OF THE FRENCH BY THE GRACE OF GOD AND THE WILL OF THE NATION.'

HIS SOCIAL HABITS AND APPEARANCE ASSOCIATED HIM WITH THE MIDDLE CLASS.

Potentially, the most important changes were those affecting the political system. A revised constitution, the so-called Charter of 1830, embodied these alterations. The King lost his right to suspend laws and to rule by decree, and the Assembly was accorded the right to propose legislation. The electoral system was also reviewed. To qualify for a vote in elections to the Assembly, Frenchmen now had to pay 200 francs per year in direct taxation as opposed to 300 francs under the Bourbons. As a result the electorate increased from 94,000 to almost 170,000.

Such changes, however, were largely superficial. Still less than 3 per cent of adult Frenchmen were entitled to participate in national elections. Moreover, since direct taxation was overwhelmingly paid on income from the ownership of land, it was a property-owning minority which enjoyed political influence in France. Significantly, the revisions to the constitution failed to embrace the urban middle class whose members derived their livelihoods from the professions or from commerce. For the moment the situation was tolerated.

In 1848, a revolution removed Louis Philippe from office. His forced departure was caused by his failure to tackle a persistent economic, social and political crisis. It has been suggested that Louis Philippe lost his throne not so much because of what he did, but because of what he failed to do. The King seemed unwilling to make alterations to the constitutional settlement which had emerged in 1830. His sympathies lay with the so-called 'Party of Resistance', while his opponents belonged to the 'Party of Movement'. (See diagram below.) The result was a prolonged period of immobility, immensely frustrating to those who wished for change and ultimately a key factor in the fall of Louis Philippe. The King's inaction in foreign affairs and his refusal to address social problems deprived him of popular support. At the same time he alienated the educated and socially-powerful middle class by continuing to deny it an active role in French politics and by behaving uncomfortably like the Bourbon he had replaced.

## Political opposition

Throughout his reign Louis Philippe was dogged by almost constant political opposition. This was the price he paid for acquiring the throne at the invitation of a narrow social élite. He was not King by virtue of hereditary right, nor did he rule by popular mandate. His promotion to royal

> **Louis Philippe's reforms**
>
> **1** Abolished censorship.
>
> **2** Guaranteed freedom of worship.
>
> **3** Reduced clerical influence in education.
>
> **4** Deprived the Roman Catholic Church of its special position in France; no longer would it be the 'religion of the State', merely that 'practised by the majority'.

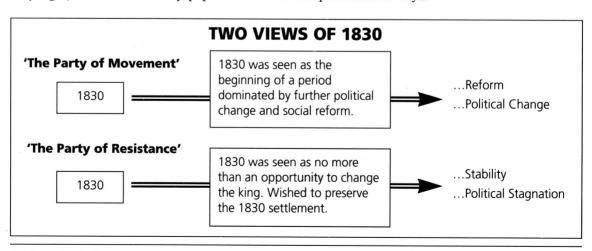

**TWO VIEWS OF 1830**

**'The Party of Movement'**

| 1830 |

1830 was seen as the beginning of a period dominated by further political change and social reform.

…Reform
…Political Change

**'The Party of Resistance'**

| 1830 |

1830 was seen as no more than an opportunity to change the king. Wished to preserve the 1830 settlement.

…Stability
…Political Stagnation

power was a carefully-engineered compromise designed to restrain the republicans and to protect property-owners from the ambitions of the Bourbons. Few Frenchmen regarded Louis Philippe as their natural leader but most had accepted him resignedly. However, while the majority did not openly oppose Louis Philippe, there were three distinct groups within France containing activists dedicated to his removal. (See diagram below.)

Political frustration was certainly one of the factors which brought down the July Monarchy in 1848. In the climate of crisis which surrounded his accession, it was expedient for the King to declare his loyalty to the constitutional principle. However, Louis Philippe had no intention of allowing parliament to dominate French affairs. He pursued an increasingly active role in government until from 1840 to 1848, with his chief minister Guizot, he was able to direct the business of the parliamentary Chamber.

As Louis Philippe tightened his control over France, there was growing disquiet amongst those middle-class citizens who were excluded from the electorate. Their case was taken up by some members of the Chamber of

---

### Challenges to Louis Philippe

### Legitimists

Defenders of hereditary monarchy and committed to restoring a Bourbon to the French throne. Widely backed by the clergy and the nobility but unable to mount an effective challenge to Louis Philippe. Their one attempt to remove the new King by force ended as an embarrassing fiasco. In 1832 the Duchesse de Berry – mother of the Bourbon heir, the Duc de Bordeaux – was arrested and imprisoned as she attempted to incite a royalist rising against Louis Philippe. In spite of this failure, the legitimist cause continued to attract clerics and aristocrats who could not accept constitutional monarchy.

### Bonapartists

Drew their inspiration from a developing phenomenon known as the 'Napoleonic Legend'. This stressed the great achievements of the former emperor and looked to reawaken the 'glorious' Napoleonic past in France by replacing Louis Philippe with a descendant of Napoleon. After 1832 their hopes became invested in Louis Napoleon Bonaparte. His ill-conceived and absurd *coups* of 1836 and 1840 betrayed his patent inability to grasp political reality. The active followers of Bonapartism comprised a small group of fanatics and their practical achievements were negligible. Yet the masses retained the capacity to be stirred by memories of Napoleon's glorious years and their ambitions for the reassertion of French supremacy in Europe remained strong.

### Republicans

The republicans did not constitute a political party; rather their ideals and objectives represented a political alternative to monarchy to which many were attracted. Republicanism appealed to large sections of the poorer classes, especially in the towns. It seemed to offer social justice and to address the problems of the labouring masses. Republicans were led by activists drawn principally from the educated middle class who looked to the republican ideal of the Revolution as the political example they wished to follow. Republicans presented the most serious threat to Louis Philippe and were responsible for a number of assassination attempts on the King.

JOSEPH HENRI FIRES TWO PISTOL SHOTS AT LOUIS PHILIPPE (AUGUST 1846). THIS WAS THE SEVENTH ASSASSINATION ATTEMPT ON THE KING.

Deputies worried by the King's encroachment on their authority. During the 1840s numerous electoral reform bills came before the Chamber, each proposing a moderate extension of the franchise to produce a broader middle-class electorate. However, the King remained unconvinced of such a need and Guizot echoed his resistance:

'I cannot find among us today, in the actual state of society, any real and serious motive, any motive worthy of a free and sensible country, to justify the proposed electoral reform.'

**Guizot speaking in 1842, quoted in A Wood, *Europe 1815–1945* (1964)**

Frustrated by their failure to make headway within the Assembly, the reformers took to holding extra-parliamentary meetings in banqueting-halls. Here they were able to debate the reform issue and publicize their cause. The first political banquet was held in Paris in the summer of 1847. It attracted 80 deputies and, significantly, more than 1000 other interested parties. Between August 1847 and February 1848 around 60 banquets were staged in towns across France. Their proceedings were fully reported in local newspapers and increasingly, as republicans began to attend, their demands became more radical. It was the prohibition of a banquet planned for 22 February 1848 in Paris which provoked mass demonstrations in the capital. By 24 February, Paris was in the throes of a full-scale revolt and the King was composing his abdication address. Through their intransigence, Louis Philippe and his ministers had succeeded in alienating a powerful and ambitious social group amongst the middle class. For this group, it became more and more unacceptable to be considered as part of the social élite, whilst remaining excluded from political involvement by a voting qualification which emphasized the possession of property. The King's stubborn refusal to consent to a moderate change in the electoral law deprived him of critical bourgeois support and drove the reform movement into the arms of the radicals.

A REFORM BANQUET IN PARIS (JULY 1847)

## Opposition propaganda

The propertied élite who sponsored Louis Philippe's candidacy in 1830 represented an influential but numerically small section of French society. Once installed on the throne, the King rapidly became aware of a determined, and largely republican, opposition which objected to his accession and viewed the events of 1830 as a royalist deception. The abolition of censorship unleashed a torrent of political propaganda directed at the King and his ministers. The principal medium for this furious assault on Louis Philippe was the caricature. Two publications, the weekly *La Caricature* and the daily *Le Charivari*, were merciless in their criticisms of him. The owner of these journals, Charles Philipon, employed a band of talented political satirists such as Grandville, Forest, Rambaud and, most notably perhaps, Honoré Daumier. Their collective efforts succeeded in giving the King a decidedly unfavourable public image. Writing in 1840, the English novelist William Makepeace Thackeray offered this observation on the effects of the caricaturists' cynical art:

The King of the French suffered so much, his Ministers were so mercilessly ridiculed, his family and his own remarkable figure drawn with such odious and grotesque resemblance, in fanciful attitudes, circumstances and disguises, so ludicrously mean, and often so appropriate, that the King was obliged to descend into the lists and battle his ridiculous enemy in form...

'...Everyone who was at Paris a few years since, must recollect the famous 'poire' [pear] which was chalked upon all the walls of the city, and which bore so ludicrous a resemblance to Louis Philippe.'

*Paris Sketchbook* (1840) quoted in The Open University study unit,
*Art and Politics in France* (1972)

The image of the 'pear', which came to be universally associated with Louis Philippe, emerged as a mischievous observation on the shape of the King's face. Such personal attacks did considerable damage to the credibility of the King. A quick sketch of a pear instantly transformed Louis Philippe into an object of ridicule and undermined public respect for his authority. The caricaturist was clearly dangerous and the King went to great lengths with arrests, prosecutions and fines to try to silence his inventive critics.

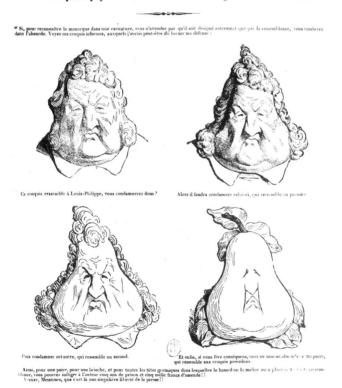

'LE CHARIVARI' DEMONSTRATED TO ITS READERS HOW LOUIS PHILIPPE'S FACE COULD BE TRANSFORMED INTO THE IMAGE OF A PEAR

The propagandists did not stop at malicious observations on the King's appearance. They utilized their talents to comment directly on the actions of the monarch.

Although the Charter of 1830 had supposedly put an end to censorship, it was not long before the King and his ministers were once again insisting upon Press restrictions. New Press laws were introduced in 1832, 1833, 1834 and 1835 making it difficult for opposition papers to operate without facing fines, confiscations and even prison terms. Some republican newspapers were forced to close down and the return to Press censorship was greeted with contempt. The image (below) appeared in 1832 and shows the Chief Prosecutor, Persil, being released from a coffin and embracing a huge pair of scissors.

**1** What is the significance of the scissors in this print?

**2** Suggest why the artists have chosen Persil to form the central figure of the print.

'THE RESURRECTION OF CENSORSHIP' BY GRANDVILLE AND FOREST

The print below appeared in December 1831. It represents an attack on the astonishing Civil List (for the King's personal expenditures) voted by the Chamber of Deputies. The sum approved totalled 18,533,500 francs. With thousands of people living in poverty, the Civil List provoked a huge outcry in the Press.

**1** There are three distinct groups of people in this picture. Try to identify whom they represent and what they are doing.

**2** What is the purpose of the long ramp?

**3** The colossal figure of Louis Philippe is seated not on a throne but on a commode. Royal commissions, licences and honours emerge from beneath it. Why has Daumier chosen to present the King in this way?

**4** Try to express Daumier's criticism of the King in a written paragraph.

'GARGANTUA' BY DAUMIER

# EXAMINING THE EVIDENCE
## Propagandists at work

On 13 April 1834 a rising broke out in Paris. Armed troops were deployed to restore order and during the fighting came under fire from snipers. The following day, soldiers stormed a house on the rue Transnonain from which the snipers were alleged to be operating. The soldiers found only families and elderly couples, yet a terrible massacre ensued.

### Source A

The soldiers rushed into the passage, and, turning half round to the right, shot my husband and M. Guitard, at the moment they reached the last step of the staircase. They fell amidst a shower of balls. The explosion was so great that the windows of the lodge, which I had not had time to shut before the soldiers ran in, were all broken to pieces. A giddiness seized me for a moment, and when I came to myself, it was to see the lifeless body of my husband stretched near that of M. Guitard, whose head was nearly separated from the neck by the numerous shots he had received. Quick as lightning the soldiers, headed by an officer, ran up to the second floor. A folding door soon gave way before them; a second door, one with glass windows, presented itself; they knocked at it furiously and it was immediately opened by an old man, M. Breffort, senior. 'We are,' he said, to the officer, 'peaceable people here; we have no arms of any sort. Do not assassinate us.' The words had scarcely passed his lips ere he fell, pierced with three bayonet wounds. He uttered a cry: 'You old ragamuffin,' exclaimed the officer, 'if you don't hold your tongue, I'll finish you.' Annette Besson rushed from an adjacent room to assist him. A soldier turned round, plunged his bayonet into her neck, just beneath the jaw, and then, firing his musket at her, blew her head to pieces, the fragments sticking against the opposite wall. A young man, Henri Larivière, was following her. He was fired upon so close that the powder set his clothes in flames; the ball was buried deep in his lungs. As he was falling, mortally wounded, a bayonet stroke cut open his forehead deeply, and exposed the skull; twenty other wounds were added to despatch him. The room was a mere pool of blood; M. Breffort, senior, notwithstanding his wounds, had managed to crawl to an alcove; he was pursued by soldiers, when Madame Bonneville came forward, and covering him with her body, her feet in the blood on the floor, her hands raised to Heaven, exclaimed: 'All my family are stretched at my feet, there remains only myself to kill, only myself!' And five bayonet wounds cut open her hands. On the fourth floor, the soldiers who had just killed M. Lepere and M. Robiquet, said to their wives: 'My poor souls! you are sadly to be pitied as well as your husbands. But we are ordered to do this, we are compelled to obey, though it makes us as wretched as you can be.'

Extract from an eyewitness account of the massacre, quoted in
The Open University study unit, *Art and Politics in France* (1972)

# TALKING POINT
## What is propaganda?

A typical dictionary defines propaganda as follows: 'books, broadcasts etc. used to propagate a set of ideas, ideals or facts; often with derogatory sense.'

Working in groups, identify features of the two prints on page 105 which might allow them to be described as examples of propaganda.

Can you now extend the simple dictionary definition above to provide a more meaningful description of the concept?

Are you aware of propaganda in our present society? In what form does it appear?

**Source B**

DAUMIER'S LITHOGRAPH 'THE MASSACRE ON THE RUE TRANSNONAIN'

**1** Study Source A. Accounts such as this were carried in newspapers and journals in the aftermath of the massacre.

(a) What is your immediate impression of this account?

(b) Comment on the following:

- The overall tone of the description;
- The vocabulary used;
- The most powerful images it conveys.

**2** What effect do you suppose such an account was expected to achieve amongst the reading public?

**3** In what sense can this account be described as propaganda?

**4** How far can this account be viewed as a reliable version of the events in the rue Transnonain?

**5** Study Source B. How does Daumier encourage us to sympathize with the victims of the massacre?

**6** Daumier did not witness the events in the rue Transnonain. Does this reduce the value of his print as historical evidence?

# **F**OCUS

## 5.1 How successful was French foreign policy (1830-48)?

Historical studies very often single out the failure of French foreign policy as an important factor in the collapse of the July Monarchy. How far can this view be accepted? First, let us examine the aims and expectations of those who shared an interest in the outcome of French foreign policy.

How far were these aims and expectations translated into positive achievements by Louis Philippe? In the section which follows you can examine four significant episodes in French foreign policy during the time of the July Monarchy.

### 1 Popular expectations

By tradition, French foreign policy was vigorous and successful. As a people, the French were accustomed to the glories of military conquest and regarded their ruler as the natural provider of prestige and influence in Europe. The defeat of Napoleon had therefore been nothing short of a national disaster. The years after 1815 witnessed an overwhelming popular wish to reverse the humiliation of military defeat and to re-establish France as the dominant Continental Power. The French were especially sensitive to the apparently smug superiority displayed by Britain in the wake of Waterloo.

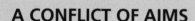

## A CONFLICT OF AIMS

### 2 Louis Philippe's aims

Among the Continental Powers, Louis Philippe was aware of being the odd man out. The rulers of Russia, Prussia and Austria owed their positions to the classic principle of hereditary monarchy; the new king of France owed his to a successful publicity campaign. He understood that an aggressive foreign policy could unite the powers against him. Accordingly his conduct in foreign affairs was restrained and unambitious. He aimed to reassure the European Powers that after the disorder of 1830, France posed no threat to inter-national peace and stability. He wished to promote an atmosphere in which middle-class commercial interests were able to flourish, and hoped to establish improved relations with Britain as a means of restraining the legitimate monarchies in the east. However, whilst not seeking to reassert French domination in Europe he *did* look for opportunities to gain any advantage and prestige which shrewd manoeuvring might secure for France.

### Belgium (1830)

In 1830 the Belgians rose against Dutch rule in an emphatic rejection of the settlement imposed by the Powers at Vienna in 1815. To many Frenchmen this incident presented Louis Philippe with an opportunity to reassert French influence in an area which had been conquered by Napoleon and contained a significant number of French-speaking people. However, Louis Philippe resisted the temptation to annex Belgium and worked with Britain to secure its independence and neutrality. Louis Philippe continued to show restraint by refusing to allow his son to accept an invitation to become king of the new constitutional Belgian state. Britain's confidence in the July Monarchy was demonstrated in August 1831 when Louis Philippe won her backing to send troops to defend Belgian independence against an abortive Dutch attack.

### The Near East (1839-40)

The Near East had been dominated by the Turkish Empire for centuries. So extensive were the Sultan's possessions that he was forced to entrust certain regions to the control of appointed governors. One such region was Egypt, ruled on behalf of the Turks by Mehemet Ali. Egypt was a traditional French sphere of influence. Under Louis Philippe, extensive French investment went to assist development here. Commercial links were established and personnel, including teachers and military advisers, put their skills at the disposal of the Egyptian government. For some time the power and influence of Mehemet Ali had been developing in the Near East and a serious challenge was mounted to the authority of the Sultan. In 1839 war between Mehemet Ali and the Turks broke out. French public opinion naturally favoured the Egyptians but Great Power interest in this politically-sensitive area quickly complicated the issue. Instability in the eastern Mediterranean threatened access to the Black Sea. Seeing their interests threatened, Britain and Russia rapidly backed Turkey and in July 1840 insisted that Mehemet Ali cease hostilities. In France, Adolphe Thiers had become Chief Minister in 1840 and was determined to take foreign policy in a direction more to the liking of popular opinion. Thiers threatened war against the Major Powers if they moved to subdue Mehemet Ali. Palmerston, the British foreign secretary, was only too pleased to call his bluff and worked with Russia to defeat the Egyptians. At the height of the crisis France was isolated and unable to act in defence of her interests. Louis Philippe removed Thiers but in doing so burdened himself with the humiliation of a resounding diplomatic defeat.

## The Spanish marriages (1846)

Palmerston had derived considerable satisfaction from humiliating France during the Mehemet Ali affair. However, in 1841 a new government under Sir Robert Peel took office and a period of harmonious Anglo-French relations began. The royal families of the two nations developed close relations and Guizot (Thiers' replacement) made co-operation the keystone of dealings between the two governments. A potential clash over the control of Tahiti was avoided in 1844 and negotiations to find a husband for the young Queen of Spain were progressing amicably. However, in 1846 Palmerston returned to office determined to arrange the marriage of a prince directly related to the British royal family to Queen Isabella of Spain. The French preferred to press the claim of Louis Philippe's son. A compromise was arranged in which Isabella was to marry her cousin. At the same time, however, Guizot seized the opportunity to marry the Queen's younger sister to Louis Philippe's son. Since Isabella was not expected to have children, it seemed only a matter of time before an Orleanist occupied the Spanish throne. The French king enjoyed a much needed, but ultimately hollow, diplomatic victory; within a short

time Isabella had a son and ensured the continuation of her own family line.

## Algeria

Continuing a process begun under Charles X, Guizot devoted considerable effort to carving out the beginning of an empire in North Africa. Steady colonization was encouraged and by 1847 around 50,000 French citizens had established themselves in Algeria. However, the achievement was not without its costs both in financial terms and in the loss of troops. Louis Philippe had little interest in colonial development, a sentiment shared by many Frenchmen who believed that success in foreign policy could only be measured in a European context. The 'glories' of global empire-building were some years in the future.

---

**Having examined these events, your task is to write two separate assessments, each from a different perspective, of French foreign policy under the July Monarchy.**

### Assessment 1: the popular perspective

This assessment should aim to show the distance between popular expectations and the conduct of the July Monarchy in foreign policy. The piece should be deliberately critical of government policy.

### Assessment 2: the King's perspective

This assessment should aim to comment on how the King might have judged his own handling of foreign affairs. Could he point to any positive achievements? The piece should contain a spirited defence of government policy.

Make detailed reference to each of the four episodes contained in this Focus section when preparing your assessments.

Now consider how you would deal with the issue of foreign policy when evaluating the reasons why French rejected Louis Philippe in 1848.

## The dangers of economic recession

The condition of the French economy posed a constant threat to the stability of the July Monarchy. It should not be forgotten that when Louis Philippe became King in 1830 the economic ills of France did not suddenly disappear. The recession which had begun in 1826 continued until 1832, and in some regions ended even later than this. The ordinary people who suffered grain shortages, inflation and unemployment did not much care who occupied the throne in Paris. The transition from Bourbon to Orleans had little practical impact upon the lives of the rural peasant or the urban artisan. In the countryside grain convoys were hijacked and prohibitions against common access to forests were ignored. The most serious manifestations of economic distress occurred in the towns of Lyons and Paris.

In November 1830 silkworkers in Lyons took to the street in demonstrations against wage cuts. They called for economic improvements: lower prices, higher wages, shorter working hours. The government responded with a law (10 April 1831) preventing unlawful assembly and by unleashing the army on the protestors. In the clashes which followed there were 275 deaths. In April 1834 the event was repeated with simultaneous disturbances in Lyons and Paris. The government again chose to apply force to silence the workers' demands. In Lyons 300 people were killed and although there were fewer casualties in Paris the government was burdened with the responsibility for a reckless massacre of innocent civilians at a house on the rue Transnonain (see *Examining the Evidence*, page 106). Republicans were outraged by such incidents and skillfuly employed scathing propaganda to attack the new king and his supporters. In the capital and in a number of smaller provincial towns, republicanism became a rallying point for the casualties of economic recession and the victims of political repression.

Louis Philippe successfully drove the republicans underground after 1835 with a series of new Press laws. However, there remained a reservoir of potential support for the republicans in towns like Paris and Lyons. The King made the mistake of believing that because the republicans were not so visible in the 1840s they had somehow been eliminated. The harvest failures of 1846–47 showed the extent of his error, and how vulnerable France was to economic recession.

In February 1848, the crisis facing Louis Philippe's government came to a head. Having failed to satisfy the popular craving for military glory, the King had compounded his troubles with an unimaginative domestic policy which offered little by way of constructive reform. Censorship, repression of political opponents and the occasional heavy-handed police action against popular demonstrations gave an unpleasant flavour to the supposedly constitutional regime. Aided by the faithful Guizot, the King's steady assumption of royal power raised calls amongst rival deputies such as Thiers for electoral reform. Louis Philippe's decision to ignore such demands produced an active and well-organized political opposition reflecting the views of the excluded middle-class. The economic recession which struck after 1846 placed him in a position which he was powerless to control. When troops opened fire on a group of demonstrators in Paris on 23 February 1848 the city rose in revolt and within 24 hours the July Monarchy was no more.

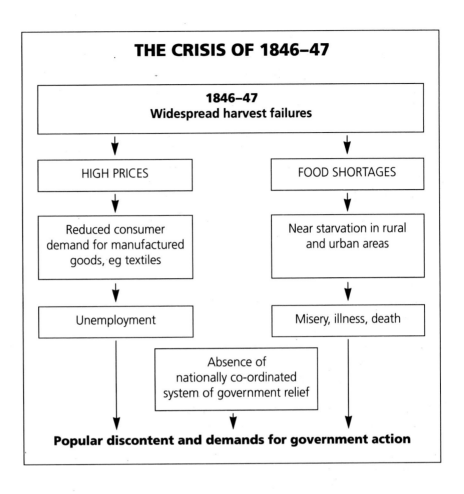

# THE CRISIS OF 1846–47

**1846–47
Widespread harvest failures**

HIGH PRICES

Reduced consumer
demand for manufactured
goods, eg textiles

Unemployment

FOOD SHORTAGES

Near starvation in rural
and urban areas

Misery, illness, death

Absence of
nationally co-ordinated
system of government relief

**Popular discontent and demands for government action**

# REVIEW

Listed below are a collection of factors covered in this chapter which may be said to have contributed to the fall of the July Monarchy. Can you add any other factors to this list?

---

**1** Louis Philippe's narrow base of support.

**2** The limitations of the revised Charter of 1830.

**3** Louis Philippe's sympathy with the 'Party of Resistance'.

**4** Republican disappointment with the outcome of 1830.

**5** Persistent political opposition.

**6** The use of repressive methods to control opposition.

**7** The King's determination to exercise royal power.

**8** The failure to satisfy middle-class demands for moderate electoral reform.

**9** The work of the political propagandists.

**10** Lack of military glory.

**11** The humiliation over the Mehemet Ali affair.

**12** Acute shortages of food.

**13** The failure of the government to address the problem of economic distress.

**14** The widespread appearance of reform banquets.

**15** The shooting of demonstrators in Paris on 23 February 1848.

---

Now consider the following question:
**'"Accidental and unexpected." Discuss this verdict on the fall of the July Monarchy in 1848.' (Oxford, 1983)**

**1** Examine your list of factors. Which of them may accurately be described as 'accidental' causes of Louis Philippe's fall from power?

**2** Using your list, can you justify the claim that the July Monarchy's collapse was 'unexpected'?

**3** How far can it be said that Louis Philippe contributed significantly to his own downfall?

**4** What were the basic structural weaknesses of the July Monarchy over which the King had little control and which threatened, under the wrong circumstances, to destabilize the monarchy?

---

# 6 France 1852–71

## PREVIEW

### The progress of Louis Napoleon: the unlikely emperor

**October 1836**
An attempt to provoke a rebellion in support of the Bonapartist cause at Strasbourg ended in farce. *The Times* commented:

> 'The ridiculous attempt at insurrection against the ruling dynasty of France…can…only have the effect of strengthening the cause which it was intended to destroy…What ridiculous dreamers must [Napoleon's] surviving relatives be if they suppose that they could satisfy France by placing any number of their race, old or young, upon the throne.'*

**August 1840**
A second attempt to raise a rebellion, this time at Boulogne, was completely unsuccessful. *The Times* reported:

> 'Within two hours the greater part…were either prisoners in the citadel, shot, or dispersed.'

**September 1848**
Louis Napoleon was elected to the revolutionary Assembly to serve as Deputy for Paris. *The Times* remained unimpressed:

> 'The choice of the first President will be the turning point of the young Republic. Who is to be the Washington of France? We will venture to predict that whoever this historical personage will turn out to be, it will most assuredly not be Louis Napoleon.'

*All extracts from *The Times* quoted in Alison Patrick, *The Empire of the Third Republic* (1973)

NAPOLEON III

**December 1848**
Presidential election results:

| | |
|---|---|
| *Lamartine* | 17,000 votes |
| *Cavaignac* | 1,500,000 votes |
| *Napoleon* | 5,400,000 votes |

# From President to Emperor

When Louis Napoleon was elected to the Presidency of the Second Republic in December 1848, it was expected that French history would record this as his greatest achievement. Constitutional law fixed his term of office to four years after which he was debarred from seeking immediate re-election. Few people could have envisaged a political life for the inexperienced President beyond 1852. But in December 1851 Louis Napoleon staged a coup and secured an extension of his Presidency. Twelve months later he dissolved the Republic, established the Second Empire and won widespread acceptance as Emperor; a position he was to hold for the next 18 years. How was this remarkable political transformation achieved?

## Creation of a power base

Following his election to the Presidency, Louis Napoleon embarked on an extensive tour of France and was seen by hundreds of thousands of ordinary people. The ceremonial tour won him the genuine affection of the masses, who appreciated his attentions and personal charm. Louis Napoleon understood that in a nation which elected its leaders through universal suffrage, the popular man would have a decisive advantage. In both the coup of 1851 and the declaration of the Second Empire, he sought and obtained popular approval through the ballot box. The President was also active in courting the support of influential figures in society. He presented himself as the defender of order and the patron of stable, disciplined government; and won the backing of powerful conservatives who found the Republic too radical. He engineered the promotion of his supporters into positions of influence so that when the time came to secure his political future, he would be able to call in debts of loyalty from his dependants.

## Popular official actions

Louis Napoleon wished to be a popular president. To this end, his response to events and his policy initiatives were designed to win him popular acclaim. In April 1849 he sent French troops to Italy to help re-establish the Pope who had been unseated by republicans. The move demonstrated his basic conservatism and proved to be very popular with the clergy and the predominantly-Catholic peasantry. In June, radical republicans staged a rising in Paris in support of the Rome revolutionaries. Louis Napoleon played a firm hand. He quickly restored order and imprisoned the conspirators, again reinforcing his association with firm, disciplined government. In 1850 he further rejected left-wing ideals by supporting a piece of legislation known as the *Loi Falloux*. This made religion a compulsory subject in all schools and permitted the development of Church schools. The measure was a blow to the republicans who had hoped to reduce the influence of the Church in the State by creating a secular education system. The President, sensitive to the Catholic majority in France, rejected this demand and won the approval of the conservative masses.

### Coup d'état (2 December 1851)

Louis Napoleon knew that his efforts to secure a firm power-base and to win public support would ultimately be futile if he could not amend or bypass the constitution. The election of a new president in 1852 would signal the end of his career in high office. When attempts to persuade the Assembly to extend his Presidency failed, Louis Napoleon resorted to the main preoccupation of his years in exile: plotting and intrigue. The *coup d'état* which he planned for 2 December 1851 was certainly his most successful venture into conspiracy politics.

**T**ALKING POINT

**2 December 1851: a successful coup d'etat**

Discuss what you understand by the term *coup d'état*. Why do you think Louis Napoleon was so successful in overthrowing the authority of the Assembly and establishing his own grip on the government of France?

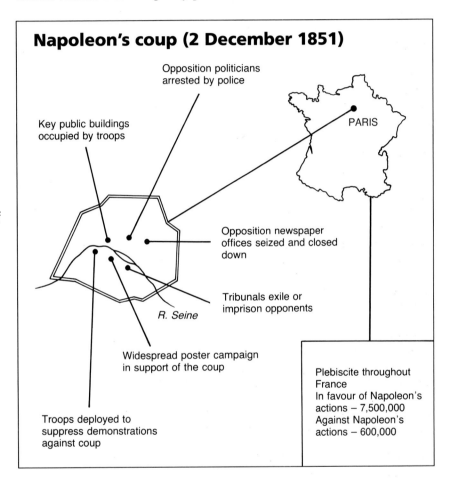

**Napoleon's coup (2 December 1851)**

Opposition politicians arrested by police

PARIS

Key public buildings occupied by troops

Opposition newspaper offices seized and closed down

Tribunals exile or imprison opponents

R. Seine

Widespread poster campaign in support of the coup

Plebiscite throughout France
In favour of Napoleon's actions – 7,500,000
Against Napoleon's actions – 600,000

Troops deployed to suppress demonstrations against coup

## Transforming the Empire

### Political developments

Following the success of the December coup Napoleon proceeded to stamp his authority on the nation. The diagram overleaf indicates the principal features of his 'Authoritarian Empire'.

The political control which Napoleon now had over the nation and, it must be said, the genuine appeal which the new regime held for many Frenchmen, were effectively illustrated through the ballot box on two occasions in 1852. In March voters went to the polls to elect their representatives to the Legislative Chamber. Thanks largely to the work of local

## THE CONSTITUTION

| | |
|---|---|
| **PRESIDENT** | The President nominated all State officials and proposed all new legislation. He controlled the army and alone had the power to make war and foreign treaties. |
| **COUNCIL OF STATE** | Consisted of 40 members nominated by the President. Its function was to draw up the legislation proposed by the President. It could discuss issues associated with government policy but it had no executive authority. |
| **LEGISLATIVE CHAMBER** | Consisted of 261 members elected by universal male suffrage. Met for just three months a year to discuss the legislation drawn up by the Council of State. Had no power to amend these proposals and served principally as a consenting chamber. |
| **THE SENATE** | The 150 senators were appointed for life by the President. It was their task to examine the laws passed by the Legislative Chamber to ensure that they were constitutional. |

## THE AUTHORITARIAN EMPIRE

### REPRESSION OF OPPOSITION

In the immediate wake of the coup there were 26,884 arrests of political opponents. The chief punishments were exile and imprisonment. Nine thousand were transported to Algeria alone.

### WINNING KEY LOYALTIES

Napoleon doubled the salaries of local prefects, the officials responsible for the administration of elections. He increased the status and salaries of army officers and indicated his support for the Catholic Church.

### GAGGING THE PRESS

New Press laws were introduced in February 1852. All publications became subject to government approval. Large sums of money had to be deposited by newspaper owners with the government to exert financial pressure on editors not to print items which criticized the government. Journals could be suspended and suppressed for repeatedly attacking the regime. Those accused of Press offences were tried without a jury.

Many histories describe the regime established by Napoleon following the December coup as a 'dictatorship'. What features can you identify from this diagram to support this description?

prefects who acted as political agents on behalf of the official 'Bonapartist' candidates, the results represented an overwhelming public endorsement for the new political system. Of the 261 representatives only eight declared themselves in opposition to the new regime. The remaining 253 were dedicated to maintaining the provincial appeal and authority of Bonapartism.

In December, Frenchmen were again given an opportunity to exercise their constitutional rights. Napoleon now proposed to end the Republic and to restore the Empire. He would cease to be the president and would become the Emperor Napoleon III. The result of the plebiscite held to determine the people's wishes on the proposal was emphatic: 7,800,000 voted in favour of the change and 250,000 declared themselves opposed. The Second Empire was born. It was clear that even allowing for around two million abstentions in the plebiscite, Napoleon's political system and personal leadership had the overwhelming approval of the French people.

How did Napoleon's actions between 1848 and 1852 help him to win such massive popular approval in the plebiscite of December 1852?

The dictatorship which Napoleon had established in 1851–52 began to be modified in the last decade of the Empire. The result was the emergence of the so-called Liberal Empire and the adoption of the principles and institutions of parliamentary government. This constitutional empire emerged through a series of amendments to the existing system; these are outlined in the following chart.

| THE LIBERAL EMPIRE (1859–70) | |
| --- | --- |
| *Date* | *Measure* |
| 1859 | Napoleon granted a general amnesty to all political opponents still under sentence following the December coup. By 1859 this applied to only 1800 individuals. |
| 1860 | The Senate and Legislative Chamber were given the right to debate and reply to the government's proposals. They were now entitled to receive a response to their observations from government ministers. Newspapers were permitted to report the debates, as long as they did so in full. |
| 1864 | Strikes were legalized. |
| 1867 | The Senate and Legislative Chamber were given the right to question government ministers and to receive parliamentary replies to their questions. This was designed to make government ministers more publicly accountable for their actions and policies. |
| 1868 | Control of the Press was relaxed. A new Press law allowed newspapers and journals to be established without the need to obtain official permission. |
| 1869–70 | The Legislative Chamber was accorded true parliamentary status with the right to initiate legislation. Government ministers were made responsible to parliament. |

In May 1870 a plebiscite allowed the French people to pass their verdict on the new Liberal Empire. Votes in favour of the changes totalled 7,336,000; 1,560,000 voted against. Napoleon III and the Second Empire continued to command huge popular support.

Why did Napoleon III relax his dictatorship and facilitate the development of the Liberal Empire? Opinion is divided on this issue. To some observers Napoleon had no choice but to move in the direction of reform. His measures are seen as concessionary responses to a growing opposition movement which reflected the inherent weakness of the regime. Others prefer to see the liberalization of the Empire as part of Napoleon's long-term plan carried out on his own initiative. This approach rejects the influence of political opposition and explains its growth during the last decade of the Second Empire as the inevitable and healthy consequence of a more open society.

The debate seems to centre on the nature and influence of political opposition at this time. In electoral terms, opposition was certainly on the increase during the last decade of the Second Empire. In the elections to the Legislative Chamber in 1852 there had been just 0.66 million votes cast in opposition to the government. By 1869 this figure had increased to 3.3 million. Opposition was evident not only in election results. Following the relaxation of the Press laws in 1868 there was a surge in opposition propaganda. Around 150 new publications, many highly critical of the government, appeared on the streets. In the cities (notably Paris and Lyons), public demonstrations and labour unrest were increasingly visible signs of urban discontent. The workers who attended such highly-charged gatherings rejected the Second Empire. Virtually all the major cities and towns in France were solidly republican.

However, opposition to the regime was not the exclusive preserve of the left. Increasingly the right – including even those who counted themselves as Bonapartists – was becoming critical of the government. This was most clearly seen in the relationship between Church and State. In 1852 most of the Catholic hierarchy welcomed the Second Empire and won from it valuable concessions. The *Loi Falloux* (see page 114) greatly extended Church control over education, clerical salaries were increased, religious orders were tolerated and offenders against religious morality were prosecuted in the civil courts. By allowing the Church a privileged status Napoleon had hoped to weld Catholic France into a nation. However, he underestimated the strength of anti-clericalism which pervaded much of French society, and earned himself opposition from those who wished to see a reduction in the Church's influence.

After 1859 it was clear that his accommodation with the Church had backfired. The chorus of clerical opposition to Napoleon's Italian campaign in 1859–60 (see page 123), and the desertion of Catholic voters to the opposition in the elections of 1868, led Napoleon to review his attitude to the Church. He appointed Victor Duruy as Minister of Education and endorsed his proposals to rescue education from the bonds of Church control. Duruy increased the number of secular schools and reduced fees. His most controversial proposal was to establish secular schools for girls. The clergy, who saw educating girls as the key to the religious devotion of future generations, objected vigorously to the suggestion.

The Church was not the only source of right-wing opposition during the 1860s. Napoleon also faced difficulties within the ranks of his own supporters. Those Bonapartists who favoured authoritarian government became alarmed by the liberalization of the Empire. Such measures, they claimed, could only serve to nurture republican opposition. Between 1857 and 1863 the total opposition vote roughly doubled, producing demands from the right to halt the reforms. The best chance Napoleon had of continuing to steer a liberal course was to rely on the talents of the Duc de Morny. As President of the Legislative Chamber, Morny was the most gifted statesman of the Second Empire. Like Napoleon, he shared the vision of a constitutional empire and possessed the political skill to move the Legislative Chamber towards this goal. His death in 1865 was a major blow to the Emperor's reform plans. After 1866 control of the government passed to Eugene Rouher who, thanks to the failing health of the Emperor, was able to manage the affairs of state virtually unsupervised. Rouher was an authoritarian Bonapartist, committed to the constitution of 1852 and opposed to any liberal concessions. His presence in government set back the development of the Liberal Empire by some five years. When

# TALKING POINT

### The control of education

In many European countries the tradition of close Church involvement in education continued during the Nineteenth Century. At certain times and in certain places – for example in Bismarck's Germany – this relationship was challenged by the State. In such circumstances, the State insisted on secular education, much to the dislike of the Church authorities. Suggest reasons why responsibility for education was so keenly contested by Church and State. In what ways may such institutional control over education be open to abuse?

the crucial reforms finally came, following his dismissal in 1869, they appeared to be the product of increasing internal opposition. Had the same reforms been sponsored and passed by Morny in 1865 they might well have been regarded as part of Napoleon's continuing commitment to liberal government.

Napoleon had always claimed that the dictatorship he established in 1852 was no more than a temporary expedient and spoke of 'crowning' the 'political edifice' with 'Liberty' once stable government had been established. It may be argued that his liberalization of the Empire after 1860 proceeded more from a desire to steer a truly liberal course than to grant self-securing concessions. When Napoleon began to liberalize the Empire in 1860 the initiative was largely with him. There was general domestic calm and a massive majority in the Legislative Chamber. The elections of 1857 had returned just 13 opposition candidates; only five of them republicans. Significantly, this 'Party of Five' took their seats in the Chamber (unlike the three republicans elected in 1852) and seemed prepared to work within the constitution. There was even republican support for Napoleon's Italian campaign in 1859. In 1860, then, Napoleon was presumably confident that a relaxation of his dictatorship would not undermine his authority.

There were also personal reasons why Napoleon initiated the Liberal Empire. The pressure of absolute power had deprived him of much of his vitality. During the last decade of the Empire his health deteriorated alarmingly. He was aware of this and concerned that in the event of his death he might not be able to guarantee the succession of his young son without the genuine support of parliament. The progress towards constitutional government has thus been interpreted as a deliberate attempt to deprive the opposition of any legitimate reason to abandon the Empire following the death of Napoleon III.

It should be remembered that although opposition *did* increase in the 1860s, and helped to motivate Napoleon to reform, the regime he had created was not in serious danger from the opposition. There was never any likelihood that the Bonapartist majority would be overturned in the Legislative Chamber and the results of the plebiscite in May 1870 were a clear indication of the support Napoleon continued to command.

---

**1** Which groups constituted the principal political opposition to Louis Napoleon?

**2** What specific reasons did these groups have for opposing the Emperor?

**3** Why did Napoleon modify his dictatorship and set up the 'Liberal Empire'?

---

### Social and economic developments

Nothing symbolizes Napoleon III's passion for self-glorification in quite the same way as his urge to rebuild Paris. The work was completed to a grand design and carried out under the vigorous supervision of Baron Haussmann, Prefect of Paris from 1853 to 1870. In the principal city-centre districts demolition gangs reduced the tangle of medieval streets to rubble. From the dust arose 136 km of carefully-planned boulevards and squares. The new avenues were wide, tree-lined and bounded by beautifully-proportioned buildings, while the broad design was punctuated by architectural treasures such as the new Opera House. Even below street-level civic improvements, in the form of a new sewer system, were part of the grand design. Paris became the civic showpiece of Europe and a centre of fashion and culture. Moreover, the rebuilding programme provided long-term work for thousands of previously unemployed labourers. Such a public works scheme had been much in demand since the demise of the National Workshops (see page 74).

BARON HAUSSMANN

The remodelling of Paris was a major achievement which enhanced the prestige of the Empire. However, Haussmann has been criticized for erecting no more than a façade. The new Paris was designed to impress the visiting dignitary or foreign tourist and its principal beneficiaries were the wealthy and cultured. Beyond the magnificence of the city-centre boulevards there remained the cramped and decaying quarters of the masses. The 20,000 houses demolished in the rebuilding programme had provided cheap accommodation for hundreds of families. They were replaced with smart shops, commercial offices and residential sites for the wealthy. No attempt was made to provide modern and affordable housing for the labouring poor. With thousands displaced from their homes and new arrivals from the provinces attracted by the prospect of employment, pressure on available stock of cheap housing became intense. In spite of the rebuilding programme (which was repeated in other French towns)

THE BOULEVARD MONTMARTRE IN PARIS. SUCH STREETS WERE TYPICAL OF HAUSSMANN'S URBAN RENEWAL PROGRAMME

the cities remained the principal centres of republican opposition to Napoleon III. In the elections of 1863, 18 of the 22 largest towns in France (including Paris) fell to this opposition.

THE NEW PARIS SEWERS WERE A POPULAR TOURIST ATTRACTION DURING THE SECOND EMPIRE. IN SPITE OF THEIR SIZE THEY HAD THEIR LIMITATIONS. THEY WERE DESIGNED TO DRAIN RAIN-WATER FROM THE STREETS AND COULD NOT COPE WITH SANITARY REFUSE. THIS WAS EITHER CARTED AWAY AT NIGHT OR DUMPED ILLEGALLY

The urban renewal programme exemplified Napoleon's approach to the problems of poverty and social deprivation. He was convinced that large-scale investment in public works and State ventures would create employment and prosperity. If a regular source of investment capital could be found, wealth would continue to be generated at all levels of society. Accordingly, he encouraged the establishment of new banks to specialize in providing venture-capital for entrepreneurs. The most notable of these new banks was the Crédit Mobilier. Such institutions were responsible for the speculative investment which helped to create the impression of the Second Empire as the most progressive regime in Europe. This was most evident in the promotion of the railway network. Napoleon inherited just 1700 km of track from Louis Philippe but by encouraging investment and rationalizing the railway companies he enabled a huge building programme to take place. By 1870 France had some 17,700 km of track. In spite of this success it was apparent that Napoleon's attempts to encourage speculative investment produced resentment among more traditional financiers. The long-established credit institutions, controlled by powerful families such as the Rothschilds, disliked the unorthodox methods of the new banks. In 1867, as the Crédit

Mobilier teetered on the edge of collapse, the conservative financial houses refused to come to its aid and happily watched as the bank and Napoleon's credit-economy went under for good. Some modest industrial development took place during the Second Empire thanks largely to the impetus provided by railway building. In 1850 French foundries produced around 390,000 tons of pig-iron per annum. By 1870 this had increased to 1,771,000 tons. Coal output and consumption also grew. However, France did not experience the same large-scale industrial take-off as Britain, Prussia or Belgium. The population expanded sluggishly while the shift to urban industrial centres was undramatic; the proportion of town-dwellers increased from 24 per cent to just 31 per cent during the years of the Second Empire. Napoleon gave little direct encouragement to industry and was in fact bitterly criticized by manufacturers for dismantling the protective tariff system in favour of freer trade with Europe.

There were some impressive achievements associated with Napoleon's social and economic policies. The availability of credit brought rapid improvements in transport and helped to promote other commercial enterprises. These were not always found at home. It was French capital which financed the construction of the Suez Canal and was behind the expansion of Russia's railway network. The urban renewal programme provided much-needed work and stimulated local industries while the free trade policy did not appear to harm French interests; between 1855 and 1867 the foreign commerce of France almost trebled. Nevertheless, as the 1860s wore on, Napoleon increasingly came to be criticized by three groups: the traditional élite who objected to his enterprise culture and sponsorship of the aspiring middle class; industrialists who continued to be nervous of his insistence on free trade; and the masses who, in both towns and countryside, found their lives to be little changed materially from the days of the Second Republic.

## The conduct of foreign affairs

The spectacular military conquests of Emperor Napoleon I continued to live in the memories of the French people long after his final defeat at Waterloo. Heroic battles and the glories of Imperial expansion gave birth to the myth of French superiority. French public opinion never doubted that the Vienna settlement of 1815 would be temporary and that in time Europe would again fall into line behind the moral, cultural and political leadership of France. Since a Napoleon created this expectation, who was better placed than his ancestral descendant to fulfil these national hopes? Invested in Napoleon III's foreign policy were the ambitions of an entire nation.

Napoleon certainly looked to reassert French prestige and influence in Europe and beyond. He was committed to destroying the Vienna settlement though he hoped to avoid antagonizing his European partners in the process. He saw himself as the champion of nationalist causes and promoted France as the protector of emerging nations. Napoleon adopted the slogan *'l'Empire, c'est la paix'* (The Empire is peace) in describing his foreign policy. He was aware of the sensitivities of the European Powers who continued to view France, especially under a Napoleon, as the most likely source of international disruption. He therefore avoided presenting France as a warmonger, thirsty for territorial expansion. At the same time he was prepared to use limited military force to obtain his objectives and liked to

**1** What were Napoleon III's principal objectives in his foreign policy?

**2** Can you detect any inconsistencies in these objectives?

insist on territorial 'rewards' for allowing other Powers to achieve their goals.

**The Crimean War (1854–56)** Napoleon's first venture into international affairs showed real promise. During the Crimean War Napoleon allied with Britain against Russian aggression in the Near East. The alliance seemed to offer the prospect of close co-operation with Britain when the war ended, an objective in itself if France were to overturn the Vienna settlement. Victory in the war bolstered French pride; when Sebastopol capitulated in September 1855 the popular mood was jubilation. French prestige was enhanced further when Paris was chosen to host the peace talks. Of greater significance was the acrimonious dissolution of the Holy Alliance. Neither Austria nor Prussia rallied to their former partner. It seemed that the prospects for challenging the Vienna settlement were better than at any time since 1815.

**1** What reasons did Napoleon have to be pleased with the conduct and outcome of the Crimean War?

**Italy (1859–60)** Napoleon's Italian adventure had quite the opposite effect to his diplomatic victories in the Crimea. Italian ambitions to drive the Austrian Habsburgs out of the peninsular fitted well with Napoleon's foreign policy objectives. He hoped that by assisting the Italians he would extend the influence and prestige of France and further weaken the Vienna arrangements. The promise of territorial gains in the shape of Savoy and Nice seemed fair reward for his assistance, though he also expected to win the gratitude of the Italians and through this to exercise influence there. At the same time, by presenting himself as the liberator of Italy, he hoped to win the support of French liberals.

When Napoleon met with Cavour, the Piedmontese Prime Minister, to discuss the terms of French involvement, it was clear that the Emperor also expected the venture to appeal to French Catholics. A confederation of Italian states under the Presidency of the Pope was accepted by both men as the more desirable outcome of the forthcoming clash with Austria. In the event Napoleon did gain Savoy and Nice for France and the decisive victories of Magenta and Solferino won popular acclaim. In spite of Napoleon's withdrawal from the war, by the Treaty of Villafranca (July 1859), Italy had become largely independent and was united the following year. With Austrian influence removed from the peninsular it was clear that the Vienna settlement had been destroyed in Italy. Despite these achievements the repercussions of the Italian venture were disastrous for Napoleon.

● His actions aroused the suspicions of Britain who viewed his involvement in the Italian affair as little more than a crude attempt to realize expansionist dreams.

● He failed to win the gratitude of the Italians, who never forgave him for his premature withdrawal at Villafranca. The situation was made worse as, in an effort to appease French Catholics, French troops continued garrisoning Rome to protect the position of the Pope. The strategy failed on all counts. French clerics viewed the action as inadequate, whilst Italian nationalists regarded it as an intolerable interference in their quest to restore their ancient capital. Far from winning the gratitude of the Italians Napoleon succeeded only in earning their contempt.

● Within France the Italian venture added fuel to the fires of opposition. The left were appalled by Napoleon's attempts to uphold the power of the Pope. More serious was the clerical response. The promise of a confederation of Italian states under the Presidency of the Pope evaporated as Italy became united. Napoleon was blamed for sponsoring a movement which resulted in the large-scale erosion of Papal territory and political power. French Catholics were outraged and many showed their feelings in the elections of 1863.

**The Polish Rebellion (1863)** When the Poles rose against their Russian masters in 1863, Napoleon was quick to express his sympathy with their nationalist aspirations. The sentiments were honest but tactless. Tsar Alexander II regarded his comments as an insult and broke off diplomatic relations with Paris. At the same time, in spite of his words, it was not possible for the Emperor to lend assistance to the Poles whose cause was popular among both French liberals and Catholics. Rhetoric was viewed as an inadequate response by these groups and, in the light of the offence caused to Alexander II, Napoleon might have been best advised to keep his views to himself.

**The Mexican Fiasco (1863–67)** As part of his foreign policy Napoleon engaged in a number of overseas projects. His most ambitious scheme was an attempt to develop Mexico as a colonial possession. Catholic support for the plan was strong since Mexico was governed by an anti-clerical administration under President Juarez. Backed by the Pope, and with the United States temporarily distracted by her own Civil War, Napoleon began his bid to establish a South American empire. In 1863 a French expedition ousted Juarez and Napoleon invited a Habsburg prince, Maximilian, to become the Emperor of Mexico. But the sweet taste of colonial glory soon turned sour. A gruelling guerrilla war ensued, with French troops finding it increasingly difficult to overhaul the Mexican patriots. Heavy losses were incurred and the Mexican adventure became very unpopular in France. In 1867 Napoleon withdrew his troops, leaving Maximilian to his fate. He was captured and executed by Mexican rebels; a tragic and humiliating end to Napoleon's colonial dreams.

**The Austro-Prussian War (1866)** As Austria and Prussia squared up for war during 1865–66, Napoleon blithely misread the situation with far-reaching consequences for the Second Empire. He regarded Austria as the stronger of the two German states and envisaged a protracted war in which the principal benefit for France would be the final collapse of the Vienna settlement. Napoleon did not regard Prussia as a threat, and was prepared to sit on the sidelines in the expectation that his services would be required in a mediation process at which he would be able to name his price.

The rapid Prussian victory presented Napoleon with some startling realities. Prussia was clearly very powerful and was confident enough to arrange peace-terms with Austria without consulting France. Accordingly, Napoleon received no territorial reward for his neutrality; when he pressed Bismarck for compensation, the Prussian Chancellor made it known in London and British suspicions of Napoleon deepened. Bismark's cursory dismissal of French claims offended national pride and earned Napoleon biting criticism. Public opinion was alarmed at the rapid emergence of a powerful and arrogant Protestant neighbour.

**The Franco-Prussian War (1870–71)** In July 1870 Napoleon III blundered into a war with Prussia and this sealed the fate of the Second Empire. The question of who should occupy the vacant Spanish throne (see page 257) hardly seemed sufficient cause for war but the French public, humiliated in 1866 and enraged now at the prospect of a German prince in Madrid, insisted that national honour be defended. With Paris gripped by hysterical war-fever and court circles urging the Emperor to action, war was declared on the upstart Prussians on 19 July 1870. The war was a catastrophe for France. Her armies were badly led, inadequately armed and quite unable to resist the superior Prussian forces. A decade of poor management in foreign affairs had succeeded in isolating France from the other European Powers. In 1870, without allies and fighting Europe's premier military power, France was doomed. On 1 September the Emperor, with 84,000 men, surrendered to the Prussians at Sedan. News of his capture brought revolutionary chaos to Paris and on 4 September a Republic was proclaimed; without Napoleon III the Second Empire ceased to exist and 18 years of Bonapartism came to a sudden and ignominious end.

BISMARCK RECEIVES NAPOLEON III FOLLOWING CAPTURE OF THE FRENCH EMPEROR AT SEDAN

# Review
## The impact of foreign policy

**1** Prepare a chart like the one opposite.

**2** Carefully review the details of foreign policy given in the section you have just read.

**3** Complete the chart opposite by ticking the appropriate boxes for each of the given events. It would be advisable to add a brief explanation for your decision to tick any particular box. For example: it would be appropriate to tick the column headed 'Alienated Russia' when dealing with the Polish Rebellion of 1863. Your explanation should indicate that Napoleon's support of the Polish cause offended Alexander II and led to the breakdown of diplomatic relations between St Petersburg and Paris.

**4** On balance, would you describe Napoleon's foreign policy as a success or a failure?

**5** How can an examination of foreign policy help to account for the growth of internal opposition in France during the last decade of the Second Empire?

## The agonies of Paris (1870–71)

### The siege
The collapse of the Second Empire precipitated a familiar sequence of events in the capital. An excited mob took to the streets and paraded noisily in the direction of the Hotel de Ville. Here, from the balcony, a Republic was proclaimed. Predictably, moderate politicians in the Legislative Chamber then acted to prevent the government falling into the hands of the extreme left. They declared a provisional Government of National Defence to be composed of the deputies for Paris.

The new government quickly announced its intention to continue the war against Prussia. It hoped to inspire the same national effort which had liberated France from her enemies in 1792. Within weeks the National Guard in Paris had doubled to some 360,000 men and it seemed as if the whole population were being put to arms:

'Everybody was a soldier. Even the waiters and cab-drivers were in uniform. All the churches and theatres were turned into ambulances and barracks. The new Opera House had been inaugurated: one wing was a hospital, another a police station, the third a barrack, while the upper part was full of stores of all kinds.'

> From *Life in Paris Before the War and During the Siege*, by an anonymous foreign resident in Paris. Quoted in Joanna Richardson, 'The Siege of Paris', *History Today* (September 1969)

By the end of September 250,000 Prussian troops had surrounded the city and the siege had begun. All hope for the relief of Paris lay with the new Minister of the Interior, Gambetta. Early in October he made a dramatic escape from Paris in a gas-filled balloon. From the town of Tours he tried to rally new provincial armies to march to the aid of the Parisians.

# EFFECTS

| EVENTS | Helped to undermine Vienna settlement | Won popular acclaim in France | Won prestige for France | Obtained territorial gains | Established inter-national co-operation | Offended French pride – national humiliation | Aroused hostility of French liberals | Aroused hostility of French Catholics | Alienated Britain | Alienated Russia | Alienated Austria | Alienated Italy |
|---|---|---|---|---|---|---|---|---|---|---|---|---|
| Crimean War (1854–56) | | | | | | | | | | | | |
| Italy (1859–60) | | | | | | | | | | | | |
| Polish Rebellion (1863) | | | | | | | | | | | | |
| Mexico (1863–67) | | | | | | | | | | | | |
| Austro-Prussian War (1866) | | | | | | | | | | | | |

PARISIAN RATION TICKETS FOR BREAD AND MEAT DURING THE SIEGE

RATION TICKETS FOR BREAD AND MEAT, ISSUED TO PARISIANS DURING THE SIEGE

Large numbers were recruited but they were inexperienced and ineffi-
ciently led. The circle of disciplined and battle-hardened Prussians was
never in serious danger of being breached.

Within the city the winter months brought great hardship. As the Seine
froze it became increasingly difficult to find supplies of firewood. Disease
took its toll amidst the crowded and insanitary tenements but perhaps the
greatest problem was hunger. Food supplies were rapidly consumed leaving the population to find alternative supplies. At first domestic pets such
as cats and dogs were consumed, but more bizarre provisions soon found

WHEN REGULAR SUPPLIES OF MEAT BECAME EXHAUSTED, BUTCHERS FOUND ALTERNATIVES TO SATISFY DESPERATE PARISIANS. THIS STALL SELLS
CATS, DOGS AND RATS

their way into the butchers' windows. Wolves, kangaroos, bears and elephants – all former exhibits at the Paris zoos – were offered for sale to the starving public. When sewer rats began to appear on market-stalls it was clear that the situation had become desperate. To compound the misery of the populace, the Prussian artillery began a regular bombardment of the city. From 5 January, for 23 consecutive nights, shells fell in the populated districts killing or wounding some 400 people. Attempts by armed detachments to break out of the city were promptly dispersed and when it became clear that Gambetta had failed to organize any effective relief, surrender was inevitable. On 28 January 1871 Paris capitulated and the Franco-Prussian War ended.

WITH PARIS DEFEATED, PRUSSIAN TROOPS ARRIVE AT THE ARC DE TRIOMPHE

## 6.1 The Paris Commune 1871

### 1 ORIGINS

**8 February:** Elections held for a new National Assembly to govern France following the demise of the Second Empire. The Assembly was overwhelmingly monarchist with republicans and Bonapartists being rejected by the voting public. Oddly, the Assembly retained the description of France as a republic and did not insist on any royalist restoration. Thiers, the leader of the newly-elected government, was determined to remove the danger from the left. In effect this threat meant Paris, still in the grip of a chaotic revolutionary situation following its capture by the Prussians. Left-wing radicals within the capital rejected the new, moderate National Assembly.

**18 March:** The National Assembly made its move against the left. Thiers ordered regular troops to enter Paris and to seize some 400 cannon held by the Paris National Guard. The strategy succeeded only in producing a revolutionary situation. There was violence and a number of deaths. Paris was abandoned by all remaining legal authorities. The government now established itself at Versailles on the outskirts of Paris.

**26 March:** The Parisian rebels held elections to form a municipal government, known as the Commune. The name of the Commune identified the actions of Paris with the spirit of the French Revolution and the Commune of 1793. To Thiers this represented a revolutionary challenge to his government which he was determined to crush.

### 2 AIMS

'...What do we ask?

'The recognition and strengthening of the Republic...

'The absolute autonomy of the Commune extended to all districts of France...

'The autonomy of the Commune shall have no limits other than the right of autonomy equally enjoyed by all other communes...

'The rights inherent to the Commune are: voting for the Communal budget, receipts and expenditure; fixing and assessment of taxes; control of local services; organization of local magistrates, police and schools; administration of property belonging to the Commune...

'Absolute guarantee of individual freedom' freedom of conscience, and freedom to work. Permanent intervention of citizens in Communal affairs by the free expression of their ideas. Organization of urban defence and of the National Guard, which elects its leaders and is solely responsible for the maintenance of order in the city.

'Paris asks for nothing further in the way of local guarantees, on the understanding that the large central administration delegated by the federation of communes shall adopt and put into practice these same principles.'

From the *Declaration to the French People* issued on 19 April 1871 on huge placards around Paris. Quoted in David Thomson, *France, Empire and Republic 1850-1940* (1968)

COMMUNARDS DESTROY THE VENDÔME COLUMN (16 MAY 1871). THE 155 FT HIGH MONUMENT – ERECTED BY NAPOLEON I TO COMMEMORATE HIS CELEBRATED CAMPAIGN OF 1805 – WAS DEMOLISHED AMID GREAT CEREMONY. TO THE COMMUNARDS IT REPRESENTED ALL THEY DESPISED ABOUT THE IMPERIALISM AND MILITARISM OF FRANCE'S RECENT PAST

RIOTERS SETTING FIRE TO BUILDINGS IN PARIS. LARGE SECTIONS OF THE CITY CENTRE WERE DESTROYED BY ARSON SQUADS

## 3 DESTRUCTION

After weeks of skirmishing and hostage-taking by the two sides, government troops finally broke into the city through an undefended section of wall on Sunday 21 May. In the seven days which followed - 'Bloody Week' - the Communards were hunted down and ruthlessly eliminated. The Communards murdered hostages, including the Archbishop of Paris, and set fire to whole sections of central Paris. There were atrocities on both sides but the Communards sustained heavier casualties. Government troops took few prisoners; anyone suspected of sympathy with the Commune was summarily executed. As the Versailles troops dislodged the Communards from their barricades with cannon-fire, many of the ordinary citizens greeted the soldiers as liberators. In the three weeks following the entry of government troops into Paris the authorities received almost 380,000 letters from citizens denouncing the Commune and known Communards. The last significant action in the battle for Paris occurred in the cemetery of Pére-Lachaise. Here 147 captured Communards were lined up against the wall and shot. The final death toll in the destruction of the Commune was around 20,000.

WOMEN WERE OFTEN AMONG THE MOST PASSIONATE COMMUNARDS. THE 'WOMEN'S BATTALION' FOUGHT FIERCELY ON THE BARRICADES. THIS PHOTOGRAPH SHOWS LOUISE MICHEL, THE 'RED VIRGIN' OF THE COMMUNE. SHE LED SQUADS OF WOMEN AGAINST GOVERNMENT TROOPS AND TOOK PART IN THE BURNING OF PARIS. SHE WAS TRANSPORTED FOR TEN YEARS TO A PENAL COLONY IN NOUMEA

## QUESTIONS

**1** Why would Thiers have considered it of great importance to destroy the Commune?

**2** What political system did the Communards hope to encourage in France by their example?

**3** Suggest reasons why the destruction of the Commune was so brutal.

# EXAMINING THE EVIDENCE
## The novels of Émile Zola

One of the most important commentators on life in France during the Second Empire was the novelist Émile Zola. Between 1871 and 1893 Zola published 20 novels in the so-called *Rougon-Macquart* series. This followed the fortunes of a single family in the France of Napoleon III. The extracts which follow come from three of the best-known books in the series, and each illustrates a particular aspect of France during the Second Empire. What value have such works for the historian of the period?

### Source A

[This extract describes a typical Parisian tenement; home to large numbers of working-class families during the Second Empire.]

Gervaise looked up at the front of the building. On the street side it had five doors, each one with fifteen windows in a line, the black shutters of which, with their broken slats, gave the huge wall-space a look of utter desolation. But below that there were four shops on the ground floor: to the right of the doorway a huge sleazy eating-house, to the left a coal merchant's, a draper's and an umbrella shop. The building looked all the more colossal because it stood between two low rickety houses clinging to either side of it and, foursquare, like a roughly cast block of cement, decaying and flaking away in the rain, it thrust the silhouette of its vast cube up into the pale sky above the neighbouring rooftops. Its unplastered sides, mud-coloured and as interminably bare as prison walls, showed rows of toothing-stones like decaying jaws snapping in the void. But Gervaise's attention was mainly caught by the doorway, an immense arched entrance going up to the second floor level and opening like a deep porch, at the further end of which could be seen the dim light of a large courtyard. In the middle of this porch, which was paved like the street, ran a gulley along which some pale pink water was flowing.

'Come on in,' said Coupeau, 'nobody's going to eat you.'

She wanted to wait in the street, but couldn't help going into the porch as far as the concierge's lodge on the right. At the entrance to the courtyard she raised her eyes again. On the inside it went up six storeys, with four identical walls surrounding the vast square yard. The walls were grey and eaten away with yellow leprous patches, streaked with drips from the roof, and rose straight from the ground to the slates, with never a single moulding, broken only by the drainpipes, with bends at each storey, where the gaping heads made rusty iron stains. The shutterless windows showed bare panes, greenish-grey like muddy water. Some were open, and out of them blue check mattresses were hanging out to air, and across others stretched clothes-lines with things drying – a whole family's washing – the man's shirts, the woman's bodices, the children's knickers – and there was one on the third floor with a baby's napkin caked with filth. From top to bottom the narrow living quarters were bursting and letting bits of their miserable poverty escape through every crack.

Émile Zola, *L'Assommoir* (1877)

## Source B

[This extract is a description of conditions faced by miners in a typical French coal-pit]

From the coal face to the incline was about sixty metres, and the rippers had not yet widened the tunnel, which was a mere pipe with a very uneven roof, bulging at every moment. At some points a loaded tub would only just go through, and the haulage man had to flatten himself and push kneeling down so as not to smash his head...For one journey he followed her and watched; she ran along with her behind so high and her hands so low that she seemed to be trotting on all fours, like one of those dwarf animals in a circus. She sweated and panted and her joints cracked, but she never complained, for familiarity had brought apathy, and you would have thought that being doubled up like that was part of the normal course of human suffering...Movement began again at all nine levels, and nothing could be heard but the regular calls of the boys and the snorting of the haulage girls as they reached the incline, all steaming like overloaded mares...With each journey back to the coal face, Étienne found the same stifling heat, the soft, regular taps of the picks and the painful gaspings of the miners as they obstinately pushed on with the job. All four had now stripped, and were covered with black mud up to their caps, so that they were indistinguishable from the coal.

Émile Zola, *Germinal* (1885)

## Source C

[The final extract chronicles some of the atrocities which occurred during the final days of the Paris Commune. Each of the events mentioned can be found in the historical record of the Commune.]

But on Sunday Jean was horrified. It was the last day of that hateful week ['Bloody Week']. As soon as the sun rose in glory on a clear and warm holiday morning he had the eerie sensation that this was to be the final agony. News had only just broken of renewed slaughter of hostages. The archbishop, the parish priest of the Madeleine and others had been shot on the Wednesday at La Roquette, and on Thursday the Dominicans of Arcueil had been picked off on the run like hares, on Friday more priests and forty-seven gendarmes had been shot point blank in the rue Haxo sector, and a fury of reprisals had flared up again, the troops executing *en masse* their most recent prisoners. All through that lovely Sunday the crackle of the firing-squads had never stopped in the courtyard of the Lobau barracks, which was full of death-cries, blood and smoke. At La Roquette two hundred and twenty-seven wretched creatures, rounded up more or less at random, were machine-gunned in a heap, riddled with bullets. In Père-Lachaise, [a cemetery] which had been bombarded for four days and finally captured grave by grave, one hundred and forty-eight were thrown against a wall, and the plaster dripped great red tears.

Émile Zola, *La Débâcle* (1892)

**1** What words and images does Zola use to stimulate the imagination of the reader?

**2** Would you expect a historian writing a textbook on the Second Empire to employ similar literary devices? Explain your answer.

**3** What advantages can you identify in using novels as a means of gaining a greater knowledge and understanding of a period of history?

**4** Can you identify any potential disadvantages in using novels for this purpose?

Now consider the following observations on Zola's work.

### Source D

Zola is one of the greatest novelists of Paris, in or near which he spent all his adult life. He knew the city in all her moods and aspects, her hard ugliness as well as her seductive charm...

From the introduction to the Penguin edition of *L'Assommoir* (1970)
translated by L Tancock

### Source E

Zola had never visited a coalfield, let alone gone down a mine or talked with colliers. His imagination may have been stimulated by one or two books: notably L.L. Simonin's *La vie souterraine, ou les mines et les mineurs* (1867), a non-technical but informative and readable work by a mining engineer; and possibly the odd novel, like Malot's *Sans famille*...

FWJ Hemmings, *Émile Zola* (1966)

### Source F

Étienne's age and his family tree [in the novel *Germinal*] date the action at about 1867. Zola accordingly darkens his picture of life in the mines by harrowing descriptions of the agonies of women and children used as beasts of burden, but at the same time, omitting to state that most of this has since been put right, he makes the general industrial slump governing the actions of the Directors of the Montsou Company depend upon all sorts of international factors, such as radical change in the American market which did not yet apply in 1867...The resulting composite picture of events at Montsou [the coal-mine in the novel] contains old abuses long since modified or put right and modern developments of socialism unknown in 1867. It is a grandiose epic poem of human misery and the revolt of the oppressed, but in no sense a true account of affairs as they could have existed at a given time.

From the introduction to the Penguin edition of *Germinal* (1954),
translated by L Tancock

### Source G

But Zola had...the advantage that he was there [in Paris during the Commune]. He saw it all, for he was not only present but a journalist, having returned to Paris a few days before the revolution of 18 March, after a spell reporting the doings of the Bordeaux government. He even got into trouble twice and in the atmosphere of indiscriminate killing might have lost his life. To that extent *The Débâcle* is an eye-witness account.

From the introduction to the Penguin edition of La Débâcle (1972),<br>translated by L Tancock

---

**1** In the light of the observations contained in Sources D–G, which of the three extracts from Zola's novels do you find the most reliable for use as historical evidence? Explain your answer carefully.

**2** In *Germinal,* Zola appears to manipulate time in order to present particular images to his readers. Does this reduce the value of such material as historical evidence?

**3** What are the advantages and disadvantages of *La Débâcle* being 'an eye-witness account'?

**4** Zola's observations on the Second Empire are retrospective. (Look at the dates of publication for the three novels selected here.) To what extent does this restrict their value to a historian of the period?

**5** What is your view on the place of the novel in the study of history?

---

# 7 Russia 1801–55: A Study in Autocracy

## PREVIEW

### The autocratic principle

'If there is one single factor which dominates the course of Russian history...it is the principle of autocracy.'

Hugh Seton-Watson, *The Russian Empire 1801–1917* (1967)

The Russian Tsar is the classic example of the autocrat in history. Invested in the position was the absolute authority to determine the fortunes of the State. The Tsar was not restricted by a constitution, and there was no sharing of powers. All citizens, regardless of social rank, were subject to the pronouncements of these eastern Caesars. Their powers devolved directly from God. Among the many titles possessed by the Tsar he was the 'Chosen One of the Almighty'. Such a recommendation entitled him to direct the Church as well as the State; the potential of such power was awesome. He might be benevolent, firm yet just or he could be capable of the basest tyranny, brutal and arbitrary. Autocracy was about power and on this the Tsar traditionally offered no concessions:

'No social group [in Russia] held political power, or made policy. This role was reserved to the autocracy, which used nobles as its instruments, rewarding them materially but not compromising on matters of power.'

Hugh Seton-Watson, as above.

### Types of government

Consider the three diagrams opposite. The first represents the autocratic form of government; the second, oligarchic; the third, democratic. Through discussion, describe how a state would be governed under each of these three systems. Try to comment on:

(a) the extent to which there is fair representation for those who are governed;

(b) whether powers of government are held collectively or individually.

In what ways, if any, might these forms of government be subject to abuse?

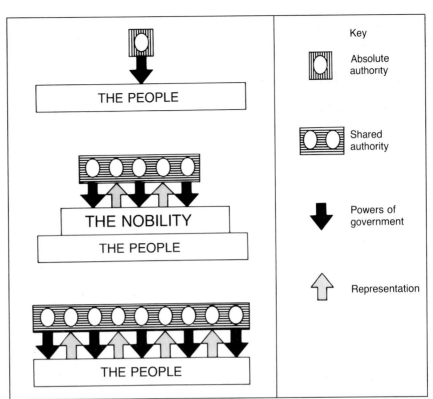

**Key**

| | |
|---|---|
|  Absolute authority | |
| Shared authority | |
| Powers of government | |
| Representation | |

## Russia's autocrats (1801–55)

Russia was steered through the first half of the Nineteenth Century by two tsars; Alexander I (1801–25) and Nicholas I (1825–55). By coincidence, both were initially reluctant to assume their titles, offered as they were in bizarre circumstances. However, once installed they observed the autocratic tradition and governed with considerable tenacity. There were reforms: projected, adopted and rejected. There was economic progress and the development of an intelligentsia. But there was also reaction, repression and brutality. The period was punctuated by peasant revolts, and in 1825 a noble-led uprising so serious it has become known as 'The First Russian Revolution'.

Both men have been subject to simplified historical assessments: Alexander was at first a liberal who passed in later life to reaction; Nicholas had no saving graces, being 'merely repressive'. Such simplification, of course, serves only to blur the image of these men. In the sharp focus offered by close historical scrutiny, they become infinitely more complex in character and policy.

## Alexander I

Tsar Alexander ascended the throne of Russia in circumstances which would haunt him for the rest of his life. On the evening of 23 March 1801 his father, the Tsar Paul, was surrounded in his palace by young army officers and high-ranking officials including his closest adviser,

TSAR ALEXANDER I

TSAR NICHOLAS I

Count Pahlen. The group demanded the Tsar's abdication: after five years of uncompromising tyranny Paul could be tolerated no longer. With considerable courage the Tsar refused the demands of his captors whereupon he was struck on the head with a heavy gold snuffbox and fell senseless to the floor. Defenceless, he was beaten, kicked and strangled. He died within minutes but the attack continued, his corpse being mutilated almost beyond recognition. To his everlasting regret, Alexander had agreed to the conspiracy and to his own succession, somehow convincing himself that his father would simply be deposed, not murdered. At 9am the following morning, as court officials assembled at the Winter Palace to swear an oath of loyalty to the new Tsar, Alexander nursed his grief in a private room and confessed to his wife:

'I cannot fulfil the duties that are imposed on me; how shall I have the strength to rule with the constant remembrance that my father has been assassinated? I cannot, I resign my power to whoever will wish it.'

Quoted in Allen McConnell, *Tsar Alexander I* (1970)

In spite of his reservations Alexander did assume the Russian Crown and was to rule as Tsar until his death in 1825.

During his formative years Alexander had been subjected to a seemingly incompatible mixture of liberal and military influences. From his grandmother, the enlightened Empress Catherine the Great, he received an education in contemporary politics and thought. At her knee, Alexander was taught to recite not nursery rhymes but the paragraphs of the first French constitution. It was she who provided him with the Swiss tutor La Harpe, a republican sympathetic to the ideals of the French Revolution. La Harpe taught Alexander that governments which failed to observe the rule of law, resorting instead to arbitrary despotism, were apt to be justifiably removed by their citizens. For ten years Catherine and La Harpe moulded Alexander's view of the world, a process which he grew steadily to resent.

CATHERINE THE GREAT

But Catherine was not the only influence in the life of the young Prince. Equally significant was his father Paul, in whose murder he was to connive in 1801. Paul offered a complete contrast to Catherine's world of court elegance and philanthropic discussion. His was the world of the parade-ground and the barrack room. At Gatchina near St Petersburg, where he commanded several battalions, Paul introduced Alexander to the concepts of discipline and obedience. Allowed to drill and inspect troops, Alexander came increasingly to enjoy the power of command and the spectacle of uniformed order. As a young man he found it difficult to reconcile the opposing forces which fought to shape his outlook and ideals.

# Examining the Evidence

**Alexander I** Historians have placed considerable emphasis on the apparent contradictions which characterize the reign of this enigmatic tsar. Consider the following assessments of Alexander.

LA HARPE, ALEXANDER'S SWISS TUTOR

### Source A
Napoleon called Alexander 'the Northern Sphinx' and 'a real Byzantine', and it is true that Alexander was easy to misunderstand. But his apparent

inconsistency was perhaps due to a conflict of two consistencies, his fear of disorder and his wish for improvement (a conflict which plagued his successors too). In retrospect, it seems that his ideas and his thoughts led their own lives independently of what Alexander happened to say at any particular time. Superficially, he seemed at different times to be an ardent liberal or a reactionary militarist. In conversation he was usually charming and agreeable. To some he seemed a complete diplomat, and to others a complete hypocrite.

JN Westwood, *Endurance and Endeavour* (1973)

### Source B

The new ruler [Alexander] had been both a pupil of La Harpe and a product of Gatchina. The contradictions in his make up are multiplied endlessly – humility mixing with pompousness, studiousness with frivolity, candour with secretiveness, companionability with withdrawal, determination with vacillation, kindness with harshness, humanitarianism with militarism, and liberalism with conservatism. His suite nicknamed him Alexander the Charmer, for the emperor did have an extraordinary ability to approach people, to say what his listeners wished to hear, and to cajole people into doing what he wanted. A 'consummate actor' is another description of the man who had received unusual training as grand duke in the arts of dissimulation and self-control.

John Bergamini, *The Tragic Dynasty* (1970)

### Source C

Contemporary accounts agree that he [Alexander] had great charm. His manner was friendly and modest, even ostentatiously so, to the point of deliberately scorning pomp and ceremony. But on the parade ground he showed himself a worthy pupil of Gatchina. He all too readily expressed agreement with those with whom he talked, but when it came to translating his words into action, delays and obstacles soon appeared, chief among these his own caution. The need to be all things to all men, and in particular to make a good impression on both his grandmother and his father, had developed in him at an early age great ability as an actor. Those who knew him best insisted on his extreme distrustfulness. It was not so much that he was insincere, or that he changed his opinions...It was rather than he formed his opinions slowly and secretly, trusting no one...In his political outlook, liberalism and autocracy...existed side by side. His reforming zeal was genuine, but abstract. It existed in him at a different level from practical political action. Sometimes the two levels intersected, but often they did not.

Hugh Seton-Watson, *The Russian Empire 1801–1917* (1967)

---

**1** Contemporaries and later commentators have been responsible for the variety of titles by which Alexander I has become known. In the sources above he is referred to as 'the Northern Sphinx' and 'the Charmer'. Having considered these assessments, how appropriate do these titles appear to you? What do they suggest about Alexander as a man?

**2** Using the assessments by the three historians above, identify the apparent inconsistencies in Alexander's character and behaviour. How is it possible to account for these contradictions?

### TALKING POINT

**What's in a name?**

Throughout history significant individuals have become identified with a particular description: Charles the Good; Ivan the Terrible; William the Silent; Peter the Great.

Consider how such titles become attached to people in history. (You could try this by selecting three or four prominent individuals in contemporary world politics and in turn suggesting appropriate names for them.) Are such names of any real use to the historian? In what ways might they be misleading to a historian?

**3** According to these assessments, why would it be unwise for the historian to place too much emphasis on the reported words of Alexander I?

**4** In some simplified accounts, Alexander I has been presented as a liberal who later in life developed into a reactionary. Given the information contained in these assessments, how is it possible to challenge such a view?

**5** You should now be in a position to present your own assessment of Alexander's character and style as Tsar. In writing your evaluation remember that he was a complex individual who was shaped by contradictory influences; it would be wise to avoid presenting him simply as a two-dimensional character.

---

## The liberal honeymoon

The death of Paul brought mass relief to the Russian people. Released from their nightmare they looked to Alexander to restore the paternalism characteristic of those tsars whom they had most admired and respected in the past. Initially the signs were hopeful. Alexander's liberal reputation preceded him and in his coronation manifesto he declared his intention to rule 'in accord with the laws and heart of the Great Catherine'. Within days the worst excesses of Paul's reign began to be undone (see diagram below).

In addition to these concessions, Alexander introduced a number of more significant measures. Three weeks after becoming Tsar he formally acknowledged the Charter of the Nobility. This important document, which gave official recognition to the rights and privileges of the Russian nobility, had been introduced by Catherine the Great in 1785. Tsar Paul had ignored it but its restoration meant that the nobility were once again allowed to travel abroad and to enjoy exemptions from corporal punishment and the poll tax. They were once more entitled to trial by their peers, to elect officials and to establish provincial assemblies. Another major move was abolition of the Secret Expedition (secret police) whose

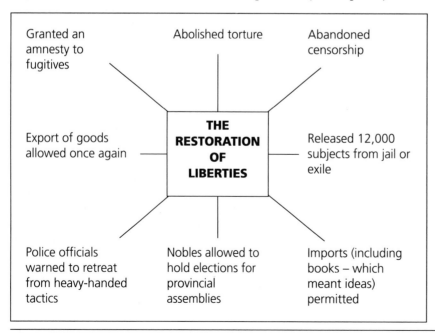

Granted an amnesty to fugitives

Abolished torture

Abandoned censorship

Export of goods allowed once again

**THE RESTORATION OF LIBERTIES**

Released 12,000 subjects from jail or exile

Police officials warned to retreat from heavy-handed tactics

Nobles allowed to hold elections for provincial assemblies

Imports (including books – which meant ideas) permitted

Created in 1711 by
Peter the Great. Initially
a council of ten high-
ranking officials, it
became the chief
authority for the
drafting and
interpretation of laws.

In what ways do you think
Alexander's liberal
reputation was enhanced
by the measures and
proposals of his first three
months in power?

sinister activities had brought fear to many Russian citizens. In accordance with his belief that good laws must lead the State, Alexander established on 5 June 1801 a law commission with instructions to prepare a new legal code. He also convened a Permanent Council, similar in membership and purpose to the council created by Catherine the Great. Its function was to advise the Tsar in matters of government business. Finally, Alexander declared his intention to restore the position of the Senate to its former prominence in Russian affairs.

At this point it is worth asking the question: to what extent were the Tsar's early concessions and proposals the product of genuine liberal sentiment? A number of Alexander's contemporaries believed that he was being directed by the conspirators who had plotted the assassination of Paul. Alexander believed this too and was especially fearful of Count Pahlen, still a very powerful figure in court circles. There were suggestions that Pahlen and Count Zubov, another of the plotters, had plans to limit the authority of the Tsar by forcing a constitution on him. Zubov is even credited with a proposal to give legislative powers (strictly reserved for the Tsar) to the Senate. Had these projects been adopted the character of the Russian autocracy would have been quite fundamentally changed. Faced with such a challenge, Alexander acted swiftly and decisively. On 29 June 1801, Count Pahlen was summoned to the Winter Palace. He was served with an Imperial order to retire at once to his estate in Courland and to consider himself relieved of all responsibilities.

Alexander never again allowed potential challengers of his authority to get so close. This determination to ensure that his authority remained undiluted indicates a consistency of purpose with which he is rarely credited. Alexander's performance in the months following Pahlen's fall offers some confirmation of the view that his liberal intentions for the practical reform of Russia were extremely limited. True, he did not go back on minor items such as the release of political prisoners, but he *did* begin to distance himself from the creations of the early months of 1801. He ignored the Permanent Council for example, and gave no encouragement to the law commission. His neglect of this body was so disappointing to Alexander Radishchev – the only competent individual on the commission – that he killed himself in 1802, convinced that Alexander was assuming the characteristics of a despot.

### The tentative reformer

After Alexander had freed himself from Pahlen he came to rely for advice on a close circle of friends, commonly referred to as the 'unofficial committee'.

Alexander met regularly with the committee, usually after coffee, in his private chambers at the Imperial palace. Here they earnestly discussed matters of general policy and specific schemes for reform. Conservative commentators who knew of the committee attacked the group as Jacobins. In fact, the Tsar and his young confidants were far more restrained than this label suggests. While they certainly discussed, for example, the idea of a constitution for Russia, its introduction was in no sense imminent. All were agreed that the existing machinery of government must first be streamlined before the ambition of a constitutional regime could be realized.

The practical changes which were made to the administration

## Adam Czartoryski

A member of Poland's most prominent aristocratic family. Time spent in England and France left him with liberal sympathies.

## Victor Kochubey

Former Russian ambassador at Constantinople and adviser to Alexander during his youth.

**THE UNOFFICIAL COMMITTEE**

## Paul Stroganov

Son of an influential magnate and landowner. Spent time in France during the early years of the Revolution. A pupil of the French Jacobin, Romme.

## NN Novosiltsov

A respected friend of the Stroganov family. Gifted administrator and reputedly of liberal persuasion.

demonstrate Alexander's reluctance to modify the autocratic tradition in favour of oligarchy. His reform of the Senate, for instance, fell far short of the relatively moderate proposals made by senators such as Derzhavin. The election of senators, the right to propose taxes and to put up candidates for certain government positions, were dismissed by Alexander. The decree on the Senate which appeared in September 1802 was clearly limited. The Senate remained the highest court of justice under the Tsar and was given authority to draw his attention to conflicts between new and existing laws. In practice this function was soon rendered invalid. In December Count Severin Potocki attempted to obtain an Imperial review of a new law originating from the Minister of War. After a frosty meeting between Tsar and senators a new decree was issued which stated that the right of remonstrance would no longer apply to new laws. Those who had hoped that a reformed Senate might spearhead the movement towards oligarchy were soon disappointed; the Senate under Alexander remained a purely judicial body with no executive powers.

A further administrative project which revealed Alexander's refusal to depart from the autocratic tradition was the creation of the Ministries. Eight new Ministries were created, each under the direction of a minister nominated by and directly responsible to the Tsar.

The new system certainly made the administration more efficient but even Alexander's close circle of friends was concerned about the implications of the reforms. The decree of 8 September 1801 which established the Ministries included the provision for them to be monitored by the Senate. In practice, ministers bypassed the Senate and directed any reports of their actions to the Tsar. Neither did they perform as a cabinet; Alexander did not wish for his decisions to be challenged by the collective voices of his ministers, and they remained strictly independent of each other and responsible

**The Ministries**

Foreign affairs

Finance

Education

Commerce

War

Navy

Interior

Justice

only to him. The practical effect of the ministerial system was to organize the authority of the Tsar in a much more effective manner. Far from limiting the powers of the autocracy, the reform achieved quite the reverse as Alexander, writing to La Harpe in November 1802, was quick to point out:

'...the Ministry is formed and has functioned well for more than a month. Affairs have, as a result, acquired more clarity, are more orderly, and I know immediately whom to call for when something does not run the way it should.'

Quoted in AG Mazour, *The First Russian Revolution* (1937)

Alexander's constitutional reforms largely confirm the judgement of the historian A McConnell that 'his liberalism was in the main sentimental' (from *Tsar Alexander I: Paternalistic Reformer* (1970)). Thus, while the Tsar spoke of the 'rights of humanity' in his coronation address, in practice his actions were those of a despot. He refused, for example, to abandon the internal passport system which restricted the movement of his people; and he would not replace military governors with civilians in order to reduce the pervasive influence of the armed forces in local government. Above all, he refused to approve a proposed 'Charter for the Russian People'. This liberal document, assembled by the 'unofficial committee', defined the purpose of monarchical rule as being always to consider the wider interests of the nation. It also propounded certain basic rights (including freedom of speech and freedom to own property) and suggested certain legal safeguards: the right to trial by one's peers; the limiting of detention in custody to three days; and the principle that the accused must be considered innocent until proven guilty. Some alterations to the political system were also proposed such as allowing the Senate to ratify laws and to levy taxes. The Charter offered no real threat to the Tsar and, if adopted, could have provided the basis for a more open society and prevented the abuse of police powers. However, Alexander remained uncommitted to the proposals and they were consigned to the archives, his autocratic instincts once more outweighing liberal rhetoric.

---

Study the points below which list some of the features of Alexander's reign in the immediate period following Pahlen's dismissal.

- Treatment of the law commission
- Treatment of the Permanent Council
- The reform of the Senate and its role in Russian government
- Refusal to grant the Charter for the Russian People
- The function of the Ministries in the administration

In each case show how Alexander appeared to be moving away from his earlier liberal stance and more towards the undisputed authority of the traditional Russian autocrat.

Suggest reasons why the Tsar was prepared to revive the Charter of the Nobility but refused to allow a similar statement of rights for the ordinary Russian citizen.

---

## Two reform issues: serfdom and education

During the informal discussion of the 'unofficial committee' two issues consistently arose: the need to create an educated class capable of filling positions of responsibility in the administration and other areas requiring trained personnel; and the unanimous condemnation of serfdom, the foundation upon which the whole of Russian society was based. In the period 1801–08, a number of measures were taken by Alexander and his ministers to reform these features. (See diagram below. An assessment of the reforms appears opposite.)

| Reform of Serfdom | Reform of Education |
|---|---|
| *1801:* the advertising of serfs for sale made illegal | Financial commitment to education substantially increased: by 1804, 740 million roubles (four times the allocation under Catherine the Great) was appropriated for educational purposes. |
| *1802:* landowners forbidden to exile serfs to hard labour as punishment | During Alexander's reign the number of universities was increased from three to six. |
| *1803: The Free Cultivators Law* allowed the emancipation of serfs if mutually agreed by serf and master | The Tsar ordered education to be open to all classes. Forty-seven new 'gymnasiums' (secondary schools) were opened. |
| *1808:* The sale of serfs in open markets was prohibited. The Tsar made and adhered to an undertaking not to grant away any more State peasants into serfdom | The University Statute of 1804 gave universities self-rule through faculty councils, and so made them independent of the nobility. |

### Alexander's 'lost opportunity': the schemes of Mikhail Speransky

In the years after 1805 Alexander became increasingly preoccupied with foreign policy, in particular the war against Napoleon. It was not until 1807, when he arranged peace-terms with his adversary at Tilsit, that the Tsar turned his attention once again to internal issues. In the intervening time some developments had occurred which altered the tone of Russian government.

The most notable of these was the voluntary disbanding of the 'unofficial committee' after 1803. In its place, though never as influential, emerged the Committee of Ministers. During the Tsar's absence with his armies in Europe after 1805, it was this Committee which effectively conducted the government of Russia. Also in 1805 the Tsar gave instructions for the secret police to be restored. Once again the close surveillance of potentially subversive individuals and societies became a feature of the Russian autocracy.

Having concluded the Peace of Tilsit with Napoleon in 1807, Alexander returned to domestic policy. By the time Napoleon's armies crossed the River Niemen on 24 June 1812 to begin the invasion of Russia, the Empire had witnessed the rise and fall of one of the most

| **Assessment of Reform of Serfdom** | **Assessment of Reform of Education** |
|---|---|
| Alexander disliked serfdom but was reluctant to challenge the institution with any real commitment for fear of rousing the antipathy of the landowning nobility. The measures he *did* introduce were merely cosmetic, easily circumvented by the serf-owners. Landlords wishing to sell serfs had little trouble in making the fact known, and if exile was a prohibited punishment there was never any shortage of alternatives which they could legally enforce. The most ambitious reform, *The Free Cultivators Law,* placed too much emphasis on the goodwill of the landowners – a rare commodity in such individuals. As a result, by 1825 only about 37,000 male serfs were freed under the terms of this law; there were 10 million male serfs in Russia! No attempt was made to address the real solution to the serf problem: emancipation. For Alexander, always aware of the fate of his father, the hostility of the nobility was a real concern. He may also have been persuaded by those who predicted economic chaos or a mass peasant uprising in the event of the serfs being freed; he certainly paid attention to the advice of his old tutor, La Harpe, who recommended a highly cautious approach to the peasant problem. Whatever the motive for his reluctance, Alexander's measures had little impact on the miserable existence of most Russian serfs. | The reform of education was undoubtedly one of Alexander's more substantial achievements. However, there were real practical problems in making the reforms work. There were, for example, shortages of Russian textbooks and competent Russian teachers. Funding was inadequate to provide well-equipped reference libraries and laboratories. Attitudes too were difficult to change: the gentry objected to schools being opened up to all social classes, and children from the higher ranks were contemptuous of those from more humble origins. The principle of self-government for the universities became increasingly unworkable. In the later part of his reign education was badly abused by the Tsar and his ministers; at least in these early years the prospect of developing an educated class seemed refreshingly hopeful. |

gifted reformers ever to serve her: Count Mikhail Speransky. Speransky's reform proposals touched at the heart of many of Russia's principal problems: finance, the legal system, privilege and, above all, the government of the nation. His programme of constitutional reform, announced in 1809, had the potential to mark a turning point in the history of the Russian autocracy. In the words of one historian:

'It would have averted the despair which in December, 1825, turned hundreds of the flower of the empire's young (Decembrists) into hopeless rebellion against autocracy and serfdom; it might also have averted 1881 [assassination of Tsar Alexander II], 1905 [revolution], and 1917 [collapse of Tsarist system] and achieved the emancipation [of the serfs] of 1861 much earlier.'

Allen McConnell, *Tsar Alexander I* (1970)

**Count Mikhail Speransky (1772–1839)**

Born the son of a village priest. Educated at Suzdal and St Petersburg. An exceptionally talented student, he became a teacher of mathematics in his own college at just 18 years of age. Progressed to minor administrative posts during the reign of Tsar Paul.

Under Alexander he served on the Permanent Council before being transferred at the request of Kochubey to the Ministry of the Interior in 1802.

In 1806 he came to the Tsar's attention and subsequently accompanied him to Erfurt in 1808 for his meeting with Napoleon. Became Alexander's State Secretary (the principal adviser in the land), a position which he held until his dismissal and exile in 1812.

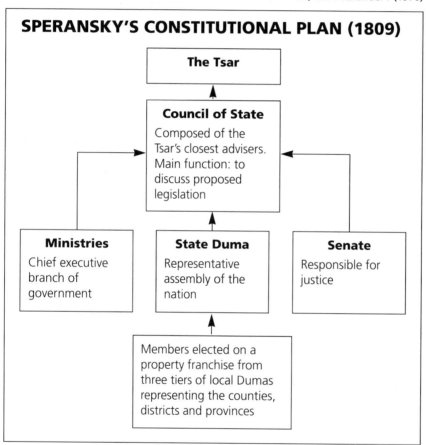

**SPERANSKY'S CONSTITUTIONAL PLAN (1809)**

**The Tsar**

**Council of State**
Composed of the Tsar's closest advisers. Main function: to discuss proposed legislation

**Ministries**
Chief executive branch of government

**State Duma**
Representative assembly of the nation

**Senate**
Responsible for justice

Members elected on a property franchise from three tiers of local Dumas representing the counties, districts and provinces

A hesitant Alexander chose to ignore Speransky's plan and later to have him exiled; his successors were to be regularly and often violently reminded of this squandered opportunity.

Speransky's proposals were dramatic for the time but *did* have their limitations as the chart opposite demonstrates.

In spite of these reservations the system devised by Speransky would have begun to involve many thousands of Russian citizens in the basic functions of government. Their active participation in helping to direct

| Positive aspects of Speransky's constitutional plan | Negative aspects of Speransky's constitutional plan |
|---|---|
| State Duma convened annually by right – not at invitation of Tsar | Tsar could dissolve State Duma at will |
| All legislation had to come before State Duma before passing into law | Duma given no legislative power – simply received reports from ministers |
| A law rejected by majority in the State Duma would be invalid | Lower Dumas met only once every three years |
| State Duma could raise matters of State importance with the Council of State | State Duma had no say in the appointment of ministers |

the development of Russia might have been sufficient to defuse the growing resentment felt by influential sections of society.

Alexander proceeded with only one part of Speransky's constitutional project by instituting the Council of State in 1810. Deprived of the other features of the plan, the Council was able to function but never as Speransky had intended; it certainly failed to modify the monarchy in any meaningful way. Speransky came increasingly to make enemies, especially from amongst the nobility. This powerful class resented the taxes which he had devised for them to help pay for the high costs of defence, and they objected to his insistence on promotion by merit through the ranks of the Civil Service. A campaign to present Speransky as unpatriotic developed. His criticism of Russian law and his preference for the Napoleonic Code resulted in him being labelled a French sympathizer; this at a time when Russia faced an imminent threat from Napoleon's armies. His reform proposals brought the charge of Jacobin and the Tsar came under growing pressure to dismiss him. With war against France almost certain Alexander needed to be able to count on a united Russia. It seems likely, then, that Speransky was dismissed in March 1812 to appease the offended nobility and to ensure their support in the forthcoming clash with Napoleon.

### The last decade (1815–25)

Alexander's military victories against Napoleon brought glory to Russia and earned her an elevated place among the ranks of the Great Powers. However, such international status had little positive effect on the internal condition of the Empire. Russia remained in need of effective reforms to liberalize the administration, to relieve the burden of serfdom, and to end the disillusionment which many Russians felt after 14 years under Alexander. Yet following his return to St Petersburg, the Tsar turned increasingly to religious extremism and gradually withdrew from progressive intellectual discussion.

The period 1815–25 has subsequently been presented as one of extreme reaction with Alexander abandoning the liberal hopes and projects of his earlier years. In fact, just as the years 1801–12 did not witness an uninterrupted flow of liberal reforms, so this last decade was not exclusively devoted to reaction and repression.

**Constitutionalism** It would be quite wrong to identify 1815 as the year in which Alexander's interest in constitutionalism expired. On numerous occasions thereafter he promoted its virtues and even established the concept in practice (see map).

In 1819 Novosiltsov was commanded to draw up a constitutional project for application in Russia itself. The draft, which went further than Speransky's earlier scheme, was approved by Alexander but never adopted

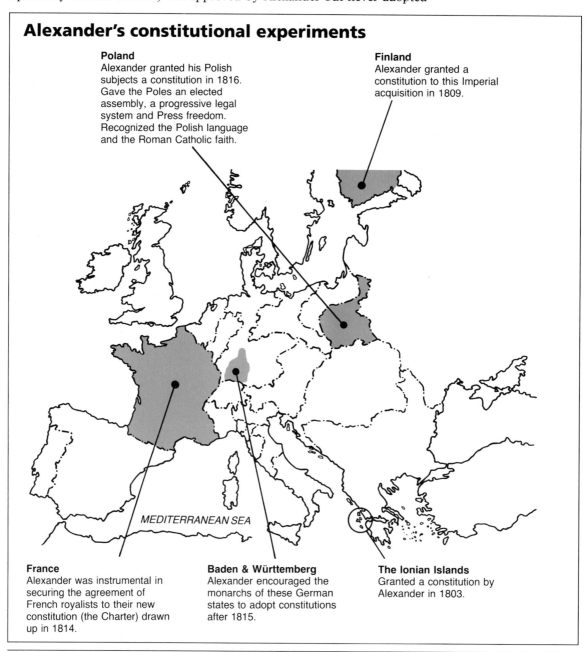

## Alexander's constitutional experiments

**Poland**
Alexander granted his Polish subjects a constitution in 1816. Gave the Poles an elected assembly, a progressive legal system and Press freedom. Recognized the Polish language and the Roman Catholic faith.

**Finland**
Alexander granted a constitution to this Imperial acquisition in 1809.

MEDITERRANEAN SEA

**France**
Alexander was instrumental in securing the agreement of French royalists to their new constitution (the Charter) drawn up in 1814.

**Baden & Württemberg**
Alexander encouraged the monarchs of these German states to adopt constitutions after 1815.

**The Ionian Islands**
Granted a constitution by Alexander in 1803.

in practice. The Russian people, particularly those of the educated class and army officers who had knowledge of Western ideas, became more and more irritated at Alexander's refusal to allow them the same rights as his non-Russian subjects.

**Serfdom** Russia's greatest social issue continued to occupy the Tsar's thoughts after his return from Europe. However, just as with his constitutional experiments, achievements in this area were restricted to the more distant outposts of the Empire. Between 1816 and 1819 three regions – Estonia, Courland and Livonia – with Alexander's blessing proceeded to free their serfs, albeit without land.

In Russia itself, however, plans for emancipation progressed rapidly from the drawing-board to the archive shelf. The most notable of these was commissioned by Alexander in 1818. Its author, Count Arakcheyev, proposed to establish an annual purchasing fund of five million roubles to buy up private serfs, along with portions of land, from the landowners. The scheme would have resulted in the gradual emancipation of Russia's serfs and might well have avoided the Decembrist Revolt of 1825. In the event, revolution in Spain, Naples and Portugal in 1820 caused Alexander to retreat from his plans for a constitution and emancipation, and to adopt a more reactionary posture against the liberals.

## The military colonies

The most ambitious reform of Alexander's last decade, and the one which has come to symbolize the reaction of his later years, was the creation of the military colonies. With these institutions Alexander sought to combine the military duties of the army with the daily routine of the peasant, and to create self-sufficient, armed communities ready to do military service for Russia at a moment's notice. (See *Focus* section 7.1.)

# FOCUS

## 7.1 The autocratic extreme: Arakcheyev and the military colonies

### In Command: Count Arakcheyev

The man whom Alexander appointed to direct the military colonies could scarcely have been more provocative. Count Alexis Arakcheyev assumed his new position with a reputation as a brutal perfectionist. Under Tsar Paul he had developed into a brilliant artillery officer. He was able, loyal and scrupulously honest. However, he was also known as a rigid disciplinarian and was at times uncontrollably violent; in a fit of rage he once bit off a soldier's ear on the parade ground! His unstable nature produced a somewhat twisted sentimentality; his fondness for the song of the nightingale, for example, caused him to order the public hanging of all cats on his estates.

In 1796 Arakcheyev acquired an estate at Gruznio as an Imperial gift from Tsar Paul. Within a short time he had transformed the 35 square kilometres of unproductive marshland into a well-cultivated estate with paved streets and brick-built dwellings. The lives of the people bequeathed with the property also underwent dramatic change. Strict discipline was enforced and the peasants were forced to submit to their master's obsession with cleanliness by keeping their model-homes spotless. The drinking of alcohol was forbidden except for an official ration provided on feast days; the keeping of pigs was prohibited on lands adjoining the main roads of the estate in case passing travellers should be offended by their dirty appearance. Even more extreme was his insistence on the regular breeding of his subjects. His instructions to the women of Gruznio were clear and chillingly insensitive: 'Every woman on my estate must give birth every year, preferably a son to a daughter. If someone gives birth to a daughter I exact a fine; if a dead child is born, or a miscarriage, a fine also;

and if there is a year that a woman does not deliver a child, then she is to present ten *arshin* [*arshin* = about 28 inches in length] of linen.' (Quoted in AG Mazour, *The First Russian Revolution* (1937)). With such practices being adopted throughout the military colonies it is perhaps not surprising that they became enormously unpopular.

### Inspiration for the colonies

The principal advocate of the military colonies was not, as might be supposed, Arakcheyev, but the Tsar himself. In one categoric statement on the issue he announced, 'There will be military colonies whatever the cost, even if one has to line the road from St Petersburg to Chudovo with corpses.' A combination of factors inspired his decision to promote the colonies. In 1810 Alexander visited Arakcheyev's estates at Gruznio and was deeply impressed by what he saw. 'It really is a charming place. But what is unique is the order prevailing here. The arrangement of the villages has aroused my admiration above all...the cleanliness, the construction of the roads and plantations, the symmetry and elegance which we saw on all sides. The streets of the villages have precisely that kind of cleanliness which I have been trying so hard to see established in the towns...How I wish the streets of Novgorod, Valdai, Vishny Volochek, Torzhok and Krestzy were kept in the same way! What a difference! I repeat, the villages here are proof that it is possible.'
(Quoted in *History Today* [September 1969])

The idea of establishing a nationwide network of self-sufficient settlements in direct imitation of Gruznio became an absorbing ambition of the Tsar. His resolve was no doubt strengthened by his knowledge of the massive costs being incurred to maintain the army of Russia. More than half the entire national budget was devoted annually to this purpose and Alexander desperately needed a way to reduce this crippling military expenditure. Installing the army on the land and making its soldiers provide for themselves seemed the ideal solution.

## The regime: organization and daily life in the colonies.

In November 1810, Arakcheyev was ordered by the Tsar to establish a military colony in the Mogilev district. This pilot operated as follows:

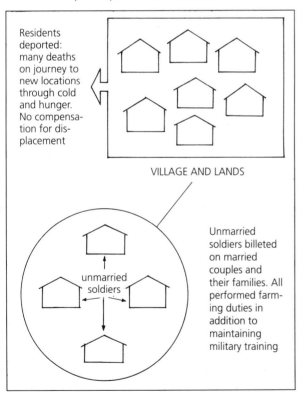

Residents deported: many deaths on journey to new locations through cold and hunger. No compensation for displacement

VILLAGE AND LANDS

Unmarried soldiers billeted on married couples and their families. All performed farming duties in addition to maintaining military training

unmarried soldiers

Napoleon's invasion of Russia in 1812 caused a temporary shelving of the plan to build a network of colonies. When the idea was revived in 1816 there was an important modification to the original scheme. The following diagram identifies some of the principal features of the military colonies as they operated between 1816 and 1831.

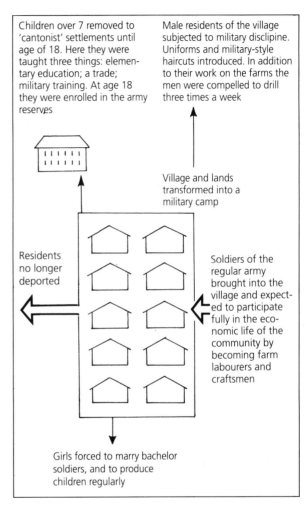

Children over 7 removed to 'cantonist' settlements until age of 18. Here they were taught three things: elementary education; a trade; military training. At age 18 they were enrolled in the army reserves

Male residents of the village subjected to military discipline. Uniforms and military-style haircuts introduced. In addition to their work on the farms the men were compelled to drill three times a week

Village and lands transformed into a military camp

Residents no longer deported

Soldiers of the regular army brought into the village and expected to participate fully in the economic life of the community by becoming farm labourers and craftsmen

Girls forced to marry bachelor soldiers, and to produce children regularly

## Response 1: appeals

The new system was badly received by most ordinary Russians. In the autumn of 1817, the Grand Duke Nicholas was intercepted by a group of peasants as he journeyed near the Novgorod colony; their plaintive appeal to him indicates the strength of popular feeling against the new settlements. 'Increase our taxes, conscript for military service a son from every house, take from us everything and send us into the Steppes; we should more gladly consent to this. We have arms, we will work and be happy there; but do not take our effects, the customs of our fathers, and do not turn us all into soldiers.'
(Quoted in AG Mazour, *The First Russian Revolution* [1937])

# 7.1 The autocratic extreme: Arakcheyev and the military colonies *continued*

## Response 2: violence

Petitions and appeals were frequent but moderate manifestations of public opposition to the colonies. More serious were outbreaks of violence, especially evident in the period 1817-19. The most serious disturbances occurred in 1819 at Chuguev. Around 9000 peasants rose in protest against the colonies. It required a detachment of troops under the personal command of Arakcheyev to suppress the revolt.

In the aftermath of the rising 313 people were sentenced to corporal punishment including 40 individuals who were forced to run a gauntlet of 1000 men, 20 times. This involved being stripped to the waist, secured to two rifles and dragged through the rows of soldiers who each administered a blow with a birch whip. In the Chuguev punishment, 25 people subsequently died of this ordeal. The severity of Arakcheyev's response to the peasants' grievances did nothing to enhance his own popularity or that of the colonies themselves.

## The Balance Sheet

### Positive achievements

1 The military colonies supported one-third of the peacetime army.

2 The colonies made a profit: by 1826 they had accumulated 30 million roubles.

3 New, stone-built dwellings were often provided for the inhabitants of the colonies.

4 Churches, schools and hospitals were features of the best colonies.

5 The villages were paved, clean and well ordered.

6 Some military colonies developed modern, efficient farming techniques and the yield of cereals increased.

7 The general standard of living for colonists was better than that of the ordinary serf or peasant.

### Negative features

1 The death-rate exceeded the birth-rate in the colonies.

2 Peasants resented the harsh military discipline and the lack of leisure.

3 Soldiers found it difficult to become farmers.

4 The commanders of the colonies were often brutal and unimaginative; a posting to one of the colonies was very unpopular amongst the army high command.

5 Few colonies ever became truly self-sufficient; most had to be subsidized by the government.

6 Peasant wages were well below the accepted level outside the colonies; 10 kopeks per day within the colonies, 50-100 kopeks per day without.

7 The colonies became one of the principal focal points of complaint for the Decembrists who inspired a major revolt in 1825.

A TYPICAL VILLAGE IN NORTHERN RUSSIA

# QUESTIONS

**1** What were Alexander's principal motives for introducing the military colonies?

**2** Why did Alexander select Arakcheyev, a known reactionary, to command the military colonies?

**3** Arakcheyev was enormously unpopular among the Russian peasantry; in 1825 his serfs slit the throat of his beloved mistress, Anastasia Milkina. What aspects of his character and methods made him such a despised figure?

**4** Historians refer to the last decade of Alexander's reign, when the forces of reaction became more prominent, as the 'Age of Arakcheyev'. Why do you suppose this term has come to be used?

**5** Compare the illustration of the typical Russian village (above) with the description of Arakcheyev's `model'

community at Gruznio. What specific improvements appear to have been made?

**6** Why, in spite of the physical and environmental improvements, did the inhabitants of the colonies so resent their situation?

**7** In what ways might the military colonies be regarded as a progressive experiment in improving social welfare?

**8** The military colonies were not abolished until 1857; what aspects of these institutions made them so attractive to the Russian autocrats?

**9** How consistent are the military colonies with your perception of the autocratic principle?

## The abuse of education

One of the more graphic illustrations of Alexander's retreat from progressive thought was his treatment of the schools and universities. The admirable achievements made in the field of education during the first decade of his reign began to be systematically undone after 1815. In 1817 education and religion were fused together in the new Ministry of Spiritual Affairs and Education. Headed by Prince A N Golitsyn, who was also Procurator of the Holy Synod, the new Ministry transformed public education into a vehicle for the transmission of religious fanaticism.

The universities suffered especially. There were purges of professors who had studied abroad and neither students nor teachers were any longer permitted to attend foreign schools. The curriculum was revised in favour of bible study and at the expense of practical or progressive courses. The worst of these abuses occurred at Kazan University. Here an inspector, Mikhail Magnitsky, had produced a report in 1819 condemning the neglect of religion in the curriculum and expressing grave concerns about allegedly subversive professors. He had gone on to recommend the closure and demolition of the university. Although this advice was not followed, Alexander chose a course of equal destruction by appointing Magnitsky curator of the Kazan educational district. Academic purges rapidly followed and a Director was appointed to supervise the religious and moral development of all students. Subjects which were considered dangerous – such as philosophy and political science – were stripped of their academic status and presented as inferior to the 'positive sciences' such as religion, law and mathematics. Even here the infiltration of religious ideas was evident; the triangle in geometry, for example, was presented as a symbol of the Trinity.

## Death at Taganrog

As Alexander neared the end of his life it was clear that he had failed to respond positively to the domestic needs of the Russian people. Millions of serfs continued to toil without relief to meet the unremitting demands of their feudal masters. Thousands of State peasants were subjected to the cruel impositions of the military colonies, one of the most despised institutions in Russian history. There were regressive educational changes; and the insult of the Polish constitution which, by giving rudimentary political rights to many Poles, infuriated the educated classes in Russia to whom no constitutional concessions were offered.

As the Tsar's reactionary outlook became more pronounced, so the educated élite's resolve to rid Russia of the autocratic system hardened. Alexander's reign witnessed the steady growth of organized opposition through a variety of secret societies. Three weeks after his death two of these societies were to stage the historically-significant Decembrist Revolt (see page 155). After 1822 Alexander came more and more under the influence of the religious fanatic, the Archimandrite Foty. Foty played on Alexander's fears of political conspiracy, causing him to clamp down on the secret societies and the relatively benign Masonic lodges. Increasingly, intelligence reached Alexander of impending plots against his person and there was frequent talk of abdication. However, his reign ended with a natural death on 19 November 1825 at the town of Taganrog on the Azov Sea. Persistent rumours circulated that the Tsar had faked his death and retreated to Siberia where he assumed a new identify in the shape of the hermit Fyodor Kuzmich. The legend lived on amongst the Russian people, helping to complete the impression of Alexander as an enigmatic and unpredictable Tsar.

# Nicholas I

The death of Alexander was followed by a dynastic crisis. The Grand Duke Constantine, governor general of Poland and Alexander's eldest brother, was next in line to the throne. However, he had secretly renounced his claim in 1817 leaving the succession open to the next brother, Nicholas. When news of Alexander's death reached Warsaw, Constantine declared his loyalty to Nicholas. In St Petersburg Nicholas, unsure of his position, declared his loyalty to Constantine. A period of confusion followed until it became apparent that Constantine would not return to St Petersburg. It was not until 14 December, more than three weeks after Alexander had died, that Nicholas finally agreed to have himself proclaimed Emperor.

GRAND DUKE CONSTANTINE

### The Decembrist Revolt

The undignified chaos surrounding the succession had severe political consequences in the shape of the Decembrist Revolt. The Decembrists were not in fact a single unified group, as this label of convenience suggests, but were made up of two societies: the Northern Society based in St Petersburg, and the Southern Society led by Colonel Pestel in the Ukraine. Their specific aims differed but there were broad similarities including the desire to replace the autocracy with some form of representative government, and the wish to abolish serfdom. Significantly, the Decembrists were alike in their social composition being drawn principally from the officer and noble class.

The Decembrists already possessed plans for the assassination of Alexander in a full-scale military coup which they had scheduled for May 1826. However, Alexander's natural death forced a rapid reassessment of this conspiracy and it was decided to act swiftly amidst the confusion caused by the succession. On the same day that Nicholas proclaimed himself Emperor, some 3000 mutineers assembled in the Senate Square in St Petersburg. Faced with around 9000 loyal troops, the rebels took up the chant 'Constantine and Constitution' (some apparently under the impression that Constitution was Constantine's wife!). After discussions had failed to end the protest peacefully, Nicholas calmly gave the order for the square to be cleared with cannon-fire. Within two hours the conspirators had been driven from the city and the revolt was over. The subsequent trials of the Decembrists dominated the first few months of Nicholas's reign. All five of the principal leaders were executed, 31 were exiled for life with hard labour to Siberia, 85 received the same sentence but for shorter terms.

COLONEL PAUL PESTEL

The memory of 14 December remained with Nicholas throughout his reign. The involvement of the nobility in the rising left him with an obsessive distrust of this class and the constant fear that his authority might again be challenged. Nicholas was not unaware of the injustices over which the Decembrists based their complaints but he failed to do very much about them; his reign was characterized by repression not reform. The Decembrists occupy a special place in Russian history. Their revolt represents the first expression of a new and highly articulate social group whose loyalties were not to themselves but to the wider ideal of an improved society; they constitute the beginnings of the Russian intelligentsia. This intellectual élite would be at the vanguard of all subsequent attempts to challenge the power of the autocracy including that which successfully drove out the Romanovs less than one hundred years later.

# Examining the Evidence
## Understanding the Decembrists

In the aftermath of the revolt of 14 December, many individual Decembrists were quite prepared to give frank accounts of their actions, possibly in the hope that their explanations might move the new Tsar to attempt the reforms Russia so urgently needed. In this section you can read the statements of three prominent Decembrists explaining their perceptions of the origins and motivation of the revolutionary movement.

### Source A: extract from Colonel Pestel's testimony

*Question 6:* How did the revolutionary ideas gradually develop and become implanted in men's minds...?

*Answer 6:* ...Political books are in the hands of everyone; political science is taught and political news spread everywhere. These teach all to discuss the activities and conduct of the government, to praise one thing and assail another. A survey of the events of 1812, 1813, 1814 and 1815, likewise of the preceding and following periods, will show how many thrones were toppled over, how many others were established, how many Kingdoms were destroyed and how many new ones were created; how many Sovereigns were expelled, how many returned or were invited to return and were then again driven out; how many revolutions were accomplished; how many *coups d'états* carried out – all these events familiarized the minds of men with the idea of revolutions, with their possibilities, and with the favourable occasions on which to execute them. Besides that, every century has its peculiar characteristic: ours is marked by revolutionary ideas. From one end of Europe to the other the same thing is observed...Here are the causes, I think, which gave rise to revolutionary ideas and which have implanted them in the minds of people.

Quoted in AG Mazour, *The First Russian Revolution* (1937)

### Source B: extract from a letter written by A Bestuzhev to Nicholas I

...The beginning of the reign of Emperor Alexander was marked with bright hopes for Russia's prosperity. The gentry had recuperated, the merchant class did not object to giving credit, the army served without making trouble, scholars studied what they wished, all spoke what they thought, and everyone expected better days. Unfortunately, circumstances prevented the realization of these hopes, which aged without their fulfilment. The unsuccessful, expensive war of 1807 and others disorganized our finances, though we had not yet realized it when preparing for the national war of 1812. Finally Napoleon invaded Russia and then only, for the first time, did the Russian people become aware of their power; only then awakened in all our hearts a feeling of independence, at first political and finally national. That is the beginning of free thinking in Russia. The government itself spoke such words as 'Liberty, Emancipation!' It had itself sown the idea of abuses resulting from the unlimited power of Napoleon...The war was still on when the soldiers, upon their return home, for the first time disseminated grumbling among the masses. 'We shed blood,' they would say, 'and then we are again forced to sweat under feudal obligations. We freed the Fatherland from the tyrant, and now we ourselves are tyrannized over by the ruling class.' The army, from generals to privates, upon its return, did nothing but discuss how good it is in foreign lands. A comparison with their own country naturally brought up the question, Why should it not be so in our own land?

At first, as long as they talked without being hindered, it was lost in the air, for thinking is like gunpowder, only dangerous when pressed. Many cherished the hope that the emperor would grant a constitution, as he himself had stated at the opening of the Legislative Assembly in Warsaw, and the attempt of some generals to free their serfs encouraged that sentiment. But after 1817 everything changed. Those who saw evil or who wished improvement, thanks to the mass of spies were forced to whisper about it, and this was the beginning of the secret societies. Oppression by the government of deserving officers irritated men's minds. Then the military men began to talk: 'Did we free Europe in order to be ourselves placed in chains? Did we grant a constitution to France in order that we dare not talk about it, and did we buy at the price of blood priority among nations in order that we might be humiliated at home?' The destructive policy towards schools and the persecution of education forced us in utter despair to begin considering some important measures. And since the grumbling of the people, caused by exhaustion and the abuses of national and civil administrations, threatened bloody revolution, the Societies intended to prevent a greater evil by a lesser one and began their activities at the first opportunity...

Quoted in AG Mazour, as above

## Source C: Memoirs of MA Fonvizin

During the campaigns in Germany and France our young men had become acquainted with European civilization, which impressed them all the more since they were able to compare everything they saw abroad with what they encountered at every step at home – the slavery of the vast majority of Russians, the cruel treatment of subordinates by their superiors, every kind of abuse of power, and the arbitrariness that reigned everywhere. All this roused the indignation of educated Russians and outraged their patriotic feelings. During the campaign many of them had met German officers and French liberals, members of the Prussian secret society (the Tugendbund), which had so successfully prepared the uprising in Prussia and furthered its liberation. In frank discussion with them our young men, ashamed of a Russia that was so greatly abased by autocracy, imperceptibly adopted their free manner of thinking and desire for constitutional government. Returning to Petersburg, our liberals could not remain content with the trivial regimental life and the tedious petty tasks and details of army drill which were strictly demanded of them by their superiors...Moreover, the Russians were offended by the obvious preference the emperor showed, in general, to all foreigners over his own subjects, whom he openly treated with disrespect; he granted annexed Poland constitutional rights of which he considered Russia unworthy. However nothing at the end of the war provoked as much public indignation against Alexander, not only among liberals but throughout Russia, as the compulsory establishment of the military settlements [colonies]. Of all the actions of the emperor Alexander after the change in his point of view, the establishment of the military settlements was the most despotic and hateful.

Quoted in George Vernadsky (ed.), *A Source Book for Russian History from Early Times to 1917* (Vol 2, 1972)

The individuals who participated in the Decembrist Revolt clearly did so for a variety of reasons. Historians call these reasons motives, and the study of motivation helps us to explain and understand events in the past. An examination of motivation can reveal information about the wider social, political and economic context in which the event occurred. It can suggest specific grievances arising from that context which drove individuals to act, and it can assist in explaining the success or failure of groups like the Decembrists who work together for a common purpose.

Consider the following factors which can be said to have motivated the Decembrists to revolt in 1825; in each case complete the exercise given.

## 1 Factors deriving from the political climate of the early Nineteenth Century

Colonel Pestel in Source A sets out some of the general features of political activity in the first quarter of the Nineteenth Century. Use Source A to *extend the descriptions* of features given in the left-hand column of the chart which follows. Use the right-hand column to *record your own understanding of the effect* of that feature. An example is provided for you.

| Feature of Political Activity | Effect on Decembrists |
| --- | --- |
| Reading and discussion of political ideas and news through books and at places of learning. | To stimulate a general awareness of alternative methods of government and to emphasize the deficiencies of the Russian autocracy. |
| The experience of recent events... (you should extend this description through reference to Source A) | |
| The 'spirit of the age'... (you should extend this description through reference to Source A) | |

(a) How would you describe the function of these features in motivating the Decembrists to revolt? Select from the list the description or combination of descriptions which you think best summarizes their function

- Provided the ideological pre-conditions for the revolt.

- Provided specific grievances upon which the Decembrists acted.

- Provided examples of what could be achieved through revolution.

- Provided an unfavourable comparison between Russia and other European nations.

(b) Are these features *by themselves* sufficient to explain the Decembrist outburst of 1825? Outline the deficiencies of these features in accounting for the rising.

### 2 Features deriving from the nature of the Russian autocracy

Sources B and C make numerous references to the conduct of the Russian government and the ruling élite.

(a) Select words and phrases from these Sources which illustrate the authors' feelings towards the autocratic system.

(b) What do these opinions suggest about the motives of the Decembrists in their revolt of 1825?

(c) Does dislike of a system of government necessarily lead to revolt?

(d) Can you establish a relationship between the political climate of the time (Feature 1 above) and the nature of the Russian autocracy (Feature 2)? How does this make a stronger case for suggesting that the Decembrists were motivated by their political circumstances?

### 3 Features deriving from Western contact through the Napoleonic Wars

Sources B and C point to the experience of the Napoleonic Wars as being important in the development of the Decembrist movement.

(a) What did educated Russians learn from their experience in Western Europe?

(b) What role did this knowledge play in motivating the Decembrists to revolt?

### 4 Features deriving from the specific policies of Tsar Alexander I

Sources B and C point to a number of specific measures taken by Alexander I which provoked the Decembrists.

(a) From the Sources, identify these measures. (There are at least four.)

(b) In what sense can these measures be said to have motivated the Decembrists to revolt?

(c) Unpopular policies do not always result in open revolt. Why did they appear to do so in Russia in 1825?

**Orthodoxy, Autocracy and Nationality** Nicholas I was a far less complicated individual then his brother had been. The new Tsar showed little interest in academic pursuits, preferring the simplicity of military organization and discipline. As a youth his education had been chiefly directed by a Baltic nobleman, General Matthew Lamsdorff. The General won obedience through his lavish use of the whip and succeeded in encouraging Nicholas's stubborn nature and his hostility to the unfamiliar. Nicholas as Tsar was hardworking and honest but he trusted no one and refused to delegate his authority. He insisted on attending to every item of business personally, a process which rendered the administration of Russia both slow and inefficient.

Nicholas despised the progressive ideas which circulated in Europe during his reign. Liberalism and constitutionalism were his sworn enemies and much of his administration was directed towards the containment of such poisonous notions. After the 1830 revolutions in France, Belgium and Poland, Nicholas redoubled his efforts to hold back the tide of change which appeared to be sweeping across the Continent. In this context the slogan 'Orthodoxy, Autocracy and Nationality' came to be adopted. First used in 1833 by Count Uvarov, the Minister of Education, the formula came to represent the official ideology of the regime and was its recipe for preserving the *status quo*.

**'Orthodoxy'** The Orthodox Church, with the Tsar as its supreme head, demanded faith and obedience from the Russian people. The ultimate objective was to have all citizens of the Empire living according to its rules of conduct. During Nicholas's reign dissenters were identified and persecuted in an effort to secure religious uniformity. Jews and Catholics represented particular targets.

**'Autocracy'** This was the concept of absolute authority which the Tsar possessed by virtue of divine right. Nicholas refused to compromise his God-given authority in any way and expected the total submission of the people to his will.

**'Nationality'** This concept emphasized the unique character of the Russian nation and sought to defend it against Western encroachment. At the same time it implied the conversion of non-Russian subjects to ensure uniformity of outlook and loyalty to the Crown.

When Uvarov's formula was translated into practical measures under Nicholas, Russia visibly regressed to a time when the absolute definition of autocracy was observed. All Alexander's constitutional projects were consigned to the archives, and the institutions of his reign – the Senate, the Council of Ministers and the Council of State – became redundant as Nicholas simply ignored them. The business of government was centred on the Personal Chancellery of His Imperial Majesty. This was subdivided into Sections, each responsible through its bureaucratic staff for particular functions including the allocation of personnel to civic offices, the codification of the law, and the surveillance of political enemies. In local government Nicholas copied the practice of his father, Paul, by removing the independence of the nobility and bringing them into the direct service of the State.

## The Third Section and censorship

The most notorious element of the Tsar's Personal Chancellery was the Third Section. This was the regime's infamous political police force which stood at the forefront of the crusade against free-thinkers. Under General Benkendorff and later Prince Orlov, the Third Section was charged with the task of maintaining the Empire's internal security. With a uniformed militia and a network of informers Benkendorff was able to maintain a watch on potentially subversive individuals and societies. As a result, regular surveillance was carried out on some 2000 citizens annually. In addition to its considerable powers of investigation and arrest, the Third Section was also able to act as its own court of law with the authority to place suspects on trial and to punish those found guilty.

After 1830 censorship came increasingly under the jurisdiction of the Third Section. The process was arbitrary, unfair and at times quite absurd. All writers were closely shadowed and were liable to be imprisoned, exiled or declared insane if found guilty of producing inappropriate material. The publication of items on serfdom or poverty was prohibited, and the printing of Western news was strictly controlled. Ridiculous instructions often emerged from the Censor's office: writers were not permitted to leave spaced marked by dots; medical anatomy texts were not to include details which might be considered indecent; and cookery books could not refer to 'free air' in an oven since the term sounded revolutionary!

THE RUSSIAN 'KNOUT'. THIS TYPE OF FLOGGING WAS A COMMON PUNISHMENT DURING THE REIGNS OF ALEXANDER I AND NICHOLAS I.

The influence of the Third Section pervaded all aspects of Russian life and has come to symbolize the suffocating repression practised by Nicholas throughout his reign. However, it would be wrong to judge Nicholas by the standards of our time, and the activities of the Third Section should be considered in context. The Tsar experienced a traumatic shock when faced with the Decembrist Revolt largely because of the involvement of so many of Russia's leading noble families. Although no similar rising was to occur again in Russia for many years, Nicholas could not have predicted this. As Tsar he saw his principal task as preserving his authority and protecting it from further conspiracies. It was in these circumstances that the Third Section and strict censorship measures were introduced. It is also important to appreciate that the Third Section was never able to operate as effectively as its twentieth-century counterpart. In the absence of railways, telegraphs and telephones, the police were without the communications network needed to operate in a comprehensive and systematic manner. Between 1823 and 1861, 290,000 individuals were transported to Siberia for terms of exile; but only about 5 per cent of these people had been found guilty of political crimes.

## Developments

The Tsar was no reformer; for the most part he was a committed conservative who looked to the distant past for inspiration in the conduct of Russian affairs. In spite of this his reign was not completely dominated by repression and developments did occur which must not be overlooked.

**The Law** Shortly after becoming Tsar, Nicholas had the most reactionary figures from the previous reign – men such as Arakcheyev and Magnitsky – removed from office. Speransky was recalled and placed at the head of a commission charged with the task of codifying the law. By 1832

CONVICTS BEING TRANSPORTED TO SIBERIA. THE JOURNEY WAS MADE ON FOOT AND MANY FELL VICTIM TO EXHAUSTION AND THE INTENSE COLD

Speransky had published 45 volumes containing all laws enacted in Russia between 1649 and 1830. This monumental work finally achieved what every tsar since Peter the Great had promised but subsequently failed to deliver. Although the new code could certainly be used by Nicholas to clarify the extent of his power, it also brought benefits to the peasants. The fresh recording of ancient laws reminded landowners that they had obligations to the peasants. Where abuses were discovered the Tsar insisted upon severe punishments for those nobles concerned.

**Serfdom** The issue of serfdom was investigated by Nicholas though never to any satisfactory conclusion. The Tsar spoke often of his dislike for serfdom and went so far as to establish six secret commissions to examine its practice. In 1834 he established the Ministry of Imperial Domains under General Kiselev to supervise the treatment of State peasants. This substantial group was subsequently freed from personal serfdom and permitted to live as free citizens. The government also began to purchase land from landowners for distribution among the peasants. This was the kind of arrangement Kiselev and Nicholas would have liked to see extended to privately-owned serfs. Some minor amendments to accepted practice were made, preventing, for example, the sale of serfs without land in order to clear private debts, and also the sale of serf families except as complete units. However, on the real issue of emancipation from private landlords there was no progress. The Tsar's fear of a noble backlash to this radical proposal was sufficient to render it a dead letter for his entire reign.

**Education** This experienced mixed fortunes under Nicholas. As the breeding-ground for new ideas, educational establishments – especially the universities – were subjected to close supervision. After 1835 they were brought under direct State control, thus losing the partial autonomy they had enjoyed through the university councils. Students and teachers had to endure official interference in their lives and studies. Student uniforms and haircuts were introduced and professors were required to have the content of their lessons officially cleared before they could be delivered in the lecture hall.

Nicholas also took exception to the principle of equal access to education for all classes, and raised tuition fees in an effort to place education out of the reach of the ordinary citizen. In spite of these restrictions intellectual life flourished in certain areas. Astronomy, mathematics and chemistry were all pursued with some distinction by Russian scientists, while the practical applications of electricity and magnetism were investigated by individuals who did pioneering work in the development of electric motors and telegraph systems. Perhaps more significantly, the reign of Nicholas I witnessed the emergence of an intellectual élite known later in the century as the intelligentsia. This new social group included nobles and commoners who had received a complete education and who were driven by ideas to demand an improved society. While Nicholas did not actively encourage the development of this group, his policies were never sufficient to prevent its appearance and steady evolution throughout his reign.

**The economy** The value of foreign trade increased by about 250 per cent between 1826 and 1830, and 1856 and 1860, although Russia's share of world trade hardly changed. Railway construction was begun under Nicholas with the first line being opened in 1837 between Moscow and Tsarkoe Selo. By 1851 a line operated between Moscow and St Petersburg. Although progress was made in railway construction, Russia in 1855 still had only about one-sixth of the total length of track laid in Germany by this time. There was also some modest industrial development. In 1804 there had been 2402 factories in Russia; by the late 1850s there were 14,000. The cotton industry in particular experienced rapid growth through its use of Western technology and hired (as opposed to serf) labour. Despite this, in comparison to the developing Western economies Russia was still enormously backward.

**Literature** Finally, it is perhaps somewhat ironic that a reign characterized by most observers as wholly repressive should have witnessed the flowering of Russian literature. The fine poet Pushkin, probably unequalled in his mastery of the Russian language, produced his masterpieces *Boris Godunov* (1825) and *Eugene Onegin* (1823–31) during the reign of Nicholas. The novelist Gogol, like Dickens, revealed in his work the corruption and brutality of his times. His novel, *Dead Souls* (1842), represents a bitter condemnation of the serf system. On one occasion Nicholas even saved Gogol from the censor who wished to ban his play *The Government Inspector* (1836). Other prominent names in Russian literature – Lermontov, Turgenev and Dostoyevsky – all emerged during this period to add a quite different dimension to the reign of Nicholas I.

ALEXANDER PUSHKIN

NIKOLAI GOGOL

# REVIEW
## Preserving the autocracy

Alexander and Nicholas shared an aim to preserve the Russian autocracy, and it is not uncommon to see 'repression of opposition' cited as the principal method by which this was achieved. Of course, both men did employ repressive methods to protect themselves and to ensure that their wishes were carried out.

| Alexander | Nicholas |
|---|---|
| Reintroduced the secret police in 1805. Insisted on the harsh regime of the military colonies. | Violently suppressed the Polish Revolt of 1830. Persecuted religious dissenters such as Jews and Catholics. Introduced the notorious Third Section and rigid censorship. |

However, was repression the only method used by the tsars in their domination of Russian life? The list below contains measures adopted by Alexander and Nicholas which can be said to have assisted in the preservation of the autocracy. Through discussion, possibly in small groups, try to explain how each of these measures could have helped the tsars to maintain their absolute authority.

### Alexander

**1** The restoration of liberties in 1801 (page 140).

**2** The acknowledgement of the Charter of the Nobility (page 140).

**3** The creation of the Ministries (page 142).

**4** Dismissal of Speransky (page 146).

**5** Treatment of serfdom (page 144).

### Nicholas

**1** Adoption of 'Orthodoxy, Autocracy and Nationality' (page 160).

**2** Government through the Personal Chancellery (page 160).

**3** Removal of the nobility's independence (page 160).

**4** Speransky's codification of the law (page 161).

**5** Treatment of serfdom (page 162).

Which groups did Alexander and Nicholas appear to depend on for the maintenance of their authority?

How would you argue that, in the long-term, some of these measures could have helped to fuel opposition to the autocratic system?

# 8 Alexander II: The 'Tsar Liberator'

## Preview

THE ASSASSINATION OF TSAR
ALEXANDER II (1 MARCH 1881)

THE PARADOX OF
ALEXANDER II'S
REIGN

'His achievement was substantial; by 1881 Russia's international position
had been restored so that she again ranked as one of the European
Great Powers, whilst at home Alexander had implemented a series of
reforms unparalleled in their scope and impact since the time of Peter
the Great.'

Martin McCauley and Peter Waldron,
*The Emergence of the Modern Russian State 1855–81* (1988)

## Talking Point

**What motivates assassins?**

The assassination of public figures is a theme which runs through the whole of
recorded time. In groups, compile a list of assassination victims and attempt to
determine why they were violently removed from public life.

Using your discussion as a starting point, produce a list of factors which can be
said to motivate assassins to commit their crimes. You can begin with the
following items:

● religious fanaticism;

● personal dislike.

As you conclude the chapter on Alexander II, it would be useful to return to this
list to try and determine which factor, or combination of factors, could be said
to be responsible for the murder of the Tsar. In doing so you will enhance your
understanding of the period and may go some way towards resolving the
apparent paradox of Alexander's reign.

# The need for change

'I am handing you command of the country in a very poor state.' This simple admission of the ageing Tsar Nicholas I to his son and heir, Alexander, speaks volumes about the decades of neglect the autocratic system had shamelessly presided over in the first half of the Nineteenth Century. In 1855, when Alexander II took possession of his ramshackle inheritance, the last traces of national pride were being snuffed out by British, French and Turkish troops on the Crimean peninsula. Defeat in this war revealed fundamental deficiencies in the Russian system. The national debt was high and rising steadily, the army was inefficient in both its structure and operations, central administration was inept and the countryside was seething with 50 million disaffected peasants grimly mourning the loss of 600,000 fellow Russians. In the villages, popular disturbances multiplied, sending shock waves reverberating around Russia to the gates of the Winter Palace itself.

TSAR ALEXANDER II

Alexander II assumed responsibility for an empire whose political and social systems were not just 'in a very poor state' but in fact, as history would reveal, in a terminal condition. Alexander, of course, did not have this knowledge but he understood fully that the State was seriously diseased and that remedial treatment was urgently needed to restore the patient. The new Tsar acted instinctively to save the autocratic system to which he was bound by honour and tradition. While representing a major progressive phase in nineteenth-century history, his reforming efforts were designed to modernize the autocracy and to ensure its preservation, rather than to create an alternative system. As a result his reforms, though ambitious in appearance and scope, were often limited in practice. His reluctance to go beyond a basic rescue mission produced resentment and encouraged political opposition. Eventually Alexander fell victim to forces which he had unwittingly released and was unable to restrain. The most significant of Alexander's projects, and the one which earned him the unofficial title 'Tsar Liberator', was the abolition of serfdom in 1861. The nature of Russian serfdom and the principal factors involved in its demise are explored in the following section.

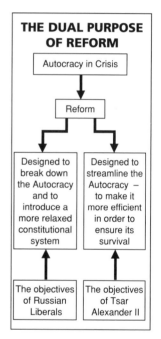

# $\mathbf{E}$XAMINING THE EVIDENCE

## Section 1: the material condition of the Russian serf

### Source A

Serfs cultivated the land allotted to them, and in recompense for the use of this land they were required to work also on the land reserved for the use of the landowner. Three days a week was probably the average requirement but in the worst cases, and in busy weeks, this might be doubled (which meant that the serf could not properly look after his own land). There were no fixed rights or obligations for the peasantry. A landowner could increase his serfs' dues and duties, he could seize their property, he could forbid their buying from, selling to, or working with persons outside the estate, he could make them into domestic servants, sell them either separately or with their families, force them to marry so as to breed more serfs, or forbid them to marry disapproved partners.

Except in cases of murder or banditry, the landowner administered rural justice and could send troublesome serfs to Siberia or into the army. Whipping was commonplace. Although there were many landowners who were kindly, educating and sometimes liberating favoured serfs, there were others who were brutal; social isolation and almost absolute power led some landowners to excesses which in other circumstances they would have found revolting. Probably the worst off peasants were those with an absentee landlord. Some nobles had never even seen their estates, and many more visited them only rarely. Such estates were entrusted to bailiffs who all too often were dishonest and tyrannical.

JN Westwood, *Endurance and Endeavour: Russian History 1812–1971* (1973)

## Source B

RUSSIAN SERFS

## Source C

…If, however, I were to relate what I heard of in those years [during his childhood] it would be a much more gruesome narrative: stories of men and women torn from their families and their villages and sold, or lost in gambling, or exchanged for a couple of hunting dogs, and then transported to some remote part of Russia for the sake of creating a new estate; of children taken from their parents and sold to cruel or dissolute masters; of flogging 'in the stables', which occurred every day with unheard of cruelty; of a girl who found her only salvation in drowning herself; of an old man who had grown grey haired in his master's service and at last hanged himself under his master's window; and of revolts of serfs, which were suppressed by Nicholas I's generals by flogging to death each tenth or fifth man taken out of the ranks, and by laying waste the village, whose inhabitants, after military execution, went begging for bread in the neighbouring provinces, as if they had been the victims of a conflagration. As to the poverty which I saw during our journeys in certain villages, especially in those which belonged to the imperial family, no words would be adequate to describe the misery to readers who have not seen it.

Peter Kropotkin, a Russian nobleman, quoted in WE Mosse, *Alexander II and the Modernization of Russia* (1958)

## Source D

Serfdom was an economic institution not a closed world created for the gratification of sexual appetites. Isolated instances of cruelty are no evidence to the contrary. It is simply not good enough to cite the notorious case of one Saltykova, a sadistic landlady immortalized by historians, who whiled away her idle hours by torturing to death dozens of her domestic servants. She tells us about as much about imperial Russia as does Jack the Ripper about Victorian London. Where statistics happen to be available they indicate moderation in the use of disciplinary prerogatives. Every landlord, for example, had the power to turn unruly peasants over to the authorities for exile to Siberia. Between 1822 and 1833, 1283 serfs were punished in this fashion; an annual average of 107 out of over twenty million proprietary serfs is hardly a staggering figure.

Richard Pipes, *Russia Under the Old Regime* (1974)

## Source E

Read the complaints of the English factory workers; your hair will stand on end. How much repulsive oppression, incomprehensible sufferings! What cold barbarism on the one hand, and what appalling poverty on the other. You will think we are speaking of the construction of the Egyptian pyramids, of Jews working under Egyptian lashes. Not at all: we are talking about the textiles of Mr Smith or the needles of Mr Jackson. And note that all these are not abuses, not crimes, but occurrences which take place within the strict limits of legality. It seems there is no creature in the world more unfortunate than the English worker...

In Russia there is nothing like it. Obligations are altogether not very onerous. The soul tax is paid by the *mir;* the *corvee* is set by the law; the *obrok* is not ruinous (except in the neighbourhood of Moscow and St Petersburg, where the diversity of industry intensifies and stimulates the greed of owners). The landlord, having set the *obrok,* leaves it up to the peasant to get it whenever and by whatever enterprises he can think of and sometimes travels two thousand kilometres to earn money...Take a look at the Russian peasant: is there a trace of slavish degradation in his behaviour or speech? Nothing need be said of his boldness and cleverness. His entrepreneurship is well known. His agility and dexterity are amazing. A traveller journeys from one end of Russia to the other, ignorant of a single word of Russian, and he is everywhere understood, everyone fulfils his requests and enters into agreements with him. You will never find among the Russian people that which the French call *un badaut* [an idler or loafer]: you will never see a Russian peasant show either crude amazement or ignorant contempt for what is foreign. In Russia there is not one man who does not have his own living quarters. A poor man who goes into the world leaves his *izba* [peasant hut]. This does not exist in other countries. Everywhere in Europe to own a cow is a sign of luxury; in Russia not to have one is a sign of dreadful poverty.

Alexander Pushkin, extract from *Journey from Moscow to St Petersburg*
quoted in Richard Pipes, *Russia Under the Old Regime* (1974)

## Source F

On the whole...so far at least as mere food and lodgings are concerned, the Russian peasant is not so badly off as the poor man amongst ourselves [in Britain]. He may be rude and uneducated – liable to be ill-treated by his superiors – intemperate in his habits, and filthy in his person; but he never knows the misery to which the Irish peasant is exposed. His food may be coarse; but he has abundance of it. His hut may be homely; but it is dry and warm. We are apt to fancy that if our peasantry be badly off, we can at least flatter ourselves with the assurance that they are much more comfortable than those of foreign countries. But this is a gross delusion. Not in Ireland only, but in parts of Great Britain usually considered to be exempt from the miseries of Ireland, we have witnessed wretchedness compared with which the conditions of the Russian boor is luxury, whether he live amid the crowded population of large towns, or in the meanest hamlets of the interior. There are parts of Scotland, for instance, where the people are lodged in houses which the Russian peasant would not think fit for his cattle.

Robert Bremner, extract from *Excursions in the Interior of Russia* (1839) quoted in Richard Pipes, as above

## Section 2: the pressure for emancipation

### Source G

This measure [proposal for emancipation] is more necessary for the welfare of our class itself [landowning nobility] even than for the serfs. The abolition of the right to dispose of people like objects or like cattle is as much our liberation as theirs: for at present we are under the yoke of a law that destroys still more in us than in the serfs any human quality.

Al Koshelyov (Russian landowner) quoted in Hugh Seton-Watson, *The Russian Empire 1801–1917* (1967)

### Source H

Just as in Western Europe before enclosures, the land was divided into strips allocated amongst the peasant families. There were commons and pastures or meadowland whose use was regulated by the community [the *mir*]. All this was the antithesis of the agrarian individualism which was to make possible great increases in production and productivity in the West...From an economic point of view the agrarian system was wasteful and unproductive, giving little scope for improvement and providing the peasant mass with little above the barest minimum necessary for existence. The surplus extracted from the peasantry went to support a nobility not interested in improving the productivity of the land and essentially a parasitic consuming class. The state likewise, though needing to promote some forms of industry for its own purposes, was not concerned to carry through any changes in the agrarian sector which would disturb the social equilibrium with which its own existence was bound up. For both the lords and the state maintenance of their position appeared to enjoin the preservation of serfdom as the only means of extracting a surplus from the peasantry.

Tom Kemp, *Industrialization in Nineteenth Century Europe* (1969)

### Source I

Serfdom is the stumbling block to all success and development in Russia...All significant internal changes in Russia are without exception so closely linked to the abolition of serfdom that one is impossible without the other…Thus, for example, the reform of the conscription system is impossible, because it would lead to the abolition of serfdom; it is impossible to change the present tax system because its roots lie in serfdom; for the same reason we cannot introduce a different and more rational passport system; it is impossible to extend education to the lower classes of society, to reform the legal system and civil and criminal proceedings, to reform the police, the administration in general, the existing censorship which is fatal for science and literature – all because these reforms would directly or indirectly lead to the weakening of serfdom, and the landowners do not want this on any account. Russia is condemned to fossilise, to remain in its present position, without making any step forward. And nothing is strong enough to change this position whilst serfdom lies at the foundation of our social and civil life, for this is the Gordian knot which ties together all our afflictions.

KD Kavelin (a Russian university professor writing in 1856), quoted in Martin McCauley and Peter Waldron, *The Emergence of the Modern Russian State 1855–81* (1988)

## Source J

Instances of violent peasant disturbances:

| | |
|---|---|
| 1845–1855 | 400 outbreaks |
| 1855–1860 | 400 outbreaks |
| 1835–1854 | 230 serf owners or bailiffs killed by serfs |
| 1858–1861 | 53 serf owners or bailiffs killed by serfs. |

Figures quoted in Hugh Seton-Waton, *The Decline of Imperial Russia* (1952)

## Source K

I have learned, gentlemen, that rumours have spread among you of my intention to abolish serfdom. To refute any groundless gossip on so important a subject I consider it necessary to inform you that I have no intention of doing so immediately. But, of course, and you yourselves realise it, the existing system of serf owning cannot remain unchanged. It is better to begin abolishing serfdom from above than to wait for it to begin to abolish itself from below. I ask you, gentlemen, to think of ways of doing this. Pass on my words to the nobles for consideration.

Tsar Alexander II addressing the Moscow nobles (30 March 1856), quoted in George Vernadsky (ed.), *A Source Book for Russian History from Early Times to 1917* (Vol 3, 1972)

## Section 1

**1** Examine Sources A, B and C. What impression of serfdom do they convey?

**2** Examine Sources D, E and F. How do these sources challenge and contradict the impression given above?

**3** Consider the following information.

*Source   Origin*

A       JN Westwood – historian.

B       Nineteenth-century French engraving.

C       Peter Kropotkin – liberal nobleman – account taken from his memoirs, written many years after the serfs had been freed.

D       Richard Pipes – historian.

E       Alexander Pushkin – Russian poet with first-hand experience of the Russian village. This extract is from a book written as a parody of an earlier work by the Russian author Radishchev which likened serfdom to slavery.

F       Robert Bremner – British traveller who journeyed to Russia in search of data to use against serfdom.

Given the origins of these sources, which view of serfdom do you find the most convincing?

**4** 'The Russian serf was the most unfortunate of Europe's labouring masses. How far do these sources support or contradict this opinion?

---

### Section 2
In 1856 Alexander II declared to a meeting of Moscow noblemen: '…the existing system of serf owning cannot remain unchanged.' Sources G–K provide evidence to explain the Tsar's decision to examine the serf problem.

**1** From Source K select the phrase which seems to summarize Alexander's principal motive for granting liberty to the serfs.

**2** How does Source J bear out the fears implicit in this phrase?

**3** According to Sources H and I how did serfdom inhibit:

(a) economic progress?

(b) political change?

(c) social and cultural development?

Why did intellectuals like Kavelin, the author of Source I, want the serfs to be freed?

**4** The author of Source G represents the minority view of the Russian land-owning nobility. Why would most landowners have disagreed with this opinion?

**5** 'Emancipation was conceived as a means of safeguarding the social order' (Tom Kemp, historian). How far do Sources G–K demonstrate this to be true?

---

## The Emancipation Edict (1861)

In March 1861 the liberation of the serfs was officially announced. Almost five years had elapsed since Alexander instructed the nobles to examine ways of freeing their serfs. Now, after much debate and considerable hostility, emancipation became a reality for millions of Russian peasants. However, the precise terms of the settlement soon gave cause for great concern. (See *Focus* section 8.1.)

# FOCUS

## 8.1 Deliverance or deception? The impact of emancipation on the Russian peasantry

### Peasants become free citizens

Freedom to marry
...to own property
...take legal action
...engage in trade or business
...could not be bought or sold
women were free to choose a husband

## Paying for land

**Stage 1 – Government**
Government pay landowners 80% of agreed price for their land in the form of treasury bonds.

**Stage 2 – Landowner**
20% of land value paid direct to landowner by peasant.

**Stage 3 – Peasant**
Peasants repay the government advance in annual instalments over 49 years. These sums were known as Redemption Payments.

## Redeption cost and land value

The Redemption cost of the land purchased by the peasants was generally much in excess of its real value.

| | Redemption cost | Land value* |
|---|---|---|
| Black-soil Provinces | 341 | 284 |
| Non black-soil provinces | 340 | 180 |
| Western provinces | 183 | 184 |

*Figures in millions of Roubles*    Statistics based on Russian estimates in 1906
*Based on average land prices for 1863-72

## The burden of Redemption Payments

Peasant arrears in Redemption Payments and Taxes for the 50 provinces of European Russia 1876-80

| Groups of provinces | Sums due (roubles 000s) | Arrears (roubles 000s) | Arrears as % of sum due |
|---|---|---|---|
| Northern | 8527 | 3968 | 46 |
| Baltic | 1686 | 161 | 10 |
| N. Western | 11,999 | 2646 | 22 |
| S. Western | 12,928 | 1125 | 9 |
| Industrial | 24,344 | 5402 | 22 |
| Central Black-soil | 40,574 | 6443 | 15 |
| Eastern | 22,220 | 7975 | 36 |
| Southern | 9,329 | 3128 | 33 |
| Ukraine | 11,408 | 1021 | 9 |
| **TOTAL** | 143,015 | 31,869 | 22 |

1881: Redemption Payments reduced by 25%
1907: Redemption Payments abolished and arrears cancelled.

**Allocation of land 1**

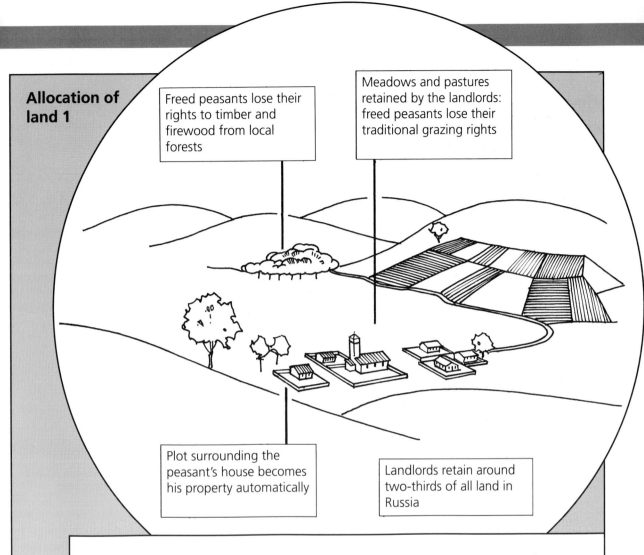

Freed peasants lose their rights to timber and firewood from local forests

Meadows and pastures retained by the landlords: freed peasants lose their traditional grazing rights

Plot surrounding the peasant's house becomes his property automatically

Landlords retain around two-thirds of all land in Russia

## The Mir

The organized village community or MIR, administered the peasants and their lands.

- The mir was collectively responsible for paying redemption costs.
- The mir had the right to issue (or withhold) passports for peasants wishing to travel distances over 20 miles.
- In some types of commune, land could be redistributed by the mir to take account of changes in family size.
- Peasant lands were allocated in small, scattered strips in order to ensure that no peasant received land of only one type and quality.
- The mir decided upon the crop rotation for the whole village.
- Titles to village lands given to the mir not to individual peasants. Only upon completion of Redemption Payments could titles be handed over to individuals.
- The mir was collectively responsible for paying taxes.

## 8.1 Deliverance or deception? The impact of emancipation on the Russian peasantry

*continued*

### Allocation of land 2

In most regions of Russia the freed peasants received smaller plots of land than they had traditionally farmed as serfs.

**Total area cultivated by serfs in 43 provinces of European Russia**

| Before 1861 | In 1877 |
| --- | --- |
| 94.5m acres | 91m acres |

Regionally, the situation was even worse. The black-soil region in the south contained some of the most productive farmland in Russia. Here, the landlords retained large quantities of land for themselves. On average the peasants received 25% less land than they had cultivated as serfs.

Only in the Western provinces was the peasant favoured when the land was distributed. This was in accordance with the official policy of discrimination against Polish landowners who tended to dominate in the Western regions.

A report from the Central Statistical Committee in 1878 revealed the following:

| | |
| --- | --- |
| % of former serfs well supplied with land | **13%** |
| % of former serfs adequately supplied with land | **40%** |
| % of former serfs inadequately supplied with land | **47%** |

## QUESTIONS

**1** To help you clarify the basic features of the Emancipation Edict, describe the following:
(a) the practical impact on the Russian peasant of becoming a free citizen;
(b) the type of land to which the peasant became legally entitled;
(c) the method of payment for that land.

**2** In pre-emancipation times, the Russian peasantry shared a common belief that the land belonged to them by right. Given this, what major criticism of the new arrangements would you expect the peasants to have made?

**3** In what specific ways was the allocation of land unfair or unsatisfactory to the majority of Russian peasants?

**4** Twenty per cent of the purchase price for the land had to be paid directly by the peasant to the landlord. If cash were not available to make this payment (and in most cases it was not), the peasant would have to discharge the debt in services. Why would the peasants have objected to this particular aspect of the redemption arrangements?

**5** Suggest reasons why the authorities deliberately fixed Redemption Payments in excess of the real value of the land being purchased. Which region of Russia was the exception to this rule? Why was the practice not followed in these provinces?

**6** Was the redemption scheme a success or failure?

**7** How did the mir restrict the freedom of the newly-liberated peasants?

**8** Historians claim that the interference of the mir held back the development of modern agriculture in Russia for the remainder of the Nineteenth Century. What arguments would you advance to support this claim?

A SERF BEING FREED FOLLOWING THE EMANCIPATION EDICT

## QUESTIONS

**1** What does this scene suggest to you about the nature of Russian society in 1861?

**2** How far do you think it would be possible for the Emancipation Edict to change the conduct and attitudes of landowners and peasants?

# The people's response

The Emancipation Edict was a major piece of social legislation carried through by the Tsar in the face of entrenched landowner opposition. It extended basic rights to millions of Russian citizens and seemed to suggest that Alexander would steer a progressive course for the remainder of his reign. However, the terms of the Edict provoked considerable disappointment amongst the two great social classes most closely touched by the changes.

## The peasants

Russia's vast size and rudimentary communications meant that precise information was always difficult to obtain. Consequently, one of the most potent enemies of the Empire was the confusion created by rumour and conjecture. Typically, the official announcement of the Edict was pre-empted by gossip and guesswork, resulting in widespread misunderstanding. Most peasants assumed that emancipation was a dual package of freedom and land-ownership; the concept of Redemption Payments simply did not occur to them. Therefore when the terms of the Edict began to be spelled out from the pulpits of their churches, jubilation was replaced by disbelief and anger. Large numbers of peasants convinced themselves that these arrangements were temporary and that true emancipation would be granted following an interim period. At Bezdna in Kazan Province a peasant rising led by Anton Petrov (and based on this expectation) resulted in the massacre of over 100 villagers by armed troops. In 1861 there were 499 incidents of serious rioting in which soldiers were deployed to restore order. Alexander himself was forced to intervene to correct the confused peasants:

THE TERMS OF THE EMANCIPATION EDICT ARE READ FROM THE CHURCH PULPIT

Reports have reached me that you expect a new emancipation. There will be no emancipation except the one I have given you. Obey the laws and the statutes: work and toil! Obey the authorities and the landowners!

Incidents of disorder declined but the peasants remained deeply disappointed. After two years almost half of the charters setting out local arrangements for land settlement had to be imposed by the government without the agreement of the peasant communities to which they applied. In the atmosphere of bitterness and resentment which emanated from the Edict, few peasants would have toasted Alexander as their 'Tsar Liberator'.

### The landowners

Emancipation dealt a serious blow to many members of the land-owning nobility. They lost land and the labour of their serfs, and found their compensation payments being swallowed up by debts. In the years before 1861, 62 per cent of privately-owned serfs had been mortgaged to state credit institutions. Accordingly the government deducted the amounts owed directly from Redemption Payments. By 1871, although 543 million roubles had been paid in redemption sums by the peasants, 248 million roubles had been absorbed by creditors. To make matters worse, the bonds paid by the government as compensation depreciated in value, reducing further the real value of the compensation paid to the landowners for the loss of their serfs. To make ends meet the gentry sold more land. Between 1861 and 1905 the acreage of land in noble possession fell by 41 per cent. The Edict badly damaged the economic fortunes of the land-owning class and signalled a significant down-turn in their social and political status.

Alexander's most celebrated reform had succeeded in alienating the principal classes in Russian society, a disastrous outcome given his initial hopes for the scheme:

'The peasant should immediately feel that his life has been improved; the landowner should at once be satisfied that his interests are protected; and stable political order should not be disturbed for one moment in any locality.'

Quoted in L Kochan and R Abraham, *The Making of Modern Russia* (1962)

## Emancipation and subsequent reform

The 1861 Edict had consequences which went far beyond immediate concerns about land-distribution and Redemption Payments. Emancipation removed the mechanism which had regulated society for centuries. Major reforms were now required to establish a new framework in which society could function. The 'lateral impact' of abolition can be traced in the diagram overleaf.

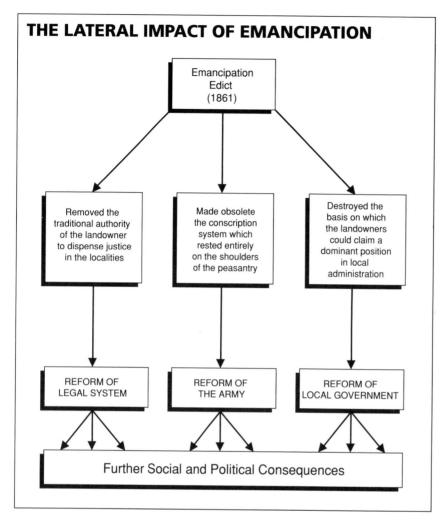

**THE LATERAL IMPACT OF EMANCIPATION**

Emancipation Edict (1861)

- Removed the traditional authority of the landowner to dispense justice in the localities
- Made obsolete the conscription system which rested entirely on the shoulders of the peasantry
- Destroyed the basis on which the landowners could claim a dominant position in local administration

REFORM OF LEGAL SYSTEM

REFORM OF THE ARMY

REFORM OF LOCAL GOVERNMENT

Further Social and Political Consequences

The key elements of the three broad reform areas are set out opposite, and should be studied before moving on to the section below.

### Social and political consequences

Such a package of reforms had not been seen in Russia since the time of Peter the Great. They affected millions of Russian people and struck out against privilege, centralization and outdated feudal traditions. They initiated Russia's gradual transformation into a modern State. In spite of this the reforms caused problems for Alexander. They were criticized as being incomplete and they unleashed dissident forces which ultimately resulted in the Tsar's assassination in 1881.

**Legal reforms** The reforms did not remove the rural 'cantonal courts' which were exclusively concerned with resolving peasant disputes. This was something of a blow to the liberals who wanted the complete removal of all class differentiation from Russian justice. Similarly, the use of 'administrative arrest' did not disappear with the new reforms. This arbitrary police power to detain anyone considered to be a threat to State

## LEGAL SYSTEM

New system introduced in 1864

(a) Borrowed heavily from Western practice.

(b) Introduced concept of a judiciary independent of the government.

(c) Introduced concept of equality before the law for all citizens.

(d) Introduced trial by jury.

(e) Made courts open to the public.

(f) Judges paid a substantial salary.

(g) Judges required to have professional qualifications.

## ARMY

Reforms the work of War Minister Dmitiri Milyutin.

(a) Most of the barbaric forms of punishment were abolished.

(b) Educational programme introduced to improve standards of literacy.

(c) All males – irrespective of class – made subject to conscription upon reaching age of 20.

(d) Recruits chosen by ballot.

(e) Length of service reduced from 25 to 15 years (6 years on full-time active service, 9 years in the reserve).

(f) Predominance in officer training of the noble-based Cadet Corps was reduced; increasing numbers taken from non-noble institutions.

## LOCAL GOVERNMENT

New institution – the *zemstva* (local councils) – set up after 1864 to be responsible for local affairs.

(a) Members elected directly by local people. All classes voted and had seats on the councils.

(b) The *zemstva* were multi-functional: they maintained roads and arranged military conscription; they supervised prisons and hospitals and attended to public health and poor relief; they assisted with the development of industry and agriculture, and assisted in financing education.

(c) Followed in 1870 by the introduction of municipal councils (*dumas*), the urban equivalent of the *zemstva*.

How do these three areas of reform appear to modify:

(a) the autocratic system of government?

(b) the tradition of class privilege in Russia?

security meant that the independence of the judiciary was somewhat compromised. In practice also, the government found itself embarrassed by the jury system which frequently returned verdicts at odds with the 'official' position. Too often for the liking of the Tsar, the open court system allowed a public platform for dissidents to make political speeches. After 1864, the government persisted in its attempts to have political offences dealt with by non-jury courts.

One important result of the reforms was to create a need for a properly-trained body of professional lawyers. Alexander was accordingly compelled to submit to the establishment of the Russian Bar. The political consequences of this were far-reaching. The Bar produced talented and dedicated legal professionals who not only improved the quality of Russian justice, but contributed substantially to the growth of articulate opposition to the autocracy. Accustomed to the complexities of officialdom, exposed regularly to society's darker side and, in their professional capacity, permitted unprecedented freedom of speech; lawyers became the champions of the liberal cause, adding their persuasive voices to demands for greater reform. Some even became revolutionary leaders, the source of the most dangerous challenges to the established government.

**The army** Milyutin's army reforms were vital to the recovery of Russian military prestige, and in the war against Turkey (1877–78) their practical effects were successfully tested in the field. However, there were also important social side-effects. The reform represented an attack on class privileges and helped to initiate a trend towards greater social equality. The democratization of the army helped to encourage those who aimed for the achievement of greater political equality in society as a whole.

**Local government** Alexander took care to ensure that his new local government assemblies did not encroach significantly on the autocracy. They were charged with essentially minor responsibilities, given no executive authority and organized in such a way that peasant representation in the assemblies was always proportionately smaller than that of the nobility.

In spite of the limitations these local institutions worked. Their success offered tangible proof that the Russian people had the skills and commitment to be masters of their own affairs. Inevitably this led to demands for more far-reaching political reform. If local self-government could be shown to succeed, educated Russians argued that the next logical step was to permit public participation in national government. The years following 1864 witnessed repeated calls for some form of national representative assembly. At the forefront of the groups making such demands were the 'professional' class of workers created by the spread and success of local government. Recruited from the developing intelligentsia and often drawn from non-noble backgrounds, these doctors, teachers, surveyors, engineers and economists spoke out against continuing rural poverty, and demanded further political change to remedy social distress.

Alexander, however, was unwilling to allow local government institutions to encroach on his authority. In 1865 and again the following year, the St Petersburg *zemstvo* demanded that a central representative body be established to further Russian constitutional progress. The Tsar responded by dissolving it and exiling several of its more outspoken members.

# The rise of revolutionary opposition

Following the failure of the Decembrist Revolt in 1825, intellectual discussion was kept alive in Russia by the exponents of opposing intellectual trends known as Westernism and Slavophilism. The Westerners believed that Russia would only make progress if she adopted the principle features of Western civilization: political liberty, technological advances and the Christian faith. The Westerners were opposed by the Slavophiles who believed Russia had already moved too close to the West, thus forsaking the qualities of her own distinctive Slav culture. The Slavophiles promoted the traditions of the Russian Orthodox Church and rejected the concept of individual liberty in favour of the traditional village commune.

The activities of the Westerners and Slavophiles were restricted to intellectual debate and had little practical impact on Russian politics. However, from the early 1860s the radical movement began to change. Intellectuals became increasingly dissatisfied with theoretical discussion about political ideas, and moved to a serious consideration of the methods which could be employed to achieve practical changes in Russia. From this there developed committed revolutionary movements and groups which came increasingly to challenge the concept of the autocracy. The *Focus* section which follows traces the establishment and progress of the Russian revolutionary movement under Alexander II.

## 8.2 The development of the Russian, revolutionary movement (1855-81)

### The moderates

The foremost political theorist of Alexander's early reign was the exile **Alexander Herzen**. He promoted the commune as the basis for Russian socialist development. Through his influential journal *The Bell* he made clear his opposition to violent change and advocated patient education of the masses as the means of achieving a social revolution. His writings called on the educated classes to go 'to the people'.

Another influential theorist was **Dmitri Pisarev**. He regarded the notion of a peasant revolution as premature, and urged the development of an intellectual elite in order to provide effective leadership for the future. Pisarev accepted the title 'nihilist'; a term invented by the novelist Turgenev to describe an individual 'who does not bow before any authorities, who does not accept any single principle on trust however much respect surrounds this principle.'

Completing this trio of theorists was **Petr Lavrov**. In direct opposition to the ideas of Bakunin, Lavrov stressed the need to educate the peasantry to enable the people themselves to direct their own liberation. Lavrov favoured propaganda and opposed revolutionary anarchism.

---

In the early 1870s informal student-based groups developed in the major cities. They rejected the extremism of Bakunin and his disciples, taking their inspiration instead from theorists such as Lavrov. They invested all their hopes for change in Russia in the peasantry, and regarded the existing structure of the village commune as the ideal basis for a new society. Their immediate objective was self-education and the extension of this learning to the popular masses. These were the **Populists** (or 'Narodniks') and their revolutionary slogan, borrowed directly from Herzen, was 'To the People'.

Between 1873 and 1874 some 2-3000 students journeyed to the countryside and with missionary-like fervour began to preach socialism. They received a mixed reception from the peasants, ranging from acceptance to suspicion and hostility.

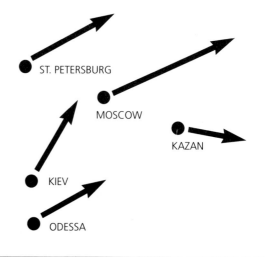

# The extremists

Inspiration for the younger generation of radical revolutionaries was provided by the romantic figure of **Mikhail Bakunin**, the founder of Anarchism and now in exile. He preached violence and destruction as the means of achieving change.

The 1860s witnessed the appearance of young, extreme radicals whose views were publicized through a journal called *The Contemporary*. The socialist editor of this review, **Nikolai Chernyshevski**, assumed a high profile among Russian radicals of the 1860s. Chernyshevski's disappointment with the terms of the Emancipation Edict caused him to promote force as the means of introducing socialism into Russia.

The violent appeals of the radicals inspired the appearance of embryonic revolutionary organizations. One such group – with the purposely sinister name **Hell** – produced the would-be assassin **Karakozov** who shot at the Tsar in **1866**. Alexander was unhurt but Karakozov was captured and executed.

The failure of Populism to win mass support led to a resurgence of the small-scale organized group dedicated to provoking a revolution in Russia. In 1876 a secret society calling itself **Land and Liberty** set out its programme. Its primary aim was to lead a social revolution and to establish the commune as the basis of the new order. The emphasis of Land and Liberty increasingly passed to terrorism and especially to the high-profile technique of political assassination.

> **'YOUNG RUSSIA'**
> 'Take up your axes!....Kill the men of the Imperial party without pity...kill them on the square if that foul scum dares to come out, kill them in their houses, kill them in the narrow alleys of the towns, kill them in the wide streets of the capital cities, kill them in the villages and hamlets.' – *Zaichnevsky, 1862*

THE NEW SPIRIT OF RADICALISM PRODUCED REVOLUTIONARY APPEALS OF A VIOLENTLY UNCOMPROMISING NATURE.

> **'TO THE YOUNGER GENERATION'**
> 'The Sovereign has betrayed the hopes of the people: the freedom he has given them is not real...We do not need a tsar...We want to have as our head an ordinary mortal...If we have to slaughter a hundred thousand landowners...we would not be afraid of that.' – *Mikhailov, 1861*

The increasing use of terrorist activities brought about a split in the 'Land and Liberty' movement:

| **BLACK PARTITION** | **THE PEOPLE'S WILL** |
|---|---|
| The minority group which emerged from the split. Led by George Plekhanov, the group concentrated on spreading peaceful propaganda among the peasants. Black Partition rejected terrorism. | This group was sceptical about the chances of a spontaneous mass rising beginning amongst the people. They believed it was their duty to trigger the revolution, and to do so in the most dramatic manner available to them: the assassination of the autocrat Alexander II. |

## TERRORISM

**January 1878** General Trepov, Governor of St Petersburg, shot and wounded by Vera Zasulich.
**August 1878** General Mezentsev, head of the Third Section, killed by Stepniak.
**February 1879** Murder of Prince Kropotkin, Governor General of Kharkov.
**March 1879** Unsuccessful attempt on the life of General Drenteln, new head of the Third Section.
**April 1879** Tsar shot at by Solovgov - the Emperor escaped unhurt.

Two years of planning and abortive attempts on the Tsar's life, eventually bore fruit for the terrorists. On 1 March 1881, Alexander was fatally wounded by an explosive device thrown as he returned home to the Winter Palace in St Petersburg.

## 8.2 The development of the Russian, revolutionary movement (1855-81) *continued*

## From thaw to reaction

### 'Thaw'

**1855**

Alexander's accession began a 'thaw' in Russian political life:

- censorship was relaxed;
- political prisoners were released;
- foreign travel was permitted;
- universities were liberalized.

**1861-64**

Major reforms were introduced, including:

- emancipation of the serfs;
- creation of a new legal system;
- establishment of representative local government;
- conscription and promotion in the army made more equitable.

### Backlash

Soon after the Emancipation Edict had been issued:

- the Tsar dismissed those officials who had been most closely associated with it;
- prominent radicals, including Pisarev and Chernyshevski, were arrested for sedition in 1862;
- imprisonment and exile to Siberia were revived to deal with political opposition.

The backlash was intensified in 1866 following an assassination attempt on the Tsar by Karakozov.

- leading radical journals were closed down;
- zemstvos were forbidden to communicate with each other;
- arrests of suspected revolutionaries were made;
- police supervision of the universities became more intensive;
- courts were urged to interpret the law in favour of the government.

POLICE RAID ON THE NIHILIST JOURNAL 'NATIONAL WILL'

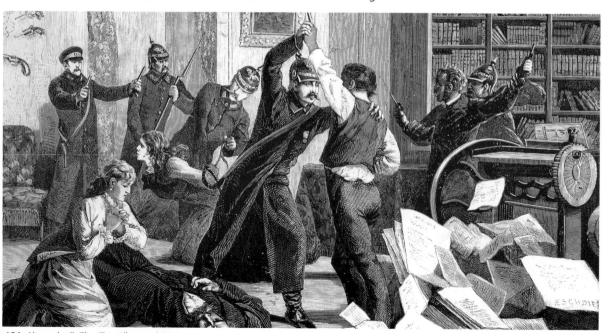

In 1866 the Tsar appointed two known reactionaries to important ministerial positions:

**COUNT PETER SHUVALOV**

**1866** Appointed head of the Third Section. Shuvalov held this post for seven years. He engineered the dismissal of progressives in the administration and had them replaced with dedicated conservatives. He was able to sabotage new reform proposals and to frustrate the implementation of existing reform schemes.

**COUNT DMITRI TOLSTOY**

**1866** Appointed as Minister of Education. His policies placed disproportionate emphasis on the classics. The almost uninterrupted diet of Greek and Latin which he served up in Russian schools impaired the development of progressive education. Tolstoy's actions served to harden opinion against the classics and to transfer demands for progressive education into the hands of the revolutionary intelligentsia.

Further reaction occurred in response to the Populist, 'To the People' movement.

The government viewed the 'To the People' movement as an attempt to incite revolution: hundreds of students were arrested. Two mass trials followed – the 'Trial of the Fifty' in Moscow in **1877** and the 'Trial of the 193' in St. Petersburg, **1877-78**. The accused won much public support through impassioned speeches made before the juries of the new open courts. Sentences were light and there were many acquittals. However, the government invoked its power of 'administrative arrest' and deported many of the acquitted to Siberia. Soon after, offences deemed to be political in nature were transferred to military courts: here there was no jury.

## QUESTIONS

**1** Identify the principal characteristics of:
(a) the moderates;
(b) the extremists.

**2** Did these two broad groups share any similarities?

**3** Consider the following:
(a) the 'thaw' in Russian political life (1855);
(b) the Emancipation Edict (1861);
(c) the repressive backlash (1866);
(d) the show-trials (1877-78).
Outline a case in support of the contention that the actions of Alexander's government were directly responsible for the development of the revolutionary movement.

# Industrial progress

The revolutionary forces unleashed during Alexander's reign continued to plague tsarist Russia long after 1881. In 1917, the last of the Romanovs, Nicholas II, was forced to abdicate by those who had inherited the revolutionary tradition from the pioneers of the 1860s and '70s. Another trend discernible during Alexander's reign, and one which was to have similar long-term consequences, was the development of the economy and the growth of the industrial city.

The rudimentary progress made by Russian industry during the reign of Nicholas I (see page 163) had, by 1860, prepared the ground for a more substantial period of industrialization. Assisted by foreign investment, Russian industrial production underwent modest expansion.

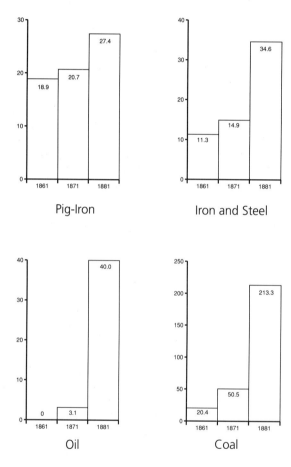

Pig-Iron

Iron and Steel

Oil

Coal

All figures in millions of puds (1 pud=16.3kg)

Russian industry was stimulated by the rapid development of the State railway network. Between 1866 and 1883 the tonnage of freight being carried by rail increased eightfold, while the total length of track in service rose from 1404 km in 1861, to 19,957 km in 1881.

In spite of these achievements, the extent of Russian industrialization was slight when compared with the economies of Britain, France and Germany.

One by-product of Russia's expanding industrial economy was the growth of her main urban centres. The population of cities such as Moscow and St Petersburg increased by about 30 per cent between 1861 and 1881. With the majority of city-dwellers employed by demanding fact-ory-owners and living in squalid conditions, a combustible situation began to develop amongst the tenements and sweatshops of the industrial centres.

# TALKING POINT

'The urban problem which was to confront the tsarist authorities at the end of the Nineteenth Century did not reach its full force under Alexander II, but all the ingredients were in place by the time of his assassination.'

In groups discuss how the features described here could be said to constitute a recipe for urban unrest.

| Town | Year | % Literate | | |
| --- | --- | --- | --- | --- |
| | | Men | Women | Overall |
| St Petersburg | 1869 | 62 | 46 | 55 |
| Kiev | 1874 | 52 | 33 | 44 |
| Moscow | 1871 | 49 | 34 | 43 |
| Kharkov | 1879 | 47 | 31 | 40 |

NB The average literacy rate in the rural provinces at the beginning of the 1880s was a little over 10%.

'Of the 181 industrial enterprises which I have inspected, it appears that correct wages are being paid in only 71 factories...There are thus more than 100 factories...in which wages are completely unregulated and depend completely on the whim and pocket of the boss...'

Moscow Factory Inspector, 1882

'The sanitary conditions of workshops is much the same as that of living accommodation, that is for the most part unsatisfactory...In confectionary factory number 11, the workshops are extremely dark and dirty: most of the chocolate section is located in an extremely dark basement where all the dirt from the yard penetrates...In cloth factory number 48, as in many other such factories, the air in the dye-shop was so full of steam that nothing was visible...there was evidently no sort of ventilation...'

Moscow Factory Inspector, 1882

'Nearest to me was a peasant with a swollen face and a red beard, wearing only a torn jacket and worn galoshes on his bare feet. It was 8 degrees below freezing...He was from Smolensk and had come to look for work so that he could buy food and pay his taxes...he had been a worker but the job had come to an end and his money and identity card had been stolen in the doss-house. Now he could not leave Moscow...All he was waiting for was for the police to come around: as he had no identity card he would be arrested and then sent back to his village.'

Leo Tolstoy (Russian novelist)

# 1 March 1881

On Sunday 1 March 1881, Alexander II left the Winter Palace to attend a review of troops; it was to be his last official duty as Emperor of Russia. As he passed slowly down the ice-bound Catherine Street on his way home from the parade, a bomb was thrown at the royal escort. The explosion immobilized the Tsar's carriage and fatally injured a Cossack bodyguard. Alexander was unharmed and insisted on taking time to offer words of comfort to his wounded men. Asked by some bystanders if he was hurt, the Tsar replied 'Thank God, no'. A moment later another bomb exploded and Alexander took its full force. Covered by blood-stained furs and cradled in his brothers' arms, the dying Tsar was taken by sledge to his palace. Inside, members of the royal family looked on in silent horror as Alexander's life slipped away.

'The Emperor lay on the couch near the desk. He was unconscious. Three doctors were fussing around, but science was obviously help-less…He presented a terrific sight, his right leg torn off, his left leg shattered, innumerable wounds all over his head and face. One eye was shut, the other expressionless…Princess Yurievsky burst in, half dressed…She fell flat on the couch over the body of the Tsar, kissing his hands and screaming, 'Sasha, Sasha!' A few minutes later the Emperor was dead. The princess dropped to the floor 'like a felled tree'. Her pink negligé was soaked in blood.'

Account of the Tsar's death by Grand Duke Alexander Mikhailovich

## TALKING POINT

The harrowing scene described opposite was witnessed by Alexander's son and heir, the future Alexander III. What impressions might this have made on his mind? How might this episode have affected the tone of his monarchy?

Ironically, the murder of the Tsar coincided with a distinct retreat from the reactionary policy adopted by the authorities in the face of revolutionary pressure. In 1880, Alexander had appointed a Supreme Commission headed by General Loris-Melikov. The Commission was invested with authority over the entire administration. Loris-Melikov, known to have certain liberal leanings, began to address the crisis which faced the autocracy with a new leniency. Press censorship was relaxed and Tolstoy was replaced as Minister of Education by the liberal Saburov.

Six months later, with the Commission dissolved and Loris-Melikov installed as Minister of the Interior, plans began to take shape to allow the participation of elected representatives in the making of legislation. There were to be two commissions with responsibility for administrative and financial matters. Their drafts would come before a General Commission composed of individuals elected by the *zemstvo* assemblies and city councils. The proposals of the General Commission would then be presented to the Council of State for ratification. Fifteen persons elected by the voting public were to be added to this body. The Loris-Melikov plans did not aim to establish a 'constitution', as some observers have claimed, but they did represent a positive step in the direction of representative institutions; a development which might ultimately have saved the tsarist system. It is perhaps the supreme irony that on the morning of his assassination, Alexander had signed the documents authorizing the implementation of Loris-Melikov's proposals; his final attempt to come to terms with liberal Russian opinion ended that very afternoon in carnage.

MEMBERS OF 'THE PEOPLE'S WILL' – FOUND GUILTY OF CONSPIRING TO ASSASSINATE THE TSAR – ABOUT TO BE HANGED IN ST PETERSBURG

# REVIEW

Alexander II introduced major reforms which pushed Russia firmly in the direction of modernization. His achievements have been compared with those of Peter the Great and Lenin. Yet this reforming Tsar was never popular. He was opposed at every level of society and was eventually killed by a group who believed that the key to progress in Russia lay in his murder. How is it possible to explain the consistent opposition to Alexander in spite of his far-reaching reforms?

## 1 Unfavourable circumstances

**1** In what ways did the 'thaw' manifest itself in Alexander's reign?

**2** How far was the opposition which emerged during his reign inevitable?

Some historians have argued that Alexander was the victim of circumstance. Consider this observation by WE Mosse:

'The Tsar was fated to preside over one of the recurring and normally abortive 'liberal' interludes in the history of Russia. After the reign of Nicholas, as after those of Peter I, Paul I, or Stalin, a 'thaw' had become an imperative necessity…Yet as soon as Alexander lifted the tight lid of repression, the compressed steam began to escape.'

WE Mosse, *Alexander II and the Modernization of Russia* (1958)

## 2 Alexander's perception of reform

Consider the diagram on page 166. How does this help to explain why the reforming Tsar continued to face opposition.

## 3 The nature and scope of Alexander's reforms

Examine the major reforms detailed in this chapter:
- emancipation of the serfs;
- legal reforms;
- creation of the *zemstva* and the *dumas*.

In each case show how the terms of the reforms disappointed the expectations of society. What specific types of opposition emerged from these reforms?

## 4 Industrialization

Alexander II's reign coincided with an intensification of capitalist activity in Russia. This produced a demand for urban workers which was met through the new mobility of the labour force. What social problems were associated with this development?

## 5 Repression

At various points throughout his reign, Alexander attempted to stifle demands for reform by using the traditional repressive devices of the autocracy: arrest, exile, and censorship. What reaction did this tend to provoke?

---

Structured examination of this chapter, using the guidance points above, should enable you to devise a convincing response to one of the central issues in the study of Alexander II. The essay question which follows could form the basis of a formal written assignment on this topic.

## 'Describe and account for the continuing opposition to Alexander II in Russia despite his major reforms.' (Cambridge, 1981)

# 9 The End of Imperial Russia 1881–1914

## PREVIEW
### A prediction of disaster

In November 1913 AI Guchkov, leader of a political grouping of modern conservatives known as the Octobrists, delivered a speech to a conference of Party activists.

'Whither is the government policy, or rather lack of policy, carrying us? Towards an inevitable and grave catastrophe! In this general forecast all are agreed; people of the most sharply opposed political views, of the most varied social groups, all agree with a rare, an unprecedented unanimity...

Let those in power make no mistake about the temper of the people; let them not take outward indications of prosperity as a pretext for lulling themselves into security. Never were those revolutionary organizations which aim at a violent upheaval so broken and impotent as they are now, and never were the Russian public and the Russian people so profoundly revolutionized by the actions of the government, for day by day faith in the government is steadily waning, and with it is waning faith in the possibility of a peaceful issue from the crisis.'

Quoted in Martin McCauley, *Octobrists to Bolsheviks: Imperial Russia 1905–1917* (1984)

Guchkov felt unable to elaborate on the form the 'grave catastrophe' he predicted would take. Yet his general fears were already close to realization. In November 1913, when Guchkov delivered his speech, the Russian autocracy had a little more than three years to live.

What sort of crisis faced Tsar Nicholas II on the eve of the First World War? If Guchkov's observations can be believed then it was surely a situation of the gravest magnitude; a crisis which touched all social groups as they increasingly despaired of the government's ability to find a solution. Certainly, the crisis was not the result of short-term factors. It had taken decades of arbitrary government and social neglect to isolate the people from their leaders.

# Rural discontent

At the beginning of the Twentieth Century slightly less than three-quarters of Russia's working population made their living from the land. Most were peasant farmers, freed now from serfdom but still firmly attached to the village commune (the *obshchina*). Cereal crops such as wheat, rye and oats were the mainstay of most village economies. Between 1881 and 1913 grain output in European Russia rose by an annual average of 2 per cent per year and, in spite of persistent population growth (see opposite), an increase in *per capita* production was registered. From 1909 to 1914 Russia was the world's premier cereal exporter, selling an annual average of 11.5 million tons to foreign markets.

Such favourable statistics must not, however, be allowed to obscure the chronic land problems and rural poverty which existed throughout the Russian countryside. Farming methods remained primitive and agricultural machinery was a rarity. As a result, agricultural yields were low when compared with those of Western economies (see below).

| Population growth | |
|---|---|
| 1897 | 125 million |
| 1900 | 133 million |
| 1910 | 160 million |
| 1914 | 175 million |

| Comparative agricultural yields (1911–15): puds per desyatina | | | | | |
|---|---|---|---|---|---|
| | *Wheat* | *Rye* | *Oats* | *Maize* | *Potatoes* |
| *Russia* | 45 | 54 | 52 | 74 | 489 |
| *USA* | 69 | 68 | 77 | 111 | 440 |
| *France* | 86 | 68 | 83 | 81 | 570 |
| *Britain* | 146 | – | 119 | – | 1012 |
| *Germany* | 146 | 120 | 127 | – | 904 |

1 *pud* = 16.3 kilograms
1 *desyatina* = 2.7 acres

Source: Martin McCauley, *Octobrists to Bolsheviks: Imperial Russia 1905–1917* (1984)

RUSSIAN PEASANT AGRICULTURE RELIED HEAVILY ON TRADITIONAL METHODS AND BACKBREAKING WORK

The most serious problem facing the Russian peasantry was land-hunger. Between 1877 and 1905 the population increased by some 25 per cent, placing enormous strains on the supply of cultivatable land. Some relief was provided by an increase in urban migration but the movement to the towns had only marginal impact; between 1880 and 1913 the proportion of the labour force engaged in agriculture only dropped from 74 per cent to 72 per cent. The total land in peasant ownership *did* increase but the average size of an allotment held by peasant households fell from 35 acres in 1887 to 28 acres in 1905. The resulting pressure on the available land had serious consequences: plots were overworked and often became exhausted; land rents and purchase prices were often inflated above their true value; and wages became severely depressed. Nor did Russia escape the European agricultural crisis of the 1880s and '90s which resulted in low grain prices. The peasant producers were compelled to sell as much grain as possible in order to meet government taxes and pay for essential goods.

STARVING PEASANTS QUEUE FOR HANDOUTS OF BREAD DURING A FAMINE NEAR KAZAN (1907)

In such circumstances harvest failure had catastrophic effects. During the famine of 1891–92, hunger and disease claimed 400,000 lives. Not surprisingly the peasants regularly defaulted on their financial commitments to the State. In the period 1896–1900 direct tax arrears averaged 119 per cent of expected collections while arrears on Redemption Payments reached 138 per cent in 1903. The Ministry of the Interior responded with chilling insensitivity by dispatching special punitive expeditions to the countryside to coerce payment. The Russian writer and scientist Prince Kropotkin described such an expedition in 1909:

'Last summer there was a famine in several provinces of European Russia…At the present time the conditions are still worse, the crop of the year 1908 having been 35,000,000 cwts. below the average crop of the four preceding years, 1902–1906. Nevertheless the Ministry of the Interior has given orders to levy, in the most stringent way, all the arrears which have accumulated for the last few years, both in regard to the payment of the taxes and in the repayment of famine loans…

The result is that in these provinces a wholesale flogging of the peasants, men and women alike – although this is contrary to the existing law – has been going on in order to recover the arrears…Acting upon commands received from superiors, the district chiefs *(Zemskiy natchalniks)* [Land Captains], when they do not resort to flogging, order a sale of the peasants' property…The sales are said to have become the occasion of a special traffic, the net result of which will be to ruin a great number of peasants; for, as there are often no ordinary buyers at the sales, the only bidders are the police authorities themselves, and they buy for five or six shillings a barn or a stock of grain, and afterwards resell the property to the peasant for three or four times the price they have paid.'

Prince Kropotkin, *The Terror in Russia: an Appeal to the British Nation* (1909)

The institution of the Land Captain, referred to by Kropotkin, added further cause for peasant discontent. Introduced in 1889 to replace peasant officials in the villages, the Land Captains were little more than bureaucrat-administrators sent to do the bidding of the Tsar. Hans Rogger has described the function of the Land Captain as being to 'check the arbitrariness of peasant over peasant by carrying the bureaucratic arbitrariness of St Petersburg to all' *(Russia in the Age of Modernisation and Revolution 1881-1917* (1983))

RUSSIAN PEASANTS IN 1906. THE VILLAGE OF JASNAYA POLYABA CAN BE SEEN IN THE BACKGROUND. COMPARE THIS WITH THE PICTURE OF A RUSSIAN VILLAGE ON PAGE 153. HOW MUCH MATERIAL PROGRESS HAD THE PEASANT CLASS MADE DURING THE 19TH CENTURY?

## Functions and powers of the Land Captains

- To oversee the rights of the peasants
- To preserve public order, safety and decency
- Could impose fines of up to 5 roubles
- Could imprison individuals for up to 7 days
- Could suspend court officials and recommend their dismissal
- Acted as judges in certain civil and lesser criminal cases
- Interfered in local elections of deputies to the district *zemstva*
- Until 1905 hereditary nobles were given preference when applicants for the posts were considered

Although peasant poverty was not universal in Russia, it undoubtedly affected the lives of large numbers and helped to drive many towards direct action. During the 1890s rent and labour strikes increased and illegal seizures of land from private landowners became more common. In 1901 there were serious crop failures. In the following year the Ukraine, the Volga and Georgia witnessed major peasant disturbances.

The last decades of tsarist rule were also of significance to the Russian noble class. Gradually, the status and power of this group were eroded as the effects of Alexander II's reforms spread through society. Between 1861 and 1905 noble land-ownership declined by some 41 per cent. The land was disposed of by sale or, all too often, as a result of bankruptcy. Of course, many nobles continued to own land and there were some who became successful capitalist-farmers, but many regarded the government's priority as being the promotion of industry. Industrial progress, they believed, was being achieved at their expense. They were critical of government measures such as high protective tariffs which kept the price of agricultural machinery high. In addition, State service no longer offered an assured alternative to the exploitation of a rural estate. It became more common for merit, not social rank, to be the qualification for entry into the State bureaucracy or officer corps. By 1897 only 51 per cent of army officers and 30 per cent of the civil service were nobles by birth. The decline of this class, and their perception that the government had too little concern for their fortunes, undermined their traditional loyalty to the autocracy.

## Industrial progress

In the years following the death of Alexander II Russia experienced rapid industrial development. By 1914 the Russian Empire was the fifth largest industrial power in the world. During the 1890s industrial output expanded at an annual rate of 8 per cent. A European recession from 1900 to 1903 slowed the pace but between 1907 and 1914 growth rates continued at around 6 per cent per annum. Heading the industrial take-off was railway construction, typified by the massive Trans-Siberian project; a 4000-mile link between Chelyabinsk in the Urals and Vladivostok which took 12 years to build and cost 250 million roubles. Government-sponsored railway-building galvanized the whole industrial economy. In concentrated regions of western Russia (see map) traditional manufacturing industries such as textiles expanded with the introduction of new machinery. Coal and iron production increased and the output of oil from the Caucasus was rivalled only by Texas in the USA.

| Railway construction (1880–1914) | |
|---|---|
| 1880 | 22,865 km |
| 1890 | 30,596 km |
| 1904 | 59,616 km |
| 1914 | 77,246 km |

| Annual production (millions of tons) | | | |
|---|---|---|---|
| | Coal | Pig Iron | Oil |
| 1870 | 0.68 | 0.33 | 0.03 |
| 1880 | 3.24 | 0.42 | 0.50 |
| 1890 | 5.90 | 0.89 | 3.90 |
| 1900 | 16.1 | 2.66 | 10.20 |
| 1910 | 26.8 | 2.99 | 9.40 |
| 1913 | 35.4 | 4.12 | 9.10 |

## Main industrial regions in Russia to 1917

FINLAND

BALTIC SEA

St Petersburg

Riga

PRUSSIA

POLAND

Warsaw

Czestocnowa

Dombrowa
Basin

Polish
industrial
area

AUSTRIA

HUNGARY

ROUMANIA

Yaroslav

Tver

Kaiuga

Kiev

Kharkov

Krivoy Rog

Odessa

Kostroma

Ivanovo

Vladimir

Moscow

Tula

Bryansk

Ekaterinoslav

Taganrog

Lugansk

Yuzovka

Rostov

Urals

Perm

metallurgical
region

Ura

Ekaterinburg

Zlatoust

Volga

Ural

BLACK SEA

Grozny

Baku

CAUCASUS

CASPIAN SEA

RUSSIA

○  Various industries
□  Textiles
△  Metallurgy
■  Iron ore
▲  Coal

P  Petroleum
●  Other towns
   Central industrial region
   St Petersburg and Riga industrial and
   engineering areas
   Caucasus petroleum areas

Hugh Seton-Watson, *The Russian Empire 1801–1917* (1967)

INDUSTRIAL PROGRESS: THE NOBEL BROTHERS' OIL REFINERY AT BAKU IN THE CAUCASUS (1886)

## Urban discontent

At the turn of the century less than a quarter of the working population was occupied outside agriculture, and only about 2 million were employed in factories and mines. However, the concentration of a landless working class in relatively confined areas (about 60 per cent of all industrial workers were employed in the industrial districts around Moscow, St Petersburg, the Ukraine and in Poland) created social problems out of all proportion to the numbers involved.

The principal complaints focused on the dreadful living and working conditions in the industrial centres. Wages were low and job security non-existent. Factories were dangerous and run by disciplinarian overseers. Hours were long and there was little comfort at the end of the daily shift as workers returned to squalid rooms and cellars; or worse, to factory dormitories. Even in Russia's civic showpiece – the capital, St Petersburg – basic standards of sanitation were grossly lacking:

'...Nobody will be able to deny that the government should take special measures to deal with a city where the number of deaths exceeds the number of births, where one third of the deaths are caused by infectious diseases, where typhoid claims more victims than in any West European city, where smallpox is still rife, where recurrent typhus, a disease long eradicated in the West, is still occasionally seen, and which is a favourable breeding ground for both cholera and plague bacteria.'

Speech by Stolypin to the Third Duma (January 1911), quoted in Martin McCauley, *Octobrists to Bolsheviks: Imperial Russia 1905–1917* (1984)

Such conditions produced an increasingly militant working class. The most potent weapon of the industrial workers was strike action. From the mid-1880s industrial disputes became more frequent, reaching a peak in 1899 with 97,000 workers withdrawing their labour. Such numbers, however, were small when compared with the opening years of the Twentieth Century. In 1902 and 1903 there were mass strikes in several southern cities including Baku, Odessa and Rostov-on-Don; rehearsals for the huge protests associated with the Russian Revolution of 1905.

## The role of the government

### The policies of Sergei Witte

How far was the government responsible for the difficulties faced by the poorer classes in Russian society? Certainly there were factors beyond the control of the State such as the weather and increases in population. Nevertheless, government policy, especially that designed to encourage industry, has not escaped criticism. The most active champion of industrial expansion in Russia was Sergei Witte, Minister of Finance from 1892 to 1903. Witte built on the groundwork laid by his predecessors, Bunge (1881–86) and Vyshnegradskii (1887–92). These ministers had been responsible for the initial progress made in railway construction, the stabilization of the currency, and the achievement of a trading balance which enabled Russia to borrow successfully from abroad. Witte's policies went further and were applied with greater intensity.

- He encouraged direct State investment in industrial projects, especially railways.

SERGEI WITTE

- He maintained high protective tariffs to encourage the development of domestic industry.
- He insisted on a tax revenue adequate to the needs of government expenditure.
- Above all, Witte actively sponsored foreign investment in Russian industry; his motive, outlined in 1899, was clear: 'The inflow of foreign capital is, in the strong conviction of the Minister of Finance, the only way to bring our country's economy quickly up to the level where it can provide us with cheap and plentiful goods.' (Sergei Witte, quoted in Martin McCauley, Octobrists to Bolsheviks: Imperial Russia 1905–1917 (1984))

Foreign investment did indeed flow quickly into Russia, especially after 1897 when Witte put the currency on the gold standard, thus making it readily convertible on the international money markets. Between 1893 and 1896 foreigners invested 144.9 million roubles in Russian enterprises (domestic investment for the same period was 103.7 million roubles). Witte presided over the most dramatic industrial boom the country had ever seen, but at what price?

Opposition voices criticized Witte for making Russia too dependent on foreigners. More significantly, high protective tariffs were attacked for restricting the freedom of the consumer to purchase cheap imports. High indirect taxes – especially on basic goods such as matches, vodka, tobacco, sugar, tea and kerosene – were seen as part of an official policy to 'squeeze' the peasantry in order to finance industrial expansion. High taxes, it was claimed, forced peasants to sell as much grain as possible, leaving them vulnerable to harvest failure and subject to famine. Some of the criticisms of Witte were valid. There was underinvestment in agriculture and a strong feeling prevailed in the countryside that industry would be promoted whatever the cost to agriculture. Nevertheless, the encouragement of industry did not *cause* the peasants problems. It is true that it probably added to their difficulties, but by far the greater portion of the tax burden was levied for the traditional purposes of servicing the army and the administration, not for industrial investment.

## The appeal of Marxism

The revolutionary movement which had gathered pace under Alexander II and eventually provided his assassins (see Chapter 8), underwent fundamental changes in the period after 1881. The old Populist belief that the Russian peasantry would, through the commune, lead Russia to socialism had become largely discredited. It was clear that the peasantry had little interest in their appointed role and that the rapid industrial transformation of the State created conditions which did not fit Populist theory. The idea, for example, that Russia would avoid the capitalist stage of its economic development and move straight to peasant socialism was no longer tenable. As Populist theories became obsolete, Russian intellectuals became increasingly attracted to the ideas of Karl Marx.

In 1848 Marx had written the *Communist Manifesto* with his collaborator Frederick Engels, but it was the publication of his book *Capital* in 1867 which had the greater impact on socialist development. Marxist theory identified the conflict between social classes as the principal factor

KARL MARX

in historical development. The class which controlled the dominant means of production would, it claimed, hold sway over the rest of society. At the time of the French Revolution, Marx saw that society had undergone a critical transformation:

|  | System | Means of production | Dominant class |
| --- | --- | --- | --- |
| Pre-1789 | Feudalism | the land | the nobility |
| Post-1789 | Capitalism | commerce and industry | the middle class |

The capitalist middle class made its wealth by exploiting the workers, the so-called proletariat. Marx believed that this exploitation would inevitably become so intolerable that the proletariat would overthrow the capitalist system in a revolution and replace it with a communist society.

Marxism had enormous appeal to Russian intellectuals. It seemed to offer a scientific analysis of social development which could be applied to the changes currently taking place in the State. A brutally-exploited, land-less proletariat was emerging in Russia as part of the process of industrialization. Russian Marxists argued that the way to ensure the over-throw of the decaying tsarist regime was to organize the workers to carry out their 'inevitable' revolution.

The founding texts of Russian Marxism were written by George Plekhanov during the 1880s. From the early 1890s Marxism was taken up by young radicals and its adherents soon outnumbered the Populists. Marxists were involved in the St Petersburg strikes of 1895, 1896 and 1897 though some of their more promising activists, including Lenin and Martov, were arrested and exiled for short terms to Siberia. In 1898 the Russian Social Democratic Labour Party was founded to unite the various Marxist groups. Police activity forced the Social Democrats to operate outside Russia. Thus the Marxist journal *Iskra* (The Spark), founded in 1900, had to be smuggled into Russia from Western Europe. In 1902 agents of *Iskra* began to distribute a pamphlet entitled *What is to be Done?* This political tract, written by Lenin, was highly significant. It adapted the ideas of Marx and produced a hybrid later to be called Marxism-Leninism. In it, Lenin rejected the theory that oppressed workers would spontaneously turn to socialism and eventually overthrow the State.

LENIN, PHOTOGRAPHED IN PARIS (1910)

Lenin believed that workers were more likely to agitate through organiz-ations such as the trade unions for improved conditions within the capitalist system. Accordingly he stressed the need for a small group of dedicated professionals who would assume responsibility for the detailed planning of the revolution. This group would be controlled by a strong central committee which would ensure absolute loyalty and obedience. In 1903 the Social Democrats met for a party congress in London. Immediately, the new direction proposed by Lenin in *What is to be Done?* caused a major split in the party. Those of the majority, the Bolsheviks (who supported Lenin), were challenged by the Mensheviks ('those of the minority') who were ranged behind Martov. The Mensheviks were con-cerned that the development of a narrow, professional party would isolate them from the working masses, the very class the Marxists sought to rep-resent. The Bolshevik-Menshevik split was never mended and eventually, in the winter of 1917, it was to be Lenin's professional revolutionaries who seized control and began to build the modern Soviet State.

## The 1905 Revolution

### Background

In 1905 massive tremors of popular discontent shook the autocracy to its foundations. The 'revolution' of that year was in fact a composite of workers' demonstrations, peasant disturbances, strikes, naval mutinies, assassinations and nationalist risings. It forced political concessions from a frightened Tsar and was hailed by political activists – including Lenin and Martov – as the beginning of the great proletarian revolution predicted by Marx.

The immediate background to the chaos of 1905 was provided by economic recession and an unpopular war with Japan. The down-turn in Russia's economic activity during the depression of 1899–1903 caused unemployment and an intensification of poverty both in the towns and the countryside. In 1902 there were major peasant disturbances in the Ukraine, Georgia and the Volga. Strikes and street disturbances in industrial cities such as Baku and Rostov-on-Don resulted in the deployment of troops to restore order. The Socialist Revolutionaries, a neo-Populist organization which rejected the methods of revolutionary Marxism, had an active terrorist wing. They added to the instability of the regime with a series of well-planned political assassinations. In 1904 they claimed their most prominent victim: the unpopular Minister of the Interior, VK Plehve. In a change of tactics the government tried to appease its critics with a more relaxed attitude to censorship and public associations. The move backfired as a torrent of propaganda poured forth from liberal and revolutionary organizations. A police-backed experiment to channel workers' grievances into supervised trade unions failed when the leadership organized large-scale strike action. Finally, the war against Japan which had begun in 1904 was going badly. Government incompetence in the handling of the armed forces and a series of humiliating defeats provoked uncompromising criticism.

It was in these circumstances that on 9 January 1905 a huge crowd assembled in St Petersburg to petition the Tsar at the Winter Palace. The crowd was peaceful, unarmed and contained women and children. Their petition called for social improvements: better pay, an eight-hour working day, fairer taxes and the right to form trade unions. There were political demands too for universal and secret suffrage and a representative assembly. Led by Father Gapon, an Orthodox priest and founder of the police-sponsored Assembly of Factory Workers, the crowd was suddenly halted by rows of armed troops. Paralysed by fear and total disbelief, the marchers watched as the soldiers raised their rifles, and fired.

The soldiers of the Preobrazhensky regiment, without any summons to disperse, shoot down the unfortunate people as if they were playing at bloodshed. Several hundred fall; more than a hundred and fifty are killed. They are almost all children, women and young people. It is terrible. Blood flows on all sides. At 5 o'clock the crowd is driven back, cut down and repelled on all sides. The people, terror stricken, fly in every

**T**ALKING POINT

**The appeal of Marxism**

Why did Marxism become popular in Russia? Discuss those aspects of the Russian social and political system which gave Marxism its appeal to educated Russians.

TROOPS OPEN FIRE AT THE NARVA GATE. THIS ACTION SPARKED OFF THE 1905 REVOLUTION

direction. Scared women and children slip, fall, rise to their feet, only to fall again farther on. At this moment a sharp word of command is heard and the victims fall *en masse*.

*Le Matin* (January 1905), quoted in GMD Howat, *European History 1789–1970* (1973)

This astonishing act of autocratic brutality, rapidly christened 'Bloody Sunday' and described by the historian Edward Acton as one of the 'greatest political blunders' of the Romanov regime, had instant and widespread consequences. (See map overleaf.)

### The Tsar's concessions

In October, with Russia paralysed by strikes, Tsar Nicholas II had been compelled to offer concessions in the shape of the *October Manifesto*. The Tsar promised to take the following measures:

'1 Fundamental civil freedoms will be granted to the population, including real personal inviolability, freedom of conscience, speech, assembly and association.

2 Participation in the Duma will be granted to those classes of the population which are at present deprived of voting powers, insofar as is possible in the short period before the convocation of the Duma, and this will lead to the development of a universal franchise. There will be no delay to the Duma elections which have already been organized.

3 It is established as an unshakeable rule that no law can come into force without its approval by the State Duma and that the elected representatives of

# Events of 1905

**Finland and Poland**

Nationalist demonstrations. Martial law declared – brutal suppression of protestors,

**St Petersburg**

*January*
'Bloody Sunday' followed by a general strike in the city.

*October*
St Petersburg Soviet (Council) of Workers set up. Deputies elected from local factories. Soviets set up in other towns in imitation.

*December*
Deputies arrested – Soviet destroyed.

**Black Sea**

*June*
Mutiny on board the battleship *Potemkin*. Many officers murdered. Ship pursued around the Black Sea after bombarding Odessa. Sought assylum in Roumania.

**Moscow**

*February*
Assassination of Grand Duke Sergei (the Tsar's uncle and Governor of Moscow).

**Widespread peasant disturbances**

Arson of noble property – seizures of noble land – labour and rent strikes. All-Russian Peasants' Union to articulate the complaints of peasant Russia. There were 3300 peasant disturbances during 1905.

During 1905 there were 13,995 strikes in Russia, involving close to 3 million people.

**Moscow**

*September*
New wave of strikes began. Quickly spread to St Petersburg and many provincial cities. Many employers showed sympathy. Railways ground to a halt as the Union of Railwaymen called strike action.

In October the Tsar issued a historic manifesto (see page 191).

*December*
Armed uprising in Moscow spread to other cities. Army remained loyal and gradually crushed opposition.

ASSASSINATION OF THE GRAND DUKE SERGEI IN MOSCOW (FEBRUARY 1905)

the people will be given the opportunity to play a real part in the supervision of the legality of the activities of government bodies.'

> Nicholas II, *The October Manifesto* (1905), quoted in Martin McCauley, *Octobrists to Bolsheviks: Imperial Russia 1905–1917* (1984)

The manifesto got a mixed reception from the Russian people. A loose political grouping of moderate landowners and industrialists, the Octobrists, agreed to work with the Tsar on the basis of his proposals. The other principal party which emerged, the Kadets, was not fully satisfied with the manifesto but regarded its terms as a platform upon which it could build real parliamentary democracy. The Tsar's proposals were seriously flawed. The Duma (or parliament) which he proposed had limited powers. It could not appoint ministers or initiate legislation, though it could prevent a law from entering the statute books. The Emperor could dissolve the Duma and government ministers were not answerable to the elected body.

The concessions failed to appease workers and peasants. The most serious peasant disturbances occurred in the three weeks *after* the issue of the October Manifesto and continued through 1906 and 1907. In many towns strikes continued and workers' councils (soviets) were established. Nationalist protests in Poland and the Baltic States persisted, and at the Kronstadt naval base near St Petersburg troops had to be used to crush a mutiny. Gradually, however, the forces of order gained the upper hand, establishing a degree of calm in a situation which nevertheless remained potentially combustible.

### The Dumas (1906–14)

Tsar Nicholas II was not pleased with the concessions he had been forced to make to the constitutionalists. Before the first Duma met in 1906 he dismissed Witte, blaming him for the crisis which had produced the October Manifesto. He was also careful to ensure that the powers of the Dumas were limited, and in a speech in 1906 he warned:

'Let it be known to all that I…shall maintain the principle of autocracy just as firmly and unflinchingly as did my unforgettable dead father.'

> Quoted in SJ Lee, *Aspects of European History 1789–1980* (1982)

The performance of the Dumas in the period 1906 to 1914 reflected Nicholas's reluctance to allow real constitutional progress in his empire.

**The First Duma (April–July 1906)** Nicholas had hoped that the peasants would return a majority of conservative representatives. Instead, the First Duma contained large numbers of radicals including Kadets, Socialist Revolutionaries and Social Democrats. The moderate Octobrists won only 17 seats. The Duma soon clashed with the government over the rural land crisis. Troops occupied the chamber and broke up the Duma.

**The Second Duma (February–June 1907)** This contained even more extremists (both on the left and the right) than the first assembly. Moderates, especially the Kadets, found their representation reduced considerably. Once again the Duma was unco-operative with the government, being especially critical of proposals made for land reforms by Stolypin, Chairman of the Council of Ministers (see page 204). As a result, the government devised a

**T**ALKING POINT

**Comparing revolutions**

How does the 1905 Revolution compare with others you have studied, eg 1830 (France), 1848 (general European outbreak)?

Do you notice any common features? Could events in Eastern Europe (1989-90) be described as revolutionary?

plan to discredit the Duma. The police fabricated evidence accusing its representatives of conspiring to incite a revolution. This provided the Tsar with an excuse to dissolve the troublesome assembly.

**The Third Duma (1907–1912)** Because the political complexion of the first two Dumas did not suit the government, Stolypin took steps to ensure that the new assembly would be more acceptable. The electoral system was revised to ensure greater representation for the urban rich and the country gentry. This conservative weighting was achieved at the expense of the peasants and the urban proletariat. Accordingly, the Third Duma was far less radical, being dominated instead by the moderate Octobrist Party (120 seats); the Kadets were reduced to just 45 seats.

This Duma was the first to serve its full five-year term, and for most of this time the government made a genuine attempt to work with it. Some achievements were recorded. Improvements in the army and navy were secured by Duma committees, justices of the peace (abolished by Alexander III) were re-established, and health and accident insurance schemes for industrial workers were introduced. However, even this conservative body did not escape government interference. Stolypin did not hesitate to use his powers of suspension to bypass the Duma when presented with resistance.

**The Fourth Duma (1912–17)** The last Duma was elected on the same basis as its predecessor and had a similar political complexion. However, its relationship with the government was far from harmonious. Stolypin's suspension of the Third Duma angered even the moderates, who attacked the Tsar unreservedly. Stolypin's assassination and the resignation in 1911 of Guchkov (Octobrist president of the Third Duma) removed the two key figures whose mutual respect had made the assembly viable. The legacy of mistrust bequeathed by the Third Duma meant that after 1912 its relationship with the government deteriorated badly. It was presented with no substantial legislation as the Tsar and his compliant ministers closed ranks against the representatives of the people.

Increasingly, the Tsar alienated even the most conservative elements in society, especially by his obsessive devotion to one Gregori Rasputin. An intimate of the royal family who enjoyed a reputation as a holy man with mystical powers, Rasputin's debauched private life was well known amongst St Petersburg society. The royal couple kept him close, however, convinced of his apparently 'miraculous' ability to stop the uncontrolled bleeding of their haemophiliac son Alexis. Rasputin's political influence at court was limited before the First World War, but his behaviour reduced further the popularity of the royal family. In addition the Tsar's apparent preference for the advice of such disreputable characters convinced the Duma that its days were numbered.

# The work of Peter Stolypin

In 1906 Tsar Nicholas II appointed a new prime minister. Peter Stolypin was a loyal and able statesman who had, until his promotion served as Minister of the Interior. His approach to government was to combine discipline with moderate reform. In the circumstances of his appointment – with a troublesome Duma, political assassinations, a naval mutiny and

**1** What do the duration and political composition of the first three Dumas suggest about the attitude of the Tsar to the 'constitutional experiment'?

**2** Would it be accurate to describe Russia from 1906 to 1914 as a constitutional monarchy?

**3** 'The Dumas helped to stabilize Russia in the period 1906–14 and improved the prospects for the survival of the monarchy.'

'The Dumas increased social and political tensions within Russia and helped to alienate the Tsar from all social classes.'

What is your opinion of these conflicting judgements?

CAPTION 9.10: RASPUTIN CARICATURED IN A RUSSIAN MAGAZINE

Comment on: (a) the size; (b) the appearance of the three figures.

What political point is the cartoonist making?

continuing peasant disturbances – Stolypin moved swiftly to the counter-attack. He established the notorious field courts-martial to deal with terrorists and rural trouble-makers. In ten months some 1400 people were executed by order of these administrative courts. A further 2000 people went to the gallows by order of ordinary courts between 1905 and 1908. The hangman's noose became known as the 'Stolypin necktie' and earned the Prime Minister a reputation as a ruthless and brutal reactionary.

There was, however, another aspect to Stolypin's work as Prime Minister. Between 1906 and 1911, a series of measures designed to address the peasant problem (known collectively as the Stolypin Reform) was introduced. The principal aim of the reforms was to stimulate the appearance of a class of prosperous land-owning peasants. It was hoped that independence from the commune would breed enterprise and lead to improved agricultural yields. Moreover, Stolypin aimed to counteract peasant disturbances by encouraging a class which would have a vested interest in the *status quo*. The focus of his attention was the commune. Instead of redistributing land held by the nobility (the demand at the centre of the rural disturbances), Stolypin decided to allow the peasants to opt out of communal land management. His legislation enabled them to leave the control of the commune and to consolidate their scattered strips of land into a single farm. By 1914 nearly two million peasant households had consolidated their holdings (there were between 10 and 12 million peasant households in Russia at this time), though applications to do so had declined considerably after 1909 with most peasants preferring the relative security of communal farming. Many of those who consolidated their lands did so in order to sell it and relocate to the towns. The class of prosperous middle-peasants which Stolypin had hoped to encourage never materialized.

| **Number of peasants leaving the commune (1907–15)** | | |
|---|---|---|
| Year | Number of households applying to leave | Number of households finally leaving |
| 1907 | 211,922 | 48,271 |
| 1908 | 840,059 | 508,344 |
| 1909 | 649,921 | 579,409 |
| 1910 | 341,884 | 342,245 |
| 1911 | 242,328 | 145,567 |
| 1912 | 152,397 | 122,314 |
| 1913 | 160,304 | 134,554 |
| 1914 | 120,321 | 97,877 |
| 1915 | 36,497 | 29,851 |
| TOTAL | 2,755,633 | 2,008,432 |

Source: SM Dubrovsky, *Stolypinskaya zemelnaya reforma* (1963). Quoted in Martin McCauley, *Octobrists to Bolsheviks: Imperial Russia 1905–1917* (1984)

Politically, too, the reform missed its target. Peasants maintained an overwhelming desire to see the redistribution of noble estates, regarding this as the only real solution to the problem of land-hunger. In addition, the appearance of independent farmers – whose ambitions had disrupted the traditional work patterns of the village community – provoked resentment amongst those who remained within the commune. Instead of relieving the situation in the countryside, Stolypin's Reform added a new dimension to peasant tensions.

Stolypin supplemented his major land-reform initiative by encouraging the relocation of peasants from the overpopulated regions of European Russia to vast tracts of vacant land in Siberia.

| Migration to Siberia (1905–13) | | |
|---|---|---|
| Year | Total migrants and scouts | Returners |
| 1905 | 44,029 | 11,524 |
| 1906 | 216,648 | 46,262 |
| 1907 | 567,979 | 117,518 |
| 1908 | 758,812 | 121,204 |
| 1909 | 707,463 | 139,907 |
| 1910 | 353,000 | 70,000* |
| 1911 | 226,100 | 64,000* |
| 1912 | 259,600 | 34,000* |
| 1913 | 327,900 | 23,000* |

*These figures do not include returning scouts.

Source: DW Treadgold, *The Great Siberian Migration* (1957). Quoted in Martin McCauley, *Octobrists to Bolsheviks: Imperial Russia 1905–1917* (1984)

According to these figures, how successful was Stolypin's migration scheme?

## Nicholas II and the autocratic legacy

On 14 May 1895 a magnificent coronation ceremony was staged in the Uspensky cathedral in Moscow. Nicholas II, who had inherited the throne the previous year, was installed as the new Tsar of Russia. It was to be the last coronation in Russian history. Four days after the ceremony, with the festivities still in full swing, tragedy struck. A crowd of over half a million eager subjects had gathered on Khodynka field to await the traditional distribution of coronation gifts. The authorities failed to take adequate precautions and were quite incapable of handling such a large assembly. As the people surged forward, whole sections of the crowd collapsed under the weight of numbers. Thirteen hundred people were crushed to death in the disaster and many hundreds more were seriously injured.

The incompetence of officials in charge at Khodynka was to blame for the huge loss of life. A few simple measures would have enabled the event to pass off without incident. With hindsight, Khodynka might be regarded as symbolic of the reign of Russia's last tsar: the revolutionary disaster which ended centuries of autocratic rule might have been prevented had those in charge recognized the danger signs and taken precautions to avert their potential consequences. As it was, the relentless advance of social and political discontent never commanded the full attention of the Tsar. His refusal to acknowledge anything other than the autocratic principle created a situation in which people from all social ranks despaired more and more of his ability to respond to their needs. Why was Nicholas II so unwilling to react constructively to the clear demands for social and political change voiced by his desperate subjects?

Nicholas II was never a popular tsar. Increasingly he avoided contact with his people, rarely venturing far from the security of his immediate

TSAR NICHOLAS II AND THE
TSARINA ALEXANDRA. THIS
PHOTOGRAPH WAS TAKEN
SHORTLY AFTER THEIR WEDDING

TSAR ALEXANDER III

family circle. In 1913 public celebrations to mark the tercentenary of the Romanov dynasty were poorly attended. Those who did find time to view the royal entourage often merely stood and stared at this rather uninspiring stranger who was their master and, to many, their oppressor. Nicholas did little to help his cause. He never approved of the Duma, seeing it as a vulgar intrusion into his running of State affairs. But he himself was weak-willed, of no particular intellect, and easily influenced by the assortment of ill-chosen advisers who gathered around him. Hence it was easy for the opposition to present the Tsar as a puppet whose strings were pulled by men such as Rasputin. Nicholas was not a complex man. He possessed the simple impulses common to many of his ancestors: a fondness for the discipline and pageantry of the army; a racial bigotry which expressed itself in aggressive anti-semitism; and, above all, an unshakeable belief in the God-given power of the autocracy.

Nicholas was primed with such beliefs by the two most important influences of his youth; his father Alexander III and his tutor Pobedonostsev. Following the assassination of Alexander II in 1881, Alexander III had retreated from the reforms initiated by his father. The Loris-Melikov proposals which Alexander II had approved on the morning of his death (see page 180) were rejected. Police activity increased and there was a major offensive against the revolutionary movement. There was persecution of religious and national minorities and a purging of 'liberal' ministers. Under Alexander III the autocracy reverted to a harsh and inflexible regime characteristic of the reign of Nicholas I.

Underpinning this period of reaction was the pervasive influence of Pobedonostsev, royal tutor and (from 1881) Chief Procurator of the Holy Synod. Until 1906, Pobedonostsev faithfully served Russia's last tsars. As one of the most complete reactionaries in Russian history his advice did much to undermine the position of the autocracy in its twilight years. Pobedonostsev was passionately committed to the values of the Russian Orthodox Church, believing that it offered an impoverished peasantry all the guidance and comfort it could need. He was anti-semitic and supported the Holy League, an extreme organization which planned and executed vicious pogroms. He was a devoted Slavophile and rejected all Western ideas as false and corrupting. Accordingly, he poured scorn on the principles of liberalism, condemned parliamentary government and refused to acknowledge the value of a free Press. His belief in the absolute autocracy of the Tsar was unassailable. Such was the man who served as tutor and adviser to both Alexander III and Nicholas II. Through Pobedonostsev's direct influence, Russia was furnished with two tsars cast in the classic autocratic mould. They were devoted to an outdated and discredited form of government at a time when the State required fundamental and far-reaching reforms. Nicholas's refusal to adapt to changing circumstances isolated him from all social classes. Only the loyalty of the secret police and the army guaranteed his position. Eventually, in 1917, even this was lost and the great history of the tsars was ended.

# 9.1 Anti-semitism in tsarist Russia

**By 1905 there were 5 million Jews in Russia**

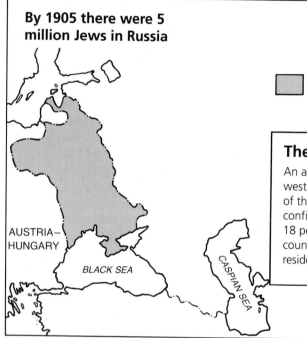

☐ The Pale of Settlement

### The Pale of Settlement

An area made up of 15 administrative districts of western and south-western Russia and ten provinces of the kingdom of Poland. Jews in Russia were confined to this region by law. By 1900 only about 18 per cent of Russian Jews remained in the countryside - official policy was to 'encourage' their residence in urban districts.

AUSTRIA–HUNGARY

BLACK SEA

CASPIAN SEA

### Anti-Jewish regulations

- After 1882 no new Jewish settlers were permitted in rural areas of the Pale.
- Jewish doctors or medical assistants serving in the army were limited to 5 per cent of total personnel.
- Laws of 1890 and 1892 removed the right of Jews to vote for *zemstvo* assemblies.
- Admission of Jewish lawyers to the Bar was suspended.
- Jews faced expulsion from towns such as Kiev (1886) and Moscow (1891).
- Jewish trade on Christian holidays, including Sundays, was banned.
- Educational quotas limited the number of Jewish university students to 10 per cent of total enrolment in the Pale, 5 per cent outside and 3 per cent in Moscow and St Petersburg. The same quotas applied to secondary-school pupils.

### Organized violence – the Pogrom

'Essentially a pogrom consisted of the assembly of a mob which would throng into the Jewish parts of a town, break into houses and shops to loot, beat, rape, burn and frequently kill the inhabitants. Local police and even sometimes the local troops seemed reluctant to intervene except against those Jews who were successfully defending themselves.'

JW Westwood, *Endurance and Endeavour* (1973)

**Principal outbreaks**

**1881** Attacks across the Pale. Numerous deaths and widespread damage to property.

**1903** Kishinev in Southern Russia. Scene of 2 days of violence – some 50 deaths.

**1905–06** 600 Jewish communities attacked – 1000 Jews killed.

## A Pogrom described

'Then a rumour started that there had been a decree that for three days you could do whatever you wanted to the Jews. For three days there was no check on the looting. After the three days were up, the police, who along with the Black Hundreds had taken advantage of the workers' primitive mentality to incite the pogrom in the first place, started to restore order. But nothing was done about all the looting and rampage. The powers who had decreed the pogrom kept their word: three days had been put at the disposal of the Black Hundreds, and all the pillage and murder went unpunished. I heard that many of the Jews who had been beaten were in the factory infirmary. I decided to go there and have a look with one of my friends, another little boy. We found a horrible scene. The corpses of Jews who had been beaten to death were lying in rows on the floor.'

NS Khrushchev, quoted in Martin McCauley, *Octobrists to Bolsheviks: Imperial Russia 1905–1917* (1984)

## Jewish responses

**1 Emigration**   Between 1881 and 1914 some 2 million Jews left Russia - most bound for the USA. 200,000 settled in Briatin.

**2 Political activity**   As an urban-based, oppressed community the Jews were drawn to the revolutionary movement and socialist politics. Jewish activists became prominent in the Socialist Revolutionary and Social Democratic parties. A socialist Russia offered Jews the hope of obtaining the same rights as other citizens.

In 1897 Russian Jews set up their own workers' movement known as the Bund. The movement was very popular in the Pale: by 1905 it had 35,000 adherents.

**3 Zionism**   Zionists believed that Jews would continue to be persecuted wherever they lived until they had a homeland of their own. Within Russia, the idea of establishing a Jewish State in Palestine found wide appeal amongst Jews.

## Explanations

**1 Religion**   The Jews maintained a religion distinct from the Orthodox Christianity of most Russian people. Jews were reviled as the killers of Christ.

**2 Occupations**   Most Jews earned a living as traders, shopkeepers, landlords' agents, commercial dealers and craftsmen. Few were engaged in the primary productive sector: agriculture. Jews were often attacked as parasites.

**3 Conspiracy**   Jews were often presented as being part of an international conspiracy to infiltrate money markets, the Press, the legal system, the bureaucracy and the banks in order to assume control of the State.

## QUESTIONS

**1** Consider the dates of the principal pogroms. From your knowledge of Russian history, do they appear to coincide with any events which placed the autocracy in apparent danger? If so, how might this explain official complicity in the violence?

**2** By requiring Jews to live in towns, how did the authorities reinforce the common believe that Jews were non-productive 'parasites' on the rest of society? At times of crisis (eg famine), how might the occupational composition of most Jewish communities have intensified anti-semitic feeling?

**3** How did official anti-semitic policy help to generate recruits for those groups which opposed the tsarist system?

# EXAMINING THE EVIDENCE
## Stability or strife (1905–14)?

### Source A

Historians disagree on whether revolution was inevitable by mid-1914. Many regard 1905–14 as a period of stabilization and progress brought to a premature end at Sarajevo; in short, that if there had been no 1914 there might not have been a 1917. Soviet historians, on the other hand, regard the revolution as historically logical, as inevitable, and discern a 'revolutionary upsurge' in the industrial unrest which began in 1912. They claim that by August 1914 Russia was ripe for an imminent revolution, for which the Bolsheviks had begun to plan in 1913, and that the war in reality delayed this revolution until 1917.

JN Westwood, *Endurance and Endeavour: Russian History 1812–1971* (1973)

### Source B

| Year | Strikes | Strikers | Political strikes | Political strikers |
|------|---------|----------|-------------------|--------------------|
| 1905 | 13,995 | 2,863,173 | 6024 | 1,082,576 |
| 1906 | 6114 | 1,108,406 | 2950 | 514,854 |
| 1907 | 3573 | 740,074 | 2558 | 521,573 |
| 1908 | 892 | 176,101 | 464 | 92,694 |
| 1909 | 340 | 64,166 | 50 | 8863 |
| 1910 | 222 | 46,623 | 8 | 3777 |
| 1911 | 466 | 105,110 | 24 | 8380 |
| 1912 | 2032 | 725,491 | 1300 | 549,812 |
| 1913 | 2404 | 887,096 | 1034 | 502,442 |
| 1914 | 3534 | 1,337,458 | 2401 | 985,655 |

Figures compiled by the Russian Ministry of Trade and Industry for strikes in factories covered by factory inspection. Quoted in Martin McCauley, *Octobrists to Bolsheviks: Imperial Russia 1905–1917* (1984)

### Source C

Peasant disorders

| 1905 | 3228 |
|------|------|
| 1913 | 128 |

Figures quoted in JN Westwood, as above

### Source D

The general decline in rural disturbances after 1907 suggested to some observers that Stolypin had successfully diverted the peasantry from their quest for noble land [through his land reforms]. Yet the view that the reform was jeopardized only by the outbreak of war in 1914 no longer seems tenable. Applications to leave the commune declined long before the war began...The relative tranquillity of the countryside in the period before 1914 owed little to social change or technical improvement in the village. It is to be explained more in terms of a rapid increase in the amount of land sown, the recovery of grain prices, and a series of excellent harvests.

Edward Acton, *Russia* (1986)

## Source E

Numbers killed or wounded by terrorist attacks (1905–09)

| Year | Killed | Wounded | Total | |
|------|--------|---------|-------|---|
| 1905 | 233 | 358 | 591 | |
| 1906 | 768 | 820 | 1588 | |
| 1907 | 1231 | 1312 | 2543 | |
| 1908 | 394 | 615 | 1009 | |
| 1909 | 202 | 227 | 429 | (Figures available up to 1.6.1909 only) |

Figures originally included in telegrams from Sazonov, Minister of Foreign Affairs, to Benkendorff, Ambassador to London; quoted in Martin McCauley, as above

## Source F

Wages [in industry] rose, but barely kept up with living costs, and the work day remained long, an average of ten hours in 1913. Housing conditions in the industrial centres deteriorated with the dramatic increase in the workforce by about a third between 1910 and 1914. In the working class districts of Moscow the average apartment accommodated 9 persons in 1912, and four couples were crowded into one room of a model barracks at one factory. In Petersburg the number of factory workers grew from 158,000 in 1908 to 216,000 in 1913. Many of them were fresh arrivals from the villages whose frustration at finding again the privations they had hoped to leave behind made them particularly prone to violence.

Hans Rogger, *Russia in the Age of Modernisation and Revolution 1881–1917* (1983)

## Source G

In the spring of 1911 the dead body of a thirteen-year-old boy was found in Kiev and widely spread rumours of a Jewish ritual murder led to the arrest of a Jew named Mendel Beilis. There was prolonged uproar in the press and a final great surge of public feeling before the accused man was brought to trial in Kiev towards the end of September 1913. Hundreds of foreign correspondents were present. As the trial proceeded a damaging weight of evidence was accumulated of official instigation of rumour and the corruption of witnesses. Behind all the plotting and perjury, a policy of diverting criticism from the government to the Jews was revealed. The person responsible was no other than the Minister of Justice for the previous seven years, IG Shcheglovitov. Feelings of acute embarrassment had been aroused in conservative quarters by the time the charge of ritual murder was dropped a month later and the accused man acquitted.

Richard Charques, *The Twilight of Imperial Russia* (1958)

## Source H

By 1914 former reformists were beginning to regard violence as the only means left to loosen a regime which seemed more and more intolerant, intolerable and, worse, untalented. This trend meant that the political parties were splitting at all possible seams. The Octobrists' left wing split away, the Kadets were uneasily divided into left, right and centre, while the businessmen's new Progressist Party actually made overtures (neither accepted nor rejected) to the Bolsheviks. Had there been no war it seems likely that a realignment of parties would have occurred, with the emergence of a strong and 'respectable' movement prepared to support violent change.

JN Westwood, as above

**1** Briefly summarize the historical debate outlined in Source A.

**2** Why do you suppose Soviet historians present the 1917 Russian Revolution as being 'inevitable'?

**3** How far do Sources B, C and E support the view that the period 1905–14 was one of stability in Russia? What are the specific limitations of these sources.

**4** How does Source D explain the apparent calm in the countryside in the period 1905–14?

**5** What does Source G reveal about public confidence in the Imperial government on the eve of the First World War?

**6** 'After 1912 the situation in Russia deteriorated and by 1914 the country was on the verge of revolution.' To what extent do Sources B, F, G and H support this statement?

# REVIEW

## What were the most significant events and developments in Russia during the period 1881–1914

The list below details many of the events and developments which occurred during the last years of tsarist Russia. Working in small groups (3–4 students), divide the list up under three headings: 'very important', 'moderately important' and 'relatively unimportant'. In each case, be prepared to justify your decision.

- Assassination of Alexander II (1881)
- Influence of Pobedonostsev (1881–1906)
- Accession of Nicholas II (1894)
- Intensification of anti-semitism
- Rise in population to the year 1914
- Periodic harvest failure and famine
- Introduction of the Land Captains (1889)
- Industrial development (1881–1914)

- Growth of urban industrial centres
- Decline of the Russian nobility
- Policies of Sergei Witte (1892–1903)
- 'Bloody Sunday' (1905)
- The *October Manifesto* (1905)
- Performance of the Dumas (1906–14)
- Influence of Rasputin
- Development of Russian Marxism
- Stolypin's land reforms

**1** Each group should report back to the whole class in turn. Groups should identify two things:
(a) the items which appear in the 'very important' column;
(b) the criteria used by the group to compile this list.

**2** From the 'report back' session, was it possible to identify a common perception of the most significant events in Russia between 1881 and 1914?

**3** How did groups decide which events were the most significant?

# 10 Independence and Unification: Italy 1815–70

## PREVIEW

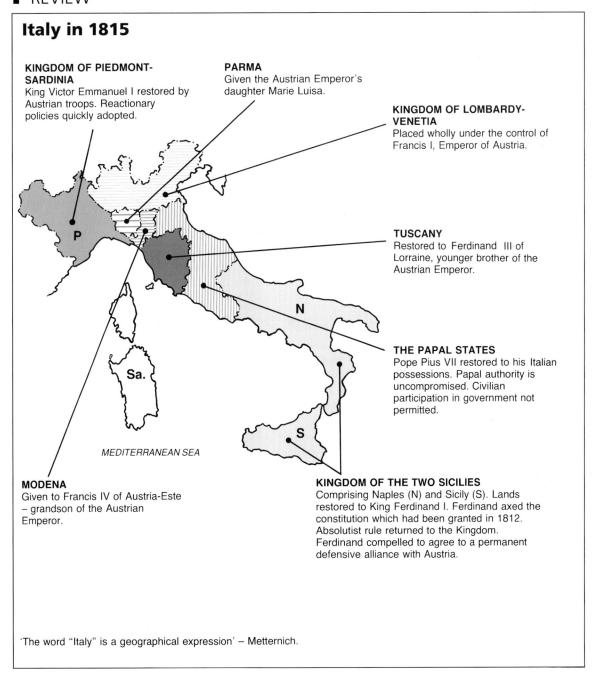

### Italy in 1815

**KINGDOM OF PIEDMONT-SARDINIA**
King Victor Emmanuel I restored by Austrian troops. Reactionary policies quickly adopted.

**PARMA**
Given the Austrian Emperor's daughter Marie Luisa.

**KINGDOM OF LOMBARDY-VENETIA**
Placed wholly under the control of Francis I, Emperor of Austria.

**TUSCANY**
Restored to Ferdinand III of Lorraine, younger brother of the Austrian Emperor.

**THE PAPAL STATES**
Pope Pius VII restored to his Italian possessions. Papal authority is uncompromised. Civilian participation in government not permitted.

**MODENA**
Given to Francis IV of Austria-Este – grandson of the Austrian Emperor.

**KINGDOM OF THE TWO SICILIES**
Comprising Naples (N) and Sicily (S). Lands restored to King Ferdinand I. Ferdinand axed the constitution which had been granted in 1812. Absolutist rule returned to the Kingdom. Ferdinand compelled to agree to a permanent defensive alliance with Austria.

*MEDITERRANEAN SEA*

'The word "Italy" is a geographical expression' – Metternich.

# The end of Napoleonic Italy

In 1815 the Italian peninsula presented the Vienna peacemakers with particular problems. Since 1799 the whole of the mainland had been under the control of the French and had experienced a social and political transformation which alarmed the conservative rulers of Europe's Great Powers.

The experience of the French occupation offered hope to Italian nationalists. The welding of the peninsula into a more coherent unit – albeit at the direction of an invader – demonstrated that the dream of a united Italy, not seen since the Sixth Century, could become a reality. The Vienna peacemakers thought differently. They wanted a divided Italy under the supervision of Austria. Thus, in the interests of the 'balance of power', and in an attempt to silence liberal and nationalist voices, Italy was broken up and returned to the possession of minor sovereigns. Many of the Napoleonic developments were abandoned, including precious constitutional experiments. In the aftermath of the 1815 settlement, the notion of a united and independent Italy was little more than political fantasy.

# The Risorgimento

In October 1870 the city of Rome became the capital of a united Italy. The acquisition of Rome from the Pope represented the final phase of a prolonged Italian struggle to become an independent nation free from internal political divisions. Italians call this process the Risorgimento; a great national revival which led to the creation of a united Italian kingdom. The use of this term, however, can be misleading. It implies a certain consistency of purpose and approach among those who participated in and directed the revival. In practice, the progress of the movement was never smooth and the outcome, a united Italian state, was by no means inevitable.

In the Nineteenth Century the Risorgimento began with an uncoordinated reaction against the Vienna restorations. The period 1815–32 was characterized by local risings directed against the absolutist rule of restored monarchs. Those who participated in these revolutionary outbursts had no common programme and precious little popular support. They were drawn chiefly from the educated middle class and driven by widely different objectives.

---

**Napoleon in Italy**

**1** *Territorial rationalization:* peninsula reduced from 11 to three states.

**2** *Legal uniformity:* introduced the French legal codes to standardize the practice of law throughout Italy.

**3** *Representative government:* set up elected assemblies based on the moderate French constitution of 1795.

**4** *Improved communications:* built new roads across the Alps and Apennine mountains.

**5** *Improved commerce:* internal trade barriers began to be dismantled.

**6** *Social change:* land redistributed; a commercial middle class began to develop.

**7** *The Church:* the power and influence of the Pope and the Catholic Church were reduced.

---

| THE EXTREMISTS | THE RADICALS | THE MODERATES |
|---|---|---|
| • Wished for Italy to become a single nation under an elected president.<br><br>• Looked to replace monarchical government with an elected parliament.<br><br>• Aimed to introduce democracy – one man, one vote. | Invested their hopes in the adoption of the 1812 Spanish constitution throughout the Italian states. This would provide for:<br>• the retention of the monarch, with limited powers;<br>• an elected assembly;<br>• one man, one vote;<br>• freedom of the Press;<br>• the guarantee of individuals' freedoms. | Wished to see the French Charter of 1814 introduced into the Italian states. This would provide for:<br>• the retention of the monarch with considerable powers<br>• two parliamentary Chambers, one of which would be elected;<br>• right to vote restricted to the wealthy. |

## The secret societies

The closest these early Italian revolutionaries came to having a shared identity was through the closed world of the secret societies. Scattered throughout Italy and having their origins in eighteenth-century Freemasonry, these sects became the natural focal point for individuals with grievances against the restored monarchies. The most notable of these secret fraternities was the Carbonari. This was supposedly an international movement but its strongest base was in Naples. However, the Carbonari (like other secret societies) had ill-defined and often contradictory aims. The groups were organized on a local basis, had parochial ambitions and limited membership; they possessed neither the competence nor often the desire to work for a united Italian state. For most, the vision of a changed Italy extended no further than regional demands for constitutions and liberal reforms; at best the secret societies shared the common but vague ambition of somehow liberating Italy from the grip of Austria.

A GROUP OF CARBONARI REVOLUTIONARIES

# The early revolutions

In 1820–21 and again in 1831, there were revolutionary outbursts in a number of Italian states. The table below details some of the main features of these risings.

| Date | State | Details of rising | Outcome |
|------|-------|-------------------|---------|
| 1820 | Naples | Members of the Carbonari and the army rose against King Ferdinand, who quickly agreed to grant a constitution. | Ferdinand appealed to the Powers at the Congress of Laibach (1821). Austrian troops sent to southern Italy; defeated the rebels at Rieti. |
| 1820 | Sicily | Rising directed by the trade guilds (*maestranze*) and aimed at obtaining separation from Naples. Rebels took over the capital (Palermo) and expelled the governor. | The rebels in Naples wished to suppress the revolution and reinforced government troops on the island. The rising was duly put down. |
| 1821 | Piedmont | Revolution aimed at creating a constitutional kingdom. King Victor Emmanuel I abdicated and was temporarily replaced by Charles Albert, second in line to the throne, who agreed to introduce a constitution. (The heir to the throne, Charles Felix, was out of the country when the rising occurred.) | Charles Felix denounced Charles Albert and appealed to Metternich for help against the rebels. Charles Albert fled as Austrian troops suppressed the revolutionaries. |
| 1831 | Parma and Modena | Minor risings with vague constitutional objectives. | Rulers of the Duchies fled but later returned with loyal troops to oust the rebels. |
| 1831 | Papal States | Provisional government set up in Bologna with the aim of dismantling oppressive papal rule. | Austrian troops dispatched to the region. Provisional government soon broken up. |

The task of unseating unpopular monarchs had not been difficult. In all the states affected by revolutions, legitimate rulers had agreed to the demands of the liberals or had fled in alarm. However, with Austria dutifully playing the role of Europe's policeman, it was never long before the old order was restored. The early revolutionaries made no substantial gains and succeeded only in revealing their own shortcomings. It was clear that the secret societies, with their poor organization and lack of common purpose, were not up to the task of directing the national revival. Rebels operating in different regions failed to acknowledge each other. In Naples, the rejection of Sicilian grievances led to one revolutionary group conspiring in the suppression of another. The provisional government at Bologna in 1831 refused to assist fellow conspirators in Modena.

Perhaps the most serious defect in the early revolutionary movement was the failure to generate mass support. The middle-class liberals who tended to lead the risings were suspicious of democracy and refused to court popular involvement in their protests. When 'rightful' rulers returned to their kingdoms they were often welcomed back by the peasant masses.

# REVIEW
## The failure of the early revolutions

Having read this far you should spend some time reflecting on the abortive revolts of 1820–21 and 1831. Work in groups, feeding-in ideas which could help to answer the following questions.

---

**1** Why did the early revolutionaries achieve no permanent successes in their struggles against the restored monarchies?

**2** What lessons could Italian nationalists have learned from the failure of these revolutions?

Collect together the groups' ideas and present them, from the perspective of an Italian nationalist, in a written statement which might be titled: 'Reflections on the Failed Revolutions of 1820–21 and 1831.'

---

## New directions (1831–47)

The failure of the early revolutions made clear the futility of localized protest. Unable to demonstrate any practical achievement, the secret societies became redundant. The nationalist scene now came to be dominated by writers and thinkers who proposed broader solutions to Austrian domination and regional despotism (See Focus 10.1).

# FOCUS

## 10.1 Paths to unity

### Giuseppe Mazzini

Mazzini was probably the most dedicated Italian revolutionary of his time. His disappointment with the objectives and methods of the Carbonari prompted him to develop a new approach to the problems of Italy. Mazzini spoke to all Italians, not just the educated middle class. He believed Italians possessed within them the ability to lead their own national revival; to rise against the petty despots and foreign masters and to establish a united, republican Italy. He spoke for democracy and freedom and viewed patriotism as a religion. His vision went beyond purely national boundaries to the creation of a United States of Europe, shaped by the civilizing influence of the Italian nation. His methods were simple: propaganda and insurrection. In both fields he worked tirelessly to awaken the national consciousness of the Italian people. In 1831 he founded his own association to work towards these goals, named 'Young Italy'.

### Vincenzo Gioberti

Mazzini was not the only political thinker to propose new solutions to the Italian problem. Gioberti, an exiled priest, presented a moderate programme in his work, *Of the Moral and Civil Primacy of the Italians*, published in 1843. He rejected revolutionary methods and saw no future for republicanism in Italy. Instead he invested all his hopes in the Pope, whom he envisaged as the President of a federation of existing rulers.

## Cesare Balbo

A variation on Gioberti's proposals appeared in 1844 in a book titled *Of the Aspirations of Italy*. Its author, Cesare Balbo, agreed with Gioberti that a united democratic Italy was undesirable. He accepted the idea of a federation of Italian states but saw no special role for the Pope in this arrangement. Balbo emphasised the expulsion of Austria from the peninsula as the essential pre-condition to political change in Italy. He claimed that the only Italian state capable of achieving this feat was Piedmont-Sardinia and that its king should assume the leadership of a new Italian federation.

**1** Complete your copy of this summary chart by ticking the appropriate boxes.

| Proposals for the future of Italy | Mazzini | Gioberti | Balbo |
|---|---|---|---|
| Expel Austria | | | |
| Unify all the Italian states | | | |
| Introduce democracy | | | |
| Establish a republic | | | |
| Establish a federation of existing Italian states | | | |
| Employ revolutionary methods | | | |
| Adopt the leadership of the Pope | | | |
| Adopt the leadership of the Piedmontese King | | | |

**2** Working in groups, design two diagrams to illustrate the concepts of republic and federation. Your models should incorporate all the features contained in the definitions on the right.

| Republic | Federation |
|---|---|
| A state or country in which the supreme ruling power is vested in representatives elected by the people. The head of state, usually a President, is also elected by popular vote. | A system of government comprising a collection of states where each retains its internal independence whilst joining together with others for the purpose of administering certain common interests, eg foreign policy. |

# 1848

In spite of the optimistic rhetoric of the 1840s, the political theorists failed to devise practical ways of achieving their goals. Mazzini's attempts to stimulate popular insurrection in 1833 and 1834 ended in complete failure. In 1836 he was forced to disband 'Young Italy'. In 1837 he left for England where he pursued his dream in exile. Mazzini continued to influence the Italian nationalist movement but his impact was as a classic romantic revolutionary, symbolic yet ultimately of no practical account. The proposals outlined by men such as Mazzini, Gioberti and Balbo were significant because they contained a clarity of purpose absent from the vague intentions of the Carbonari. However, the appeal of such ideas was strictly limited, with the majority of the Italian people yet to be moved by the same nationalist impulses. In 1848 revolutions once again swept over Italy (see map). However, unlike the earlier outbreaks of 1820–21 and 1831, there seemed to be real hope that these revolts might succeed. Three developments in the years 1846–48 provided the basis for this optimism.

**1 A liberal Pope** Pius IX was elected to the Papacy in 1846. His reputation as a liberal was widely known and he quickly won popular acclaim by granting an amnesty to all political prisoners in the Papal States. Reforms followed in the administration, the law and education; and in 1847 Press censorship was curtailed. In the same year he introduced a new advisory body (the *Consulta*) to assist him in the task of government. Significantly, members of this council were elected and included representatives from outside the ranks of the clergy. Reform in the Papal States was imitated in other areas, notably Piedmont and Tuscany. The actions of the new Pope appeared to signal the commencement of Gioberti's plans for Italy. Throughout the country interest in reform and the Risorgimento became acute; the Italian people seemed to have found a leader through whom they could articulate their discontent.

POPE PIUS IX

**2 Economic crisis** Disastrous harvests in 1846 and 1847 revealed the instability of a society dependent for its survival on agriculture. The failed harvests produced food shortages in both rural and urban districts. High prices and static wages combined to produce a revolutionary situation. While the crisis lasted the involvement of the masses in the protests was assured.

**3 General revolutionary outbreak** 1848 was the year of revolutions throughout Europe. The minor monarchs of the Italian states experienced the same popular upheaval as the mightier sovereigns of countries such as France and Austria. When revolution struck in Vienna – the very heart of the Habsburg Empire – and caused the fall of Metternich, Italy was presented with an opportunity to determine her own future without the corrective intervention of Austrian troops.

# The Italian revolutions of 1848

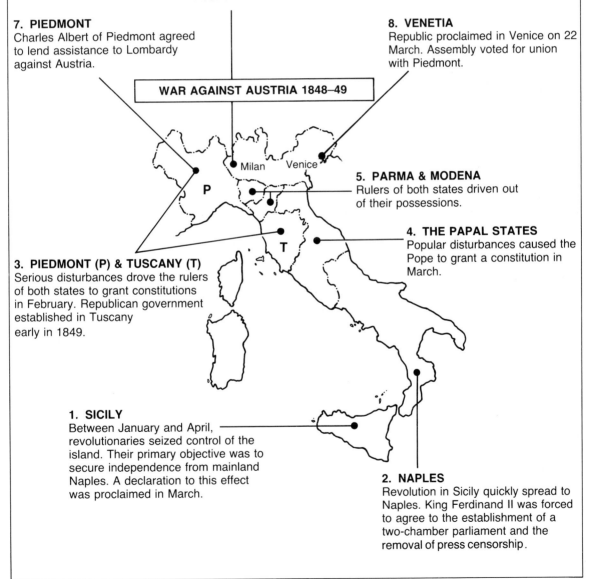

**6. LOMBARDY**
Rising in Milan directed against the Austrian occupation of Lombardy. Austrian garrison driven out of Milan during the 'Five Days' (17–22 March). Provisional government set up. Help sought from Piedmont to continue the fight against the Austrians.

**7. PIEDMONT**
Charles Albert of Piedmont agreed to lend assistance to Lombardy against Austria.

**8. VENETIA**
Republic proclaimed in Venice on 22 March. Assembly voted for union with Piedmont.

**WAR AGAINST AUSTRIA 1848–49**

Milan    Venice

**P**

**5. PARMA & MODENA**
Rulers of both states driven out of their possessions.

**4. THE PAPAL STATES**
Popular disturbances caused the Pope to grant a constitution in March.

**T**

**3. PIEDMONT (P) & TUSCANY (T)**
Serious disturbances drove the rulers of both states to grant constitutions in February. Republican government established in Tuscany early in 1849.

**1. SICILY**
Between January and April, revolutionaries seized control of the island. Their primary objective was to secure independence from mainland Naples. A declaration to this effect was proclaimed in March.

**2. NAPLES**
Revolution in Sicily quickly spread to Naples. King Ferdinand II was forced to agree to the establishment of a two-chamber parliament and the removal of press censorship.

## The defeat of the revolutions

The optimism of 1848 was short-lived. Across Italy the temporary gains made by the revolutionaries began to dissolve. The chart below summarizes the main developments of the period 1848–49.

VICTOR EMMANUEL II

| State | Events |
| --- | --- |
| Naples and Sicily | King Ferdinand II managed to suppress the rising in Naples by September 1848. The following spring Sicily was reunited with the mainland by force of arms. All traces of parliamentary government were erased from the dual kingdom. |
| Piedmont | The Piedmontese army was decisively beaten by Austrian troops under Radetzky at Custozza in July 1848. Charles Albert was forced to agree to an armistice which left Lombardy and Venetia to the mercy of the Austrians. In March 1849 Charles Albert restarted the war against Austria but was again defeated at Novara. In April he abdicated in favour of his son Victor Emmanuel II. |
| Tuscany | Following the defeat of Piedmont, Austrian troops entered Tuscany and restored the Grand Duke to the throne he had abandoned in January 1849. |
| Parma and Modena | Rulers restored by Austrian troops. |
| Papal States | Pius IX refused to co-operate with Piedmont in the war against Austria. By November 1848 he had left Rome and turned his back on the Italian liberal and nationalist movements. In his absence a republic was established (February 1849) with Mazzini returning to share the leadership of the government. The Pope appealed for help. Some 20,000 French troops arrived and with assistance from Naples the republic was crushed. After heroic resistance Rome finally fell in June 1849. The Pope was duly restored to his possessions. |
| Venetia | Following the defeat of Piedmont at Custozza, Venetia reverted to a republic and continued to fight against Austria. Venice was besieged and finally surrendered to Austrian troops in August 1849. |

# REVIEW

## The failure of 1848

**1** The revolutions of 1848 like those of 1820–21 and 1831 failed. Consider the following factors and in each case explain how they contributed to the failure of the risings. (The first one is done for you as an example.)

| Factor | Contribution to failure of revolutions |
|---|---|
| Austrian recovery from internal upheaval | Once Austrian troops had regained the initiative from the revolutionaries at home, they were able to pursue their traditional role as protectors of the Italian monarchies. No Italian state possessed an army capable of resisting Austrian military might. Before long, bombardments and battlefield routs had crushed the revolutions and reinstalled rulers to their thrones. |
| Desire of the new French ruler, Louis-Napoleon, to secure the support of French Catholics. | |
| Defection of the Pope from his role as champion of liberal causes. | |
| Peasant masses excluded from participation in new political systems established by the revolutions. Liberals had no social policy; conditions for peasants did not improve. | |
| Revolutions characterized by local ambitions: ie to drive out Austria; to obtain a constitution; to establish a republic; to become independent. | |

**2** 'By 1849 the supporters of the Risorgimento had made no progress towards achieving a united and independent Italy.' How far would you agree with this comment?

FRENCH TROOPS ENTER ROME (JULY 1849). THEIR INTERVENTION ENSURED THE COLLAPSE OF THE ROMAN REPUBLIC.

# The unification of Italy (1858–70)

### A narrative outline

Following the failures of 1848–49, the kingdom of Piedmont-Sardinia became the focal point of those who continued to pursue independence and unity for the Italian nation. After 1852 the Prime Minister of Piedmont was the ambitious and able Count Camillo Benso di Cavour. Cavour wished to be rid of Austrian interference in Italy and to extend the power and influence of Piedmont. He was certain that this would never be achieved without foreign assistance.

During the Crimean War, Piedmont fought with France and Britain against Russia. At the Paris peace conference in 1856, Cavour tried to canvass international support for his plans to end Austria's domination of the Italian states. In this he failed, but he was successful in making important personal contacts, especially with the French Emperor, Napoleon III. Cavour committed himself to the goal of securing an alliance with France in order to accomplish the expulsion of Austria from the peninsula. Oddly enough it was an assassination attempt on Napoleon by the Italian nationalist Felice Orsini (14 January 1858) which persuaded the Emperor to support the Italian cause. At his trial, Orsini made an impassioned plea for Italian freedom which so impressed Napoleon that by May arrangements had been made for a secret meeting with Cavour to discuss the Italian question.

The meeting between the two men took place at Plombières on 20 July, and after lengthy negotiations a deal was struck. In return for Nice and Savoy, and providing Austria was seen to be the aggressor, France would

CAVOUR

ORSINI'S ATTEMPT TO ASSASSINATE NAPOLEON III (1858)

assist Piedmont with 200,000 troops in a war against the Habsburgs. A formal treaty was signed in January 1859 and Cavour began the task of luring Austria onto the battlefield. The Piedmontese army was mobilized and when in April the Austrian government issued an ultimatum demanding it be returned to a peacetime footing, Cavour had his excuse. The ultimatum was rejected and war was declared.

THE BATTLE OF SOLFERINO

Two battles decided the first war of the Risorgimento: Magenta on 4 June and Solferino three weeks later. The defeat of the Austrians on both occasions provoked an outbreak of popular disturbances in Central Italy. The sovereigns of Tuscany, Parma and Modena were once more compelled to leave their territories, and in parts of the Papal States the authority of the Pope was violently challenged. The rebels in these regions sought fusion with Piedmont as the surest way of preserving their gains. For Napoleon, however, events were moving too fast. He had no desire to see Piedmont extend into Central Italy and was becoming worried by the threat of a Prussian army mobilizing on the Rhine. Ignoring the arrangements made at Plombières, he unilaterally concluded an armistice with the Austrians at Villafranca. Lombardy was to be ceded to France to pass on to Piedmont, Venetia would remain Austrian, and the sovereigns of Tuscany, Parma and Modena were to be restored. Without France, Piedmont could not hope to continue the war and Victor Emmanuel was forced to accept the armistice. Cavour, furious at the arrangements, resigned.

Villafranca did little to change the political geography of Italy (see maps below).

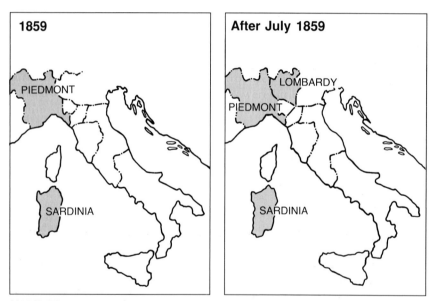

SOURCE: STEPHEN J LEE, *ASPECTS OF EUROPEAN HISTORY 1789–1980* (1982)

However, by March 1860 Italy had moved a step closer towards nation status. In Tuscany, Parma, Modena and parts of the Papal States, the popular mood was unmistakable; the former sovereigns were not acceptable and the call was for immediate union with Piedmont. In January 1860 Cavour returned as Prime Minister and offered Napoleon III Nice and Savoy in return for the states of Central Italy. Napoleon was unsure and plebiscites were arranged for March 1860. Universal suffrage applied, voters being given a choice between fusion with Piedmont or continuation as a separate kingdom. In each case the majority in favour of annexation to Piedmont was overwhelming. The states became part of the Piedmontese-Sardinian kingdom and in April Savoy and Nice were duly handed over to France.

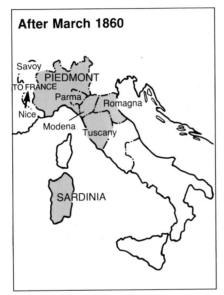

SOURCE: STEPHEN J LEE, *ASPECTS OF EUROPEAN HISTORY 1789–1980* (1982)

In May 1860 a new phase in the unification process began. Giuseppe Garibaldi – the charismatic Italian patriot who had organized the heroic defence of Rome in 1849 – led a small group of volunteers known as 'the Thousand' by boat to Sicily. His immediate objective was to assist a revolution which had broken out on the island. By 6 June he had captured the capital, Palermo, and began preparations for an assault on the mainland. During the evening of 18–19 August 1860, Garibaldi crossed the Straits of Messina and struck north for Naples. He entered the city on 7 September, already with plans to liberate Rome. Cavour knew the proposed march on Rome carried with it the serious danger of provoking war with France. To avoid this the Piedmontese army was sent south to intercept Garibaldi. Cavour organized a plebiscite in the former Bourbon kingdom now occupied by Garibaldi's supporters. A massive majority in favour of union with Piedmont was returned (voters were not given the option of a separate kingdom). Garibaldi was forced to accept the result. At Teano on 26 October 1860, the hardened revolutionary met King Victor Emmanuel II and handed over his conquests. The Kingdom of

Italy was proclaimed in March 1861. Unification was now almost complete (see map below).

SOURCE: STEPHEN J LEE, *ASPECTS OF EUROPEAN HISTORY 1789–1980* (1982)

GARIBALDI (TOP, CENTRE) LEADS HIS REDSHIRTS TO VICTORY OVER THE NEAPOLITAN FORCES AT THE BATTLE OF CALATAFIMI (1859)

THE HISTORIC MEETING AT TEANO. GARIBALDI SHAKES THE HAND OF VICTOR EMMANUEL AND SURRENDERS HIS CONQUESTS TO THE HOUSE OF SAVOY (OCTOBER 1860)

Only two territories – Venetia and Rome – remained outside the new kingdom. Venetia was added in 1866 as a result of the Austro-Prussian War. Victor Emmanuel had hoped to acquire the territory without assistance, but a series of military disasters meant Venetia could only be taken from Austria because the Habsburgs were so comprehensively beaten by Prussia. In 1870, with France preoccupied in the war against Prussia, Italian forces seized control of the city of Rome and proclaimed it the new capital of Italy.

ITALIANS CAPTURE ROME AND RE-ESTABLISH THE ANCIENT CITY AS CAPITAL OF A UNITED ITALY (SEPTEMBER 1870)

## What factors determined Piedmont's special role?

### The constitution

Alone among the Italian states after 1849, Piedmont-Sardinia possessed a constitution. Although limited, it offered to some of its citizens opportunities for political participation which could not be found anywhere else in the peninsula. Piedmont's status as a constitutional state won her sympathy outside Italy, notably in Britain, and attracted the attention of all those political hopefuls – the democrats, the liberals, the nationalists and the republicans – who sought some practical means of transforming Italy. During the 1850s Piedmont's free Press acted as a magnet attracting political exiles from other Italian states. Agitation for change in Italy began to be powerfully concentrated in one area.

### The National Society

During the 1850s many Italians came to reject the republican idealism of Mazzini. His methods had clearly failed and it seemed appropriate to seek an alternative. The new direction which emerged in the decade after 1848–49 was articulated and developed by Giorgio Pallavicino, founder of the National Society. Although initially a radical republican, Pallavicino became convinced that the goal of political unification would most likely be achieved by Piedmont-Sardinia, and that the House of Savoy would govern Italy. Leadership of the Society (founded in 1857) was provided by Daniele Manin, the former President of the Venetian Republic during the revolutions of 1848–49. Manin, like Pallavicino, had turned his back on republicanism and invested his hopes for Italian unification in the

Piedmontese monarchy. The Society worked hard to organize support for Piedmont throughout Italy. In its propaganda and policy statements Piedmont was presented as the only Italian state capable of delivering national unity. The Society remained small, having between 4000 and 8000 members. However, since it attracted the support of both Garibaldi and Cavour, its influence was substantial. Cavour's motives for supporting the National Society have been questioned, and it seems likely that he approved more of its ability to attract the critics of Mazzini than of its hopes for unification. Nevertheless, Cavour could not ignore an association capable of raising 20,000 volunteers in three months, nor the assistance of these patriots, fighting alongside Garibaldi on the Alpine front against Austria in 1859.

## Cavour

Cavour's appointment as Prime Minister of Piedmont in 1852 was an important stage in Italy's progress towards nationhood. He was known as an able politician who favoured liberal causes. Vehemently opposed to the revolutionary republicanism of Mazzini and his followers, he did not take seriously the idea of national unification. Yet he was determined to rid the peninsular of Austrian influence and to allow Italians to determine their own fortunes. He envisaged a modern and extended Piedmont at the head of the drive towards independence. With these aims in mind he initiated the economic transformation of the state. He concluded trade treaties with France, Britain, Belgium and Austria, and the merchant fleet was enlarged. During the 1850s Piedmont's foreign trade trebled in value. Cavour promoted the use of the latest techniques in farming and in the factories, and encouraged the development of a railway network. By 1860 Piedmont possessed 800 km of track; a third of the total for the entire Italian peninsula. In addition to constructing a firm economic platform upon which to base Piedmont's development in Italy, Cavour also engineered a political partnership which allowed him to remain firmly in control of government and thus able to pursue his objectives unfettered by parliamentary opposition. By bringing his own Centre-Right party into coalition with Ratazzi's Centre-Left group, he produced the *connubio* (marriage) of Piedmont's politically moderate middle-ground. The *connubio* enabled Cavour to resist the opposition of both the extreme clerical right and the extreme revolutionary left.

# Examining the Evidence
## Cavour's commitment to unity

An important issue in the study of the Risorgimento centres around Cavour's attitude to the notion of a united Italy. Was he an Italian nationalist working always with his eyes on the prize of a unitary state; or was he a Piedmontese expansionist who wished merely to extend the power and prestige of Piedmont-Sardinia?

### Source A

Cavour is known in history as the architect of the modern kingdom of Italy...It was Cavour who by wise domestic policy first won the respect and confidence of Europe, and later by a bold and hazardous statesmanship sent the flower of the little Sardinian army to the aid of France and England in the Crimea, raising the prestige of Italy and earning the gratitude of the Western Powers. It was Cavour who pilloried Austria in the eyes of Europe at the Congress of Paris (1856) and knew how to utilise the defeat of Russia to wean England from her traditional alliance with Austria to become the warm supporter of Italian freedom. Finally it was the same clear brain and firm hand which brought Napoleon III into Italy in 1859, broke the power of Austria and kept Italy free from foreign interference while Garibaldi won the Kingdom of Naples for Italy and Victor Emmanuel...Italy found in Cavour...a man who, uninfluenced by the squabbles and jealousies of the various Italian states, viewed Italy and the Italian question as a single problem, and thus lifted the whole complex controversy from the lower level of a mere redistribution of Italian soil (as Napoleon III and others regarded it) on to the higher plane of the creation of a nation.

Arthur J Whyte, *The Early Life and Letters of Cavour, 1810–1848* (1925)

**Source B**
As a parliamentary liberal...Cavour did not, like Mazzini and Garibaldi, believe in Italian unification. For him the idea was tainted with radicalism, and his diplomat's sense of realities told him there were too many insurmountable obstacles in the way...All that can be safely said is that Cavour wanted to get as much as could reasonably be obtained [for Piedmont], but no more. He certainly envisaged the acquisition of Tuscany and the Romagna [in the Papal States]...but his acquiescence in the proposal [at Plombières] to cede Savoy and possibly Nice indicates how very far indeed Cavour was from being the apostle of Italian Nationalism...The truth about Cavour is not that he dared all for the national ideal, never once stopping until the dream of a united Italy had been fulfilled. Cavour did not think national unity an aim that justified the contemptuous violation of all the normal rules of political and international conduct.

LCB Seaman, *From Vienna to Versailles* (1956)

---

**1** How do the historians Whyte and Seaman (Sources A and B above) differ in their interpretations of Cavour?

**2** How is it possible for historians to present such contradictory impressions of the same historical figure?

**3** 'Seaman's interpretation of Cavour is more likely to be accurate because it was written later than Whyte's.' How far would you agree with this contention?

---

## Testing the theory

The views expressed in Sources A and B can be tested against the evidence available from the time. What do the letters, diaries, speeches and agreements of the 1850s reveal about Cavour's intentions for Piedmont and Italy? The following sources will allow you to begin clarifying this issue.

---

### Source C

Between you [Cavour] and us, sir, an abyss yawns. We represent Italy – you the old, covetous, faint hearted ambitions of the House of Savoy. We desire above all National Unity – you territorial aggrandizement for Piedmont.

Mazzini (1856), quoted in WG Shreeves, *Nationmaking in Nineteenth Century Europe* (1984)

### Source D

Foresti writes again to me as follows:

'Our Garibaldi went to Turin on the thirteenth and I went with him. Cavour welcomed him with courtesy and friendliness and hinted that he could rely on considerable official help. Cavour even authorized Garibaldi to pass on these hints to others. It seems that he is seriously thinking about the great political redemption of our peninsula. Garibaldi took his leave of the minister on very friendly terms and with these encouraging promises of help for the cause.'

It was all an act! What Cavour wants, and I am sure of it, is just for Piedmont to be enlarged by a few square miles of Italian soil.

Pallavicino to Manin (24 August 1856), quoted in Denis Mack-Smith *The Making of Italy 1796–1866* (1988)

### Source E

The Emperor [Napoleon III] readily agreed that it was necessary to drive the Austrians out of Italy once and for all, and to leave them without an inch of territory south of the Alps or west of the Isonzo. But how was Italy to be organized after that? After a long discussion, which I spare your Majesty, we agreed more or less to the following principles, recognizing that they were subject to modification as the course of the war might determine. The valley of the [river] Po, the Romagna, and the Legations [in the Papal States] would form a kingdom of upper Italy under the House of Savoy [the royal house of Piedmont-Sardinia]. Rome and its immediate surroundings would be left to the Pope. The rest of the Papal States, together with Tuscany, would form a kingdom of central Italy. The Neapolitan frontier would be left unchanged. These four Italian states would form a confederation on the pattern of the German Bund, the presidency of which would be given to the Pope to console him for losing the best part of his States. This arrangement seems to me fully acceptable.

Cavour reporting on the Plombières discussion to Victor Emmanuel (24 July 1858), quoted in D Beales, *The Risorgimento and the Unification of Italy* (1981)

### Source F

Piedmontism is for us an extremely dangerous opponent, an implacable enemy. Everyone in Piedmont…is tarred with the same brush. Instead of a single Italian nation with its centre in Rome, they would prefer a Kingdom of Northern Italy with two capitals, Turin and Milan. Camillo Cavour is one of the most Piedmontese of all; and we shall harness him to our chariot only when we have a knife at his throat.

Pallavicino to Manin (1 October 1856), quoted in Denis Mack-Smith, as above

**Source G**

We must leave Naples out of it. United Italy will be our children's achievement. I'm satisfied with what we've got, so long as we can reach Ancona. [See map on page 227.]

Reported comment made by Cavour recorded by Massari in his diary (29 December 1859), quoted in Denis Mack-Smith, as above

**Source H**

Count Cavour's strength does not lie in his principles; for he has none that are altogether inflexible. But he has a clear, precise aim, one whose greatness would – ten years ago – have made any other man reel: that of creating a unified and independent Italy.

F Petruccelli della Gattina, backbencher in Italian parliament (1861), quoted in Denis Mack-Smith, as above

---

**1** According to Sources C, D and F, was Cavour an Italian nationalist or a Piedmontese expansionist?

**2** Do the statements of the republicans Mazzini and Pallavicino (Sources C, D, and F) offer convincing proof that Cavour was uninterested in Italian unification?

**3** Suggest reasons why Cavour encouraged Garibaldi to believe that he was 'seriously thinking about the great political redemption' of Italy (Source D).

**4** How do the Plombières arrangements (Source E) help to confirm the suspicions of Cavour expressed in Sources C, D and F?

**5** As late as December 1859, Cavour spoke of leaving the unification of Italy to a later generation (Source G). How, then, would you explain the assessment of his intentions given in Source H?

**6** As a historian, what would be your criticisms of this selection of sources in attempting to determine the extent of Cavour's commitment to Italian nationalism?

---

# A recent view

In spite of the reservations about Cavour's feeling for unification, it is beyond dispute that when the new Kingdom of Italy was proclaimed in March 1861, Cavour was still the Prime Minister of Piedmont and had overseen each stage of the unification process. Did Cavour become 'converted' to the idea of Italian unity? If so, how did this occur? A recent historian, Stephen J Lee, offers us this concise and convincing analysis:

'During the 1850s Cavour considered unification of the entire peninsula neither possible nor desirable; he therefore differed fundamentally from Garibaldi, who argued that a 'single Italy must be our first goal'...

Cavour however, envisaged only an enlarged Piedmont, which would include Lombardy and Venetia. At its most ambitious, his scheme was for an Italian Confederation; this was explicitly stated in a confidential memorandum to Victor Emmanuel explaining the contents of the secret Pact of

Plombières with Napoleon III in 1858. Mazzini, fully aware of Cavour's caution, described him as 'the ministerial liberator who taught his master how to present the union of Italy'. It does, indeed, appear that Cavour was willing to halt the growth of the Italian nation at a stage already reached by Germany in the loosely constructed Confederation.

Between 1859 and 1860, however, Cavour was pushed along irresistibly by the sequence of events and had to adapt his former proposals. His original dislike of total unification had been due largely to his fear of the radical republicans who had made it their ultimate aim. But when Napoleon III withdrew France prematurely from the war with Austria by the Treaty of Villafranca in 1859, Cavour threatened to 'turn revolutionary and conspirator' himself and he resigned his office of prime minister. Until his recall a few months later, Cavour now found himself approving and depending on the activities of Ricasoli, Farini and Azeglio to gain popular acceptance for the incorporation of Tuscany, Modena and Romagna into Piedmont in defiance of the Villafranca settlement. Once reinstalled as prime minister, this time of a greatly enlarged kingdom in Northern Italy, Cavour was again carried forward by the momentum of change. He was seriously concerned about the activities of Garibaldi and the 'Thousand' in Sicily and Naples (1860) and their threat to the Papal States in Central Italy. He realized that to oppose Garibaldi directly would incur the wrath of Italian patriots everywhere, including Piedmont. To take no action would enable Garibaldi to establish a rival state in the south or, at best, give him the credit for the unification of Italy. Cavour found this prospect abhorrent and was quite adamant that 'The King cannot accept the crown of Italy at the hand of Garibaldi'. The only solution to this dilemma was to take direct military and diplomatic action: to annex the Papal States and to outmanoeuvre Garibaldi into relinquishing his hold on the south. The overall result would have to be a kingdom covering the entire peninsula.'

Stephen J Lee, *Aspects of European History 1789–1980* (1982)

---

**1** When, if ever, do you think Cavour became convinced that Italy would have to be united?

**2** Why was Cavour so reluctant to adopt a policy of unification from the outset?

**3** Why could Cavour not allow Garibaldi to continue unchecked towards Rome in 1860?

**4** Older histories present Cavour as a master planner whose scheme for unification was worked out in advance and followed to the letter in practice. What is your view of this theory?

---

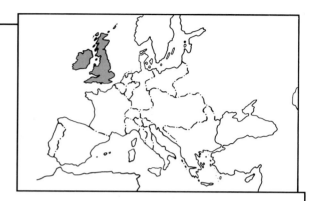

# FOCUS

## 10.2 The international situation

### Britain

Following the Crimean War, Britain withdrew from European affairs in order to avoid being caught up in another expensive and destructive war. This was an essential pre-condition to any territorial revision in Europe. Within Britain public opinion was highly influential and overwhelmingly in support of the Italian cause. The image of a constitutional state struggling to secure national independence was irresistible to the British public. Even Queen Victoria spoke in favour of the Italians and Garibaldi was seen as a great national hero. When war broke out in 1859, Britain was prepared to guarantee Piedmont against a territorial carve-up in the event of her defeat. Palmerston, Gladstone and Russell all favoured unification - a stronger Italy, they believed, would act as a counterweight to

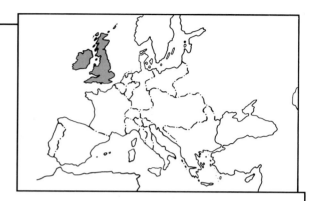

Napoleon III's ambitions in Europe. Accordingly, Britain backed the Piedmontese annexation of Central Italy in 1860 — a fact which helped to secure Napoleon's acquiescence. In July 1860 Britain rejected a French proposal to block Garibaldi's assault on Naples - the crossing was made and southern Italy conquered.

### France

Napoleon III maintained a long and sincere interest in Italian affairs. He was keen to act as the champion of liberal causes and believed that support for Italian independence would be popular at home. This interest also fitted in with his desires to see the power of Austria reduced, and to secure a favourable revision of the 1815 Vienna settlement. During the 1850s Napoleon frequently spoke of `doing something for Italy'. By this he probably did not mean unification. Instead he wished for a federated Italy with an enlarged Piedmont in the north acting as a benevolent ally: a united Italy was rejected since it could pose a threat to France. In the war with Austria, France gave substantial practical assistance; without the 200,000 French troops Cavour's chances of defeating Austria were slim indeed. Subsequently, however, Napoleon

abandoned Piedmont when it seemed she was going beyond the terms of the Plombières pact. Unification was left to Cavour and Garibaldi, with France adopting a neutral position both in Garibaldi's expedition and Cavour's invasion of the Papal States.

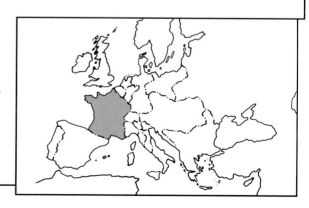

## Russia

The Crimean War had dealt a serious blow to Russian pride. Defeat in the war, and the settlement of the Black Sea (1856) which followed, transformed Russian into a revisionist power. Tsar Alexander II was now prepared to accept Napoleon III's schemes to revise the 1815 settlement in order that the 1856 settlement might also be reconsidered. Russia was unfavourably disposed to Austria after 1856 because the Habsburgs had failed to support her in the Crimean War. Russia was now prepared to see her former ally pay for her treachery. In September 1857 Napoleon met with Alexander II at Stuttgart. This produced a secret alliance in March 1859 containing Alexander's agreement to remain benevolently neutral in the event of an Italian war. When war broke out, Alexander remained faithful to his promise even when Naples - a long-standing friend of Russia - was attacked by Garibaldi. Russia

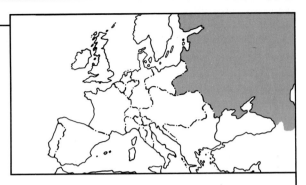

also played a significant role by restraining Prussia in the years 1859-60. In October 1859 Prussia accepted Russian guarantees for the protection of her Rhine frontier and in return declared herself neutral over Italy. In March 1860 it was the Tsar who persuaded Prussia to accept the Piedmontese annexation of Central Italy. Finally, in July 1860, Habsburg plans to re-form the Holy Alliance against Italy were wrecked by Alexander's opposition and his efforts to secure Prussian hostility to the scheme.

## Prussia

During the 1850s Prussia and Austria became rivals for the leadership of the German states. In 1851 Austria engineered the collapse of the Erfurt Union, a Prussian attempt to unite the German states and exclude Austria. This humiliation left Prussia with little inclination to assist her neighbour. When Piedmont declared war on Austria in 1859, Prussian neutrality was secure.

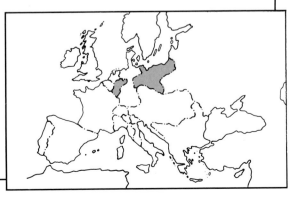

## QUESTIONS

**1** Why was the Crimean War an important factor in the unification of Italy?

**2** Specify the ways in which the cause of Italian unity was given positive assistance by the attitude and actions of the four Powers described in this section.

**3** What was the attitude of Napoleon III to Italian unity? What was his purpose in associating himself with the Italian cause? Could he be said to have hindered unification?

**4** 'Without a favourable international situation, Italian unification would probably not have occurred.' What is your opinion of this suggestion?

# REVIEW

**Why was the Kingdom of Piedmont-Sardinia able to secure political control over so much of Italy in the years 1859–61?**

The following questions could be used as a basis for small group discussion.

**1** Make a list of the Italian states which came under the control of Piedmont-Sardinia in the years 1859–61. How did each of these states come to be controlled by Piedmont-Sardinia?

**2** In what ways was the European situation different in 1859–61 to that in 1848–49? How does this help to account for the success of Piedmont-Sardinia?

**3** How important was the attitude of Napoleon III to the success of Italian unification?

**4** Would Italian unification have happened when it did without:
(a) Cavour?
(b) Garibaldi?

**5** Why did Piedmont-Sardinia achieve such prominence in progress towards the political unification of Italy?

# 11 The Unification of Germany

## PREVIEW
## The evolution of a nation

THE 39 STATES OF THE GERMAN CONFEDERATION
ESTABLISHED BY THE VIENNA SETTLEMENT OF 1815

| | |
|---|---|
| ▨ | Prussian territories |
| ▢ | Habsburg territories |
| —— | Limits of the German Confederation |
| —·—·— | State boundaries |

THE RESULTS OF PRUSSIAN EXPANSION DURING THE SEVEN
WEEKS WAR OF 1866 AND THE CREATION OF THE NORTH
GERMAN CONFEDERATION

THE GERMAN EMPIRE IN 1871

# The birth of the Empire

On 18 January 1871 the final act in a long-running and complex European drama was played against the magnificent backdrop of the Versailles Palace near Paris. Before an audience of assorted German princes and State dignitaries the King of Prussia, William I, accepted the Crown of the new united German Empire. Otto Von Bismarck, William's Chief Minister and a prime mover in the unification process, delivered the proclamation:

We William, by the Grace of God, King of Prussia, and after the German Princes and free cities have unanimously appealed to us to renew the Imperial dignity, which has been in abeyance for more than sixty years, hereby inform you that we regard it as our duty to the whole Fatherland to respond to this summons of the allied German Princes and free cities to assume the German Imperial title.

The announcement of the new German Empire was unquestionably significant. With it disappeared a Central European map of bewildering complexity. The dozens of independent and semi-independent states, which had filled the space loosely termed 'Germany' since the Middle Ages, were finally replaced by a single nation with a common name and an Emperor whose authority applied to some 41 million people. After 1890 the impact of this creation was to be felt on a global scale, a fact which renders the emergence of Germany one of the most important developments of the Nineteenth Century.

OTTO VON BISMARCK

# **E**XAMINING THE EVIDENCE
## How was unity achieved?

The process by which Germany came to be unified has been an area of constant debate amongst historians of the period. The following sources will provide you with an introduction to some of the main issues surrounding the achievement of German unification.

### Source A

Germany doesn't look to Prussia's liberalism, but to its power: Bavaria, Württemberg, Baden can indulge in liberalism, but no one will expect them to undertake Prussia's role; Prussia must gather and consolidate her strength in readiness for the favourable moment, which has already been missed several times; Prussia's boundaries according to the Vienna treaties are not favourable to a healthy political life; not by means of speeches and majority verdicts will the great decisions of the time be made – that was the great mistake of 1848 and 1849 – but by iron and blood...

Otto Von Bismarck in a speech to the budget commission of the Prussian Landtag
(September 1862)

### Source B

The German Empire was created more by coal and iron than by blood and iron.

JM Keynes, *The Economic Consequences of the Peace* (1919)

### Source C

When the army has been brought to such a state as to command respect, then I shall take the first opportunity to declare war with Austria, burst asunder the German Confederation, bring the middle and smaller states into subjection and give Germany a national union under the leadership of Prussia.

Bismarck to Disraeli in 1862, quoted in *William Carr, Germany 1815–45* (1969)

### Source D

In later life he [Bismarck] gave out that he had always intended to fight Austria and to unify Germany; and this version was generally accepted by his admirers and by most historians. In reality, Bismarck's greatness lay not in mastering events, but in going with events so as to seem to master them.

AJP Taylor, *The Course of German History* (1945)

### Source E

Bismarck owed his success to the disunion and lack of will of his opponents. A coalition, or even a prolonged war, would have ruined him.

AJP Taylor, as above

---

**1** What does Bismarck's phrase 'iron and blood' (Source A) suggest about the method by which he expected Germany's future to be settled?

**2** How do Sources B and E account for the establishment of a united German Empire?

**3** Bismarck's ideas about unity had little to do with German nationalism; he was more interested in the Prussian conquest of the other German states. How do Sources A and C support this view?

**4.** The role of Bismarck in the unification process is an area of intense debate. Some regard him as a master-planner, others as an opportunist. Which of these descriptions best fits the content of Sources C, D and E?

**5** '…Bismarck was an expert at the well-chosen phrase that was intended not only for his audience but also, in part at least, for posterity.' (Cowie and Wolfson, *Years of Nationalism* (1985)) Assess the value of Source C in the light of this information.

**6** In isolation, are any of these sources likely to provide the definitive explanation of German unification? How useful are such sources to the historian?

---

# The barriers to unity

Bismarck's claim that it had always been his intention to fight Austria and to unite the German states under Prussian leadership carried the suggestion that unification was merely the inevitable consequence of strong leadership and war. However, there was almost certainly nothing inevitable about the emergence of a united German Empire. For the first half of the Nineteenth Century at least, nothing could have been further from the minds of those who determined the fortunes of Germany's leading states.

During this period the barriers to national unity seemed insuperable. In 1815 'Germany' consisted of little more than a loose grouping of states known collectively as the German Confederation. This artificial creation of the Vienna peacemakers was composed of 39 units; each independent, and each with its own government, army and ruler. The suggestion that their princes and kings should give up their independent existence in the interests of national unity was rejected absolutely. There were other, deep-seated divisions which stood in the way of unification. The states were, for example, incompatible on religious grounds with the north consisting mainly of Protestants and the south and west being chiefly Roman Catholic. But perhaps the greatest obstacle to creating a single German nation was the attitude of Austria and Prussia, the two leading states of the Confederation. Both were conservative and fiercely absolutist. Both wished to preserve their general influence among the states and largely respected each other's position. Neither at this stage had any interest in uniting the German states; they were content to exist side by side in what the Austrian Chancellor Metternich called 'peaceful dualism'.

In addition, they both regarded movements associated with the goal of national unity as being subversive and dangerous, and they reacted accordingly. Crippling censorship and rigid police-state tactics ensured the containment of nationalists and democrats, and when in 1819 the notorious Carlsbad Decrees were issued, the demise of the national move-ment was assured. The measures were introduced by Metternich in response to the assassination of the writer Kotzebue by a radical student, Karl Ludwig Sand. Throughout the German states all printed matter of less than 20 pages was subject to official scrutiny. Liberal newspapers were banned and individuals associated with radical movements were hunted down and frequently imprisoned. Such measures did not eradicate the national movement completely, but they made it very difficult for such sentiment to develop in Germany in the first half of the Nineteenth Century.

FREDERICK WILLIAM IV, KING OF PRUSSIA (1840–58)

## The Zollverein

If the achievement of German political unity in the first half of the Nineteenth Century seemed a remote possibility, the progress being made towards closer ties in the economic sphere was impressive indeed. In the years immediately after 1815, the 39 states of the Confederation managed their own economies, protecting them by means of customs duties against the challenge of their neighbours. As a result, economic stagnation charac-terized many of the states as innumerable customs barriers and internal tariffs restricted the development of commercial exchange.

Then in 1818, Prussia abandoned its domestic tariff system. In the years which followed, the success of the Prussian Customs Union encour-aged other German states to follow her example and join an expanding tariff-free zone. Progress was so rapid that by 1834 the German Customs Union (or Zollverein) was launched. The pioneering work begun by Prussia had, in just 16 years, succeeded in creating a single economic unit consisting of 18 states which touched the lives of some 23 million people. The lessons of the Zollverein did not, of course, escape the attention of those who sought a similar political arrangement in the German states.

**The Extent of the Zollverein in 1834**

NORTH SEA

BALTIC SEA

HOLSTEIN

THE MECKLENBURGS

HANOVER

THE ZOLLVEREIN

NASSAU

LUXEMBURG

BADEN

Non-Zollverein states

By 1836 the Zollverein had been extended still further to include 25 states with a total population of 26 million. Within the Union all internal customs barriers were dismantled and a common system of protective duties applied around its international boundary. Significantly, Austria – opposed to the idea of free trade and intent on maintaining the protection of her industries and markets – refused to be part of this arrangement. The political consequences of this decision were not yet apparent to the Austrians, but as the Habsburgs clung to their *political* leadership of the Confederation, domination in *economic* terms was already a Prussian responsibility.

Austria belatedly turned its attention to the Zollverein in the aftermath of the 1848 European revolutions. Under Minister President Schwarzenberg, she pursued a policy which sought to revitalize her position as the leading German state. To this end Schwarzenberg addressed himself to the challenge of the Prussian-dominated Customs Union. He proposed to establish a Zollunion between Austria and the Zollverein, the leadership of which would be in the hands of the Habsburgs. Baron von Bruck, the Austrian Minister of Commerce, gave his enthusiastic support to the scheme and the take-over bid began. Austrian hopes suffered prompt and comprehensive reversal. Whatever their political affiliations, the majority of German states did not regard Austria as an economic force in Europe. They were compelled to look to Prussia with its rapidly-developing economy as the state best equipped to direct their commercial fortunes. Well before war between Prussia and Austria excluded the latter from Germany altogether, Austria had already been isolated from the economic coalition of the German states.

The attitude of one Zollverein member to its leadership is expressed in the following extract:

Württemberg's trade routes go in the main towards the North Sea…a breach of the tariff links with Prussia, who rules the Rhine for a long stretch on both banks would cause the most damaging disturbance of trade…During the 18 years that the Zollverein has existed contacts in trade have become so many and the interests of the business men have so interlocked with each other that the tearing apart of these countries would be accompanied by the most damaging effect upon industry and trade and connected with enormous losses of capital…

Württemberg Office for Industry and Trade (1851), quoted in WG Shreeves,
*Nationmaking in Nineteenth Century Europe* (1984)

**1** What specific reason is given by the state of Württemberg for maintaining a close economic link with Prussia?

**2** What is there in this extract to suggest that the Zollverein was a force for unity?

# EXAMINING THE EVIDENCE
## Historians and the Zollverein

In their efforts to account for the emergence of a united Germany, historians have been compelled to consider the contribution of the Zollverein. Some of their conclusions are examined here.

### Source A

Many modern historians support the view that from the 1830s onwards Prussia was using the Zollverein to achieve 'a Prussian solution to the German question'. The argument is that those who found financial advantage in an economic union under Prussian leadership might be expected to take a favourable view of similar arrangements in a political union. The Zollverein was a force for unity in the 1840s and therefore a focal point for nationalist sentiments. As a result, Prussia, despite her reactionary political sympathies, came to be regarded by many as the natural leader of a united Germany.

Andrina Stiles, *The Unification of Germany 1815–90* (1986)

### Source B

Few would dispute that the Zollverein was a powerful factor in the eventual exclusion of Austria from a Prussian dominated Kleindeutschland [a united Germany minus Austria], but it is also by no means clear that it could have achieved German unity unaided by other factors. The lesser German states clung tenaciously to their independence, which was guaranteed by the rule that decisions within the Zollverein could only be taken unanimously, and suspiciously blocked any attempts by Prussia to streamline the voting procedure. In 1866 the South German States were not deterred by their membership of the Zollverein from allying with Austria against Prussia.

DG Williamson, *Bismarck and Germany 1862–1890* (1986)

## Source C

The lesser princes objected to any general German tariff union as a diminution of their sovereignty. On the other hand they were beginning to fear that the capitalist middle class which was at last developing in Western Germany would regard the internal tariffs of the German states as an intolerable imposition and would turn in irritation and despair to the radical programme of a single German republic. The princes, in other words, reversed their position and actually favoured tariff unions as the sole means of winning the middle classes back from Jacobinism, and these unions, far from envisaging a united Germany, were created with the deliberate purpose of making a united Germany unnecessary.

AJP Taylor, *The Course of German History* (1945)

## Source D

...although Prussia had succeeded by 1860 in preventing Austria from modifying the economic arrangements of the Zollverein, Austria had managed, equally effectively, to veto any constitutional change in the Confederation. The progress towards a united Germany had, therefore, reached a political impasse which would have to be resolved by political means.

Stephen J Lee, *Aspects of European History 1789–1980* (1982)

## Source E

The struggle over the customs union came to be of central importance for the further development of the German problem, and it can be asserted that the Kleindeutsch national state arose chiefly from the Prussian defence against Austrian plans for a great economic order in central Europe. For, in defending itself against the Schwarzenberg-Bruck conception, Prussia laid the foundation for its own later hegemony.

Helmut Bohme in *The Unification of Germany 1848–1871* (ed. Otto Pflanze, 1968)

---

**1** Summarize the points contained in Source A which suggest a direct relationship between the Zollverein and German unification.

**2** What evidence is used in Source B to show that the economic unity of the Zollverein was not equalled by a feeling of political unity?

**3** In Source A, Andrina Stiles described the Zollverein as 'a force for unity'. How does AJP Taylor in Source C challenge this view?

**4** The impact of Austro-Prussian rivalry for the leadership of the Zollverein is discussed in Sources D and E. How do Lee and Bohme differ in their interpretations of its effects on the eventual unification of Germany?

**5** Consider these descriptions:

'He sees German History primarily in terms of the ebb and flow of economic life and of the pressures it creates on politics.'

Otto Pflanze describing Helmut Bohme

'...in general Taylor's work is characterised by scepticism and distrust of theory...'

Arthur Marwick describing AJP Taylor

The arguments advanced by Taylor and Bohme in Sources C and E are, to some extent, controversial. How do the descriptions above help you to account for their views? Do you consider it important to have some knowledge of the historian whose work you are studying? Explain your response.

**6** Show by reference to all the sources:
(a) the positive contributions made by the Zollverein to the achievement of German unity;
(b) the limitations of this factor.

What is your assessment of the impact of the Zollverein?

## The end of dualism

The failure of German liberals and nationalists to establish a united democratic empire in the revolutions of 1848–49 created confusion in the German states. In the absence of any strong suggestions to the contrary, it was widely assumed that the old German Confederation was dead. In what form it was to be replaced became the object of intense rivalry between the leading states. The Prussian King, Frederick William IV, continued to be attracted to the idea of a united Germany providing he wore its Crown with the consent of the princes and the blessing of Austria. William's adviser, General von Radowitz, was entrusted with the task of devising an appropriate plan. He proposed to set up a united German Empire under Prussian leadership. Austria would be excluded from this 'Kleindeutschland' but not from German affairs since it was intended that a permanent union should exist between the Empire and Austria.

In 1849 the Prussian army represented the most potent authority in the German states. Austria was temporarily distracted from German affairs by disturbances in Piedmont and Hungary. Prussia seized the opportunity and announced the creation of the Erfurt Union, the first step in the direction proposed by Radowitz. Helpless in the face of Prussian military strength, the German princes were compelled to accept the Prussian plan. Twenty-eight states joined the Union and thus came under the authority of the King of Prussia.

Austria viewed the Prussian scheme with deep suspicion, seeing it as an attempt to advance the power and prestige of her North German rival. Encouraged by success in Piedmont and Hungary, Schwarzenberg (the Austrian Chief Minister) announced an alternative solution to the German problem. He proposed the creation of a 'Middle Europe' incorporating all 70 million inhabitants of the German states and the Habsburg Empire, and confidently advanced Austria as its leader. As Austria began to reassert her position in German affairs the Erfurt Union crumbled. States which had adhered to the association because of Prussian intimidation defected, looking to Austria for protection.

The situation came to a head in the Autumn of 1850. In Hesse-Cassel, a member state of the Erfurt Union, a rising prompted its ruler to request help from the recently-revived Diet of the German Confederation. Prussia claimed rights of intervention and dispatched troops. The Diet claimed equal rights and entrusted Bavarian troops, supported by Austria, with the task of restoring order. On the brink of armed conflict, Prussia backed

# TALKING POINT

Discuss the view that the collapse of the Erfurt Union represented a turning point in the progress towards a united German State.

**1** What was the 'German problem' when the failure of 'peaceful dualism' became evident?

**2** What does Bismarck see as the only solution to this problem? How accurate do you think his assessment of the situation was in 1856?

down. At Olmutz on 29 November 1851, the Erfurt Union was terminated. Although this represented an important diplomatic victory for the Habsburgs, the revival of Austria was not allowed to go as far as Schwarzenberg had planned. At a meeting in Dresden in 1851 his proposal for an Austrian-dominated 'Middle Europe' was rejected. In May the old German Confederation was officially restored.

For Prussia, the surrender at Olmutz represented a profound humiliation; for Austria it demonstrated the potency of her revival. The resurrection of the Confederation seemed to herald a return to Metternich's 'peaceful dualism'. However, that system had, like its author, lost its former stature and influence. In the 1850s Prussia harboured a deep desire to reassert her dignity and power; Austria deliberately stood in her path, frustrating her in the Diet, determined to retain the advantage. This conflict signalled the removal of one of the more significant barriers to unity. The failure of Austria and Prussia to co-operate developed into open antagonism and thence to war as it began to be appreciated that the only way for Prussia to re-establish her position would be to exclude Austria from the German states by force. In April 1856 an emerging Prussian statesman, Otto von Bismarck, articulated the feelings of many Prussians when he wrote:

'...Germany is clearly too small for us both; as long as an honourable arrangement concerning the influence of each cannot be concluded and carried out, we will both plough the same disputed acre...In the not too distant future we shall have to fight for our existence against Austria...it is not within our power to avoid that, since the course of events in Germany has no other solution.'

Bismarck to Manteuffel and Gerlach (April 1856)

# 11.1 Bismarck – 'the mad Junker'

In the years after the creation of the German Empire, it became fashionable to erect huge monuments to celebrate the achievements of Otto von Bismarck. He had become a great national hero, winning the respect and admiration of large sections of German society. However, for the first 32 years of his life such a destiny would have seemed far from likely. Bismarck was born in 1815, the son of an unremarkable Junker (land-owning nobleman). He attended university where he developed a reputation as an accomplished duellist. (In one year alone at Gottingen University he fought 25 duels.) He left university with qualifications in law and entered the civil service. In 1839, unable to find any appeal in the State bureaucracy, he returned to manage the family estates. Here, his passion for practical jokes earned him the title 'the mad Junker'. He ate, drank and smoked to excess and suffered miserably with indigestion as a result.

Then, in 1847, the life of this 'mad Junker' assumed an altogether more serious purpose. He married and became a Deputy in the Prussian United Diet, thus launching a long and illustrious political career.

### The development of Bismarck's political ideology

Bismarck was intensely proud of his Junker background and believed firmly in the traditional system of government of which his class was a fundamental part. New political forces such as liberalism and nationalism he regarded as dangerous and subversive. In the revolutions of 1848, therefore, he defended the old order against these forces. The triumph of conservatism in 1849 led to his appointment as the Prussian delegate at the revived Diet of the Confederation in Frankfurt. Bismarck hoped for a return to close co-operation with Prussia's conservative neighbour, Austria; but a short time in the Diet convinced him that such a restoration was impossible. He came to realize that Austria meant to subdue Prussia along with all the other German states, and make them obedient to Vienna. As a result he became an outspoken critic of Austria. At the time of the Crimean War he commented:

> I should be very uneasy if we sought refuge from a possible storm by hitching our trim and sea-worthy frigate to that worm-eaten old Austrian man-of-war.

Bismark became an unlikely advocate of nationalist schemes for a united German State which would exclude Austria. He had not become a nationalist, he remained firmly a Prussian patriot. As late as 1865 he asserted: 'I am much less German than Prussian...' Instead, be believed he could make use of the nationalist movement as a means of ridding the North German states of Austrian influence.

In 1857 Frederick William IV was declared officially insane and a Regency was established under William I. Bismarck was sent as Prussian ambassador first to St Petersburg and then to Paris. However, in 1862, with the King struggling to get proposals for army reforms through the Prussian parliament, Bismarck was recalled and asked to serve as Prime Minister. It was from this high office that he embarked on his mission to promote the interests of Prussia at the expense of the Austrians.

WILLIAM I WITH HIS WIFE, MARIE LOUISE

# The Prussian economy

The failure of the 1848 revolutions, the collapse of the Erfurt Union, the ascendency of Austria; in 1851 the prospect of a national solution to the German problem seemed as remote as ever. It was true that the idea of a unified state persisted in the hearts and minds of German liberals and nationalists, but as the historian EJ Feuchtwanger pointed out, '1848 demonstrated crushingly the impotence of ideas without power...' This was a lesson well learned by Bismarck who, in his 'blood and iron' speech of 1862, signposted the way to eventual unification: 'Germany doesn't look to Prussia's liberalism but to its power.'

The basis of Prussian power was, to a large extent, economic. Domination of the Zollverein was important but perhaps equally significant was the period of rapid industrialization which occurred after 1850. As it came to be acknowledged by men like Bismarck that Prussia would probably have to fight Austria, the ability to do so became the responsibility not so much of the Prussian generals as of the captains of Prussian industry.

Prussia's industrial resources were unrivalled on the Continent. In the Ruhr, the Saar and Silesia, deposits of coal and iron were abundant. It was in these regions, with their mines, steel works and blast furnaces, that Prussian power was forged.

KRUPP'S FACTORIES AT ESSEN

It was certainly significant that at the Great Exhibition of 1851, one of the proudest exhibits of the industrialist Alfred Krupp was a superbly-made field-gun with a cast-steel barrel. During the coming decades, Krupp's foundries in the Ruhr displayed, with equal pride, an ever increasing capacity for the production of high-quality armaments. Financially, Prussia was in a very healthy condition. Money was raised from a wide selection of sources including trading revenues from the Zollverein and interest from railway investment.

RAILWAYS BEGIN TO BIND THE GERMAN STATES TOGETHER. THIS PICTURE SHOWS THE PADERBORN-MARBURG LINE IN 1855

The railways were also significant in their own right. In 1845 there had been some 3280 km of track in Germany. By 1860 11,633 km had been completed. The railways acted as a binding agent, bringing together the scattered territories of Germany. Prussian military chiefs were quick to see their potential for the rapid mobilization of troops and equipment. As a result, the railways were constructed to a strategic plan determined by the needs of the army.

Since Prussia's challenge to Austria would ultimately come on the battlefield, it was essential she should possess the financial and physical resources to deploy well-equipped troops quickly to the place of need. Prussia's industrial revolution provided this capacity.

## Unification by force (1864–71)

For half a century German liberals and nationalists had chased after an illusive prize: a united German state. For the greater part of that time the quarry had remained hidden from sight and in 1848, after a brief period of capture, was released by Europe's gamekeepers, the conservative ruling class. Unification was not to be the product of discussion and consensus and it could not be maintained by liberal principles and parliaments. Unification was the immediate result of war. Prussian soldiers on foot and on horseback, with rifles and with cannon, made Germany a reality by force. In three short wars against Denmark (1864), Austria (1866) and France (1870–71), Prussian power subdued the resistance of the minor German states and excluded Austria from a Prussian-dominated German Empire.

However, the apparent simplicity of the unification process during these seven years is enormously deceiving. The period has provided exceptionally fertile ground for discussion and debate amongst historians. The key issues centre around three important questions:

- Did Bismarck possess a blueprint for unification; an overall plan which he followed step by step to its inevitable and predicted outcome?

- Did Bismarck owe his success to a coincidental gathering of favourable international and domestic circumstances?

- Was Bismarck merely an opportunist, cleverly exploiting the mistakes of his adversaries and taking calculated risks which happened to be successful?

The remainder of this chapter will consider these questions.

### The Polish Revolt (1863)

**Events** In 1863 disturbances occurred in Russian Poland. The great European Powers sympathized with the Poles but Bismarck did not. He dispatched an envoy to Russia where discussions produced an agreement known as the Alvensleben Convention. This allowed for co-operation in the suppression of the rising. Prussia was condemned by the other European Powers but succeeded in securing the gratitude of an otherwise isolated Russia.

POLISH REBELS ON THE MARCH

**The Bismarckian interpretation** According to the Bismarck blueprint, this event offered the opportunity to secure Russian neutrality in the forthcoming clash with Austria. Bismarck had to be certain that the Holy Alliance was truly dead since he could not risk engaging Russia as well as Austria on the battlefield. This, then, was the first stage in the process of unification.

**Commentary** In a letter to his sister in 1861, Bismarck revealed his feelings towards the Poles:

Strike the Poles so that they despair for their lives. I have every sympathy for their plight, but if we want to survive we cannot but exterminate them.

Bismarck disliked the Poles for their Catholic faith and feared them for their radical tradition. The Alvensleben Convention was in all probability an attempt to gain security against possible disturbances in Prussia's Polish territories. Bismarck was concerned that Tsar Alexander II might pursue a more liberal policy towards Poland and thus encourage demands for similar treatment amongst Prussian Poles. Above all, a more relaxed Russian policy might lead to the realization of Bismarck's greatest fear: a Franco-Russian friendship.

Bismarck's interpretation of the Polish Revolt (as the first stage of a calculated plan to wage war on Austria and unite the remaining German states under Prussian leadership) must be challenged. At the time of the revolt the Prussian accord with Russia led to international hostility as Britain and France unreservedly attacked Bismarck's actions. William I lost confidence in his chief minister and Bismarck was forced to belittle publicly the importance of Alvensleben. His elevated position in Prussian affairs was placed in considerable jeopardy by the Polish episode. The outcome of these events was favourable. Bismarck *did* manage to secure the friendship of Russia which was to be useful in the war of 1866. However, it seems most unlikely that he actually planned to arrive at this destination via such a potentially dangerous path.

### Schleswig-Holstein (1864)

**Events** The Duchies of Schleswig-Holstein had traditionally been ruled by Denmark. However, since Holstein was mainly German-speaking and Schleswig too had a German element, they had become the focus for German nationalist ambitions. In 1863 the King of Denmark, Frederick VII, died without an heir. By prior international arrangement, the vacant throne was to pass to Christian of Glucksburg. However, in the event his claim was challenged by the German Prince of Augustenburg, a move passionately supported by German nationalists. A war to settle the issue seemed imminent. Bismarck's attitude to Augustenburg's claim was clear:

...I cannot regard it as in the interest of Prussia to wage a war in order, as the most favourable result, to install in Schleswig-Holstein a new Grand Duke, who in fear of Prussian lust for annexation, will vote against us in the Diet and whose government, in spite of the gratitude due to Prussia for its installation, will be a ready object of Austrian machination...

**1** What were Bismarck's reasons for not supporting the claim of Augustenburg?

**2** Does Bismarck's conduct over this issue lend support to the criticism that he had no real interest in German nationalism?

**Schleswig-Holstein**

NORTH SEA

Aalburg

JUTLAND

DENMARK

Copenhagen

ZEALAND

FÜNEN

SCHLESWIG

BALTIC SEA

LAALAND

Eider

Canal    Kiel

HOLSTEIN

Elbe

LAUENBURG

HANOVER    Hamburg    MECKLENBURG

SWEDEN

Bismarck wanted the territories for Prussia and successfully enrolled Austrian assistance in achieving his goal. Austria, aware of the intense nationalist feeling aroused by the issue, was unable to resist Prussia's invitation to join it in settling the argument by force. Early in 1864, Prussian and Austrian troops moved into the Duchies. Denmark failed to obtain the support of any Great Power and was soon defeated. The Duchies were then placed in the joint custody of Prussia and Austria although the question of their long-term fate became a source of acute tension between the two Powers. The situation was resolved in August 1865 with the Convention of Gastein, which gave Austria responsibility for Holstein and Prussia the right to administer Schleswig.

**The Bismarckian interpretation** Having decided upon the necessity of fighting Austria, Bismarck required a pretext upon which to go to war. In later years he claimed to have deliberately provoked Austria over the Schleswig-Holstein affair in order to draw her onto the battlefield.

**Commentary** In one sense at least, Bismarck's interpretation of the Schleswig-Holstein issue, and its role in the process of unification, is accurate. When war between Austria and Prussia broke out in June 1866, it was the question of the future of the Duchies which provided the immediate cause. However, it must be considered doubtful whether this had been Bismarck's deliberate intention all along. Bismarck's only clear policy was his determination to prevent any attempt by the Austrians to reassert their leadership of the German states. Bismarck certainly entertained the idea of a united 'Kleindeutschland' under Prussian domination, but he was not committed to fighting a war to make this possible; a diplomatic solution would have been quite acceptable. It seems likely that Bismarck was not following a set plan but pursuing a 'wait-and-see' policy:

'I think it more useful to continue for a while the present marriage despite small domestic quarrels, and if a divorce becomes necessary, to take the prospects as they then prevail rather than to cut the bond now...'

Bismarck in 1865 on the Austro-Prussian alliance

When Bismarck agreed to the Convention of Gastein he was keeping his options open. The Gastein proposals originated from Austria and were viewed by Bismarck as being something of a concession. By delaying the final decision over the future of the German states, he hoped to extract further concessions; perhaps Austria would even give up the states of the north without a fight. The historian AJP Taylor sums up Bismarck's 'policy':

'Bismarck was a diplomatic genius, inexperienced in war and disliking its risks. He may well have hoped to manoeuvre Austria out of the duchies, perhaps even out of the headship of Germany, by diplomatic strokes; marvels of this sort were not beyond him in later life. His diplomacy in this period seems rather calculated to frighten Austria than to prepare for war.'

AJP Taylor, *The Struggle for Mastery in Europe* (1954)

It was not until 28 February 1866, at a meeting of the Prussian Crown Council, that war with Austria was acknowledged to be inevitable; but even as late as May 1866, Bismarck was prepared to consider a proposal to settle the issue diplomatically. The suggestion made by Anton von Gablenz to partition the German states foundered because Austria required Bismarck to guarantee the position of the Habsburgs in Venetia, something Bismarck felt unable to undertake.

## War with Austria (1866)

**Events** Bismarck was aware that if a war with Austria became necessary, then the attitude of the French would be important in deciding the outcome. In October 1865 he made an informal visit to Biarritz and met with the French leader, Napoleon III. No binding arrangements were made at Biarritz, but in sounding out the French Emperor, Bismarck was able to convince himself that if Venetia could be secured for Italy then Napoleon was unlikely to intervene on behalf of Austria. On 8 April 1866, Bismarck arranged an alliance with Italy to remain in force for three months. Italy was to support Prussia if war broke out during that time, and in return Italy would be allowed to absorb Venetia into her territories. Bismarck's actions alarmed the Habsburgs who were forced to begin mobilizing their troops. In this way Bismarck was able to claim that Austria had acted as the aggressor.

On 1 June 1866, Austria appealed to the Confederation to settle the question of the Duchies. This broke with the terms of the Convention of Gastein and Bismarck responded by occupying Holstein. Austria made an appeal to the Diet for assistance. This was granted and the states of the Confederation were ordered to begin mobilizing against Prussia. Bismarck reacted by declaring the Confederation dissolved and sent troops to occupy the northern states of Hesse-Cassel, Saxony and Hanover. The major engagement between Prussian and Austrian troops came on 3 July at Königgrätz (Sadowa) and resulted in defeat for the Habsburgs. Bismarck insisted on bringing hostilities to an end at this point and concluded a moderate peace with Austria. By the Treaty of Prague (August 1866) Austria was forced to give up Venetia to Italy, to agree to the annexation of Schleswig-Holstein by Prussia, and to acknowledge the ending of the German Confederation. This was partially replaced by a North German Confederation which comprised all the German states north of the River Main in a union dominated by Prussia.

KING WILLIAM I (CENTRE) AT THE BATTLE OF KÖNIGGRÄTZ

**The Bismarckian interpretation** According to Bismarck's calculations, a successful war with Austria was only possible if the French could be persuaded not to intervene. This he claimed to have achieved at Biarritz. Then, as part of his pre-planned scheme, it would be essential to treat Austria moderately after she had been defeated:

'We had to avoid wounding Austria too severely; we had to avoid leaving behind in her unnecessary bitterness of feeling or desire for revenge; we ought rather to reserve the possibility of becoming friends again with our adversary of the moment, and in any case to regard the Austrian state as a piece on the European chessboard and the renewal of friendly relations with her as a move open to us. If Austria were severely injured, she would become the ally of France and of every opponent of ours...'

Bismarck, *Reflections and Reminiscences* (1898)

**1** What were Bismarck's reasons for arranging a non-punitive peace with Austria?

**2** If Bismarck could achieve a restoration of friendly relations with Austria, how might this help in the final war of unification which he claimed to have been planning against France?

**Commentary** When Bismarck went to war with Austria, he was taking advantage of an exceptionally favourable international situation. He was indeed fortunate that:

'Both Russia and Great Britain had virtually eliminated themselves from the European balance; this gave the years between 1864 and 1866 a character unique in recent history.'

AJP Taylor, The Struggle for Mastery in Europe (1954)

In Bismarck's bid to advance Prussia's position in Germany, he was able to count on Russia remaining neutral. Alexander II was appreciative of the support given during the Polish Revolt of 1863, but more important, the old Austro-Russian partnership had been acrimoniously dissolved during the Crimean War; a development over which Bismarck had no control but which he was able to exploit skilfully. Russia never forgave the Habsburgs for their anti-Russian stance during the war, and welcomed any opportunity to see them humiliated.

British observers failed to detect any significant danger in the Prussian bid for power. The real threats to a stable Europe came, according to British opinion, from Russia and France; a strong Central European Power offered the prospect of a counterbalance to the ambitions of these traditional rivals.

Contrary to Bismarck's later version of events, the meeting at Biarritz did not guarantee the neutrality of the French in a forthcoming war with Austria. Bismarck believed that he had temporarily bought the neutrality of France with the promise of Venetia for Italy, but he could not be certain how long this would last. Indeed, on 12 June 1866 Napoleon signed a secret agreement with Austria in which he was offered territory in the Prussian Rhineland if Austria were victorious. In the war with Austria Bismarck was taking a considerable chance. He could not accurately predict a rapid victory and therefore ran the risk of the international situation changing. This was probably the real reason why he fought so hard to bring the war to an end after Königgrätz and insisted on a moderate peace. In a letter to his wife in July he wrote:

'If we are not excessive in our demands and do not believe that we have conquered the world, we will attain a peace that is worth our effort. But we are just as quickly intoxicated as we are plunged into dejection, and I have the thankless task of pouring water into the bubbling wine and making it clear that we do not live alone in Europe but with three other Powers that hate and envy us.'

Bismarck, quoted in Gordon Craig, Germany 1866–1945 (1978)

Bismarck wanted to end the war before the other Powers intervened to reverse the victory of Königgrätz. It seems highly unlikely that he was looking ahead to a war with France to complete the unification of Germany.

### The final stage: war with France

The Peace of Prague brought considerable gains to Prussia and concluded the first major political unification of the German states north of the River Main. For the time being Bismarck was content to allow the states of the south to remain independent. Despite this there were strong forces in existence which appeared to suggest that this arrangements would not last for long. Pressure was mounting on Bismarck from nationalists and liberals within Prussia to finish the job. Bismarck had certainly not given up all influence in the south; even before the Treaty of Prague was signed, he had arranged secret military alliances with the southern states which committed them to fight with Prussia if she were attacked. In 1867, the south was incorporated into the new Zollparlament, an extension of the Zollverein which, it was hoped, would encourage the idea of close co-operation between north and south.

For France, the outcome of the Prussian victory was disturbing. She gained nothing from the peace settlement and found that she now had a powerful and ambitious Protestant neighbour. French public opinion was humiliated and demanded territorial compensation. However, Napoleon's attempts to gain land (first in Belgium and later Luxembourg) were rejected by Bismarck. He understood that a war with France was a real possibility, and that its appeal to German nationalism could bring the south German states into a German Empire. However, there is little to suggest that he was planning to go to war with France in order to conclude the unification process.

PRINCE LEOPOLD

**The Hohenzollern candidature** The episode which provoked the war between France and Prussia began in 1868 in Spain. Here, a revolution had deposed the monarch, Isabella II. A new king was sought to head a constitutional government, and a request was made to Prince Leopold, a member of the same Hohenzollern family as William I of Prussia. Bismarck was a keen supporter of the candidature:

'Acceptance of the Spanish Royal Crown by a Prince of Your Majesty's illustrious House would strengthen existing sympathies between two nations…The Spaniards would have a feeling of gratitude towards Germany…For Germany it is desirable to have on the other side of France a country on whose sympathies we can rely…French peaceableness towards Germany will always wax or wane in proportion to the dangers of war with Germany. We have in the long run to look for the preservation of peace not to the goodwill of France but to the impression created by our position of strength…The prosperity of Spain and German trade with her would receive a powerful impetus under Hohenzollern rule…In the event of a rejection, the wishes of the Spaniards would probably turn to Bavaria…Spain would have a ruling house which looked for support to France and Rome, maintaining contact with anti-national elements in Germany and affording them a secure if remote rallying point…'

Bismarck to William I (9 March 1870)

**1** What were Bismarck's reasons for supporting the Hohenzollern candidature?

**2** Bismarck was concerned to show Prussia in a position of strength in order to dissuade France from contemplating war. Why did he believe a war with France might be likely?

**3** What is your opinion of the suggestion that Bismarck supported Leopold in order to provoke a war with France by which he could complete the unification of Germany?

The French found the candidature of Leopold completely unacceptable, fearing that it would place a Prussian puppet on the throne of their southern neighbour. War-fever gripped the popular imagination and Napoleon found himself compelled to demand assurances that Prussia would detach herself permanently from Spanish affairs. When Bismarck doctored the Ems Telegram which contained William I's reply (see *Examining the Evidence* opposite), Napoleon could only follow the outraged demands of his people and declare war on Prussia.

PARISIANS CELEBRATE THE DECLARATION OF WAR AGAINST PRUSSIA

# **E**XAMINING THE EVIDENCE

## **Did Bismarck plan the Franco-Prussian War?**

### Source A

Do not believe that I love war. I have seen enough of war to abhor it profoundly. The terrible scenes I have witnessed, will never cease to haunt
my mind. I shall never consent to a war that is avoidable, much less seek
it. But this war with France will surely come. It will be clearly forced
upon us by the French Emperor. I see that clearly.

Bismarck (1867)

### Source B

That German unity could be promoted by actions involving force I think
is self-evident. But there is a quite different question, and that has to do
with the precipitation of a powerful catastrophe and the responsibility of
choosing the time for it. A voluntary intervention in the evolution of history, which is determined by purely subjective factors, results only in the
shaking down of unripe fruit, and that Germany unity is no ripe fruit at
this time leaps, in my opinion, to the eye. If the time that lies ahead works
in the interest of unity as much as the period since the accession of
Frederick the Great has done…then we can look to the future calmly and
leave the rest to our successors.

Bismarck to the Prussian envoy in Munich (February 1869)

## Source C

His Majesty writes to me: 'Count Benedetti spoke to me on the promenade, in order to demand from me, finally in a very importunate manner, that I should authorise him to telegraph at once that I bound myself for all future time never again to give my consent if the Hohenzollerns should renew their candidature. I refused at last somewhat sternly, as it is neither right nor possible to undertake engagements of this kind *à tout jamais*. Naturally I told him that I had as yet received no news, and as he was earlier informed about Paris and Madrid than myself, he could clearly see that my government once more had no hand in the matter.' His Majesty has since received a letter from the Prince. His Majesty having told Count Benedetti that he was awaiting news from the Prince, has decided, with reference to the above demand, upon the representation of Count Eulenburg and myself, not to receive Count Benedetti again, but only to let him be informed through an aide-de-camp: That his Majesty had now received from the Prince confirmation of the news which Benedetti had already received from Paris, and had nothing further to say to the ambassador. His Majesty leaves it to your Excellency whether Benedetti's fresh demand and its rejection should not be at once communicated both to our ambassadors and to the press.

WILLIAM I AND BENEDETTI AT EMS

Original text of the Ems Telegraph, from Heinrich Abeken to Bismarck (13 July 1870)

## Source D

After the news of the renunciation of the hereditary Prince of Hohenzollern had been officially communicated to the Imperial government of France by the Royal government of Spain, the French ambassador further demanded of his Majesty, the King, at Ems, that he would authorise him to telegraph to Paris that his Majesty, the King, bound himself for all time never again to give his consent, should the Hohenzollerns renew their candidature. His Majesty, the King, thereupon decided not to receive the French ambassador again, and sent the aide-de-camp on duty to tell him that his Majesty had nothing further to communicate to the ambassador.

Bismarck's text of the Ems Telegram edited for publication

## Source E

I went on to explain: 'If in execution of His Majesty's order, I at once communicate this text...not only to the newspapers but by telegraph to all our embassies it will be known in Paris before midnight...and will have the effect of a red rag on the French bull...Success, however, depends essentially upon the impression which the origination of the war makes upon us and others: it is important that we should be the ones attacked.

Bismarck, *Reflections and Reminiscences* (1898)

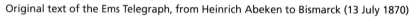

**1** What evidence is contained in Source B to suggest that Bismarck was not planning a war to complete the process of German unification?

**2** Examine Source C carefully, then arrange the following events in the correct chronological sequence.

- William I informed of Hohenzollern decision not to accept the Spanish throne.
- Benedetti asks William I for permission to send a telegram to Paris containing an undertaking on behalf of William not to consent to any future Hohenzollern candidature.
- Benedetti informed by Paris of Hohenzollern decision not to accept the Spanish throne.
- William I communicates to Benedetti his intention to say nothing more about the Hohenzollern candidature.
- William I refuses to give permission for telegram to be sent by Benedetti to Paris in the absence of any direct information on the Hohenzollern decision.

3 (a) Attempt a similar sequencing exercise using the information in Source D.

(b) Which specific stages of the Ems negotiations does Bismarck omit from his version of events?

(c) What effect do these omissions have on the tone of the Ems Telegram?

(d) Suggest what effect this might have had on French public opinion?

4 Does the fact that Bismarck amended the Ems Telegram provide conclusive proof that he alone was responsible for causing the Franco-Prussian War?

5 Using your conclusions to questions 2 and 3 and the information in Source E, present a counter-argument to Bismarck's statements in Source A.

6 In Source E Bismarck appears to be keen to take responsibility for engineering the French declaration of war on Prussia. Given the source and date of this extract explain:

(a) why Bismarck assumes this responsibility;

(b) how reliable you believe this extract to be when determining Bismarck's role in provoking the Franco-Prussian War.

**Unification: Variations on a theme**

For Bismarck and the German liberals the concept of unification had different meanings. Consider the chart below and decide which interpretation was most appropriate to the German state which emerged in 1871.

*Bismarck*

Exclusion of Austria from German affairs and the establishment of a Kleindeutschland.

Prussian absorption of lesser German states.

Universal adoption of Prussian system of government – authoritarian monarchy.

*Liberals*

Exclusion of Austria (but some supported a Grossdeutsch solution).

Voluntary surrender of regional sovereignty.

Adoption of constitutional parliamentary government – development of liberal institutions.

### The Franco-Prussian War (1870–71)

As Bismarck had hoped, nationalist feeling led the south German states to fight alongside Prussia against France. The French, facing a better organized and better equipped army, quickly sustained a number of defeats. The decisive Prussian victory was won at Sedan in September 1870. Paris fell in January 1871 and a preliminary peace was arranged. The terms of this settlement were ratified by the Treaty of Frankfurt in May. The French provinces of Alsace and Lorraine were annexed by Prussia, and France was forced to pay an indemnity of 5000 million francs. An army of occupation was to remain for four years until the indemnity was paid.

Four months before the signing of the Frankfurt Treaty the German Empire was proclaimed at Versailles. The southern states, fuelled by nationalist passions and aware that their only chance of lasting security lay with Prussia, finally gave up their independence and joined with the states of the north to complete the process of German unification.

# REVIEW
## The interdependence of causes

**'The Second Reich was proclaimed in 1871. It was war – nothing more and nothing less – that was responsible for its creation.' (JMB)**

Carefully examine the statement above and then discuss it.

The problem with such a statement is that it excludes the importance of other factors in the process of German unification. War was certainly significant, but a response to this statement which chose to agree unreservedly with it would produce a rather distorted explanation of the event. The chart below lists some of the factors which can be said to have helped in the creation of the Second Reich. None of these factors, by itself, can fully account for the emergence of the German Empire in 1871. Each may be said to be dependent on a combination of other factors. Success on the battlefield in the 1860s, for example, was dependent on the strength of the Prussian economy.

Take each factor in the left-hand column in turn and pose the following question:

This factor, by itself, could not have brought about the unification of Germany; in making its contribution to unification, upon which other factors did it depend?

Working in small groups, indicate on your copy of the chart whether the contribution made by other factors was:
- vital (mark box with a V)
- significant but not essential (mark box with an S)
- peripheral (mark box with a P)

An example is provided for you. Your group should be able to justify its decisions.

| | War | Bismarck's diplomacy | Prussian army reforms | The Zollverein | French neutrality (1866) | Austrian weakness | German nationalism | The Crimean War | The strong Prussian economy |
|---|---|---|---|---|---|---|---|---|---|
| War | ✕ | | | | | | | | |
| Bismarck's diplomacy | | ✕ | | | | | | | |
| Prussian army reforms | V | V | ✕ | P | S | S | P | S | V |
| The Zollverein | | | | ✕ | | | | | |
| French neutrality (1866) | | | | | ✕ | | | | |
| Austrian weakness | | | | | | ✕ | | | |
| German nationalism | | | | | | | ✕ | | |
| The Crimean War | | | | | | | | ✕ | |
| The strong Prussian economy | | | | | | | | | ✕ |

**1** Examine your completed chart. Which combination of factors appears to be the most important in explaining the creation of the Second Reich?

**2** What are the dangers of attributing events to single explanations (mono-causal answers)?

# 12 Bismarck's Germany 1871-90

## The shape of things to come

The proclamation of the German Empire on 18 January 1871 prompted great speculation as to the future of this new and powerful element in European politics. On 20 January *The Times* newspaper editorial made this contribution to the debate:

'In 1871 Germany starts independent, ardently patriotic, almost purely national. She is about to have the most powerful instrument of unity, a great popular Assembly, an institution which seems in these days to have a more strongly centralizing influence than any despot can command. The Parliament in which Germany will be represented has not yet been constituted, but if there is anything safe in political prediction it is that this Parliament will reflect the instincts and impulses which have welded the nation into one. The Hohenzollerns must prove very different from their traditional character if they neglect to make the best use of so potent an ally. There will be, we think, an inevitable tendency in the Federal Legislature and Administration to break down the independent authorities which the Minor States have reserved for themselves or have been suffered by Prussia to retain. We do not expect that the Federal Representatives will be enthusiastic for the Imperial House; but their certain instinct will be to make Germany one and homogeneous, and this will necessitate the concentration of even more and more authority in the Imperial hands; the respective armies over which the Sovereigns have reserved to themselves considerable power, at least in time of peace, will be gradually fused; it will be found that material improvements can be much more efficiently made by a central administration; a common legal system, a common judicature will be demanded, and with each change the authority of Berlin will be increased, while the Sovereigns of Munich and Stuttgart will tend to become powerless though honourable Dignitaries of the State.'

*The Times* (20 January 1871), quoted in Anthony Hewison, *Bismarck and the Unification of Germany* (1970)

WILLIAM I

*The Times* was, like many other observers across Europe and within Germany itself, responding to the constitution of the new German State outlined by Bismarck in January 1871. It was this document which signposted the direction of Germany's political development.

## 12.1  The new Empire
### Constitutional democracy or authoritarian monarchy?

| Features of a constitutional democracy | Features of an authoritarian monarchy |
|---|---|
| Devolution of some responsibility to local government. | Heavily-centralized government – little scope for regional initiative. |
| Elected Parliament responsible for central government, foreign policy, the army, defence. | Monarch in direct control of major State responsibilities, eg foreign policy, the army, government. |
| Broad electorate – acceptance of universal manhood suffrage and periodic elections. | Restricted electorate (if any), no place for universal manhood suffrage. |
| State legislation is the product of parliamentary process. | State legislation derives from monarch and advisers. |
| The government and government ministers answerable to parliament. | Monarch not required to justify or explain actions. |

## QUESTIONS

**1** Consider the detail of the German constitution of 1871 contained in the diagram opposite. Which of the features listed in the chart (above) can be identified within the constitution?

**2** In what sense can the constitution be described as a political compromise?

**3** Which features of the constitution restricted the democratic composition of the Reichstag?

**4** How was Prussia able to dominate the Federal government (Bundesrat)?

**5** The German socialist Karl Liebknecht described the Reichstag as 'a fig leaf covering the nakedness of absolutism.' What is your opinion of this judgement?

## EMPEROR

- Always the King of Prussia
- Could appoint and dismiss the Chancellor
- Could dissolve the Reichstag
- Controlled foreign policy
- Could make treaties and alliances
- Commanded the army
- Could declare war and make peace
- Supervised the execution of all Federal laws
- Possessed the right to interpret the constitution

## CHANCELLOR

- Chief Minister of the Reich
- Not responsible to parliament, only to the Emperor
- He decided upon Reich policy outlines
- Chaired sessions of the Bundesrat
- Could 'hire and fire' State Secretaries responsible for the various government ministries
- Could ignore resolutions passed by the Reichstag
- Office was normally combined with the Minister-Presidency of Prussia

## FEDERAL

Centralized government with specific responsibilities for the Reich as a whole, eg foreign affairs, defence, civil and criminal law, customs, coinage, railways, postal service.

## REICH GOVERNMENT

## STATE

Regional government with special responsibilities for individual states, eg education, transport, direct taxation, police, local justice, health.

## BUNDESRAT

- The Federal Council
- Comprised 58 members nominated by State assemblies
- Consent was required in the passing of new laws
- Theoretically able to change the constitution
- A vote of 14 against a proposal constituted a veto
- Prussia had 17 of the 58 seats

## REICHSTAG

- The National Parliament
- Elected by all males over 25 years of age
- Operated as a consenting Chamber: could accept or reject legislation but power to initiate new laws was negligible
- State Secretaries, responsible for government ministries, were excluded from membership of Reichstag
- Members were not paid
- Could approve or reject the budget

## 12.1 The new Empire *continued*
## A unitary nation?

Berlin: Prussian capital becomes the new Imperial capital

*BALTIC SEA*

Northern Schleswig: contained, a Danish population

Eastern Germany: contained large Polish population

P R U S S I A

Prussia: constituted two-thirds of Reich territory and over half the total population

SAXONY

BAVARIA

Alsace-Lorraine contained a French-speaking population

WURTTEMBERG

BADEN

THE GERMAN EMPIRE 1871

The Empire functioned as a federation of 25 states. Each possessed its own representative assembly and was responsible for specified local provisions. Local royal families were retained.

In 1871 the Empire did not have:
- ■ a national flag;
- ■ a national anthem;
- ■ a uniform currency;
- ■ a common legal system;
- ■ a State bank;
- ■ free trade between all states.

The states of the Reich did not enjoy equal rights:
- ■ Saxony, Bavaria, Wurttemberg and Baden were exempted from taxes on alcohol;
- ■ Bavaria and Wurttemberg retained their own railway, postal and telegraph systems;
- ■ Bavaria held on to peace-time command of her armed forces and maintained her own diplomatic service.
- ■ free trade between all states.

Germans living in the Habsburg Empire (mainly Austria and Bohemia) remained excluded from the German State. Not until the aggressive nationalism of the 1930s under Hitler did all Germans become united.

# **T**ALKING POINT

## The importance of national symbols

Symbols of national pride such as flags, anthems, monuments and emblems abound in the modern world. When US astronauts landed on the Moon in 1969 they left behind the American flag, the Stars and Stripes. Winners of Olympic gold have the honour of receiving their medals to the accompaniment of their national anthem. The hammer and sickle and the swastika can be instantly associated with a nation and its ideals. What is the purpose of such symbols? How are they used and abused in the modern world?

Bismarck had little time for such symbolism. Germany did not have a national flag until 1892 and was without a national hymn until after the First World War. In fact, the most potent symbol in post-unification Germany was Bismarck himself, his image immortalized in huge monuments in cities such as Berlin and Hamburg. What does Bismarck's disregard for national symbols suggest to you about his brand of nationalism. Why do you think German artists seeking inspiration for national monuments often chose Bismarck as their subject?

# QUESTIONS

**1** Present a case to support the view that in 1871 Germany could not truly be described as a 'unitary state'.

**2** Use the information on this page and opposite to argue that in 1871 Germany was no more than an enlarged Prussia.

# The development of political parties

The introduction of universal suffrage across Germany promoted the development of well-organized mass political parties with popular appeal and distinct programmes.

| Party | Number of seats in Reichstag (1871–90) | | | | | | | |
|---|---|---|---|---|---|---|---|---|
| | *1871* | *1874* | *1877* | *1878* | *1881* | *1884* | *1887* | *1890* |
| The National Liberals | 125 | 155 | 128 | 99 | 47 | 51 | 99 | 42 |

The main support for this party was derived from the educated Protestant middle class and the industrial upper-middle class. The party had two principal aims: (a) the creation of a strong nation-state and (b) the encouragement of a liberal constitutional state; the former in practice being the priority. Until 1878 the National Liberals were Bismarck's most reliable parliamentary allies.

| | | | | | | | | |
|---|---|---|---|---|---|---|---|---|
| The Centre Party | 63 | 91 | 93 | 94 | 100 | 99 | 98 | 106 |

A political grouping consisting mainly of Catholics worried by the predominance of Protestants in the new state. They worked in opposition to Bismarck in order to defend the interests of the Catholic Church. The party also attracted support from the non-socialist lower classes, particularly in the Rhineland and Southern Germany.

| | | | | | | | | |
|---|---|---|---|---|---|---|---|---|
| The Social Democratic Party | 2 | 9 | 12 | 9 | 12 | 24 | 11 | 35 |

Composed of socialist groups and having close links with the trade unions, this was predominantly a working-class party. Its socialist programme aimed to promote complete democracy in Germany and to fight for social reforms in the interests of the German labouring masses.

| | | | | | | | | |
|---|---|---|---|---|---|---|---|---|
| The German Conservative Party | 57 | 22 | 40 | 59 | 50 | 78 | 80 | 73 |

Mainly composed of landowners. They were sceptical about the unification of Germany, preferring the comfortable familiarity of the old separate states. Gradually they came to support Bismarck after 1878.

| | | | | | | | | |
|---|---|---|---|---|---|---|---|---|
| The Free Conservatives | 37 | 33 | 38 | 57 | 28 | 28 | 41 | 20 |

Drawn from a wider geographical and social base than the German Conservatives. Contained not just landowners but also industrialists and professional and commercial interests. This group accepted Bismarck's unification and the constitution which followed. They offered Bismarck steady support.

| | | | | | | | | |
|---|---|---|---|---|---|---|---|---|
| The Progressives | 47 | 50 | 52 | 39 | 115 | 74 | 32 | 76 |

A liberal party but one which, unlike the National Liberals, remained opposed to Bismarck's pursuit of a powerful nation-state at the expense of liberal constitutional principles. Remained committed to the attainment of parliamentary government.

It would be inaccurate to suggest that such parties were able to participate in government in quite the same way as in modern democracies. The constitution limited them to being either supporters of the Chancellor or part of his parliamentary Opposition. The parties were in no position to form governments, nor to furnish the nation with a Chancellor, nor even to provide State Secretaries responsible for government ministries. In spite of these restrictions, Bismarck could not afford to ignore them. He relied on their support to steer legislation through the Reichstag and on more than one occasion found that they were prepared to challenge his proposals. The Chancellor even went as far as to identify two political groupings within the Reichstag as 'enemies of the Reich' and attempted to destroy their influence in the new state.

KAISER WILLIAM I SURROUNDED BY HIS MOST TRUSTED SERVANTS

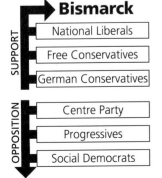

**1** Comment on the electoral performance of each of the main parties in the period 1871–90.

**2** In the period 1871–78 the political parties were roughly aligned as shown opposite.

Draw a diagram of the same design to show the alignments of the parties in the period 1878–90. (You may want to wait until you have studied the remainder of this chapter before you attempt the diagram.)

**3** What does your diagram reveal about Bismarck's political support/opposition in the Reichstag after 1878?

# 'Enemies of the Reich': socialists and the Church

For all his immense power and influence in the new Germany, Bismarck was uneasy. As he surveyed the Empire his attention was drawn to two groups who seemed to challenge his perception of the nation-state. The socialists and Roman Catholics commanded and encouraged loyalties which went beyond national boundaries, and their political programmes struck at the very heart of the new Imperial system. Bismarck spoke of both groups as 'enemies of the Reich' and conducted a determined campaign to remove their challenge.

## The clash with the Church: Bismarck and the 'Kulturkampf'

The political wing of the Roman Catholic Church in Germany was the Centre Party. Its purpose was to defend the interests of the Catholic Church in the new, largely Protestant state. Bismarck was deeply suspicious of the party and alarmed himself with visions of internationalist conspiracies supported by his European (and largely Catholic) rivals, France and Austria. The Centre Party opposed the rise of centralized Imperial authority and spoke out in favour of greater self-rule for the component states of the Reich. In addition, it objected to State interference in the Church's traditional sphere of influence: the education system. Bismarck observed that the Centre Party was fast becoming a rallying-point for anti-Imperial groups, and regarded its appeal across all social classes as dangerous. He was particularly concerned by the enthusiastic support given to it by Prussia's Polish minority. Bismarck's fears led to the conflict between State and Catholic Church frequently referred to as the *Kulturkampf*.

The conflict was initiated by Bismarck as an opportunist response to an internal dispute within the Catholic Church over education. Soon after the creation of the Empire Bismarck fired the opening shots in the feud by removing schools from clerical control and bringing them directly under the jurisdiction of State government. From 1872, however, the assault on the Church became more vigorous. In that year, the Jesuit order was forbidden to set up establishments in the Empire, and troublesome Jesuit supporters became subject to expulsion from Germany. In 1873 the Reichstag approved a package of measures known as the May Laws. Under this legislation all candidates for the priesthood were required to attend a secular university for three years before commencing training, and all religious appointments became subject to State approval. Other measures followed:

*1874*   Obligatory civil marriage introduced in Prussia.
Births, marriages and deaths to be notified to the public registrar, not to the Church. (Both measures extended to the other states in 1875.)
States empowered to limit the freedom of movement of the clergy and to expel troublesome priests.

*1875*   All religious orders dissolved

The results of this campaign against the Church were not at all what Bismarck had hoped. The 'iron Chancellor' had chosen a resourceful and resilient adversary fully capable of responding to his tough line. Presented as the victims of an authoritarian oppressor, the Church thrived on persecution and won both sympathy and support across Germany. As Catholics and other assorted opponents of Bismarck rallied to the defence of the Church, the Centre Party enjoyed widespread electoral support and the Chancellor was forced into an embarrassing defeat. An analysis of Bismarck's failure is provided by the historian C Grant Robertson in the following extract:

'...in 1871 Bismarck plainly miscalculated. The diplomacy with which he had hitherto crossed swords successfully had not had the traditions, skill, fertility in resource, and pertinacity of the Vatican. The Roman Curia could and did pull many wires throughout Europe, and it could afford to wait. It had no capital that could be stormed, leaving the defence impotent. Its capital was everywhere planted in the consciences of millions of its communion. Heads can be cut off, but the obedience of heart and will cannot be enforced by prison or the guillotine...Indeed the seven years from 1871 to 1878 were an instructive object lesson in the limits of power even when exercised by a state with the executive strength of Prussia....In 1872 he [Bismarck] apparently calculated that the Catholics would either not resist, or, if they did, would soon surrender to a rigorous coercion. He was completely mistaken. When cardinal archbishops, with the applause of their congregations, defied the law and went to prison, the state as power could only, as Windthorst remarked, bring in the guillotine – if it dared. For when a state by its own action converts law-breakers into martyrs for conscience it loses the sympathy of the law-abiding...Universal suffrage proved a terrible weapon in the hands of the Centre Party. At the general election of 1874 the National Liberals increased their numbers to over one hundred and fifty, but the Clericals polled a million-and-a-half votes and returned not sixty [58 seats in 1871] but 91 members. Bismarck had therefore to face a National Liberal Party stronger than ever and more indispensable to the government, and a Centre opposition enormously encouraged by its success.'

C Grant Robertson, *Bismarck* (1919)

**1** Why did Bismarck's attempts to subdue the Catholic Church fail?

**2** How was this failure emphasized by the results of the 1874 elections?

As the decade passed, Bismarck was made acutely aware of the failure of his campaign, even to the extent of incurring the displeasure of the royal family. He knew he must cut his losses and end the religious dispute. The opportunity came at last in 1878 with the death of Pope Pius IX. His successor, Leo XIII, was keen to end the *Kulturkampf* and re-establish good relations with Berlin. Bismarck did not miss his opportunity and arranged for discussions to begin in the summer of 1878. The negotiations lasted until 1887 and ironically produced substantial concessions in Bismarck's favour. Civil marriage remained obligatory, the Jesuits were not permitted to return to Germany, and the State continued to oversee all permanent Church appointments. Ultimately these gains were of real significance, but Bismarck's scheme to destroy the Centre Party completely backfired; his actions served to strengthen rather than weaken his political opponents.

## The assault on Social Democracy

Bismarck was uniformly hostile to the objectives of the socialists, regarding them as revolutionary and anarchic. He feared the international appeal of the ideology and was concerned by the steady electoral gains being made by the Social Democratic Party.

As the German working class became more politically aware, the implications of universal suffrage for the further development of Social Democracy did not escape Bismarck. The conservative-monarchist system which he had laboured to build in Germany seemed under threat; Bismarck's natural reflex in such circumstances was to go on the offensive. His opportunity came in 1878 following two isolated assassination attempts on Kaiser William. Bismarck was quick to present these incidents as part of a 'red' conspiracy to undermine the values and institutions of the new Reich. He dissolved the Reichstag, attacked the Social Democrats and proposed anti-socialist legislation. The storm of public indignation aroused by the attempts on the King's life enabled Bismarck to secure the passage of his anti-socialist bill in the new Reichstag. The new law declared as follows:

| Year | Number of seats in Reichstag |
|------|------------------------------|
| 1871 | 2                            |
| 1874 | 9                            |
| 1877 | 12                           |

'Associations, which further social democratic, socialist or communist aims and thus threaten to overthrow the existing state and social structure, are banned.

The same applies to associations in which social democratic, socialist or communist aims are directed at the overthrow of the existing state and social structure in a manner which threatens peace and harmony amongst the population.

The same law on associations applies to alliances of any kind.'

*Law Gazette of the Reich* (1878), quoted in *Fragen an die deutsche Geschichte* (1984)

Police activity against the socialists was intensified. Meetings were broken up and left-wing publications outlawed. Known agitators were hunted down and removed from circulation. Between 1878 and 1890 some 900 labour leaders were deported from their place of residence and around 1500 were sentenced to terms in prison. As with the *Kulturkampf*, Bismarck had launched an uncompromising assault on a political enemy, but was his approach any more successful? Consider this evaluation by William Carr:

'This law had the same traumatic effect on Socialists that the May laws were having on German Catholics. It rallied the faithful and fortified them in their beliefs…Twelve years of persecution deepened the fortress mentality of the German working class. The party became more radical and class-conscious; at the Wyden Congress, held in Switzerland in 1880, the party committed itself to use 'all means' to attain its objectives…At first the Socialist vote fell from 493,000 in 1877 to 312,000. But by 1884 it had risen to 550,000 – giving the party twenty-four seats in the Reichstag – and continued to rise until it was well over one million in 1890. The party simply went underground; it held congresses and published its journals as before but operated from outside Germany. By the

**1** How were the socialists able to survive Bismarck's attack?

**2** In what ways was the socialists' and their supporters' response to Bismarck's policy similar to that of the Catholics?

**3** How might it be argued that Bismarck's handling of the socialists did long-term damage to the development of the Reich?

1883 Sickness insurance introduced for three million workers and their families. Cost to be borne jointly by employers and workers.

1884 Accident insurance introduced for injured workers; financed wholly by employers.

1886 Accident and sickness insurance extended to seven million agricultural workers.

1889 Old age pensions made available upon reaching the age of 70. Paid for by workers, employers and the State.

# TALKING POINT

### State socialism

Working in a group of four, allocate each of the following roles to the members of your group:

(a) Bismarck
(b) A Social Democrat
(c) A radical National Liberal
(d) A German worker.

Consider your reaction to State socialism. Present and defend your case for the approval or rejection of State socialism.

beginning of the twentieth century, it had become a well disciplined and highly organised mass-party, a model for all Socialist parties. In short, Bismarck had completely failed to bring the Socialists to heel; worst of all, his blundering ill-conceived policy had seriously retarded the integration of the growing working class in the new Reich.'

William Carr, *A History of Germany* (1979)

## 'State socialism'

Bismarck's crude attempt to eliminate the socialists was accompanied by a more subtle effort to win the loyalty of the working classes. The Chancellor proposed a package of welfare measures designed to assist German workers at times of need (see left).

For Bismarck, this venture into state socialism had a broader motive than mere humanitarian concern. Its purpose was, as William Carr has said, '...to wean the working classes from revolutionary Socialism by offering them a modest stake in the Empire...' State socialism has been described as a 'taming policy', a phrase not inappropriate when considering some of Bismarck's own observations:

'Whoever has a pension for his old age, he is much more content and easier to handle than the person who has no prospects.'

In the long term, Bismarck's welfare measures must be seen as a great pioneering effort. They represented the first comprehensive welfare system in Europe, pre-dating similar developments in Britain by more than a quarter of a century. But the State programme had its critics. Not unexpectedly perhaps, the socialists scorned the measures as 'crumbs from the rich man's table' and saw in them only a cynical attempt to win the German workers away from the true objectives of socialism. The issue also raised passions within the National Liberal Party. Around 50 supported the measures, but other, radical elements within the party rejected state socialism as unwarranted state intervention which violated individual freedom.

Ultimately, Bismarck's view of the working class as a docile and essentially conservative body, which could be won over by the comforting paternalism of the State, was proved quite wrong. It was true that his legislation helped to remove the more revolutionary elements from Social Democracy, and that German workers developed a certain allegiance to the Empire, but he failed to halt the progress of the Social Democratic Party at the polls. By 1890 there were well over a million Social Democratic voters and the party had 35 seats in the Reichstag. Bismarck underestimated the nature of the social problem, and State socialism was never intended to extend into the private realm of the factory-owner where grievances associated with long hours, child labour and safety were ignored. Whilst such conditions persisted in Germany, the Social Democrats were assured of a future.

A SHANTY TOWN ON THE OUTSKIRTS OF BERLIN (1871)

# The myth of the 'liberal era'

Many histories of Germany refer to the period 1871–78 as the 'liberal era'. To the casual observer, taking this description at face value, it is quite possible to conjure an image of Germany moving steadily from the achievement of unity towards the liberal ideal of independent parliamentary government. This was certainly the long-term goal of the National Liberals but the 1870s witnessed instead the steady erosion of liberal hopes. Bismarck increasingly put his dislike of these on public display and locked horns with their adherents on several occasions in the Reichstag. In fact, the 'liberal era' can be more accurately defined as the period from 1871 to 1878 when Bismarck found himself dependent on National Liberal support in the Reichstag. The era ended when he released himself from this dependence and aligned himself with his true political associates, the Conservatives.

In 1871, most National Liberals applauded Bismarck for his bold and resolute achievement of national unity. True, there were reservations about his methods, but they were generally forgiven amidst the euphoria associated with unification. They had seen one of their principal aims realized and were fully appreciative of Bismarck's pivotal role in this process. As the largest party in the Reichstag from 1871 to 1878, the National Liberals came to be the Chancellor's main parliamentary ally. As Bismarck consolidated the Empire, they were further heartened by the rapid progress made towards economic unification.

> **Economic unification**
> - Abolished all remaining internal tariffs
> - Established a national currency
> - Set up a national bank
> - National system of railways completed
> - Established national postal and telegraph systems
> - A unified system of weights and measures was introduced

However, Bismarck was never really happy with his National Liberal supporters. Politically he was out of sympathy with much of their long-term programme, particularly their hopes for the extension of parliamentary government. He disliked having to rely on them to ensure the passage of his legislation through the Reichstag. Above all he became increasingly irritated as they exercised their constitutional rights and threw out a number of his proposals. In 1874, for example, the National Liberals refused to agree to a proposal to remove the military budget from the supervision of the Reichstag. Bismarck had to threaten to call new elections before a compromise was reached which fixed the budget for seven years. Again in 1876, the National Liberals ensured the defeat of proposals to introduce anti-treason laws which the Chancellor intended to use against the socialists. A similar bill was rejected in 1878. Bismarck had to wait until assassination attempts on the Kaiser's life later that same year produced a wave of patriotic sentiment which the National Liberals could not afford to ignore.

Bismarck's frustration was ended in 1878 over the issue of Germany's trade policy. During the 1870s he had supported free trade, a policy close to liberal hearts. However, from around 1873 a serious trade depression began to affect Europe. Germany's neighbours began to erect trade barriers to protect domestic agriculture and industry. Before long a campaign had been launched with the backing of German industrialists and landowners to introduce protective tariffs into Germany. Bismarck viewed these demands with considerable interest since they presented him with a number of tempting opportunities. First, tariffs meant an additional source of income. Federal government had to rely on indirect taxation which was always inadequate. In order to make up the budgetary shortfall, supplementary payments were made by individual states, a situation Bismarck found distasteful. The Chancellor hoped that the new tariffs would permit the Federal government to become financially independent of the states. In addition, Bismarck looked for a political advantage from the protectionist issue. In the elections of 1878, the National Liberals had lost 29 seats; the combined strength of the two Conservative parties was now sufficient to outvote them in the Reichstag. In pursuing the protectionist case (popular with the Conservatives), Bismarck saw his chance to break with the National Liberals.

In July 1879 a tariff bill passed through the Reichstag and duties began to be imposed on foreign imports. The political implications of this measure were far-reaching. The issue split the National Liberals, with those still supporting free trade leaving the party to join the Progressives. Those who remained supported Bismarck's tariff bill but he no longer needed their backing. He was now firmly established in the Conservative camp. Together, the landowners and the industrialists offered their grateful support to the Chancellor in return for his protection of their livelihoods. This so-called 'alliance of steel and rye' served Bismarck faithfully for the remainder of his term in office, and the National Liberals were becalmed in the political doldrums.

# EXAMINING THE EVIDENCE
## The myth of the 'red menace'

The following sources deal with the assassination attempts made on Kaiser William I in 1878. You will find it useful to reread the section in this chapter on Bismarck's attitudes towards the National Liberals (page 274-75).

### Source A

The noble old man [Kaiser William I], who knew no fear, drove out on Sunday, 2nd June, towards the Tiergarten as usual. It was an open carriage...Suddenly he collapsed, streaming with blood. From the windows of a house in the Unter den Linden a double-barrelled gun had fired two well aimed shots. It was buck-shot, and had injured head, shoulders, both arms and his right hand. The Emperor who throughout his whole life had never lost his self-control, retained it even now. Truly great, in dignified calm he returned to his palace, supported by his bodyguard...More than thirty pieces of shot had to be extracted one by one, many of them in dangerous spots...A great wave of shame and wrath surged over the German people. Immediately after the attack the frenzied crowd tried to tear the would be assassin limb from limb...Dr Karl Nobiling [the man responsible for the assassination attempt] appeared on the scene as an intellectual. He had turned to the Socialist Party early in his life, and at a time when they exercised great influence on the half-educated and immature...It was natural that Bismarck should make use of the atmosphere created by these attacks to dissolve the Reichstag and proceed to new elections.

Von Bulow, *The Memoirs of Prince Von Bulow* (Vol. IV, 1931)

### Source B

Nobiling's attempt was the act of a lunatic. He came from a well-to-do family, had studied economics and had taken his degree at Leipzig. He certainly had no political connections. Nobody in the Social Democratic Party even knew his name.

Erich Eyck, *Bismarck and the German Empire* (1950)

### Source C

As I stepped out of the park, I saw the Chancellor [Bismarck] walking slowly across the field in the bright sunshine, with his dogs at his heels. I went to meet him and joined him. He was in the best of tempers. After a little while I said, 'Some important telegrams have arrived.' He answered jokingly; 'Are they so urgent that we have to deal with them out here in the open country?' I replied: 'Unfortunately they are. The Emperor has again been fired at and this time he has been hit. His majesty is seriously wounded.' With a violent start the Prince stopped dead. Deeply agitated, he thrust his oaken stick into the ground in front of him and said, breathing heavily, as if a lightning flash of revelation had struck him: 'Now we will dissolve the Reichstag!' Only then did he enquire sympathetically after the Emperor's condition and ask for details of the attempt.

Tiedemann (Bismarck's secretary), quoted in Erich Eyck, as above

## Source D

All he [Bismarck] cared about was how much political capital he could make of it [the assassination attempt] in whipping up the feelings of the masses...the object of his manoeuvre was really to break the power not so much of the Social Democrats as of the National Liberals. This does not mean that he did not also desire the suppression of the Social Democrats, for he did. But unlike the National Liberals, they were not a political millstone round his neck. Hence in the coming electoral struggle...they could be held up as the men who had refused protection to the life and health of the dear old Kaiser. 'Now I've got those fellows where I want them', said Bismarck to his intimates. 'Your Highness means the Social Democrats?' somebody asked. 'No, the National Liberals', was the Chancellor's reply. A popular rumour attributed to Bismarck the saying: 'I shall squeeze the National Liberals against the wall until they squeal.'

Erich Eyck, as above

## Source E

The German people wishes to be ruled by its emperor and his conscientious advisers. A spectacle like that of the other day, when the minister who is called minister of commerce but is in fact only minister of railways is asked about the question of railway tariffs which the Chancellor has personally raised, and is obliged to reply that he knows nothing about it, constitutes an utterly damaging confirmation of the dangerous chaos prevailing in the highest government circles. It is only too true that because of the silly whims of one man a large part of the moral esteem that Germany has won among educated world opinion has already been lost...and it can only be a question of time until His Majesty finds himself obliged to transfer the government of the empire to sober persons who are less extravagant in their conduct of affairs...

Franz v. Roggenbach (German Liberal), February 1879, quoted in WM Simon, *Germany in the Age of Bismarck* (1968)

## Source F

I cannot, and the government cannot, be at the beck and call of particular parties. It must go its own way that it regards as correct; these courses are subject to the resolutions of the Reichstag, the government will require the support of the parties but it can never submit itself to the domination of any single party!

Bismarck speaking to the Reichstag (9 July 1879), quoted in WM Simon, as above

---

**1** What do the tone and language of Source A reveal about the political sympathies of its author?

**2** What does Source A imply about the reason why Nobiling attempted to assassinate the Kaiser? How does Source B challenge this interpretation?

**3** How does Source D interpret Bismarck's response to Nobiling's assassination attempt? How far does Source C support this interpretation?

**4** What value would you place on Source C as historical evidence?

**5** What do Sources E and F reveal about the wider political context in which the assassination attempt took place? How does Source F help to explain Bismarck's actions in the wake of the shooting?

---

# FOCUS

## 12.2 What kind of foreign policy?

The creation of the German Empire in 1871 caused a major shift in the European balance of power. Germany was advanced into a position of 'latent hegemony' which meant she had the potential to dominate the whole of continental Europe. It was in this context that Bismarck had to formulate and conduct his foreign policy. If the Empire were to survive and perhaps eventually realize its potential in Europe, Bismarck had to find broadly-acceptable solutions to some complex diplomatic problems. The map below details the principal difficulties with which he had to contend.

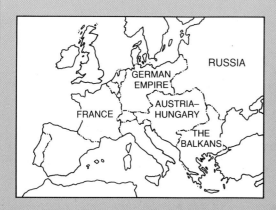

**THE GERMAN EMPIRE**   With extensive economic resources and an efficient, well-trained army the new Germany was powerful and confident. The other Great Powers looked on with a mixture of awe and suspicion. There were real fears that Germany could pose a political threat to the European balance of power. Bismarck was aware that he could face a coalition of Powers directed against him. Above all he feared a two-front war which might successfully exploit Germany's vulnerable political geography.

**FRANCE**   The comprehensive defeat of France by Prussia in the war of 1870-71 was a national humiliation. The loss of Alsace- Lorraine to Germany was bitterly resented not only because it was a valuable piece of territory, but also because its annexation represented the eclipse of French power in Europe. France could no longer honestly count herself as Europe's premier Power. The shock of this realization produced an overwhelming national sentiment - revenge!

After 1871, France was in no condition to pursue this objective alone. The only real hope was to find allies. Bismarck was aware that if Germany became involved in a serious conflict with another Power, he would have to face France also. Alsace-Lorraine and the French desire for revenge fully occupied Bismarck's diplomatic attention in the years after 1871.

**THE BALKANS**   This sensitive corner of Europe presented substantial problems for Bismarck. Turkey, the traditional master in this region, was in decline. Both Russia and Austria-Hungary viewed the Balkans with special interest. The Slav peoples who predominated in the region were becoming fiercely nationalistic. Russia encourage these demands for an independent Slav state.

Austria-Hungary, driven out of both Italy and Germany, was determined to resist Russian ambitions so close to her own territories. In addition to this the encouragement of Slav nationalism in the Balkans could serve as an example to other national groups within the Austro-Hungarian Empire. The clash of interests over the Balkans was a major concern to Bismarck who realized the diplomatic value of being able to count both Austria and Russia as friends.

Aim to work in small groups for this exercise. Carefully study the information on the page opposite. In 1871 this was the situation faced by Bismarck. Like national leaders today, he was presented with the challenge of devising solutions to complex diplomatic problems. In this exercise you are required to respond to that same challenge. The first section below outlines Bismarck's objectives in his conduct of foreign policy. The second section suggests possible actions which he might have considered pursuing. In each case discuss how far the action would have helped him to solve his diplomatic problems and achieve his diplomatic objectives. Be aware that a solution to one problem could well aggravate another.

## Objectives

■ Attempt to maintain European peace - essential for the security of the Empire and its commercial prosperity.

■ Prevent France from mounting a serious challenge to the new Empire.

■ Avoid a war on two fronts.

■ Avoid having to make a choice between Austria-Hungary and Russia in their disputes.

■ Ensure that in any grouping of the five Great European Powers (Germany, Britain, Russia, Austria-Hungary and France) Germany is in a majority of three to two.

## Actions

■ Begin to convert the 'latent hegemony' into real power by further expansion, for example in Holland and Austria.

■ Reassure neighbours of peaceful intentions through speeches, diplomatic contact, State visits.

■ Attempt to maintain cordial diplomatic relations with all Powers except France.

■ Launch a 'preventive war' against France to arrest her ambition for revenge.

■ Isolate France diplomatically - try to ensure that she does not secure European allies, especially Austria or Russia.

■ Choose either Russia or Austria-Hungary and arrange a firm defensive alliance with them.

■ Attempt to defuse the Balkan problem by encouraging Austria-Hungary and Russia to settle their differences amicably; also, try to prevent them from resorting to open conflict.

■ Attempt to persuade Austria-Hungary and Russia that a close relationship with Germany is a necessity.

## QUESTIONS

**1** Which actions did your group dismiss as potentially dangerous for Bismarck?

**2** Which actions do you think Bismarck would have been best advised to try?

**3** In his conduct of foreign policy Bismarck has been described as a 'poacher' who after 1871 became a 'gamekeeper'. How far does your analysis confirm this comparison?

## "AU REVOIR!"

GERMANY. " FAREWELL, MADAME, AND IF——"
FRANCE. "HA! WE SHALL MEET AGAIN!"

By special permission of]

THE PROPHECY.

[The Proprietors of " Punch."

A 'PUNCH' CARTOON BY TENNIEL COMMENTS ON THE CONCLUSION OF THE
FRANCO-PRUSSIAN WAR. WITH FRANCE BEING FORCED TO PAY AN INDEMNITY OF
£200,000,000, THE MOOD OF REVENGE WAS UNMISTAKABLE

# The Three Emperors' League (1873)

In the aftermath of the Franco-Prussian war, Bismarck was keen to
develop an understanding with his eastern neighbours, Austria-Hungary
and Russia. In 1872 the Emperors of these three Great Powers held meetings and discussions. The result of these consultations was an agreement
known as the *Dreikaiserbund* or Three Emperors' League. The monarchs
identified republicanism and socialism as common enemies and promised
to consult on matters of common interest. Although the *Dreikaiserbund* was
vague it suited Bismarck's purpose. It signalled the diplomatic isolation of
France without forcing him to make a choice between Austria and Russia.
It soon became clear, however, that the League offered no automatic guarantee of support for Bismarck's policies. In 1875 Germany reacted to
French recovery and rearmament by provoking a diplomatic crisis.
Bismarck prohibited the export of horses to France and in April 1875 the
*Berlin Post* carried an article asking 'Is War in Sight?' The Chancellor had
hoped to convince France of the need to scale down her rearmament by

raising the spectre of war. However, Bismarck plainly miscalculated. The 'War-in-sight' Crisis was swiftly condemned as provocative by both Britain and Russia, and Bismarck was forced to offer assurances that Germany was not contemplating a preventive war against France. The episode served to remind Bismarck that he lived amidst suspicious neighbours who would not tolerate any attempt to increase German power in Europe. Moreover, he was made to realize that a war on two fronts could, in the wrong circumstances, become a real possibility.

## The Near Eastern Crisis (1877–78)

The 'War-in-sight' Crisis resulted in a diplomatic humiliation for Bismarck but did not place him in immediate danger. In the next two years, however, the Chancellor was to be drawn into a conflict which he had always hoped to avoid; an Austro-Russian clash over the Balkans. Between 1875 and 1877 the Sultan of Turkey, whose Empire covered this volatile corner of Europe, was faced with revolts in Bosnia, Herzegovina, Bulgaria, Serbia and Montenegro. The Turks inflicted cruel reprisals including the slaughter of some 10,000 Bulgarians in 1876, and thus

THE TURKS IN DEFEAT AT KARS DURING THE RUSSO-TURKISH WAR (1877–78)

prompted Russia to aid her fellow Slavs. Austria – afraid that support for Slav nationalism could threaten her own multi-national empire, and anxious to prevent Russian encroachment in the region – found it increasingly difficult to maintain a dialogue with St Petersburg. Bismarck was clearly concerned; the failure of Austro-Russian relations would compel him to make a choice between his *Dreikaiserbund* partners, so presenting France with a potential ally.

In April 1877 Russia declared war on Turkey, having secured Austrian neutrality with a promise to respect Habsburg interests in the Balkans. Eleven months later the victorious Russians imposed the severe San Stefano Treaty on the Turks. The reaction of both Austria and Britain to the proposed treaty was uniformly hostile. Criticism was focused on the Russian proposal to create a Greater Bulgarian state from former Turkish territories in the Balkans. Austria and Britain objected, seeing in the new creation no more than a cynical Russian attempt to establish a Balkan client state with a strategically-important Aegean coastline. A British fleet was sent to Turkish waters, troops were recalled from India, and Russia faced a choice: war or a revision of the San Stefano Treaty.

## The Congress of Berlin (1878)

In the event, Russia was quite unable to fight a war against two major European Powers and was forced to submit to mediation. This was

THE CONGRESS OF BERLIN IN SESSION

provided by Bismarck, who set up an international Congress in Berlin and offered his services as the 'honest broker'. The revision of the San Stefano Treaty (see map) proved acceptable to all the Powers with the exception of Russia. The one hope of the Russian delegation had been that Bismarck would offer them his support, but this failed to materialize. Isolated and humiliated at Berlin, Russia blamed Bismarck for her diplomatic defeat. Slav nationalists bitterly criticized the Chancellor in the press and the Tsar described the Congress as 'a coalition of the European powers against Russia under the leadership of Prince Bismarck'.

In this atmosphere the Three Emperors' League dissolved completely. Bismarck had certainly assisted in creating a Balkan settlement which avoided, at least for the time being, the prospect of a damaging European war. However, his failure to support Russian interests and the animosity this generated placed him in a potentially dangerous position. A Russian approach to Italy on the possibility of an alliance was made early in 1879, and her frontier garrisons were strengthened. In August 1879 Tsar Alexander II wrote to the (pro-Russian) German Emperor:

'Decision [on remaining questions over the Balkans] rests with the majority of the European commissioners. Those of France and Italy join ours on practically all questions, while those of Germany appear to have received the word of command to support the Austrian view which is systematically hostile to us...'

Quoted in John Lowe, *Rivalry and Accord: International Relations 1870–1914* (1988)

## The revision of the San Stefano Treaty

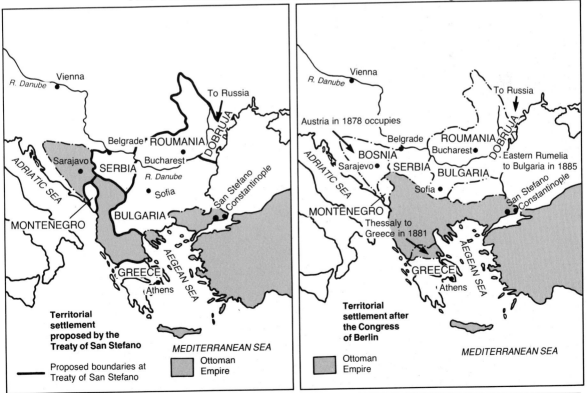

Territorial settlement proposed by the Treaty of San Stefano

— Proposed boundaries at Treaty of San Stefano

Ottoman Empire

Territorial settlement after the Congress of Berlin

Ottoman Empire

The Tsar's complaints contained the ominous reference to a shared Franco-Russian perception of the Balkan question, and can only have confirmed for Bismarck that some short-term security measure was an urgent necessity.

## The Dual Alliance (1879)

In October 1879 Bismarck and Austrian Foreign Minister Andrassy concluded negotiations for a formal alliance between their two countries. The Dual Alliance was Bismarck's response to Russia's sabre-rattling in the aftermath of the Berlin Congress. It strengthened Austria against Russia and provided Germany with a companion with whom she could weather the storm of Russian hostility (see below). The alliance was supposedly secret but its terms soon became known in St Petersburg. It was also meant to be temporary, lasting for just five years. However, the option to renew the arrangement was taken up so that the alliance continued until 1918. However, the Dual Alliance should not be regarded as Bismarck's final choice between Austria and Russia. The partnership undoubtedly meant more to the Austrians who had at last escaped from the diplomatic isolation they had been forced to endure since the Crimean War. Bismarck did not abandon his belief that friendship between Germany, Austria and Russia was the most effective method of securing the future of the Second Reich.

## Provisions of the Dual Alliance

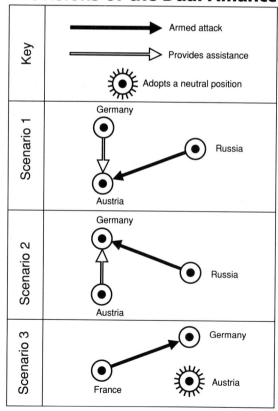

## THE GAME OF THE DAY.

BISMARCK. "COME, ANDRASSY, WE KNOW EACH OTHER'S 'FORM.' YOU AND I TOGETHER AGAINST THE LOT!!"
RUSSIA (to FRANCE). "I THINK, MADAME, *WE* MIGHT BE A MATCH FOR THEM!"
FRANCE. "THANKS! I PREFER TO SIT OUT AT PRESENT!"       ENGLAND (to ITALY). "NOBODY ASKS *US!!*"

'PUNCH' COMMENTS ON THE DUAL ALLIANCE OF 1879

**Terms of the Three Emperors' Alliance**

● If either Russia, Germany or Austria were at war with another Power, the others would remain neutral.

● The three Powers agreed to keep the entrance to the Black Sea closed to foreign warships.

● The allies would not permit territorial changes in the Balkans without prior, mutual agreement.

● The Balkans were to be divided into 'spheres of influence'. Russian interests were recognized in the eastern portion, Austrian interests in the western.

● Austria acknowledged Russian ambitions to re-create a large Bulgarian state; Russia accepted Austria's right to annex Bosnia-Herzegovina.

## The Three Emperors' Alliance (1881)

It was not long before Russia, alarmed at her increasing isolation in Europe, turned back to Germany in the hope of a reconciliation. Bismarck was only too pleased to oblige and in 1881 a revised version of the *Dreikaiserbund* was signed. The new Three Emperors' Alliance was more specific than the original statement of monarchical solidarity (see left).

The alliance aimed at resolving Austro-Russian disputes in the Balkans and at reassuring the Russians that they did not need to seek an accommodation with France. For Bismarck it offered security; if war with France became a reality, a neutral Russia was essential. Although Bismarck felt pleased with the Three Emperors' Alliance, he undoubtedly had private reservations about its durability. It attempted not to *solve* Austro-Russian hostility but to *contain* it. Bismarck could not predict for how long this fragile peace would last. The alliance was renewed in 1884, but shortly afterwards the Balkan question flared up again in a new dispute over Bulgaria. Once more Bismarck was forced to restructure his complex system of coalitions.

## The Triple Alliance (1882)

In 1881 Italy made overtures to Austria aimed at securing an alliance. The Italians were angered by the French occupation of Tunis which had frustrated Rome's plans for colonial expansion in North Africa. Austria found little appeal in the Italian bid for closer ties but Bismarck was quick to see its potential. In 1882 a leading Slav nationalist, General Skobelev, visited Paris to canvass support for a Franco-Russian alliance. Bismarck's fears for German security surfaced once again. Bringing Italy closer to the Dual Alliance partners would secure Austria's vulnerable southern flank and deprive France of a potential ally. Accordingly, in 1882 the Triple Alliance was signed.

This was not an extension of the Dual Alliance (Rome was kept ignorant of that arrangement) but a separate agreement to last for five years. It was directed squarely against France. If any of the signatories were attacked by two or more Powers, the other promised to lend assistance. In a war between Austria and Russia, Italy would remain neutral. If France attacked Germany, Italy would provide support to her partner (Austria would remain neutral); and if Italy were attacked by France, both Germany and Austria agreed to back her. The Triple Alliance helped to reassure Bismarck that an independent attack by either France or Russia could be successfully contained. However, Austria and Italy were not powerful allies and a joint Franco-Russian assault would place Germany in a very vulnerable position. Bismarck's diplomacy had not yet discovered a means of preventing such a dangerous combination.

## The Reinsurance Treaty (1887)

The Three Emperors' Alliance was fractured beyond repair by a recurrence of the Balkan problem in 1885. It was clear that Austro-Russian rivalries in the region were unlikely ever to be fully resolved. Once again Bismarck was forced to make new arrangements in order to reassure Russia and avoid the possibility of a war on two fronts. Therefore, in June 1887 he concluded the Reinsurance Treaty with Russia. The basic provisions were set out in Article I:

'If one of the high contracting parties [Russia or Germany] should find itself at war with a third Great Power, the other would maintain a benevolent neutrality, and would try to localize the conflict. The provision would not apply to a war against Austria or France resulting from an attack on one of these two Powers by one of the high contracting parties.'

Article I of the Reinsurance Treaty, quoted in WN Medlicott and DK Coveney, *Bismarck and Europe* (1971)

**1** By the terms of the Reinsurance Treaty how would Germany/Russia have responded in the circumstances shown on the right?. (Use the key given in the diagram on page 278.)

**2** Bismarck aimed to avoid:

(a) being drawn into a war between Austria and Russia;
(b) having to fight a two-front war against France and Russia.

To what extent did the Reinsurance Treaty satisfy these aims?

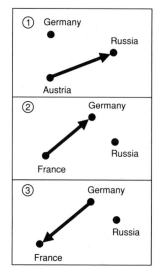

## The Second Mediterranean Agreement (1887)

In secret articles of the Reinsurance Treaty, Bismarck recognized Russia's ambitions in Bulgaria. This reassured Russia that Bismarck would not back Austria in the event of a clash over the Balkan territory. However, Bismarck was determined that this concession to Russian interests should not enable St Petersburg to challenge Austria. He therefore encouraged Britain to arrange a treaty with Italy and Austria which would guarantee the *status quo* in the Mediterranean and Near East and thus prevent Russia from precipitating a crisis in the area. The result was the Second Mediterranean Agreement of December 1887. Bismarck did not participate in this agreement, but by sponsoring its creation he had once again managed to restrain Russia from assuming a provocative posture in the Balkans.

# Review
## Foreign policy: success or failure?

Consider these assessments of Bismarck's foreign policy in the period 1871–90.

**Assessment 1** Bismarck's foreign policy should be regarded as a success because for 20 years he kept France in isolation and skilfully avoided having to defend in a European war the gains made during the 1860s.

**Assessment 2** Bismarck's foreign policy was ultimately a failure. He developed only short-term responses to problems which he never actually solved. His style was no more than crisis management and this in turn produced further problems for Germany.

Now consider the following:

- The Three Emperors' League (1873)
- The 'War-in-sight' Crisis (1875)
- The Congress of Berlin (1879)
- The Dual Alliance (1879)
- The Three Emperors' Alliance (1881)
- The Triple Alliance (1882)
- The Reinsurance Treaty (1887)
- The Second Mediterranean Agreement (1887)

**1** Which of the above were useful in:

(a) isolating France?
(b) helping to maintain the general European peace?

**2** Which of Bismarck's international arrangements were the product of short-term necessity?

**3** Which particular problems remained unsolved when Bismarck resigned in 1890?

**4** Which longer-term problems did Bismarck's diplomacy create for Germany?

**5** In conclusion, what would be *your* assessment of Bismarck's performance in foreign policy between 1871 and 1890?

'DROPPING THE PILOT'. TENNIEL'S OBSERVATION ON THE RESIGNATION OF BISMARCK APPEARED IN 'PUNCH' (MARCH 1890)

# 13 The Approach of War 1890–1914

## Guilty as charged?

One of the most persistent historical controversies of the Twentieth Century has been the debate over who was responsible for the outbreak of the First World War. The caricature right, which appeared in *Punch* magazine in 1914, represents one of the earliest contributions to this debate. It is quite clear whom the artist, Bernard Partridge, wanted his readers to condemn as the perpetrator of this terrible conflict. In 1919 the verdict of the peacemakers' meeting at Versailles was that Germany was guilty as charged; the Kaiser and his allies had premeditated the war and were held responsible for all the damage suffered as a consequence of their actions. In the decades which have followed, the question of war-guilt has been the focus of almost constant revision. How did this tragic episode in human history begin? Do the Powers who fought share responsibility for the outbreak of the war, or is it possible to accuse a single nation of deliberately planning and starting one of the most dreadful conflicts in history?

THE TRIUMPH OF "CULTURE."

KAISER WILLIAM PORTRAYED BY 'PUNCH' AS A HEARTLESS MURDERER (1914)

CAPRIVI, GERMAN CHANCELLOR
(1890–94)

# The changing pattern of international relations (1890–97)

Following the dismissal of Bismarck in 1890 the Germans began to steer a 'New Course' in the conduct of their foreign policy. The direction they chose had profound effects on the pattern of international relations, and led to a series of crises in the early Twentieth Century which made many Germans fear for their national security.

Caprivi, the new German Chancellor, sought to disengage the Reich from the web of international commitments which had been spun by Bismarck. He wanted a simplified system with a more defined purpose. The most significant decision taken following the departure of Bismarck was to allow the Reinsurance Treaty with Russia to lapse. Caprivi and the young Kaiser, William II, were persuaded by Friedrich von Holstein, a high-ranking official in the foreign ministry, that partnership with Russia was incompatible with Germany's responsibilities to her associates in the Triple Alliance. The decision not to renew the Reinsurance Treaty had far-reaching consequences. In St Petersburg, no one now doubted that in the event of a dispute over the Balkans, Germany would support her Alliance partner, Austria-Hungary. Bismarck had warned for years about the danger of isolating Russia and, in the event, his warnings proved valid. By 1894 Russia has concluded an alliance with France and raised the spectre in Germany of a two-front war. The Franco-Russian Alliance stated that if either Power were attacked by Germany, then the other would come to her aid. To counter this Caprivi sought an alliance with Britain.

In the early 1890s relations between Germany and Britain were very cordial and Caprivi thought it only a matter of time before the latter became part of the Triple Alliance. However, he failed to gauge properly the British attitude to foreign alliances. Under Lord Salisbury, the Conservative Prime Minister (1887–92) and Foreign Secretary (1895–1900), Britain pursued a policy commonly referred to as 'Splendid Isolation'. This did not mean that she preferred to remain detached from all aspects of international affairs, but that she was uninterested in the restrictive commitments of a formal alliance. Accordingly, by 1894 when Caprivi resigned, Germany was sandwiched between two potentially hostile Powers and had failed to obtain the security of an alliance with Britain. In these circumstances it might be expected that Germany would have followed a prudent course by working to maintain cordial relations with her neighbours. Instead she embarked on a rather curious and quite arbitrary policy of interference in the affairs of the European colonies. This was conducted with such self-righteous arrogance that she had soon soured relations with all the major colonial Powers.

This was particularly true of Britain who was especially sensitive about her large and therefore potentially-vulnerable Empire. In 1896 the German Kaiser caused great offence in Britain over his response to the so-called Jameson Raid in December 1895. In this incident Dr Jameson, an administrator in the British South Africa Company, commanded a force of Company police into the Transvaal State to incite a rising against the Boer Republic led by Paul Kruger. The conspiracy failed and Cecil Rhodes, the Governor of Cape Colony, was forced to resign when his

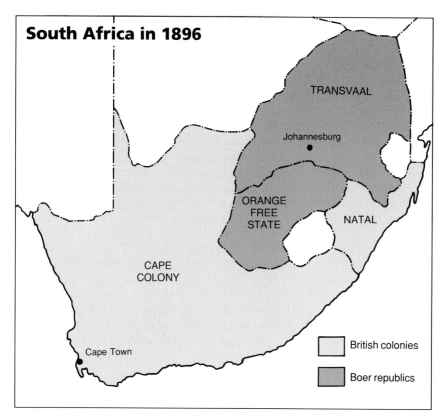

**South Africa in 1896**

TRANSVAAL

Johannesburg

ORANGE
FREE
STATE

NATAL

CAPE
COLONY

Cape Town

British colonies

Boer republics

complicity in the scheme was revealed. Germany tried to capitalize on the episode by encouraging French and Russian action against Britain. When this failed to materialize the Kaiser sent a telegram to the Boer leader congratulating him on resisting the British assault:

'I would like to express my sincere congratulations that you and your people have succeeded, without having to invoke the help of friendly powers, in restoring peace with your own resources in face of armed bands which have broken into your country as disturbers of the peace and have been able to preserve the independence of your country against attacks from outside.'

The Kruger Telegram caused outrage in Britain and took Anglo-German relations to their lowest point for many years.

## The quest for world power: German 'Weltpolitik'

From the mid-1890s German policy-makers began to raise their sights and look beyond the confines of Europe. It seemed to them that Germany had a legitimate claim to a colonial empire in imitation of the other imperial Powers such as Britain. Thus the concept of *Weltpolitik* (World Policy) was born. Germany entered an expansionist phase (the key to which was the creation of a large navy) with the ultimate goal of an overseas empire to signal her emergence as a world Power.

**1** Why do you think the Kruger Telegram caused so much offence in Britain?

**2** Why might many Germans have felt less secure about their position in Europe in 1900 than in 1890?

**3** How might the words 'insensitive' and 'miscalculated' be applied to German foreign policy in the 1890s?

The concept of *Weltpolitik* had enormous appeal for the young and flamboyant Kaiser William II. As early as 1892 he spoke of achieving 'a sort of Napoleonic supremacy' in Europe and beyond. The Germany he envisaged would dominate a new *Mitteleuropa,* a Central European customs union with extensions into the Balkans, Turkey and the Near East. In addition, and with the support of a hugely-expanded fleet, Germany would carve out an empire in central Africa. Such a vision was meat and drink to groups of patriotic extremists like the Pan-German League. This organization preached hatred of France, Britain and Russia and advocated an uncompromising policy of overseas expansion. The Kaiser saw it as his destiny to satisfy the nationalistic dreams of such groups and accordingly made *Weltpolitik* the central theme of his foreign policy: '*Weltpolitik* as a task, to become a world power as an aim and the fleet as an instrument.'

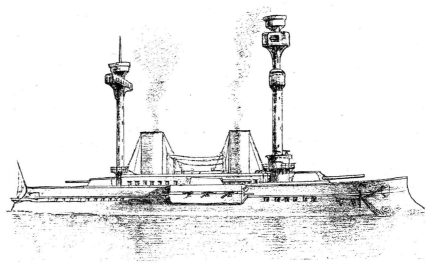

THE KAISER'S PASSION FOR NAVAL DEVELOPMENT IS REFLECTED IN HIS SKETCH FOR A BATTLESHIP OF THE FUTURE (1891)

ADMIRAL VON TIRPITZ

In 1897 William made two significant State appointments. First, Admiral von Tirpitz became the new Secretary of State for the Navy. He brought with him to the post an enthusiasm for naval expansion which mirrored the Kaiser's own ambitions. Within a year Tirpitz had steered a navy bill through the Reichstag which made provision for the construction of 17 ships-of-the-line over the next seven years. The new Foreign Secretary in 1897 was Bernhard von Bülow, a favourite of Kaiser William and an advocate of German expansionism. Together Bülow and Tirpitz acted as the Kaiser's principal agents in the promotion of German *Weltpolitik.* However, this stance was not simply the product of the Kaiser's nationalistic ambitions. Behind his international posturing and the hysterical propaganda of the Pan-German League there lay a more calculated political motive. This has been effectively described by the historian Imanuel Geiss:

'It *(Weltpolitik)* was apparently advocated for the first time at government level in July 1897 by the national-liberal Prussian Minister of Finance, Johannes von Miquel, as an indispensable part of his new policy of 'Collection' *(Sammlungspolitik)* – of rallying the well-to-do classes around the throne against Social Democracy. At the same time, the new emphasis on foreign policy was to help overcome serious differences between the industrial and agrarian wings of Germany's wealthier classes and to create a united front of the whole nation against the world. Thus German *Weltpolitik* was partly created by a domestic policy, which aimed at diverting the attention of the masses from social and political problems at home by a dynamic expansion abroad.'

Imanuel Geiss, *July 1914* (1965)

Whatever the motivation for *Weltpolitik*, it was inevitable that the Kaiser's plans to transform the international status of his Empire would impact heavily on the other Powers.

This was particularly true for Britain. By the turn of the century it was becoming apparent to politicians and the general public alike that the policy of 'Splendid Isolation' had outlived its useful life. British relations with France and Russia were not cordial. In 1898 Britain clashed with France over claims to territory around the town of Fashoda in the Sudan, leaving the French bitter and resentful. In the Far East Britain eyed Russian ambitions in China with great suspicion. With Germany unprepared to conclude an alliance with Britain and antagonizing her still further with a second Navy Law in 1900, it now seemed expedient to negotiate with other Powers for the purposes of security. Accordingly, in 1902 Britain concluded an alliance with Japan in an effort to restrain Russia in the Far East. Two years later Britain and France settled their differences over Egypt and Morocco with the Entente Cordiale. Although not a formal alliance, this arrangement represented a new direction in Anglo-French relations. From 1904 rivalry between the two nations was replaced with

| Seats won by Social Democrats in Reichstag elections (1890–1912) | |
| --- | --- |
| Year | Seats |
| 1890 | 35 |
| 1893 | 44 |
| 1898 | 56 |
| 1903 | 81 |
| 1907 | 43 |
| 1912 | 110* |

*The largest party in the Reichstag

VON BÜLOW (LEFT)

KING EDWARD VII ON A VISIT TO PARIS (1903). THE OCCASION WAS SYMBOLIC OF THE NEW SPIRIT OF FRIENDSHIP BETWEEN BRITAIN AND FRANCE

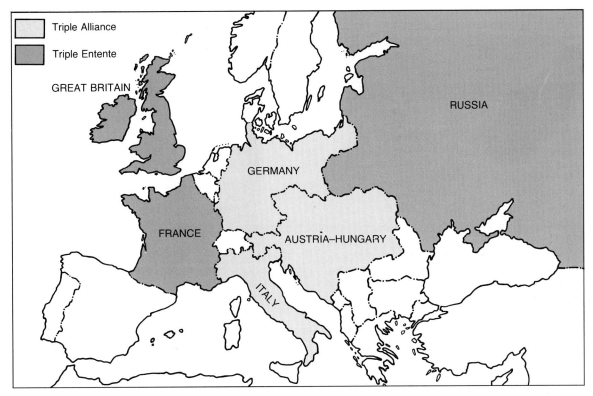

Triple Alliance

Triple Entente

GREAT BRITAIN

RUSSIA

GERMANY

FRANCE

AUSTRIA–HUNGARY

ITALY

understanding and mutual diplomatic support. In 1907 Britain and Russia reached agreement over influence in Persia, Tibet and Afghanistan. These arrangements produced the so-called 'Triple Entente'. No formal alliance existed between the three Powers but as relations between Germany and the Entente partners worsened, it became convenient to see Europe as a divided continent.

# Examining the Evidence
## The extent of German militarism

Pre-war Germany has often been accused of excessive militarism. It has been claimed that the Empire, from the Kaiser to the common people, was motivated by, and found its principal expression in, its military origins and traditions.

PROCLAMATION OF THE GERMAN EMPIRE AT VERSAILLES (JANUARY 1871)

**Source B**

KAISER WILLIAM II IN FULL MILITARY UNIFORM (1900)

### Source C

I hope Europe will gradually come to realize the fundamental principle of my policy: leadership in the peaceful sense – a sort of Napoleonic supremacy...I am of the opinion that it is already a success that I, having come to govern at so early an age, stand at the head of German armed might yet have left my sword in its scabbard and have given up Bismarck's policy of externally causing disruption to replace it with a peaceful foreign situation such as we have not known for many years.

*The Kaiser to Eulenburg (July 1892), quoted in JCG Rohl,*
*From Bismarck to Hitler (1970)*

### Source D

Give no quarter! Take no prisoners! Anybody who falls into your hands must be destroyed. Just as a thousand years ago Attila's Huns made a reputation for ruthless violence that still resounds through the ages, so let the name of Germans, through your actions in China, acquire a similar reputation that will last for a thousand years...

*Kaiser William II addressing German troops being sent to China to crush the Boxer*
*Rising in 1900. Quoted in KD Bracher, 'Kaiser Wilhelm's Germany' in Purnell,*
*Purnell's History of the Twentieth Century (1968)*

### Source E: The story of the Captain of Kopenick

On 16th October 1906, Wilhelm Voigt, a shoemaker, dressed himself as a captain in the German army and sallied forth into the streets of Berlin. He first encountered four soldiers whom he immediately ordered to fall in and follow him. They had never seen him before but such was the authority conferred upon him by his captain's uniform that he was instantly obeyed. Picking up some more troops on the way, the band arrived by train at the railway station of Kopenick, a small town outside Berlin. The captain set out for the town hall and on the way encountered three policemen. They were also peremptorily ordered to fall in, and, of course, instantly obeyed. Arriving at the town hall the Captain demanded a sum of 4002.50 marks to be paid to him. It was promptly done. The Captain handed over a receipt and then ordered the arrest of the mayor, who was despatched under escort to the new Berlin police station at Unter den Linden. The Captain's autocratic spree lasted for six hours. He was arrested and later sentenced to four years in prison.

*Purnell, Purnell's History of the Twentieth Century (1968)*

WILLIAM VOIGT, THE 'CAPTAIN OF KOPENICK' PHOTOGRAPHED IN 1906

### Source F

In regard to Germany we are confronted by certain circumstances that indisputably merit our consideration here in England. There is, for example, the annual appearance in Germany of very nearly seven hundred books dealing with war as a science. This points, at once, to an extreme preoccupation in that nation with the idea of war. I doubt whether twenty books a year on the art of war appear in this country, and whether their circulation, when they do appear, is much more than twenty!

*Professor JA Cramb in a lecture given in London (1913), quoted in JCG Rohl, as above*

**1** Look closely at Source A. What do you notice about the appearance of the participants in this ceremony?

**2** Examine Sources B, C and D. What impressions of the Kaiser are conveyed here? How would you account for the differences revealed in these sources.

**3** Source E is a true story. What does it suggest to you about the nature of German society in the early Twentieth Century? How is this impression supported by Source F?

**4** Which of the sources (E or F) provides the more reliable impression of the militaristic nature of German society in pre-war Europe?

**5** 'To the very end of its existence in 1918 the German Empire bore the deep imprint of its origins in military victory.' (William Carr, *A History of Germany* (1979)) How far can Sources A–F be used by the historian to support this view? You should answer in detail.

## The crisis years (1905–12)

### The First Moroccan Crisis (1905–06)

When French Foreign Minister Théophile Delcassé secured the Entente Cordiale with Britain and thus won what amounted to a French mandate over Morocco, there was deep concern within the German government. In particular, Holstein and Bülow worried that Germany was becoming encircled by the links which now existed through the Franco-Russian Alliance and the new Entente. In 1905 they decided to test the latter by encouraging the Moroccan Sultan to resist French designs on his country.

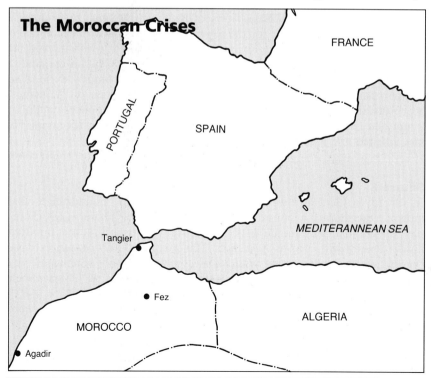

German intervention in Morocco was presented as legitimate since, by the terms of the Treaty of Madrid (1880), she had the right – along with Spain, Italy and Britain – to be consulted over the future of that country. It took Delcassé four years to obtain the agreement of these three Powers, but he failed to discuss his plans with Germany. In 1905 the Germans were determined to show that they could not be left out of any international agreement.

Encouraged by Bülow and Holstein, the Kaiser made a dramatic landing at Tangier and in a speech declared his intention to support the independence of Morocco. The gesture was a direct challenge to France and an assertion of German power. It was expected that the Entente Cordiale would crumble when the French realized that they could not depend upon British support in a crisis. In fact this proved not to be the case. In January 1906 there was a change of government in Britain. The new Liberal Foreign Secretary, Sir Edward Grey, was determined to support France in the clash with Germany. He warned the German ambassador in London that popular opinion in Britain was strongly in favour of the French and assured the French ambassador, Paul Cambon, of British diplomatic support. Although no guarantees of military assistance in the event of a Franco-German war were made, Grey continued to repeat his belief that 'in the event of an attack upon France by Germany, arising out of our Morocco Agreement, public feeling in England would be so strong that no British Government could remain neutral.' The crisis did not deteriorate into war and German diplomacy looked to have won some success. In June 1905 Delcassé was forced to resign and France conceded to German pressure for an international conference to settle the Moroccan question.

GERMAN VIEW OF THE ANGLO-FRENCH ENTENTE. ACCORDING TO THE CARTOON, HOW FIRM IS THIS NEW FRIENDSHIP?

However, the conference which met at Algeciras in January 1906 proved to be a bitter disappointment for Germany. Her claims were backed only by Austria-Hungary and Morocco; even her alliance partner Italy stood with the opposition. The result was that Germany won only guarantees of commercial freedom. France was permitted to control the Moroccan State Bank and, with Spain, was given joint authority over the police. Germany had miscalculated and her pride was injured as the international community ignored her demands. In addition it was clear that the

Entente Cordiale had not only held together but had in fact been strengthened. In the immediate aftermath of Algeciras, Grey gave official authorization to Anglo-French military conversations. The assumed enemy was Germany and the discussions were designed to consider strategies for responding to a German attack on France. Anglo-French relations had made dramatic progress since their tentative beginnings in 1904.

**1** Why was the outcome of the First Moroccan Crisis such a disappointment to Germany?

## The Second Moroccan Crisis (1911)

Although it is convenient to present the two Moroccan Crises back-to-back, this should not lead to the assumption that the intervening years were without incident. Indeed, this was the very period in which international relationships began to coalesce into the form recognizable in 1914.

The Anglo-Russian entente of 1907 suggested to Germans a conspiracy to encircle and contain them. Such views were being articulated in 1909 by Count Schlieffen, former head of the German General Staff:

'An endeavour is afoot to bring all these powers [Britain, France, Russia and Italy] together for a concentrated attack on the Central Powers [Germany and Austria-Hungary]. At the given moment the drawbridges are to be let down, the doors are to be opened and the million-strong armies let loose, ravaging and destroying, across the Vosges, the Meuse, the Niemen, the Bug and even the Isonzo and the Tyrolean Alps. The danger seems gigantic.'

Count Schlieffen, *Der Krieg in der Gegenwart* (1909), quoted in Imanuel Geiss, *July 1914* (1965)

The Balkans in 1908

To the Kaiser and many of his ministers such a danger seemed very real. Reading Schlieffen's article aloud to his commanding generals in January 1909, William concluded with the single comment: 'Bravo.' The encirclement complex forced Germany into a much closer relationship with her oldest alliance partner, Austria-Hungary. This was clearly evident in the Bosnian Crisis of 1908. Austria's decision to annex Bosnia-Herzegovina renewed the Balkan troubles which had lain dormant since the late 1890s. The proposed annexation incensed Serbia who envisaged the provinces ultimately forming part of a greater Slav state in South-Eastern Europe. Too weak to oppose Austria alone, the Serbs looked to their fellow Slavs in Russia for support. Russia, however, had still not fully recovered from defeat at the hands of the Japanese in the war of 1904–05 and was unable to lend assistance. In these circumstances Germany stood firmly behind the Austrians and watched with considerable satisfaction as both Russia and Serbia were forced to back down. The situation in Europe was again dangerous: the Balkan problem was re-opened, Germany was aligning with Austria, Russia was humiliated and unlikely to tolerate a repetition of this defeat, and Serbian nationalists were out for revenge.

### William II and the *Daily Telegraph* affair

In the summer of 1907 King Edward VII invited Kaiser William II to England with the intention of improving Anglo-German relations. The Kaiser was the house guest of Colonel Stuart-Wortley, a member of the British military establishment desperate to promote better understanding with Germany. As part of his objective, Stuart-Wortley wrote an article for the *Daily Telegraph* based on conversations he had had with the Kaiser. The article, in the form of an interview, was published on 28 October 1908. The feature provoked a storm of indignation both in Britain and Germany. Part of the text of the article is reproduced below.

'You English are mad, mad, mad as March hares…What has come over you that you are completely given over to suspicions quite unworthy of a great nation…?

I have declared with all the emphasis at my command…that my heart is set upon peace, and that it is one of my dearest wishes to live on the best terms with England. Have I ever been false to my word? Falsehood and prevarication are alien to my nature…[but]…your press…bids the people of England to refuse my proffered hand, insinuates that the other holds a dagger. How can I convince a nation against its will?

Just at the time of your Black Week, in December 1899 [during the Boer War], when disasters followed one another in rapid succession, I received a letter from Queen Victoria, my revered grandmother, written in sorrow and affliction, and bearing manifest traces of the anxieties which were preying on her mind and health. I at once returned a sympathetic reply. Nay I did more…I worked out what I considered to be the best plan of campaign under the circumstances, and submitted it to my general staff for their criticism. Then I despatched it to England and that document…is among the state papers at Windsor Castle, awaiting the serenely impartial verdict of history.'

Quoted in Purnell, *Purnell's History of the Twentieth Century* (1968)

**T**ALKING POINT

How might this article have been viewed from the perspective of the British public? Four words which are commonly used in history books to describe the Kaiser's comments are: *offensive; patronizing; tactless; arrogant.*

Through discussion in small groups, identify parts of the article which could be appropriately described by the four words above.

Suggest one or two words of your own which could be used to describe the content and tone of the article.

## Events of the Second Moroccan Crisis

In 1911 a Second Moroccan Crisis dominated the European stage. A revolt had resulted in French troops occupying the capital, Fez; a move widely seen as the first stage in the French annexation of the country. No longer interested in Morocco for political gain, Germany was nevertheless concerned that France should not be allowed to break the international agreement made at Algeciras in 1906. The German Foreign Minister, Kiderlen, demanded the whole of the French Congo as compensation for the commercial losses incurred by the transfer of Morocco to French control. A gunboat, the *Panther*, was sent to the Moroccan port of Agadir to underline this demand. Significantly, it was not the reaction of France but of Britain which created a serious international situation. Amid speculative fears that Germany was planning to establish a naval base at Agadir, the British government repeatedly requested that Germany make her intentions in Morocco clear. As a result of the ominous silence which followed, it was decided to force a reaction from Germany. On 21 July, Lloyd George, an influential member of the Cabinet, delivered a clear warning to Germany in a speech at a Mansion House banquet:

'If a situation were to be forced upon us in which peace could only be preserved by the surrender of the great and beneficent position Britain has won by centuries of heroism and achievement, by allowing herself to be treated, where her interests were vitally affected, as if she were of no account in the Cabinet of nations, then I say emphatically that peace at that price would be a humiliation intolerable for a great country like ours to endure.'

Lloyd George, quoted in MC Morgan, *Foreign Affairs 1886–1914* (1973)

Germany and Britain looked to be on the brink of war but when both Austria and Italy refused to support their alliance partner, Germany backed down. In return for recognizing a French protectorate over Morocco, Germany received two unimportant strips of territory in the French Congo. The broader consequences of this crisis are succinctly described by the historian Imanuel Geiss:

'The net effect of German endeavours was to weld together the Triple Entente, and to raise a new spirit of national defiance in France. Sir Edward Grey, the British Foreign Secretary, and Paul Cambon, the French Ambassador in London, exchanged their famous letters in which they promised to coordinate the foreign policy of their countries in future periods of crisis, while arrangements for naval and military cooperation between Britain and France were made in the event of a German attack against France...The effect of the German diplomatic defeat in the second Moroccan crisis was even more dramatic in Germany: German propaganda, from now on, loudly proclaimed that the Reich was 'encircled' by the Entente Powers, by a coalition of envious and mischievous Powers, who were only waiting for their chance to overwhelm the Central Powers.'

Imanuel Geiss, *July 1914* (1965)

**1** In the circumstances of 1911, why would the claims of the German propagandists have seemed so convincing to the general public?

**2** To what extent was Germany's vulnerable position in 1911 of her own making?

## 13.1 The origins of the Anglo-German naval race

In the summer of 1897 the Royal Navy staged an impressive review off Spithead as part of Queen Victoria's Diamond Jubilee celebrations. The fleet - which sailed past in six perfect lines, each more than five miles in length - was the greatest in history. With over 165 fully-armed warships the *Times* newspaper confidently described the battle-fleet as 'the most powerful and far-reaching weapon the world has ever seen.' The fleet was symbolic of Britain's World Power status and was viewed with great pride by the island inhabitants of the strongest maritime nation on earth. As the Nineteenth Century drew to a close, Britain remained unrivalled on the high seas. Certainly, few people could have predicted a serious naval challenge from Germany. In 1898 her naval forces were vastly inferior to Britain's; she had, for example, only seven first-class battleships – Britain had 38; Germany had two first-class cruisers – Britain had 34. However, the ambitions of Kaiser William II and his naval chief, von Tirpitz, quickly transformed the situation. Plans drawn up by von Tirpitz for an enlarged German fleet led to a full-scale naval race and contributed towards a closer alignment between Britain, France and Russia.

### 1 Why was the Royal Navy so important to Britain?

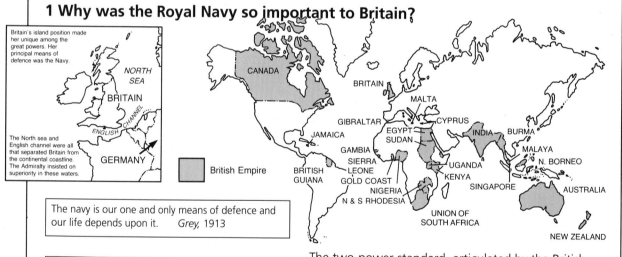

Britain's island position made her unique among the great powers. Her principal means of defence was the Navy.

NORTH SEA

BRITAIN

The North sea and English channel were all that separated Britain from the continental coastline. The Admiralty insisted on superiority in these waters.

GERMANY

ENGLISH CHANNEL

British Empire

CANADA
BRITAIN
MALTA
GIBRALTAR
CYPRUS
JAMAICA
EGYPT
SUDAN
INDIA
BURMA
GAMBIA
MALAYA
SIERRA LEONE
N. BORNEO
BRITISH GUIANA
UGANDA
GOLD COAST
KENYA
NIGERIA
SINGAPORE
AUSTRALIA
N & S RHODESIA
UNION OF SOUTH AFRICA
NEW ZEALAND

The navy is our one and only means of defence and our life depends upon it.    *Grey,* 1913

Annual value of British foreign trade in 1914: £1,223,152,000; of France £424,000,000. Britain had the largest merchant marine in the world.

THE TWO-POWER STANDARD
The minimum standard of security which the country demands is that our fleet should be equal to the combination of the two strongest navies in Europe.

The two-power standard, articulated by the British First Lord of the Admiralty (left), was an indication of the importance attached by Britain to the size of her navy.

■ In simple terms, what was the two-power standard?

■ Using the information in this section, explain why the Admiralty insisted on such a standard?

## 2 The Tirpitz Plan

### Stage 1
Concept of enlarged German battle-fleet is launched:

*1898:* First Navy Law – 17 battleships proposed

*1900:* Second Navy Law – 38 battleships proposed.

Tirpitz planned to challenge British naval supremacy by concentrating his fleet in the North Sea.

'On account of her foreign policy commitments [England] can only utilize a very small part of these ships [Royal Navy battle-fleet] in the North Sea. England's weak point is therefore the North Sea.'                    *Tirpitz*

### Stage 2
*The danger zone:* Tirpitz aimed at a quiet, almost secret, enlargement of the battle-fleet.
He wished to allay British fears and prevent a retaliatory response. Bülow was charged with the responsibility of maintaining cordial relations with Britain. The Tirpitz plan depended on Germany being able to pull clear of the danger zone (by building enough ships to make Britain think twice about engaging her at sea) before Britain reacted with a naval expansion programme of her own.

This stage could take many years.

### Stage 3
*The risk theory:* Tirpitz believed that Britain would not want to risk her navy in a clash with Germany if the German fleet were large enough to inflict serious damage. This was his famous 'risk theory'. It lay at the heart of the Tirpitz plan for once this stage was reached Germany would be able to pursue *Weltpolitik* without British interference.

---

● Examine the map at Stage 1. Why do you think Germans saw Britain as an obstacle to Weltpolitik?

● At which stage was there the greatest risk of a naval race beginning with Britain? Consider the information which follows. Use it to explain why the Tirpitz plan failed and produced an Anglo-German naval race.

■ 'It is a fundamental principle of Admiralty policy that sufficient force shall at all times be maintained in home waters to ensure the command of those seas. And in no other way than by defeat can our naval force be rendered unable to meet the enemy at sea.'

British Admiralty memorandum (1902)

■ It was impossible to hide the construction of a battle-fleet from international view.

■ The British Press was quick to report the expansion of the German fleet. *The Times* reflected the views of the British public on this issue when in 1900 it commented: 'Whatever our position may be at a given moment, we must be ready to make it still stronger, if the other sea powers build more ships.'

■ Tirpitz exploited anti-British sentiment in Germany, especially over the Boer War, to ensure public support for his Navy Bills and their safe passage through the Reichstag.

■ Britain could not be seen to compromise the power of the Royal Navy. The security and prosperity of the British Isles were almost entirely dependent upon the maintenance of an unchallenged fleet.

# The decision for war: events in Europe (June–August 1914)

### Assassination!

On 28 June 1914, the heir to the Austro-Hungarian throne, Archduke Franz Ferdinand, was shot to death with his wife while on a State visit to the Bosnian capital, Sarajevo. The assassin, Gavrilo Princip, was a member of a Serbian terrorist organization called the 'Black Hand'. Serbia, for years a thorn in the side of the Austro-Hungarian Empire, was accused of complicity in this terrible affront to the Habsburg dynasty.

ARCHDUKE FERDINAND AND HIS WIFE. THIS PHOTOGRAPH WAS ONE OF THE LAST TO BE TAKEN OF THE COUPLE BEFORE THEIR ASSASSINATION IN THE SUMMER OF 1914.

In the summer of 1914, a crisis was undoubtedly brewing. The premeditated killing of the heir to one of Europe's greatest royal houses could not be expected to pass without incident. Yet few observers could have anticipated the infamous distinction which history has since accorded Sarajevo; the spark which ignited the First World War. A hint as to the general mood prevailing in Europe in the aftermath of the assassination can be seen in the following extract:

'I shall never forget that Sunday morning in June 1914 when I found the morning papers waiting for me on my return from Church announcing the murder of Archduke Franz Ferdinand and his wife. I wondered what would be the outcome of this, but little did I think it would really mean war.'

Princess Marie Louise, *My Memories of Six Reigns* (1956)

The killings were certainly shocking and they commanded considerable attention in the press. There was much speculation about the type of punishment Serbia should accept; but for this episode to provoke a general European war would certainly have seemed an unlikely outcome. Yet, scarcely one month after the assassination, the European Powers had become embroiled in a devastating conflict which was to last for four

agonizing years. In order to understand this development, two questions have to be addressed:
- How did the Powers respond to the assassination?
- Why did they respond in these ways?

Clearly, between the assassination and the outbreak of war in late July, decisions were taken which had the effect of blowing this diplomatic incident out of all proportion. Sarajevo became a pretext for war. How did this happen?

### The response to Sarajevo: the July Crisis

**The Austro-Hungarian response** In the immediate wake of the assassination, the crucial decisions were taken in Vienna and Berlin. As the injured party, Austria-Hungary was expected to make the initial response. Within the Habsburg Empire the passing of the Archduke was received with little genuine grief; the Heir Apparent had never been popular either within Court circles or amongst the people. His life ended with a 'third class funeral' and widespread public indifference. There was international sympathy and an expectation that Austria-Hungary would legitimately make some moderate demands of Serbia. But the messages of condolence, from France and Russia in particular, contained indirect warnings that Austria-Hungary should resist the temptation to use Sarajevo as an excuse to pursue excessive claims against Serbia. It was clear that the response of the Habsburgs was crucial in determining the outcome of this episode.

In Vienna, many of the leading figures in the government listened not to the warnings of the international community, but to the middle-class Press which clamoured for decisive action against the murderous Serbs. Berchtold, the Austro-Hungarian Foreign Minister, spoke ominously of his intention to use 'the abomination of Sarajevo as the pretext for a settlement of accounts with Serbia.' Even more explicit was Conrad, the Chief of the General Staff, who viewed the assassination as an opportunity to throttle Slav nationalism through a preventive war against troublesome Serbia. Strategically, however, Conrad knew that such a war would be difficult to contain and win unless Austria-Hungary could depend on German support. Once Belgrade came under attack from the Habsburgs, the Russians were almost certain to intervene on behalf of their fellow Slavs; the attitude of Germany was therefore critical. Without the backing of Berlin, the government in Vienna was not prepared to risk a war with Russia.

**The German response** In Berlin there was no single response to news of the assassination. Broadly speaking, the Imperial Government favoured restraint whilst the military leaders in the General Staff were much less cautious (see left).

In the event, it was the Kaiser who settled the debate between the political and military leaderships. His belligerent comments, scribbled impetuously in the margin of a report from Tschirschky (the German Ambassador in Vienna), established the tone and direction of subsequent German policy. The report, with the Kaiser's marginal notes, is reproduced on the following page:

**Imperial Government**
1 Restrain Austria-Hungary in her dealings with Serbia.

2 Work with the other Powers to secure a peaceful solution to the problem.

3 Avoid a war between Austria-Hungary and Serbia which could so easily develop into a 'world war'.

**General Staff**
1 Encourage Austria-Hungary to crush Serbia.

2 Seize this incident as an opportunity to launch a preventive war while Russia and France remain some years from reaching their full military capacity.

'Count Berchtold told me today that everything pointed to the fact that the threads of the conspiracy to which the Archduke fell a sacrifice, ran together at Belgrade. The affair was so well thought out that very young men were intentionally selected for the perpetration of the crime, against whom only a mild punishment could be decreed. The Minister spoke very bitterly about the Serbian Plots.

*I hope not*

I frequently hear expressed here, even among serious people, the wish that at last a final and fundamental reckoning be had with the Serbs. The Serbs should first be presented with a number of demands, and in any case they should not accept these, energetic measures should be taken. I take opportunity of every such occasion to advise quietly but very impressively and seriously against too hasty steps. First of all they must make sure what they want to do, for so far I have heard only indefinite expressions of opinion. Then the chances of every kind of action should be carefully weighed and it should be kept in mind that Austria-Hungary does not stand alone in the world, that it is her duty to think not only of her allies, but to take into consideration the entire European situation, and especially to bear in mind the attitude of Italy and Roumania on all questions that concern Serbia.'

*Now or never*
*Who authorised him to act*
*that way? That is very stupid.*

*It is none of his business, as it is solely the affair of Austria, what she plans to do in this case. Later if plans go wrong, it will be said that Germany did not want it! Let Tschirschky be good enough to drop this nonsense! The Serbs must be disposed of, and that right soon!*

*Goes without saying; nothing but truisms.*

Tschirschky to Bethmann Hollweg (30 June 1914), quoted in Imanuel Geiss, *July 1914*, (1965)

**1** What line of action does Tschirschky recommend?

**2** What is the Kaiser's opinion of this advice?

**3** Which of the Kaiser's phrases best illustrates his attitude to Serbia?

The Kaiser's comments signalled to the civilian and military branches of government the policy which he believed should be adopted. In obedience to his wishes the military and political leaders made common cause in pursuit of a decisive action against Serbia.

William's commitment to Austria-Hungary was categorically affirmed on 5 July with the issue of the so-called 'blank cheque'. This represented an offer of unconditional support to Austria-Hungary in handling Serbia. Szogyeny, the Austrian Ambassador, reported this decisive development in a telegram to the Austro-Hungarian Foreign Minister, Berchtold:

'After lunch...the Kaiser authorised me to inform our gracious Majesty [Emperor Franz Joseph] that we might in this case, as in all others, rely upon Germany's full support.'

Nor did the Kaiser stop here. Szogyeny also reported William's recommendation that action against Serbia be taken quickly, even though this was likely to provoke Russia into action:

**T**ALKING POINT

What do you understand by the term 'blank cheque'? How appropriate is this term in the context of the Kaiser's statement of 5 July?

'...it was his [Kaiser William II's opinion that this action [against Serbia] must not be delayed. Russia's attitude will no doubt be hostile, but to this he had been for years prepared, and should a war between Austria-Hungary and Russia be unavoidable, we might be convinced that Germany, our old faithful ally, would stand at our side.'

Szogyeny to Berchtold, 5 July, quoted in Imanuel Geiss, as above

Now certain of support from Germany, the Austro-Hungarian government began to plan a vigorous action against Serbia. The scheme which emerged was to present the Serbs with an ultimatum deliberately intended to be unacceptable. Its rejection would be the pretext for an Austro-Hungarian declaration of war. In this way it was hoped that Vienna would crush Slav nationalism and sabotage Russian ambitions to dominate the Slav Balkan states. In the event, the action touched off the most devastating war the world had ever seen.

## Ultimatum, mobilization and war

Although the German 'blank cheque' was an important development it did not make the outbreak of a general war inevitable. Its principal effect was to galvanize the Austrians into preparing and delivering a forceful ultimatum to Serbia. But even this document, deliberately designed to be unacceptable to the Serbs, did not guarantee a war between the Great Powers. On a number of occasions between the sending of the ultimatum on 23 July and the outbreak of war in early August, diplomatic efforts were made to try and resolve the crisis. The table which follows charts the principal developments following the delivery of the Austrian ultimatum.

| 23 July | Austrian ultimatum sent to Serbia. Serbs given 48 hours to reply. |
|---|---|
| 25 July | Serbia replied to ultimatum. Reply was conciliatory but failed to satisfy Austro-Hungarian government. Vienna severed diplomatic relations with Belgrade. In Russia, determination to back Serbia confirmed at meeting of the Council of Ministers. Tsar ordered preparations for mobilization of the armed forces. |
| 26 July | Grey, the British Foreign Secretary, proposed a four-power conference of ambassadors to be held in London. Austria began to mobilize her forces on Russian border. |
| 27 July | France accepted Grey's proposals. Austria-Hungary took decision to declare war on Serbia. Bethmann Hollweg, the German Chancellor, rejected idea of a four-power conference. |
| 28 July | Austria-Hungary declared war on Serbia. Belgrade suffered aerial bombardment. Kaiser William appealed to Vienna to 'halt in Belgrade' and to use the Serbian reply of 25 July as basis for negotiations. Russia began partial mobilization. |

| 29 July | Vienna rejected negotiations with Serbia. |
|---|---|
| | Germany informed of partial Russian mobilization. |
| | St Petersburg warned by Berlin to suspect mobilization. |
| | Grey informed German Ambassador in London that Britain would not remain neutral in the event of a general European war. |
| | Tsar issued then revoked a general mobilization order. |
| 30 July | Austria-Hungary and Russia ordered general mobilization for 31 July. |
| 31 July | Vienna rejected an international conference and initiated general mobilization. |
| | Russian general mobilization became known in Berlin. Kaiser declared 'state of imminent war'. |
| | German ultimatum issued to Russia. |
| | France decided to order mobilization for 1 August. |
| 1 August | German ultimatum to Russia expired. Germany declared war on Russia. |
| 3 August | Germany declared war on France. |
| | Britain issued ultimatum to Germany to respect neutrality of Belgium. |
| 4 August | German forces invaded Belgium. |
| | British ultimatum expired at midnight. Britain declared war on Germany. |

The key factor in the countdown to war was the mobilization of troops. It was this which made war inevitable. German military planning rested exclusively on the management of a two-front war. The basic strategy had been drawn up in 1905 by the then Chief of the General Staff, General Count von Schlieffen. His operational plan rested on the assumption that in the event of a European war, Germany would most likely have to face France and Russia, possibly supported by Britain. The Schlieffen Plan depended for its success on speed. During the time it took to mobilize the huge Russian army, France would be rapidly taken out of the war by an attack through neutral Belgium. It is clear, then, that from the moment the Russian mobilization order became known in Berlin on 31 July, the decision for hostilities had to be taken by the German authorities if they were to stand any chance of winning a two-front war. Each day that this decision was delayed brought Russian troops closer to German soil, and reduced the time available to deliver the knockout blow to France.

Writing in 1920 the German Chancellor at the time of the July Crisis, Bethmann Hollweg, gave the following explanation for Germany's actions following the announcement of Russian general mobilization on 30 July:

'We were not in complete agreement among ourselves as to how we were to proceed officially. The War Minister, General von Falkenhayn, thought

## The Schlieffen Plan

**The main German army was to attack France through neutral Belgium and encircle Paris.**

**A diversionary attack would be simultaneously launched across the heavily defended Franco-German border.**

**③**

**Strategic planning calculated that it would take up to six weeks for Paris to capitulate and France to surrender. Attention could then be focused on Russia.**

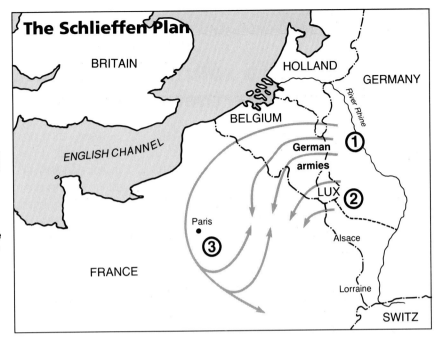

# TALKING POINT

## The issue of mobilization

For France, Russia and Austria-Hungary, the mobilization of troops did not necessarily mean war. Why did this not apply to Germany?

it was a mistake to declare war on Russia, not because he considered that war could be avoided after Russia had mobilized, but because he feared that the political effect would be prejudicial to us. The Chief of the General Staff, General von Moltke, was on the other hand in favour of declaring war, because our plan of mobilization, providing for a war on two fronts, required that military actions be immediately taken, and because our hope of success against an enormous superiority in numbers was dependent on the extreme rapidity of our movements. I myself agreed with the view of General von Moltke. I was, of course, under no illusion as to the effect on the question of responsibility for the war that our declaration would have and actually did have. But it was impossible at a moment when the existence of the country was entirely dependent on military action to oppose the military arguments, quite reasonable in themselves, of that general who was responsible for military operations.'

Bethmann Hollweg, *Reflections on the World War* (1920)

## 13.2 Was war a solution to the problems of the Dual Alliance partners?

Why did Germany and Austria-Hungary adopt such an uncompromising attitude in response to the Sarajevo assassination? Why did Vienna, with the unconditional support of Berlin, present Serbia with an ultimatum deliberately intended to be unacceptable? It is hard to avoid the conclusion that in July 1914 the leaders of the Dual Alliance had decided to use Sarajevo as a pretext for a showdown with Serbia and, if necessary, with the other European Powers. This Focus Section examines some of the pressures felt in Berlin and Vienna in the years immediately preceding the outbreak of war. How far do they help to explain why Germany and Austria-Hungary behaved as they did in July 1914?

### The problems of the Dual Alliance partners

**Diplomatic failures:** International humiliation associated with the Algeciras Conference in 1906 and the *Panther* incident in 1911. The German authorities became convinced of the existence of a conspiracy, directed by the powers of the Triple Entente, to short-circuit their plans to transform Germany into a World Power.

**Disappointment with Tirpitz's naval policy:** Britain's response to German naval expansion was to step up the pace of her own naval construction. The naval race which resulted was regarded by Germans as another attempt by Britain to sabotage their quest for *Weltpolitik*. In 1906 Britain added a further dimension to the naval race with the launch of a new class of battleship, the Dreadnought. This had the effect of making all other warships obsolete. The naval race recommenced in earnest. However, Britain had the advantage and, much to Germany's frustration, was able to retain it.

| Dreadnoughts | GB | Germany |
|---|---|---|
| 1906 | 1 | 0 |
| 1907 | 3 | 0 |
| 1908 | 2 | 4 |
| 1909 | 2 | 3 |
| 1910 | 3 | 1 |
| 1911 | 5 | 3 |
| 1912 | 3 | 2 |
| 1913 | 7 | 3 |
| 1914 | 3 | 1 |
| *Total* | 29 | 17 |

**Consolidation of the Triple Entente:** As a result of the Moroccan Crisis and Russian anger over the Bosnian Crises, the Entente partners began to draw closer together. Anglo-French military planning now clearly identified Germany as the likely enemy in the event of an armed conflict. This process of consolidation caused German fears of 'encirclement' and the prospect of a two-front war to become acute. Such fears were exacerbated by the attention given, particularly in France and Russia, to military improvements. In 1913 France increased its period of conscription by one year; while in Russia, the army was being overhauled and expanded. Full capacity was expected to be reached by 1917.

**Threats to the Triple Alliance:** Italy was generally regarded as an unreliable partner in the Alliance. More importantly, Austria-Hungary was experiencing difficulties in the Balkans which threatened her entire Imperial status. Serbia's ambitions to unite all the Balkan Slavs in a new Slav state posed a real threat to the Habsburg Empire. The defection of Austria-Hungary's southern Slavs to a new state was likely to inspire other national groups within the Dual Monarchy to demand independence from Vienna. If the Austro-Hungarian Empire collapsed, Germany would be left isolated in Europe.

**Pressure from the right:** During 1913, the German government came under intense pressure from the nationalist right in the shape of the Pan-Germans. This group criticized the government for being indecisive and failing to protect Germany's national interests. The government was accused of wishing to preserve peace at any price. The Pan-Germans urged the authorities to take the initiative and attack the other Powers who were conspiring to humiliate Germany.

**Pressures from the left:** The Reichstag elections of 1912 made the Social Democrats the largest political party in parliament. Leading Social Democrats were opposed to *Weltpolitik* and the military posturing of the government. To the Kaiser and the conservative ruling elite, the socialists presented a major challenge to the existing social and political system. A short, patriotic war was seen by some as the ideal way to encourage popular support for the Emperor and the traditional values of the Reich.

**Slav nationalism:** Balkan Slavs shared the ambition of uniting the Slav peoples of south-eastern Europe into a Slav national state. Such a development threatened the very existence of the multi-national Austro-Hungarian Empire. Vienna feared that if their southern Slavs - in provinces such as Bosnia, Herzegovina and Slavonia - were to demand their independence then this could spread to the northern Slavs, especially Czechs, Poles, Ruthenes and Slovaks. Demands for self-rule from other national groups could lead ultimately to the disintegration of the Empire.

**Serbia:** The greatest threat to the integrity of the Austro-Hungarian Empire came from Serbia. The Serbs were the focal point for Slav nationalism in the Balkans and had the backing of Russia in their quest to establish a Slav national state. Serbia was becoming increasingly powerful and ambitious. In the Balkan Wars of 1912 and 1913, she had acquired large tracts of territory and now had an army of 200,000 men. In some Austrian circles the belief existed that only a war would put an end to Serbia's schemes.

## QUESTIONS

**1** How do you think the governments in Berlin and Vienna viewed the prospects for their national security at the beginning of 1914?

**2** How does the information in this Focus Section help to explain the actions of the Germans and Austrians in response to Sarajevo?

ROSA LUXEMBURG, THE CELEBRATED GERMAN SOCIALIST, SPEAKING IN STUTTGART (1907). THE SOCIALISTS WERE ATTRACTING INCREASING SUPPORT IN THE YEARS PRIOR TO THE OUTBREAK OF THE FIRST WORLD WAR

# Did Germany plan a preventive war?

Much of the debate surrounding German war-guilt has centred on whether Germany consciously planned a war against the other Powers. Following the Second Moroccan Crisis the German authorities became convinced that the Entente Powers were conspiring to prevent Germany's progress to World Power status. Accordingly, the idea of the preventive war was born. This would involve Germany in a pre-emptive strike against her enemies in order to break out of the ring of containment. Absolute proof that Germany was planning such a war before 1914 is difficult to find. However, there is no shortage of evidence to suggest that if Germany wasn't actually *planning* a war, then she was certainly *discussing* it as a serious possibility, and considering the conditions under which a favourable result might be achieved.

Many historians, including Fritz Fischer (who breathed new life into the debate in the 1960s), have cited the so-called 'war council' of 1912 as clear evidence of German war-planning in the years immediately preceding 1914. The Kaiser, along with his top military advisers, had met to discuss the situation in the Balkans. Admiral von Muller, head of the Kaiser's naval cabinet, recorded the meeting:

'H.M. [the Kaiser] envisaged the following:

Austria must deal energetically with the foreign Slavs [the Serbs] otherwise she will lose control of the Slavs in the Austro-Hungarian monarchy. If Russia supports the Serbs, which she evidently does...then war would be unavoidable for us too...If these powers [Bulgaria, Roumania, Turkey, Albania] join Austria then we shall be free to fight the war with full fury against France. The fleet must naturally prepare itself for the war against England.

General von Moltke, Chief of the German General Staff, agreed that war was unavoidable though he did urge a vigorous press campaign to ensure popular support for the forthcoming clash with the Entente Powers. Tirpitz requested that the 'great fight' be postponed for 18 months to allow the Kiel canal, linking the Baltic with the North Sea, to be completed.

Muller concluded with the following observations on the meeting:

That was the end of the conference. The result amounted to almost nothing.

The Chief of the Great General Staff says: War the sooner the better, but he does not draw the logical conclusion from this, which is: To present Russia or France or both with an ultimatum which would unleash the war with right on our side.'

**Extracts from von Muller quoted in JCG Rohl, *From Bismarck to Hitler* (1970)**

**1** Would you conclude from these extracts that Germany was planning a preventive war from 1912?

**2** Why is the fact that war did break out 18 months after this meeting so important to those who have argued that Germany was planning a preventive war?

Working in groups consider each of the following statements. In your opinion, which of them provides the fairest and most accurate summary of responsibility for the First World War?

**1** Germany willed a war with the other European Powers and during the war council of December 1912 agreed to engineer its outbreak in 18 months' time.

**2** Germany felt compelled to go to war in 1914 because she believed her national ambitions and security were at risk from a containment policy being pursued by the Entente Powers.

**3** Austria was reckless in her dealings with Serbia in 1914. Had she exercised caution and made only moderate demands the crisis could have been resolved without recourse to war.

**4** Austria-Hungary applied pressure on Serbia in 1914 only because she was certain of German support. Therefore it was Germany who should have exercised restraint and helped to defuse the crisis.

**5** Russia made a general war inevitable by refusing to heed German warnings and continuing with mobilization.

**6** The First World War was not planned in advance. The Powers stumbled into war because they were unable to find a generally-acceptable way of settling their differences in the Balkans.

# REVIEW

### Why did the Sarajevo murder but not the Agadir Crisis lead to the outbreak of the First World War?

Work as a small group (3–4 persons) for this exercise. Consider each of the items in the list below. Each item may be said to offer a clue towards solving the problem posed by the question above.

Within your group work initially as individuals. Think about each clue in turn and note down in a few short sentences how you think this helps to explain why the war broke out in 1914 rather than 1911. Share your ideas with the rest of the group. Discuss your ideas and try to reach agreement on how you might use them in a formal written response to the question.

- The attitude of Austria-Hungary
- Britain's response to both incidents
- The effect of Agadir on the thinking of the German authorities
- The extent of German military readiness
- The strength of the French and Russian military in 1914
- Evidence of Anglo-French military co-operation following Agadir
- The German elections of 1912
- Serbian expansion during the Balkan Wars (1912–13)

This list should not be seen as exhaustive. Try to add other points of your own which could help to explain why Sarajevo and not Agadir was the spark which ignited the First World War.

# ACKNOWLEDGEMENTS

The author and publishers wish to thank the following who have kindly given permission for the use of copyright material.

Routledge for material from *Aspects of European History* by Stephen J. Lee, Methuen & Co. 1982; Stanford University Press for material from *The First Russian Revolution* by A. G. Mazour, 1937;

Every effort has been made to trace all the copyright holders, but if any have been inadvertently overlooked the publishers will be pleased to make the necessary arrangement at the first opportunity.

The following photographic sources have kindly given permission for photographs to be reproduced:

Mary Evans Picture Library: pp.2, 8 (2), 9 (3), 22, 23, 32, 36 (2), 37, 48, 49, 52, 53 (3), 55, 71, 77 (3), 80, 81, 86 (2), 92, 95, 113, 120, 121, 125, 128 (2), 129, 131, 138, 153, 155, 161, 162, 163, 165, 166, 167, 175, 176, 182, 183, 184, 189, 193, 196, 201, 202, 203, 215, 218 (2), 220, 224, 225 (2), 229, 240, 242, 249, 250, 251, 252, 256, 258, 259, 260, 263, 269, 274, 288, 291, 292, 294, 297, 311;

The Hulton – DEUTSCH Collection: pp.39, 79, 88, 137 (2), 138, 146, 150, 155, 163, 194, 207, 287, 289, 304;

The Illustrated London News/Peter Newarks Military Pictures: Cover photograph, pp. 3, 6, 7, 39, 69, 86 (2), 99, 102, 120, 131, 192, 197, 198, 199, 222, 224, 228, 229, 280, 281, 282, 294, 295, 303;

Paul Poppes: pp.207, 291, 292;

Suddeutscher Verbg: pp. 219;

Roger Vivlket: pp.74, 88, 96, 103, 104, 105 (2), 107;

# Index